THE

CAFO
—— READER ——

THE TRAGEDY OF INDUSTRIAL ANIMAL FACTORIES

EDITED BY
DANIEL IMHOFF

WATERSHED MEDIA

CONTEMPORARY ISSUES SERIES

Library of Congress Control Number: 2010925052

Printed in the United States on New Leaf Paper, 50# Frontier Offset (FSC), made with 100% recycled fiber and 100% post-consumer waste, processed chlorine free, designated Ancient Forest Friendly™ and manufactured with electricity that is offset with Green-e® certified renewable energy certificates.

Distributed by University of California Press
Berkeley and Los Angeles, California
University of California Press, Ltd.
London, England
www.ucpress.edu

Interior design by BookMatters.

10 9 8 7 6 5 4 3 2 1

*To the hundreds of billions of animals, past
and present, who have been and continue to be
tortured in the industrial food factories known as
concentrated animal feeding operations—CAFOs.*

*And to the activists, farmers, scientists, writers,
photographers, concerned citizens, and all
others engaged in creating a healthy, humane,
community-based, and sustainable food system.*

*May the real costs and impacts of mega feeding
operations and their associated economies become
more widely discussed, debated, and understood.*

*And may the time come when animal husbandry,
agricultural diversity, and wild biodiversity are
valued for their own sake as well as our own, and
when the interdependence between healthy lands,
healthy plants and animals, healthy communities,
and healthy people is universally acknowledged.*

CONTENTS

FOREWORD

DOUGLAS R. TOMPKINS

This book, along with its photo-format companion volume, *CAFO (Concentrated Animal Feeding Operation): The Tragedy of Industrial Animal Factories*, has been a long time in the making. It is not the first of its kind. Our foundation, the Foundation for Deep Ecology, has published several large-format books and companion readers over the last seventeen years documenting various ecological outrages. These volumes have exposed the fallacies and outright pathologies of industrial agriculture and industrial forestry (*Fatal Harvest, The Fatal Harvest Reader*, and *Clearcut*); mega-scale dam building for hydroelectricity (*Patagonia Sin Represas*); public lands livestock grazing in the American West (*Welfare Ranching*); ill-conceived fire suppression policy (*Wildfire* and *The Wildfire Reader*); motorized recreation (*Thrillcraft*); and mountaintop-removal coal mining (*Plundering Appalachia*). With *The CAFO Reader*, we again turn our attention to the horrors of industrial food production, this time with a focus on factory "farms," which are of course nothing of the sort, having little connection with honorable agrarianism and everything to do with cruelty and environmental abuse in the pursuit of corporate profit.

Through the years, as editors and producers of these books, we have come to recognize a common thread that ties them together. Wherever we look closely at the most egregious assaults on the Earth's beauty and integrity, we find that the abusive behavior flows from a root cause: a technological and industrial approach to production, land management, recreation, or other economic activity. Time and again we are struck by the fact that this reductionist, narrow, techno-industrial paradigm when applied to a production system ends up diminishing nature, accelerating its demise, and unbalancing ecosystems.

In short, we conclude that within this fundamental industrial framework lies the answer to why the world is falling apart and why we find ourselves, one and all, ensnared in the massive social and ecological unraveling we call the "ecosocial crisis." For it is not only natural systems that are in crisis—as manifest in burgeoning rates of extinction, collapsing fisheries, and a rapidly warming planet—but also human societies that depend on healthy ecosystems. Around the globe, natural and human communities are in decline or in some state of crisis, collapsing or having already collapsed. Industrialism, the godchild of this mechanistic worldview, lurks behind every tree and is responsible for the deeper and deeper hole we humans are digging for ourselves.

In *The CAFO Reader*, we recognize the logic of industrialism applied to domesticated food animals. The result is a tragic, pathetic, and inhumane method of raising animals in factory farms to produce meat, milk, eggs, leather, fur, and nonessential culinary luxuries such as liver pâté. Living creatures are treated as machines, reduced to "units" in an assembly line of protein production by corporate food purveyors, with the individual animal's suffering ignored. This is the kind of atrocity for which the word *evil* seems too meek and mild.

After reading this book, a reasonable person might assume that agribusiness's unethical treatment of farm animals could sink no lower. Unfortunately, the future bodes otherwise, for on the horizon we see cloning and genetic engineering emerging in full force from a Frankenstein laboratory owned and operated by giant corporations looking to make their breeding and raising of commercial/industrial animals ever more "efficient." Thus the ecosocial crisis deepens. At every juncture, the subjugation of nature by human culture is exacerbated, and the factory "farm" becomes yet another symptom of the machine mind that seeks to engineer the world—including living creatures—in service of human aims and corporate interests.

It is time to call this cold and calculated evil system by its real name: industrial animal concentration camps. This is a much more accurate term than the seemingly innocuous and technical acronym CAFO, for concentrated animal feeding operation. As you read through this book, consider how you can contribute to the abolition of this ungodly industry and its despicable treatment of other sentient beings. These concentration camps for animals simply have to go, and it will take the same kind of creative, uncompromising social change movement built by those visionaries who worked to abolish slavery, racism, torture, and other relics of inhumanity over the last two hundred years. Please lend your voice and your votes, your personal economic choices and your heart to this effort. It is quite possible to banish these animal factories from the face of the Earth; it only takes the will and determination of citizen activists.

We spent a number of years researching and assembling this book as a tool to inform the broader public of where most meat comes from and how it is produced. Now we need an army of activists who will make it a principle textbook, who will become articulate on this issue so they can forge arguments, alliances, and strategies to campaign for a change in social norms that ultimately eliminates these *food animal factories*. For anyone who takes up this noble cause, we can guarantee that this kind of activism will pay your rent for living on the planet.

INTRODUCTION

DANIEL IMHOFF

Our domesticated livestock have never been as cruelly confined or slaughtered in such massive quantities in all of history. Every year, at least four domesticated animals are raised for every person on the planet. In the United States alone, nearly 10 billion domesticated livestock—mostly chickens, pigs, and cows—are raised and slaughtered annually, a number that is dwarfed if one includes rapidly expanding land- and ocean-based fish farming. This is twice the number that America raised in 1980, and ten times more than in 1940.[1] Even more alarming is that animal food production is expanding across the globe at a staggering pace. The United Nations Food and Agriculture Organization predicts that global consumption of both meat and dairy products will double by 2050.[2] Yet already the world's lands and waters are being overwhelmed by animals that consume vast amounts of energy, foul the environment, and when eaten excessively, degrade our health.[3]

In the United States and in other parts of the world, the raising of livestock has become increasingly dominated by *concentrated animal feeding operations* (CAFOs), *intensive livestock operations* (ILOs in Canada), and smaller *animal feeding operations* (AFOs). These are essentially factorylike buildings into which animals—industrially bred for rapid growth and high output of meat, milk, or eggs—are tightly crammed, caged, and sometimes even chained or tethered. By current U.S. Environmental Protection Agency definitions, a large CAFO imports its feed and concentrates more than any of the following: 1,000 cattle; 2,500 swine over 55 pounds; 10,000 swine under 55 pounds; 55,000 turkeys; 125,000 chickens; or 82,000 laying hens.

As the name implies, a CAFO is a feeding operation. Animal density and weight gain are the primary objectives. These animal factories are quite different from small- or medium-size diversified farms that combine row or tree crops with livestock raised on pastures, using the animals' manure to fertilize the fields or orchards. Most

CAFOs shouldn't really even be described as farms—either techni-cally or legally—because they basically operate under an industrial factory framework. In a CAFO, animals are concentrated in unnatu-rally high stocking rates by the thousands or tens of thousands and under unnatural conditions, often unable to breathe fresh air, see the light of day, walk outside, peck at plants or insects, scratch the earth, or eat a blade of grass. They are fed a high-calorie grain-based diet (sometimes including reclaimed animal manure, ground-up fish, or recycled animal parts) designed to maximize growth and weight gain in the shortest amount of time. Only a select few modern breeds are chosen for these cold industrial parameters.

According to the *Oxford English Dictionary*, the first recorded use of the term *factory farming* appeared in an American journal of economics in 1890, although confinement feeding operations such as the deplorable nineteenth-century "swill" dairies—which fed milk cows the spent distillery wastes from whiskey production—had been in existence long before that. Industrial animal farming received a significant boost in the 1920s with the discovery that adding vita-mins A and D to feed rations allowed producers to keep animals indoors all year long, channeling their energy into rapid growth.[4] By the post–World War II era, the increasing confinement of livestock ultimately triggered high rates of mortality and outbreaks of disease. These problems were countered with a second technological devel-opment essential to the CAFO system—regular doses of antibiotics (or antimicrobial medicines) in feed and water to fight off infec-tious pathogens and promote weight gain.[5] As grain replaced pasture as a primary feedstock, farmers also turned to twentieth-century industrial technologies such as synthetic fertilizers, toxic pesticides and herbicides, and hybrid and genetically modified crop varieties to boost feed harvests. Factory farms grew larger, and became ever more mechanized and capitalized. Smaller independent slaughtering facili-ties closed down, and regional distribution networks dried up. With falling prices and limited access to markets, millions of independent family operators vanished from the agricultural landscape altogether. Or they became low-margin contractors or low-wage employees for the animal factories that replaced them.

Corporate agribusinesses that have revved the economic engines of the global animal factories have reduced living creatures to mere production units of milk, eggs, and meat. Every step of the way, domesticated animals have been increasingly altered and bred to meet the conditions of their confinement. Chicks' beaks can be partially seared off so they cannot fatally strike one another. The tails of piglets are "docked" to instill "avoidance behavior" inside a stall crammed with hogs: the animals do all they can to prevent an aggressive or stimulation-deprived pen mate from gnawing their sensitive backsides. The horns of young cattle are sawed off or chemically shortened before they are sent off to the overcrowded feedlots. Mother sows and dairy cows nurse their offspring for a bare minimum before they are both whisked off into animal factory food assembly lines. The CAFO industry argues that while such practices may seem cruel to some, they are done to benefit the health and welfare of the animals and to provide an abundant and safe food supply for a hungry planet.

Meanwhile, the intensive concentration of animals produces obscene amounts of waste. It is not uncommon for a CAFO on 100 acres to generate the same amount of sewage as a city of 100,000 inhabitants. The key difference is that CAFOs aren't required to set up carefully monitored sewage treatment plants. Instead, the waste—spewed onto surrounding "sprayfields" or buried directly into the soil—is often too much for the area to safely absorb and at some point becomes a toxic social and ecological liability. Stored in football field–size ponds (aka "lagoons"), massive quantities of manure often become fugitive—seeping into groundwater, released into the atmosphere, and mixing with rainwater during rain and flood events.

Inside the CAFO, animals are routinely administered antibiotics whether they need them or not. (The states of Iowa and North Carolina, for instance, each administer more antibiotics for animal production than the entire human population of the United States uses for medical purposes.) The appearance of new, more virulent forms of disease-causing organisms such as *Salmonella, E. coli*, and methicillin-resistant *Staphylococcus aureus* (MRSA) have been increasingly associated with CAFO production. Many scientists now caution that we are dangerously close to losing the effectiveness of valuable human medicines because of their overuse in industrial animal food production.

At the far end of the animal food production chain are the slaughterhouses and "disassembly lines." The pace of killing is relentless—7,000 calves, 130,000 cattle, 360,000 pigs, 24 million chickens per day in the United States at the turn of the twenty-first century—making slaughterhouse work one of the more dangerous occupations.[6] In February 2008, the Humane Society of the United States released an undercover video showing employees at the Westland/Hallmark Meat Company in Chino, California, dragging, electrically prodding, and using forklifts to move "downer cows" unable to walk to the kill floor. Slaughtering an animal unable to walk under its own power is illegal under the Humane Slaughter Act of 1958 (updated in 1978 and 2002). But without adequate regulation and enforcement (recently strengthened in 2009), an estimated 100,000 downer animals have still been slaughtered every year in the United States.[7] The Hallmark case led to the largest meat recall on record—143 million pounds—and the closure of that plant.[8] In addition to the brutality inflicted on helpless creatures, what shook many observers was that this particular firm supplied a significant amount of meat to the National School Lunch Program.

The CAFO industry has also become concentrated geographically. California and Idaho lead the country in dryland industrial dairies, and Texas and Kansas lead in cattle feedlots. Meat chicken (broiler) CAFOs are heavily concentrated along the eastern shore of the Chesapeake Bay, Arkansas, Alabama, Georgia, western Kentucky, and North Carolina, while Iowa and Ohio specialize heavily in eggs. Swine CAFOs are centralized in Iowa and North Carolina. The state of Iowa, for instance, raises an average of 11.3 hogs for every citizen in its population of just 3 million. The *New York Times* reported in 2008 that Iowa's 5,000 confinement hog facilities generate over 50 million tons of raw waste, or 16.7 tons of animal manure for every resident.[9] Many CAFO production areas are prone to cyclical flooding.

An increasing number of observers argue that such concentration has arisen as a direct result of intentional U.S. government policies that have allowed CAFOs to avoid paying the true costs of their operations.[10] For over a decade—until the recent ethanol and biofuels boom—CAFO operators were able to purchase feed at below the cost of production. These staggering discounts came about thanks to billions of dollars in annual taxpayer-funded farm bill grain subsidies, allowing animal factories to outcompete smaller independent producers and unfairly expand their operations.[11] Farm bill "conservation" programs have also doled out hundreds of millions of taxpayer dollars to build the actual infrastructure for large CAFOs to process their waste, a routine cost of business that most small- and medium-size operations normally cover out of their own operating expenses. Powerful agribusiness corporations have successfully lobbied for laws that regard CAFOs as farms rather than industries, essentially giving them a free pass on certain air, water, and solid waste emissions, and in many cases, exempting them from animal cruelty legislation. Agencies have often failed to enforce existing environmental regulations and antitrust laws despite the outright domination of nearly every sector of the industry by a small number of corporations.[12] Local control over the ability to reject a CAFO installation has been taken away from community governments in some states as the powerful industrial animal food production sector has successfully shifted authority from the local to the state level. In three states—Montana, Kansas, and North Dakota—it is actually illegal to photograph a CAFO without permission of the owner. Thirteen states have passed disparagement laws that attempt to restrict what can be said about perishable food products, meaning that our food system is now infringing on basic constitutional freedoms.

The world's increasing appetite for animal food products of all kinds—pork, dairy, beef, poultry, and eggs—is also placing unsustainable pressures on the planet's ecosystems. The Earth's atmosphere is literally heating up, and waterways and fisheries are being deluged as a result of the prolific waste output of the world's food producing animals. According to an oft-cited 2006 United Nations Food and Agriculture Organization report, the livestock sector alone accounts for 18 percent of global greenhouse gas emissions, a larger share than all of the world's transportation emissions combined.[13] A more recent study published by the World Watch Institute, however, pegs global livestock production as responsible for 32 billion tons of carbon dioxide per year, or 51 percent of all greenhouse gas emissions.[14] There are now five hundred reported "dead zones" throughout the world, aquatic regions whose biotic capacities are collapsing, largely because of agricultural runoff and waste contamination, much of it linked to the livestock sector.

At one time, the concept of industrial-scale farming seemingly held out a promise to society at large. Fewer people would be required to grow more food in less labor-intensive factorylike operations. "Economies of scale" would make food cheaper for an expanding population in a world where periodic famine and crop failures inflicted mass suffering. Today we know too well that these short-term advances in affordability and availability of animal food products have been offset by tremendous costs to the natural world, rural communities, public health, and society at large—along with a legacy of basic welfare denied to untold billions of confined livestock. A 2008 Pew Commission report on CAFOs described—and cautioned against—the rise of the "agro-industrial complex: an alliance of commodity groups, scientists at academic institutions who are paid by the industry, and their friends on Capitol Hill." The commission, overseen by the Center for a Livable Future at the Johns Hopkins University Bloomberg School of Public Health, concluded that the current method of producing food animals in the United States "presents an unacceptable level of risk to public health and damage to the environment, as well as unnecessary harm to the animals we raise for food."[15]

Clearly, the ways in which we produce our food define us as a culture and as human beings. The subject forces us to ask big questions: How did we arrive at this place where the very foundation of human society—secure and sustainable food production—has become so far removed from caring farmers and the cycles of nature? What are our ethical responsibilities as eaters, citizens, and producers in reforming a food production system that is so clearly in need of change? What does our treatment of domestic animals say about our society, our government, our food system, and our very way of life?

But this is getting ahead of our story, a complex topic that bridges a vast number of subjects: economics, food science, veterinary medicine, ecology, ethics, nutrition, food and agricultural policy, and genetics, to name just a few. The rapid growth of the animal factory and industrial food production in general stems from a pervasive philosophical framework, one that reduces the world to a mechanistic system in which the ultimate goal is the maximization of output and market share, even as animal and human health, worker and community well-being, profit margins and democratic freedoms decline.

Welcome to the world of the CAFO. Welcome to an issue for our time.

Part One

THE PATHOLOGICAL MINDSET OF THE CAFO

INTRODUCTION

From Agrarianism to Industrialism

What are the philosophical and ethical underpinnings of industrial animal food production? How did agriculture, arguably the crucible of human civilization, come to value productivity and profit over common decency and concern for the welfare of other beings? How have legions of eaters intentionally turned their backs on the grim realities that lurk behind the closed doors of concentrated animal feeding operations?

Some would argue that we have become "species-ists," ranking the interests of humanity above the well-being and flourishing of other species. Such "species-ism" serves to justify any treatment of animals used for food production, clinical testing, or other purposes because animals are deemed lesser beings than we are. Others make a strictly functional case: Livestock are here for our benefit. If we didn't eat them or the foods and by-products they generate, they wouldn't be here at all. Intensification and industrialization of food production are necessary to feed a burgeoning human population. Without a cheap and abundant food supply, many would go hungry. Why should we care about the welfare of an animal that is going to be slaughtered regardless?

A counterargument follows that as our societies and economies have become urbanized and industrialized, the majority of the population have become disconnected from the plants, animals, and places that we depend on for basic sustenance. Without such knowledge or firsthand interaction with the farming process, we have given over our moral compass to the owners of animal factory food production and find ourselves complicit in an ethical collapse.

The idea that our relationship with other members of the animal kingdom has moral relevance goes back millennia. Because food production has played such a vital role in our survival and in the organization of daily life, it became an essential topic of religious teachings. Ancient Hindus elevated the cow to sacred status, as its importance in supplying humans with fuel, milk, muscle power for plowing fields, and manure for soil fertility could not be equaled. Traditional Kosher laws restricted Jews to eating only cloven hoofed, cud-chewing mammals slaughtered according to ethical guidelines. This precluded the eating of pork (although pigs' hooves are cloven), also prohibited by Islamic code. The Old Testament forbids intentional and unnecessary infliction of pain and suffering on animals and outrageous neglect of them (such as failing to provide food and water). According to Colorado State University veterinary ethicist Bernard E. Rollin:

> Biblical edicts against cruelty helped Western societies reach a social consensus on animal treatment and develop effective laws. The Massachusetts Bay Colony, for example, was the first to prohibit animal cruelty, and similar laws exist today in all Western societies. The anticruelty ethic served two purposes: it articulated concern about animal suffering caused by deviant and purposeless human actions, and it identified sadists and psychopaths who abuse animals before sometimes "graduating" to the abuse of humans. Recent research has confirmed this correlation. Many serial killers have histories of animal abuse, as do some of the teens who have shot classmates.[1]

French philosopher René Descartes led the way toward both a species-ist and a strictly functional approach to animal exploitation in the seventeenth century. Descartes argued that all of nature existed as a toolbox for human industry. Animals, Descartes wrote, are "soulless automata": merely complex machines. Because they do not possess consciousness, they cannot feel pain or suffer. Their cries and writhing are simple reflexes. Under the banner of such modernist thought, livestock, raised for both food and clothing, eventually became soulless commodities on the assembly lines of a global industrial revolution.

Yet as questions about the morality of slavery and sexual inequality surfaced in the eighteenth and nineteenth centuries, so too did concerns about our relationships with domesticated animals. Not long after the French colonies granted fundamental freedoms to black slaves, the English philosopher Jeremy Bentham predicted a future animal welfare movement. "The day may come," he wrote in 1789, "when the rest of the animal creation may acquire those rights." While animals may not equal a human's ability to rationalize or communicate, Bentham argued, "the question is not, Can they *reason*? Nor Can they *talk*? But, Can they *suffer*?"

By the mid-twentieth century, agriculture in America was in the midst of a radical transformation. Millions of family farmers were leaving the land in the face of larger, more heavily capitalized agribusinesses. Centuries of agrarian tradition and animal husbandry gave way to land grant universities teaching animal sciences with a focus on industrial concentrated animal feeding operations (CAFOs). The addition of vitamins to feed rations, which allowed for year-round confinement of animals, the increase in grain harvests, the use of antibiotics and growth hormones to fight disease outbreaks and speed weight gain, and decades of genetic selection for animals that can be raised in intensive concentrations and confinement all fueled the growth of the animal factory and the CAFO industry.

Along the way, the flames of debate about the ethical, social, cultural, and environmental repercussions of animal factory farming blazed on through seminal works like Ruth Harrison's *Animal Machines* (1964), Frances Moore Lappé's *Diet for a Small Planet* (1971), and Peter Singer's *Animal Liberation* (1975). A legion of organizations devoted to animal rights, animal welfare, sustainable agriculture, and vegetarianism sprang up during this time.

Future historians may look back on the age of the CAFO with bewilderment and rancor. Certainly animals feel pain, certainly they have the ability to suffer, and certainly they deserve our care, respect, and mercy—even those destined to become part of the food chain. Whether or not we choose to eat them, we can probably agree that a dignified life for farm animals assumes fundamental freedoms: the ability to turn around, to groom, to stand up and lie down, to stretch the limbs freely, to not live on top of one's own waste, to live the life that a species is born to lead. If we are to evolve beyond the modern industrialized animal factory mindset, we must universally adopt a worldview that puts the health and care of all involved in the food production system above short-term profits and cheap calories at any cost.

FARM FACTORIES

The End of Animal Husbandry

BERNARD E. ROLLIN

WITH THE RISE OF INDUSTRIAL ANIMAL AGRICULTURE, *the contract between humans and livestock has been broken. Agriculture as a way of life and as a practice of animal husbandry has been replaced by agriculture as an industry, driven by the goals of efficiency and productivity. Among the most profound changes has been a major departure from traditional farming and its core values.*

❖

A young man was working for a company that operated a large, total-confinement swine farm. One day he detected symptoms of a disease among some of the feeder pigs. As a teen, he had raised pigs himself and shown them in competition, so he knew how to treat the disease. But the company's policy was to kill any diseased animals with a blow to the head—the profit margin was considered too low to allow for treatment of individual animals. So the employee decided to come in on his own time, with his own medicine, and cured the animals. The management's response was to attempt to fire him on the spot for violating company policy. Soon the young man left agriculture for good: he was weary of the conflict between what he was told to do and how he believed he should be treating the animals.

Consider a sow that is being used to breed pigs for food. The overwhelming majority of today's swine are raised in severe confinement. If the "farmer" follows the recommendations of the National Pork Producers, the sow will spend virtually all of her productive life (until she is killed) in a gestation crate 2½ feet wide (sometimes only

2 feet) by 7 feet long by 3 feet high. This concrete and barred cage is often too small for the 500- to 600-pound animal, which cannot lie down or turn around. Feet that are designed for soft loam are forced to carry hundreds of pounds of weight on slotted concrete. This causes severe foot and leg problems. Unable to perform any of her natural behaviors, the sow goes mad and exhibits compulsive, neurotic "stereotypical" behaviors such as bar biting and purposeless chewing. When she is ready to birth her piglets, she is moved into a farrowing crate that has a creep rail so that the piglets can crawl under it and avoid being crushed by the confined sow, whose maternal instinct has been lost through breeding for productivity.

Under more natural conditions, pigs reveal that they are highly intelligent and behaviorally complex animals. Researchers at the University of Edinburgh created a "pig park" that approximates the habitat of wild swine. Domestic pigs, usually raised in confinement, were let loose in this facility and their behavior observed. In this environment, the sows covered almost a mile a day in foraging, and, in keeping with their reputation as clean animals, they built carefully constructed nests on a hillside so that urine and feces ran downhill. They took turns minding each other's piglets so that each sow could forage. All of this natural behavior is inexpressible in confinement.

Factory farming, or confinement-based industrialized agriculture, has been an established feature in North America and Europe since its introduction at the end of World War II, when agricultural scientists were concerned about supplying Americans with sufficient food. After the Dust Bowl and the Great Depression, many people had left farming. Cities and suburbs were beginning to encroach on agricultural lands, and scientists saw that the amount of land available for food production would soon diminish significantly. Farmers who had left their farms for foreign countries and urban centers during the war were reluctant to go back. "How 'ya gonna keep 'em down on the farm after they've seen Paree?" a post–World War I song asked. Having experienced the specter of starvation during the Great Depression, the American consumer was afraid that there would not be enough food.

At the same time, a variety of technologies relevant to agriculture were emerging, and American society began to accept the idea of technologically based economies of scale. In a major departure from traditional agriculture and its core values, animal agriculture began to industrialize. Agriculture as a way of life and as a practice of husbandry were replaced by agriculture as an industry with values of efficiency and productivity. Thus the problems we see in confinement agriculture are not the result of cruelty or insensitivity, but rather the unanticipated by-product of changes in the nature of agriculture.

In the first place, the basic approach of confinement agriculture entails raising vast numbers of animals, limiting the space needed to raise these animals, moving them indoors into "controlled environments," and replacing labor with capital—that is, replacing humans with mechanized systems. One can tell a priori that confinement agriculture is inimical to animal husbandry, for husbandry requires naturalistic environments, relatively few animals, extensive production, and good shepherds.

Confinement agriculture is responsible for generating animal suffering on at least three fronts that are not a significant part of husbandry agriculture:

1. *Production diseases.* Veterinarians acknowledge the existence of so-called production diseases—that is, diseases that would not be a problem or that, at worst, would be a minor problem if animals were raised traditionally. One example is liver abscesses in feedlot cattle. In confinement agriculture, beef cattle are typically raised on pastures and finished by being fed grain in feedlots, where a large number of animals are crowded into relatively small spaces for the last few months of their lives. That much grain is not a natural diet for cattle—it is too high in concentrate (calories) and too low in roughage. Although a certain percentage of feedlot cattle get sick and may die, the overall economic efficiency of feedlots is maximized by the provision of such a diet. The idea of using a method of production that *creates diseases* that are "acceptable" would be anathema to a husbandry agriculturalist.

Indeed, the issue of diet in confinement operations is related to other health problems as well. In husbandry agriculture, animals eat natural forage. In industrialized agriculture, the quest for "efficiency" has led to feeding cattle poultry waste, newspaper, cement dust, and, most egregiously, bone or meat meal, which is something herbivores would not normally eat. Mad cow disease (bovine spongiform enceph-alopathy, or BSE) arose as a health problem because cattle were fed animal proteins from infected cows or sheep (a practice now prohib-ited by the U.S. Food and Drug Administration Ruminant Feed Ban).

2. *Lack of individual husbandry.* The huge scale of industrialized agriculture operations—and the small profit margin per animal—militates against the sort of individual attention that typified much of traditional agriculture. In traditional dairies fifty years ago, one could make a living with a herd of 50 cows. Today, one needs literally thousands. In parts of the United States, dairies may have 15,000 cows. People run sow operations with thousands of pigs that employ only a handful of unskilled workers. A case that speaks to this point was sent to me by a veterinarian for commentary in the column that I write for the *Canadian Veterinary Journal*:

> You (as a veterinarian) are called to a 5,000-sow farrow-to-finish swine operation to examine a problem with vaginal discharge in sows. There are three full-time employees and one manager overseeing approximately 5,000 animals. As you examine sev-eral sows in the created gestation unit, you notice one with a hind leg at an unusual angle and inquire about her status. You are told, "She broke her leg yesterday and she's due to farrow next week. We'll let her farrow in here and then we'll shoot her and foster her pigs." Is it ethically correct to leave the sow with a broken leg for one week while you await her farrowing?

Before commenting on this case, I spoke to the veterinarian who had experienced this incident, a swine practitioner. He explained that such operations run on tiny profit margins and minimal labor. Thus, even when he offered to splint the leg at no cost, he was told that the operation could not afford the manpower entailed by separating this sow and caring for her! At this point, he said, he realized that confinement agriculture had gone too far. He had been brought up on a family hog farm where the animals had names and were pro-vided individual husbandry, and the injured animal would have been treated or, if not, euthanized immediately. "If it is not feasible to do this in a confinement operation," he said, "there is something wrong with confinement operations!"

3. *Physical and psychological deprivation.* Another new source of suffering in industrialized agriculture is the physical and psychological deprivation experienced by animals in confinement: lack of space, lack of companionship for social animals, inability to move freely, boredom, austerity of environment, and so on. Since animals evolved for adaptation to extensive environments are now placed in truncated environments, such deprivation is inevitable. This was not a problem in traditional extensive agriculture.

From a public point of view, the unnatural confinement of animals is the most noticeable difference between traditional animal husbandry and modern industrial agriculture. Paul Thompson, a professor of ethics at Michigan State, has pointed out that the average American still sees farms as Old MacDonald's farm. Cows, in the public mind, should be grazing in pastures, lambs gamboling in fields, pigs happily cooling themselves in a mud wallow. As one of my colleagues put it, "The worst thing that ever happened to my department is betokened by the name change from Animal Husbandry to Animal Science." The practice of husbandry is the key loss in the shift from traditional to industrialized agriculture.

Farmers once put animals into an environment that the animals were biologically suited for and then augmented their natural ability to survive and thrive by providing protection from predators, food during famine, water during drought, help in birthing, protection from weather extremes, and the like. Any harm or suffering inflicted on the animal resulted in harm to the producer. An animal experiencing stress or pain, for example, is not as productive or as reproductively successful as a happy animal. Thus proper care and treatment of animals becomes both an ethical and a prudential requirement. The producer does well if and only if the animal does well. The result is good animal husbandry: a fair and mutually beneficial contract between humans and animals, with each better off because of the relationship.

In husbandry agriculture, individual animal productivity is a good indicator of animal well-being; in industrial agriculture, the link between productivity and well-being has been severed. When productivity as an economic metric is applied to the whole operation, the welfare of the individual animal is ignored. Husbandry agriculture "put square pegs in square holes and round pegs in round holes," extending individualized care to create as little friction as possible. Industrial agriculture, on the other hand, forces square pegs into round holes by use of "technological sanders"—antibiotics (which keep down disease that would otherwise spread like wildfire in close surroundings), vaccines, bacterins, hormones, air-handling systems, and the rest of the armamentarium used to keep the animals from dying. Furthermore, when crowding creates unnatural conditions and elicits unnatural behaviors such as tail biting in pigs or acts of cannibalism in poultry, the solution is to cut off the tail of the pig (without anesthetics) or to debeak the chicken, which can cause lifelong pain.

A few years ago, while visiting with some Colorado ranchers, I observed the ethic of animal husbandry in action, in a situation that contrasted sharply with the killing of sick pigs described at the beginning of this essay. That year, the ranchers had seen many of their calves afflicted with scours, a diarrheal disease. Every rancher I met had spent more money on treating the disease than was economically justified by the calves' market value. When I asked these men why they were being "economically irrational," they were adamant in their responses: "It's part of my bargain with the animal." "It's part of caring for them." This same ethical outlook leads ranchers to sit up all night with sick, marginal calves, sometimes for days in a row. If they were strictly guided by economics, these people would hardly be valuing their time at fifty cents per hour—including their sleep time. Yet industrialized animal production thrives while western cattle ranchers, the last large group of practitioners of husbandry agriculture, are an endangered species.

Unlike industrialized animal agriculture, husbandry agriculture is by its very nature sustainable. When pigs (or cattle) are raised on pasture, manure becomes a benefit, since it fertilizes pasture, and pasture is of value in providing forage for animals. In industrial animal agriculture, there is little reason to maintain pasture. Instead, farmers till for grain production, thereby encouraging increased soil erosion. At the same time, manure becomes a problem, both in terms of disposal and because it leaches into the water table. Similarly, air quality in and around confinement operations is often a threat to both workers and animals, and animal odors drive down real property values for miles around these operations.

Another morally questionable aspect of confinement agriculture is the destruction of small farms and local communities. Because of industrialization and economy of scale, small husbandry-based producers cannot compete with animal factories. In the broiler industry, farmers who wish to survive become serfs to large operators because they cannot compete on their own. In large confinement swine operations, where the system rather than the labor force is primary, migratory or immigrant workers are hired because they are cheap, not because they possess knowledge of or concern for the animals. And those raised in a culture of husbandry, as our earlier stories revealed, find it intolerable to work in the industrialized operations.

The power of confinement agriculture to pollute the Earth, degrade community, and destroy small, independent farmers should convince us that this type of agriculture is incompatible with common decency. Furthermore, we should fear domination of the food supply by these corporate entities. As to the oft repeated claim that industrial animal agriculture provides cheap food, this food is only cheap at the cash register—significant costs such as cleaning up pollution and increased health care costs in CAFO areas are "externalized"—that is, passed on to the public as taxes.

It is not necessary to raise animals this way, as history reminds us. In 1988, Sweden banned high-confinement agriculture; Britain and the EU have banned sow confinement. If food is destined to cost more, so be it—Americans now spend an average of only 11 percent of their income on food, whereas at the turn of the century they spent more than 50 percent, and Europeans now spend 20 percent. We are wrong to ignore the hidden costs paid by animal welfare, food safety, the environment, rural communities, and independent farmers, and we must now add those costs to the price of our food.

Some years ago Tim Blackwell, the chief swine veterinarian for Ontario, invited me to give the keynote speech on ethics and animal welfare to the swine producers of Ontario. Though I had by then given over three hundred lectures to all kinds of audiences, I had never spoken to pig producers. The group I was about to address had converted to high-confinement, highly intensive, highly capitalized, and highly industrialized production methods that had replaced animal husbandry with industry, and traditional agricultural values with an emphasis on efficiency and productivity.

I began in my usual fashion, with a few jokes, a few anecdotes. People laughed in the right places. So far so good. I continued as planned, discussing the differences between social ethics, personal ethics, and professional ethics. Ultimately, I spoke of the ethical problems that stemmed from the supplanting of an agriculture of husbandry—the practice of reciprocity and symbiosis between animals and people—by an exploitative agriculture in which animals do not benefit from being domesticated by humans.

When finally my speech ended, at first there was no applause. Oh-oh, I thought. Silence—my perennial nightmare. But then the applause began, and grew. I still could not see their faces, but Tim moved toward me, grabbing my hand. "You've done it, you son of a bitch, you've done it."

"Done what?" I asked.

"Touched their hearts! Can't you see the tears in their eyes?" Stupidly, I replaced my glasses and saw that he was right. Suddenly, one man climbed atop a picnic table and began to speak. "This was it!" he shouted. "This was the straw that broke the camel's back! I've been feeling lousy for fifteen years about how I raise these animals and so—in front of my peers, so I can't back out later—I'm pledging to tear down my confinement barn and build a barn I don't have to be ashamed of! I'm a good enough husbandman that I can do it right, make a living, and be able to look myself in the mirror!" This was Dave Linton, a leading hog farmer in the area. Tim whispered to me, "If Linton says it, he means it!"

A year and a half went by. Periodically I received progress reports from Tim, until eventually he took me to visit the new barn in person. With eyes dancing, Dave and his wife spoke of the new barn while serving us what is arguably the best strawberry-rhubarb pie in the universe. Finally, his wife said, "Enough talk, Dave—let the man see for himself."

We walked to the barn and opened the door. We went in. Mirabile dictu! There was sunshine! "The roof is hydraulic," Dave explained. "On nice days, we retract it so the animals are, in essence, outdoors.

And look! No stalls, no crates!" Indeed, in place of the crates were huge pens, lavishly supplied with straw, with fifteen or so animals to each pen. The sows lay around on beds of straw, chewing it as a cowboy chews tobacco. "They look . . . they look . . ." I groped for words. "Non-neurotic. Happy! That's it! Happy!"

Tim said, "I've been a pig vet for twenty years, and this is the first time I've seen sows smile."

"And," I marveled, "the air is sweet; at least as sweet as it could be!"

The three of us shook hands. Linton was effusive. "I'm a religious man," he said, "and God has already paid me back for doing the right thing!"

"How so?" I asked.

"It's my boy," he said. "My son." He went on to explain, "When we had the old barn, my son dropped out of school and did nothing but play video games. I couldn't interest him in the business or even get him to set foot in the barn. Since I built this one, I can't get him out!"

The key point is that there are alternatives to sow stalls. After all, we raised pigs for thousands of years without stalls! In fact, Tim Blackwell and I recently made a film entitled *Alternative Housing for Gestating Sows.* In it we portray a number of different loose-housing (i.e., noncrate) pen systems. What was notable was our discovery that not only do these systems work, but they also cost half as much to build as full-confinement systems, giving the producers a clear financial benefit.

Regardless of economic indicators, Dave Linton's story reminds us that it is a radical mistake to treat animals merely as products, as objects with no intrinsic value. A demand for agriculture that practices the ancient and fair contract with domestic animals is not revolutionary but conservative. As Mahatma Gandhi said, a society must ultimately be morally judged by how it treats its weakest members. No members are more vulnerable and dependent than our society's domestic animals.

FEAR FACTORIES

The Case for Compassionate Conservatism—for Animals

MATTHEW SCULLY

DESPITE THE HORRIFIC CONDITIONS *of mass confinement agriculture, on both the Right and Left in America's political debates there is little commentary on the issue of factory farming. The moral teachings of every major faith recognize that cruelty to animals is shameful and wrong, yet somehow these widely shared principles are seldom translated into serious policy debates over the treatment of animals. The livestock industry has a powerful interest in closing off debate about animal welfare: once the details of factory farming are known, the case for reform becomes overwhelming, and the great majority of voters take the side of mistreated animals.*

❖

A few years ago I began a book about cruelty to animals and about factory farming in particular, problems that had been in the back of my mind for a long while. At the time I viewed factory farming as one of the lesser problems facing humanity—a small wrong on the grand scale of good and evil but too casually overlooked and too glibly excused.

This view changed as I acquainted myself with the details and saw a few typical farms up close. By the time I finished the book, I had come to view the abuses of industrial farming as a serious moral problem, a truly rotten business for good reason passed over in polite conversation. Little wrongs, when left unattended, can grow and spread to become grave wrongs, and precisely this had happened on our factory farms.

The result of these ruminations was *Dominion: The Power of Man, the Suffering of Animals, and the Call to Mercy*. And though my tome never quite hit the bestseller lists, there ought to be some special literary prize for a work highly recommended in both the *Wall Street Journal* and *Vegetarian Teen*. When you enjoy the accolades of PETA and *Policy Review*, Deepak Chopra and G. Gordon Liddy, Peter Singer and Charles Colson, you can at least take comfort in the diversity of your readership.

The book also provided an occasion for fellow conservatives to get beyond their dislike for particular animal rights groups and to examine cruelty issues on the merits. Conservatives have a way of dismissing the subject, as if where animals are concerned nothing very serious could ever be at stake. And though it is not exactly true that liberals care more about these issues—you are no more likely to find reflections or exposés concerning cruelty in *The Nation* or *The New Republic* than in any journal of the Right—it is assumed that animal protection causes are a project of the Left, and that the proper conservative position is to stand warily and firmly against them.

I had a hunch that the problem was largely one of presentation and that by applying their own principles to animal welfare issues, conservatives would find plenty of reasons to be appalled. More to the point, having acknowledged the problems of cruelty, we could then support reasonable remedies. Conservatives, after all, aren't shy about discoursing on moral standards or reluctant to translate the most basic of those standards into law. Setting aside the distracting rhetoric of animal rights, that's usually what these questions come down to: what moral standards should guide us in our treatment of animals, and when must those standards be applied in law?

Industrial livestock farming is among a whole range of animal welfare concerns that extends from canned trophy hunting to whaling to product testing on animals to all sorts of more obscure enterprises like the exotic-animal trade and the factory farming of bears in China for bile believed to hold medicinal and aphrodisiac powers. Surveying the various uses to which animals are put, some might be defensible, others abusive and unwarranted, and it's the job of any conservative who attends to the subject to figure out which are which. We don't need novel theories of rights to do this. The usual distinctions that conservatives draw between moderation and excess, freedom and license, moral goods and material goods, rightful power and the abuse of power, will all do just fine.

As it is, the subject hardly comes up at all among conservatives, and what commentary we do hear usually takes the form of ridicule directed at animal rights groups. Often conservatives side instinctively with any animal-related industry and those involved, as if a thing is right just because someone can make money off it, or as if our sympathies belong always with the men just because they are men.

I had an exchange once with an eminent conservative columnist on this subject. Conversation turned to my book and to factory farming. Holding his hands out in the "stop" gesture, he said, "I don't want to know." Granted, life on the factory farm is no one's favorite subject, but conservative writers often have to think about things that are disturbing or sad. In this case, we have an intellectually formidable fellow known to millions for his stern judgments on every matter of private morality and public policy. Yet nowhere in all his writings do I find any treatment of any cruelty issue, never mind that if you asked him, he would surely agree that cruelty to animals is a cowardly and disgraceful sin.

And when the subject is cruelty to farmed animals—the moral standards being applied in a fundamental human enterprise—suddenly we're in forbidden territory and "I don't want to know" is the best he can do. But don't we have a responsibility to know? Maybe the whole subject could use his fine mind and his good heart.

What we're really looking for, when we debate animal rights issues, are safeguards against cruel and presumptuous people. We are trying to hold people to their obligations, people who could spare us the trouble if only they would recognize a few limits on their own conduct.

Conservatives like the sound of *obligation* here, and those who reviewed *Dominion* were relieved to find me arguing more from this angle than from any notion of rights. "What the PETA crowd doesn't understand," Jonah Goldberg wrote, "or what it deliberately confuses, is that human compassion toward animals is an obligation of humans, not an entitlement for animals." Another commentator put the point in religious terms: "[W]e have a moral duty to respect the animal world as God's handiwork, treating animals with 'the mercy of our Maker.' . . . But mercy and respect for animals are completely different from rights for animals—and we should never confuse the two." Both writers confessed they were troubled by factory farming and concluded with the uplifting thought that we could all profit from further reflection on our obligation of kindness to farm animals.

The only problem with this insistence on obligation is that after a while it begins to sounds like a hedge against actually being held to that obligation. It leaves us with a high-minded attitude but no accountability, free to act on our obligations or to ignore them without consequences, personally opposed to cruelty but unwilling to impose that view on others.

Treating animals decently is like most obligations we face, somewhere between the most and the least important, a modest but essential requirement to living with integrity. And it's not a good sign when arguments are constantly turned to precisely how much is mandatory and how much, therefore, we can manage to avoid.

If one is using the word *obligation* seriously, moreover, then there is no practical difference between an obligation on our end not to mistreat animals and an entitlement on their end not to be mistreated by us. Either way, we are required to do and not do the same things. And either way, somewhere down the logical line, the entitlement would have to arise from a recognition of the inherent dignity of a living creature. The moral standing of our fellow creatures may be humble, but it is absolute and not something within our power to confer or withhold. All creatures sing their Creator's praises, as this truth is variously expressed in the Bible, and are dear to Him for their own sakes.

A certain moral relativism runs through the arguments of those hostile or indifferent to animal welfare—as if animals can be of value only for our sake, as utility or preference decrees. In practice, this outlook leaves each person to decide for himself when animals rate moral concern. It even allows us to accept or reject such knowable facts about animals as their cognitive and emotional capacities, their conscious experience of pain and happiness.

Elsewhere in contemporary debates, conservatives meet the foe of moral relativism by pointing out that, like it or not, we are all dealing with the same set of physiological realities and moral truths. We don't each get to decide the facts of science on a situational basis. We do not each go about bestowing moral value upon things as it pleases us at the moment. Of course, we do not decide moral truth at all: we discern it. Human beings in their moral progress learn to appraise things correctly, using reasoned moral judgment to perceive a prior order not of our devising.

C. S. Lewis in *The Abolition of Man* calls this "the doctrine of objective value, the belief that certain attitudes are really true, and others really false, to the kind of thing the universe is and the kind of things we are." Such words as *honor, piety, esteem,* and *empathy* do not merely describe subjective states of mind, Lewis reminds us, but speak to objective qualities in the world beyond that merit those attitudes in us. "[T]o call children delightful or old men venerable," he writes, "is not simply to record a psychological fact about our own parental or filial emotions at the moment, but to recognize a quality which demands a certain response from us whether we make it or not."

This applies to questions of cruelty as well. A kindly attitude toward animals is not a subjective sentiment; it is the correct moral response to the objective value of a fellow creature. Here, too, rational and virtuous conduct consists in giving things their due and in doing so consistently. If one animal's pain—say, that of one's pet—is real and deserving of sympathy, then the pain of essentially identical animals is also meaningful, no matter what conventional distinctions we have made to narrow the scope of our sympathy. If it is wrong to whip a dog or starve a horse or bait bears for sport or grossly abuse farm animals, it is wrong for all people in every place.

The problem with moral relativism is that it leads to capriciousness and the despotic use of power. And the critical distinction here is not between human obligations and animal rights, but rather between obligations of charity and obligations of justice.

Active kindness to animals falls into the former category. If you take in strays or help injured wildlife or donate to animal charities, those are fine things to do, but no one says you should be compelled to do them. Refraining from cruelty to animals is a different matter, an obligation of justice not for us each to weigh for ourselves. It is not simply unkind behavior, it is unjust behavior, and the prohibition against it is non-negotiable. Proverbs reminds us of this—"a righteous man regardeth the life of his beast, but the tender mercies of the wicked are cruel"—and the laws of America and of every other advanced nation now recognize the wrongfulness of such conduct with cruelty statutes. Often applying felony-level penalties to protect certain domestic animals, our state and federal statutes declare that even though your animal may elsewhere in the law be defined as your property, there are certain things you may not do to that creature, and if you are found harming or neglecting the animal, you will answer for your conduct in a court of justice.

There are various reasons the state has an interest in forbidding cruelty, one of which is that cruelty is degrading to human beings. The problem is that many thinkers on this subject have strained to find indirect reasons to explain why cruelty is wrong and thereby to force animal cruelty into the category of the victimless crime. The most common of these explanations asks us to believe that acts of cruelty matter only because the cruel person does moral injury to himself or sullies his character—as if the cruel person is our sole concern and the cruelly treated animal is entirely incidental.

Yet there is only one reason for condemning cruelty that doesn't beg the question of exactly why cruelty is a wrong, a vice, or bad for our character: that the act of cruelty is an intrinsic evil. Animals cruelly dealt with are not just things, not just an irrelevant detail in some self-centered moral drama of our own. They matter in their own right, as they matter to their Creator, and the wrongs of cruelty are wrongs done to them. As *The Catholic Encyclopedia* puts this point, there is a "direct and essential sinfulness of cruelty to the animal world, irrespective of the results of such conduct on the character of those who practice it."

Our cruelty statutes are a good and natural development in Western law, codifying the claims of animals against human wrongdoing and asserting those claims on their behalf. Such statutes, however, address mostly random or wanton acts of cruelty. And the persistent animal welfare questions of our day center on institutional cruelties—on the vast and systematic mistreatment of animals that most of us never see.

Having conceded the crucial point that some animals rate our moral concern and legal protection, informed conscience turns naturally to other animals—creatures entirely comparable in their awareness, feeling, and capacity for suffering. A dog is not the moral equal of a human being, but a dog is definitely the moral equal of a pig, and it's only human caprice and economic convenience that say otherwise. We have the problem that these essentially similar creatures are treated in dramatically different ways, unjustified even by the very different purposes we have assigned to them. Our pets are accorded certain protections from cruelty, while the nameless creatures in our factory farms are hardly treated like animals at all. The challenge is one of consistency, of treating moral equals equally, and living according to fair and rational standards of conduct.

Whatever terminology we settle on, after all the finer philosophical points have been hashed over, the aim of the exercise is to prohibit wrongdoing. All rights, in practice, are protections against human wrongdoing, and here too the point is to arrive at clear and consistent legal boundaries on the things that one may or may not do to animals, so that every man is not left to be the judge in his own case.

More than obligation, moderation, ordered liberty, or any of the other lofty ideals we hold, what should attune conservatives to all the problems of animal cruelty—and especially to the modern factory farm—is our worldly side. The great virtue of conservatism is that it begins with a realistic assessment of human motivations. We know man as he is, not only the rational creature but also, as Socrates told us, the rationalizing creature, with a knack for finding an angle, an excuse, and a euphemism. Whether it's the pornographer who thinks himself a free-speech champion or the abortionist who looks in the mirror and sees a reproductive health care services provider, conservatives are familiar with the type.

So we should not be all that surprised when told that these very same capacities are often at work in the things that people do to animals—and all the more so in our $125 billion-a-year livestock industry. The human mind, especially when there is money to be had, can manufacture grand excuses for the exploitation of other human beings. How much easier it is for people to excuse the wrongs done to lowly animals.

Where animals are concerned, there is no practice or industry so low that someone, somewhere, cannot produce a high-sounding reason for it. The sorriest little miscreant who shoots an elephant, lying in wait by the water hole in some canned hunting operation, is just "harvesting resources," doing his bit for "conservation." The swarms of government-subsidized Canadian seal hunters slaughtering tens of thousands of newborn pups—hacking to death these unoffending creatures, even in sight of their mothers—offer themselves as the brave and independent bearers of tradition. With the same sanctimony and deep dishonesty, factory farm corporations like Smithfield Foods, ConAgra, and Tyson Foods still cling to countrified brand names for their labels—Murphy Family Farms, Happy Land Farms, Sunnyland Farms—to convince us and no doubt themselves, too, that they are engaged in something essential, wholesome, and honorable.

Yet when corporate farmers need barbed wire around their happy, sunny lands, and laws to prohibit outsiders from taking photographs (as is the case in three states), and still other laws to exempt farm animals from the definition of "animals" as covered in federal and state cruelty statutes, something is amiss. And if conservatives do nothing else about any other animal issue, we should attend at least to the factory farms, where the suffering is immense and we are all asked to be complicit.

If we are going to have our meats and other animal products, there are natural costs to obtaining them, defined by the duties of animal husbandry and of veterinary ethics. Factory farming came about when resourceful men figured out ways of getting around those natural costs, applying new technologies to raise animals in conditions that would otherwise kill them by deprivation and disease. With no laws to stop it, moral concern surrendered entirely to economic calculation, leaving no limit to the punishments that factory farmers could inflict to keep costs down and profits up. Corporate farmers hardly speak anymore of "raising" animals, with the modicum of personal care that word implies. Animals are "grown" now, like so many crops. Barns somewhere along the way became "intensive confinement facilities" and the inhabitants mere "production units."

The result is a world in which billions of birds, cows, pigs, and other creatures are locked away, enduring miseries they do not deserve, for our convenience and pleasure. We belittle the activists with their radical agenda, scarcely noticing the radical cruelty they seek to redress.

At the Smithfield mass-confinement hog farms I toured in North Carolina, the visitor is greeted by a bedlam of squealing, chain rattling, and horrible roaring. To maximize the use of space and minimize the need for care, the creatures are encased row after row, 400- to 500-pound mammals trapped without relief inside iron crates 7 feet long and 22 inches wide. They chew maniacally on bars and chains, as foraging animals will do when denied straw, or engage in stereotypical nest building with the straw that isn't there, or else just lie there like broken beings.

Efforts to outlaw the gestation crate have been dismissed by various conservative critics as "silly," "comical," "ridiculous." It doesn't seem that way up close. The smallest scraps of human charity—a bit of maternal care, room to roam outdoors, straw to lie on—have long since been taken away as costly luxuries, and so the pigs know only the feel of concrete and metal. They lie covered in their own urine and excrement, with broken legs from trying to escape or just to turn, covered with festering sores, tumors, ulcers, lesions, or what my guide shrugged off as routine "pus pockets."

C. S. Lewis's description of animal pain—"begun by Satan's malice and perpetrated by man's desertion of his post"—has literal truth in our factory farms because through the wonders of automation they basically run themselves, and the owners are off in spacious corporate offices reviewing their spreadsheets. Rarely are the creatures' afflictions examined by a vet or even noticed by the migrant laborers charged with their care, unless of course some ailment threatens production—meaning who cares about a lousy ulcer or broken leg, as long as we're still getting the piglets?

Kept alive in these conditions only by antibiotics, hormones, laxatives, and other additives mixed into their machine-fed swill, the sows leave their crates only to be driven or dragged into other crates, just as small, to bring forth their piglets. Then it's back to the gestation crate for another four months, and so on back and forth until after seven or eight pregnancies they finally expire from the punishment of it or else are culled with a club or bolt gun.

Industrial livestock farming operates on an economy of scale, presupposing a steady attrition rate. The usual comforting rejoinder we hear—that it's in the interest of farmers to take good care of their animals—is false. Each day, in every confinement farm in America, you will find cull pens littered with dead or dying creatures discarded like trash.

For the piglets, it's a regimen of teeth cutting, tail docking (performed with pliers, to heighten the pain of tail chewing and so deter this natural response to mass confinement), and other mutilations. After five or six months trapped in one of the grim warehouses that now pass for barns, they're trucked off, 355,000 pigs every day in the life of America, for processing at a furious pace of thousands per hour by migrants who use earplugs to muffle the screams. All these creatures, and billions more across the earth, go to their deaths knowing nothing of life, and nothing of man, except the foul, tortured existence of the factory farm, having never even been outdoors.

But not to worry, as a Smithfield Foods executive assured me, "They love it." It's all "for their own good." It is a voice conservatives should instantly recognize, as we do when it tells us that the fetus feels nothing. Everything about the picture shows bad faith, moral sloth, and endless excuse making, all readily answered by conservative arguments.

We are told "they're just pigs" or cows or chickens or whatever and that only urbanites worry about such things, estranged as they are from the realities of rural life. Actually, all of factory farming proceeds by a massive denial of reality—the reality that pigs and other animals are not just production units to be endlessly exploited but living creatures with natures and needs. The very modesty of those needs—their humble desires for straw, soil, sunshine—is the gravest indictment of the men who deny them.

Conservatives are supposed to revere tradition. Factory farming has no traditions, no rules, no codes of honor, no little decencies to spare for a fellow creature. The whole thing is an abandonment of rural values and a betrayal of honorable animal husbandry—to say nothing of veterinary medicine, with its sworn oath to "protect animal health" and to "relieve animal suffering."

Likewise, we are told to look away and think about more serious things. Human beings simply have far bigger problems to worry about than the well-being of farm animals, and surely all of this zeal would be better directed at causes of human welfare.

You wouldn't think that men who are unwilling to grant even a few extra inches in cage space, so that a pig can turn around, would be in any position to fault others for pettiness. Why are small acts of kindness beneath us, but not small acts of cruelty? The larger problem with this appeal to moral priority, however, is that we are dealing with suffering that occurs through human agency. Whether it's miserliness here, carelessness there, or greed throughout, the result is rank cruelty for which particular people must answer.

Since refraining from cruelty is an obligation of justice, moreover, there is no avoiding the implications. All the goods invoked in defense of factory farming, from the efficiency and higher profits of the system to the lower costs of the products, are false goods unjustly derived. No matter what right and praiseworthy things we are doing elsewhere in life, when we live off a cruel and disgraceful thing like factory farming, we are to that extent living unjustly, and that is hardly a trivial problem.

Factory farmers also assure us that all of this is an inevitable stage of industrial efficiency. Leave aside the obvious reply that we could all do a lot of things in life more efficiently if we didn't have to trouble ourselves with ethical restraints. Leave aside, too, the tens of billions of dollars in annual federal subsidies that have helped megafarms to undermine small family farms and the decent communities that once surrounded them and to give us the illusion of cheap products. And never mind the collateral damage to land, water, and air that factory farms cause and the more billions of dollars it costs taxpayers to clean up after them. Factory farming is a predatory enterprise, absorbing profit and externalizing costs, unnaturally propped up by political influence and government subsidies much as factory-farmed animals are unnaturally sustained by hormones and antibiotics.

Even if all the economic arguments were correct, conservatives usually aren't impressed by breathless talk of inevitable progress. I am asked sometimes how a conservative could possibly care about animal suffering in factory farms, but the question is premised on a liberal caricature of conservatism—the assumption that, for all of our fine talk about moral values, "compassionate conservatism," and the like, everything we really care about can be counted in dollars. In the case of factory farming, and the conservative's blithe tolerance of it, the caricature is too close to the truth.

Exactly how far are we all prepared to follow these industrial and technological advances before pausing to take stock of where things stand and where it is all tending? Very soon companies like Smithfield plan to have tens of millions of cloned animals in their factory farms. Other companies are at work genetically engineering chickens without feathers so that one day all poultry farmers might be spared the toil and cost of defeathering their birds. For years, the many shills for our livestock industry employed in the "Animal Science" and "Meat Science" departments of rural universities (we used to call them Animal Husbandry departments) have been tampering with the genes of pigs and other animals to locate and expunge that part of their genetic makeup that makes them stressed in factory farm conditions—taking away the desire to protect themselves and to live. Instead of redesigning the factory farm to suit the animals, they are redesigning the animals to suit the factory farm.

Are there no boundaries of nature and elementary ethics that the conservative should be the first to see? The hubris of such projects is beyond belief, only more because of the foolish and frivolous goods to be gained—blood-free meats and the perfect pork chop.

No one who does not profit from them can look at our modern factory farms or frenzied slaughter plants or agricultural laboratories with their featherless chickens and fear-free pigs and think, "Yes, this is humanity at our finest—exactly as things should be." Devils charged with designing a farm could hardly have made it more severe. Least of all should we look for sanction in Judeo-Christian morality, whose whole logic is one of gracious condescension, of the proud learning to be humble, the higher serving the lower, and the strong protecting the weak.

Lofty talk about humanity's special status among creatures only invites such questions as: What would the Good Shepherd make of our factory farms? Where does the creature of conscience get off lording it over these poor creatures so mercilessly? "How is it possible," as Malcolm Muggeridge asked in the years when factory farming began to spread, "to look for God and sing his praises while insulting and degrading his creatures? If, as I had thought, all lambs are the Agnus Dei, then to deprive them of light and the field and their joyous frisking and the sky is the worst kind of blasphemy."

The writer B. R. Meyers remarked in *The Atlantic*, "Research could prove that cows love Jesus, and the line at the McDonald's drive-through wouldn't be one sagging carload shorter the next day. . . . Has any generation in history ever been so ready to cause so much suffering for such a trivial advantage? We deaden our consciences to enjoy—for a few minutes a day—the taste of blood, the feel of our teeth meeting through muscle."

That is a cynical but serious indictment, and we must never let it be true of us in the choices we each make or urge upon others. If reason and morality are what set human beings apart from animals, then reason and morality must always guide us in how we treat them, or else it's all just caprice, unbridled appetite with the pretense of piety. When people say that they like their pork chops, veal, or foie gras just too much ever to give them up, reason hears in that the voice of gluttony, willfulness, or at best moral complacence. What makes a human being human is precisely the ability to understand that the suffering of an animal is more important than the taste of a treat.

Of the many conservatives who reviewed *Dominion*, every last one conceded that factory farming is a wretched business and a betrayal of human responsibility. So it should be a short step to agreement that it also constitutes a serious issue of law and public policy. Having granted that certain practices are abusive, cruel, and wrong, we must be prepared actually to do something about them.

Among animal activists, of course, there are some who go too far—there are in the best of causes. But fairness requires that we judge a cause by its best advocates instead of making straw men of the worst. There isn't much money in championing the cause of animals, so we're dealing with some pretty altruistic people who on that account alone deserve the benefit of the doubt.

If we're looking for fitting targets for inquiry and scorn, for people with an angle and a truly pernicious influence, better to start with groups like Smithfield Foods (my candidate for the worst corporation in America in its ruthlessness to people and animals alike), the

National Pork Producers Council (a reliable Republican contributor), or the various think tanks in Washington subsidized by animal use industries for intellectual cover.

We need conservatives, and especially our storied "values voters," to engage with the issue and get behind humane farming laws so that we can all quit averting our eyes. Such reforms, consisting of explicit federal cruelty statutes with enforcement funding to back them up, would leave us with farms we could imagine without wincing, photograph without prosecution, and explain without excuses.

The law would uphold not only the elementary standards of animal husbandry but also of veterinary ethics, following no more complicated a principle than that pigs and cows should be able to walk and turn around, fowl to move about and spread their wings, and all creatures to know the feel of soil and grass and the warmth of the sun. No need for labels saying "free-range" or "humanely raised." They will all be raised that way. They all get to be treated like animals and not as unfeeling machines.

On a date certain, mass confinement, sow gestation crates, veal crates, battery cages, and all such innovations would be prohibited. This will end livestock agriculture's moral race to the bottom and turn the ingenuity of its scientists toward compassionate solutions. It will remove the federal support that unnaturally serves agribusiness at the expense of small farms. And it will shift economies of scale, turning the balance in favor of humane farmers—as those who run companies like Wal-Mart could do right now by taking their business away from factory farms.

In all cases, the law would apply to corporate farmers a few simple rules that better men would have been observing all along: we cannot just take from these creatures—we must give them something in return. We owe them a merciful death, and we owe them a merciful life. And when human beings cannot do something humanely, without degrading both the creatures and ourselves, then we should not do it at all.

COLD EVIL

The Ideologies of Industrialism

ANDREW KIMBRELL

THE EXPLOITATION OF ANIMALS FOR PROFIT *is enabled by a cold, calculating Trinity of Science, Technology, and the Market that has stripped our public life of empathy. Countering factory farms requires going beyond legal and political strategies: what's needed is a societal reevaluation that places compassion and morality above the industrial cult of efficiency at any cost.*

❖

Pig No. 6707 was meant to be "super"—super fast growing, super big, super meat quality. He was supposed to be a technological breakthrough in animal food production. Researcher Vern Pursel and his colleagues at the U.S. Department of Agriculture had used taxpayer money to design this pig to be like no other, and to a certain extent they succeeded. Number 6707 was unique, both in his general physiology and in the very core of each and every cell. For this pig was born with a human growth gene engineered into his permanent genetic makeup, one of hundreds of thousands of animals that have now been engineered with foreign genetic material. Pursel's idea was to permanently insert human growth genes into livestock to create animals many times larger than those currently being bred. Pursel jokes of a pig "as big as a barn." He is serious, however, about merging human genes with the pig's genetic makeup to create more meat and more profit for the hog industry.

Pursel's pig did not turn into a superpig. The human growth genes injected into the animal at the early embryo stage altered its metabolism in unpredictable and tragic ways. By analogy, imagine injecting elephant growth genes into an early human embryo and the physiological changes that might accrue. The human growth genes in No. 6707 caused the creation of a huge muscle mass that overwhelmed the rest of the pig's physiology. He was crippled and bowlegged and riddled with arthritis. The genes made him impotent and nearly blind. The deformed pig could not stand up and could only be photographed in a standing position with the support of a plywood board. When Pursel was asked about his purpose in creating this suffering, pathetic creature, he responded that he was attempting to make livestock more efficient and more profitable. As for his failure, he said, "Even the Wright brothers did not succeed at first." Clearly for Pursel, there appeared to be little distinction between a machine (an airplane) and a living animal.

Pursel is not alone in his view of farm animals. The billions of animals that are slaughtered and disassembled each year throughout the factory farm system are viewed as little more than profitable commodities and production units. As most industrial factories use inanimate natural resources to manufacture various products, so animal factories dismember billions of animals annually and turn them into the neatly packaged commodities we purchase at our supermarkets and fast-food restaurants. This mechanistic mindset about farm animals is even encoded in our laws. The important protections against cruelty and mistreatment in our federal Animal Welfare Act apply to pets, exhibition animals, and research animals, but not to our farm animals.

SECULAR DOGMAS

Activists who have spent decades seeking protection for these animals have been repeatedly frustrated and angered by the coldness displayed by our legislators, policy makers, and much of the general public to the plight of these fellow creatures. How can so many blithely tolerate the unspeakable cruelties visited upon these countless sentient creatures? Part of the answer lies in the literal physical distance between the buyer of these animal commodities and the factories that produce them. "Out of sight, out of mind," is a ubiquitous if unattractive part of all our natures. Particularly when we imagine the horrors of the slaughterhouse, it's easier just to eat the burger and not think of the hidden history and suffering of the animal, made invisible by time and distance from the moment and place of eating.

But even as the nature of factory farming is masked through physical and temporal distancing, there is another, more subtle, more profound distancing that keeps the majority from challenging the realities of factory farming and the other evils of the industrial system. After all, Pursel was not physically distanced from the suffering he was creating. In fact, he was with pig No. 6707 day after day, carefully assessing each deformity and reaction. His distancing was not physical, but psychological and ideological. He and so many others—including most of our leaders—are ensconced in habits of thinking that are extraordinarily effective in making them immune to even the most terrible suffering and in suppressing their humanity and ethical responsibility.

Ideas have consequences, and the bizarre and tragic fate of pig No. 6707 is in reality the result of certain "trickle-down" ideologies that have over many generations become unquestioned habits of thought in modern industrial society. What are these dogmas? Pursel was motivated to genetically engineer pig No. 6707 by his unequivocal belief in objective science, and the requirements of efficiency. He was also driven by the hope of creating a more competitive and profitable pig. Quantitative science, efficiency, competition, and profit are the central dogmas underlying not just Pursel's experiments but also the entire industrial enterprise. These dogmas have been the underpinning of the industrial system that has spawned much of the wealth and the stunning daily "miracles" of modern technological society. The sufferings of billions in factory farms and other tragic results of applying these industrial ideologies to life have arisen not out of cruelty or passion, but rather from the impassive application of the "laws" of science, efficiency, and the market to living beings. That is why factory farms and other evils of the system are "cold" evils. They are not created by terrorists, religious fanatics, or psychopaths, persons acting out of uncontrolled "hot" violence, anger, or lust. Rather it is the businesspeople, scientists, policy makers, and consumers who are acting "rationally" by comporting themselves with these "laws" of science and economics on which our system is based. Factory farms, like environmental pollution, are representative of numerous systemic industrial evils that only 1 percent of society creates but in which the other 99 percent are complicit.

For many fighting for laws and regulations to help protect animals, a discussion of ideology may seem abstract. But I guarantee that anyone in the struggle against the factory farm system will come up against the wall of one or more of these dogmas consistently. Your view of animals and their suffering will be called "unscientific" by many animal scientists. Your suggestions for giving these animals more space or better treatment will be dismissed as grossly inefficient by economists. Your pleas to have laws passed that protect these animals will be said by legislators and their agribusiness friends to drive up costs, reduce profit, and make us less competitive in the world market. These modern shibboleths have kept the animal movement at bay and effectively marginalized advocates for decades. Unless we expose these ideological frames and find an alternative language, we will continue to flail away at these modern credos without much impact.

In the following exploration of these industrial ideologies, we will see that they date back centuries and involve some of the great thinkers of the Enlightenment and Western philosophy. I am not suggesting that purveyors of factory farms or animal research or industrial development have read up on their Descartes, Bacon, or Adam Smith. Quite the contrary: I believe that certain basic tenets of these philosophers have trickled down from the scientific and academic elite to become habits of thinking and perception for the general public. These ideologies now go virtually unexamined, yet they provide the basic rationale for much of what I have called the "cold evil" of the industrial system.

THE CULT OF OBJECTIVITY

One of the epochal moments in the history of Western science occurred on June 22, 1633, when Galileo, under extreme pressure from church inquisitors, "abjured" his heresy that the Earth revolves around the Sun. Since that time Galileo has remained an ultimate symbol of modern enlightenment martyred by the forces of superstition and prejudice. Yet if we consider the nature of the cold evil so prevalent today, we can bring charges against Galileo anew. For his real crime was not his understanding of the nature of the heavens, but rather his seminal role in creating what could be called "the cult of objectivity"—resulting in a science and scientific community that have largely been purged of subjectivity and qualitative human thought.

Galileo, a mathematician, was convinced that the natural world could not be understood through participation, relation, or metaphysical or spiritual work; rather, he maintained that the truth could be found only by means of objective, quantitative measurement and rigorous mathematical analysis. All the "warm" aspects of the human— memories, senses, kinship, empathy, relationship—he dismissed as subjective and immeasurable and therefore without value in the scientific search for truth. Galileo wrote that color, taste, and all subjective experiences were "merest opinion," while "atoms and the void are the truth." He then carried this argument one incredible step further, positing that what cannot be measured and reduced to numbers is not real. This philosophical "crime" of amputating human qualities from the search for truth is summarized by historian Lewis Mumford:

> Galileo committed a crime far greater than any dignitary of the Church accused him of; for his real crime was that of trading the totality of human experience for that minute portion which can be observed and interpreted in terms of mass and motion. . . . In dismissing human subjectivity Galileo had excommunicated history's central subject, multi-dimensional man. . . . Under the new scientific dispensation . . . all living forms must be brought into harmony with the mechanical world picture by being melted down, so to say, molded anew to conform to a more mechanical model.

The magnitude of the revolution in science inaugurated by Galileo and his fellow Enlightenment thinkers is difficult to comprehend. Perhaps philosopher Scott Buchanan best encapsulated this transformation when he described Galileo and his generation of thinkers as "world-splitters." Focusing fully on treating all of life and creation in cold, strictly mathematical and mechanical terms, they created a lasting dualism by separating the quantitative and qualitative, the objective and subjective. Regarding all the warm, individual, empathic, and feeling functions of the human as incapable of quantification and therefore of little or no importance, they elevated one value, the "cold" objective, as the only road to truth. Their dualism resulted in an attempt to completely eliminate human subjectivity from the scientific search for knowledge and truth. This cult of objectivity is thus based on the pathetic notion that somehow the observed can be separated from the observer, a fallacy that has disfigured and deformed most fields of science for centuries.

The cult of objectivity also provides the central underpinning for cold evil, offering a sure ideological defense against any attempt to reduce distancing through the infusion of qualitative human experience, whether it be feeling, relationship, participation, or culture. Its influence results in a just-the-facts, bottom-line conception of truth. Whoever seeks to break the bondage of cold evil, to strike out against it, is inevitably accused of being unscientific or, even worse (as so many animal advocates know), "emotional." When we protest against the dangers of nuclear technology, the dire effects of global warming, the massive destruction of biodiversity, the cruelties of the factory farms, or the monstrous creations of genetic engineering, we are inevitably warned not to react emotionally but rather to rely on objective "experts" using "sound science." We are intellectually bludgeoned into abandoning our protest and acquiescing to the objective "laws" and methods of science, the cold facts. As a result, the arts and philosophy are ghettoized as entertainment or academic pursuits, while love of and participation with animals and nature are dismissed as romantic and nostalgic.

Such disconnections result in a kind of social schizophrenia that separates our public lives from our private lives. If we tried to bring such objectivity into our family lives, we would correctly be viewed as insane. If a mother described her child solely in mathematical terms, stating that all the rest is "unreal," she would be an appropriate candidate for institutionalization. If someone described their beloved Labrador retriever to you solely in terms of its chemistry, you would react with laughter and disbelief. Yet this objectivist view is exactly what determines public policy in science, law, and much of our governmental and educational systems. Woe to the scientist who would speak of feeling communion with a cow, or of scientific truth received through poetry, long meditation on the spirituality of a salmon, or the experience of a Mozart piano concerto; woe to the lawyer who would ask the judge to use intuition in resolving the case, or even to the biology teacher who would teach that all of life has an "inside," a soul.

The ideological hold of the cult of objectivity is so strong that as a society we have virtually eliminated human culture and subjectivity as part of our scientific pursuit of knowledge and truth. Our policies continue to be guided by the cold values of quantification and measurability; they ignore intuition, emotional understanding, spiritual wisdom, and all the subjective human values so needed for our healing and wholeness. The continued reign of the cult of objectivity among our scientific and policy elites is a fundamental precondition of the acceptance of the industrial model of life and ensures the continuing spread of cold evils such as factory farming.

THE CULT OF EFFICIENCY

Just four years after Galileo's historic confrontation with the church, another mathematician, René Descartes, published his now famous *Discourse on Method*. Among its many provocative arguments was the revolutionary view that animals are really "beast machines," nothing more than "soulless automata." In a memorable passage, Descartes writes: "I wish . . . that you would consider all the functions [of animals] neither more nor less than the movements of a clock or other automaton . . . so that it is not necessary, on their account, to conceive within any animal any sensitive soul." This mechanistic concept of life quickly became a cause célèbre as theologians and others attacked the bête-machine theory. But the Cartesians were adamant and became active adherents and practitioners of vivisection, performing operations on live animals for the purpose of scientific research. Jean de La Fontaine gives us an account of where Descartes' theory led his followers:

> There was hardly a Cartesian who didn't talk of automata. . . .
> They administered beatings to dogs with perfect indifference,
> and made fun of those who pitied the creatures as if they had
> felt pain. They said the animals were clocks; that the cries they
> emitted when struck were only the noise of a little spring which

had been touched, but that the whole body was without feeling. They nailed poor animals up on boards by their four paws to vivisect them to see the circulation of blood, which was a great subject of conversation.

Pursel's genetic experiments, factory farming, and much of modern-day animal research are the unfortunate offspring of the centuries-old ideology of mechanism. This dogma is summed up by historian Floyd Matson, who notes: "With Descartes all of life has become a machine and nothing but a machine: all purposes and spiritual significance alike have been banished."

In the centuries since Descartes, we have fully entered the industrial/technological milieu, and as we create our great machines, they in turn re-create our images of ourselves. We speak of our soldiers as "fighting machines"; our leaders ask us to be "mighty engines of change"; and our bedroom partners call on us to be "sex machines." When we are tired, we say we are "worn out" and "run down," perhaps near a "breakdown." Cold evil thrives when all of life is viewed in terms of machinery. What dignity or responsibility inheres in a machine? How can machines love or care or feel? The habit of perceiving life as a machine ultimately distances us fully from our own humanity and from other animals and the entire living community.

The cult of efficiency is perhaps the greatest impact of Cartesian mechanism. Efficiency—maximum output with minimum input in minimum time—is an appropriate goal for the productivity of machines. Under the sway of mechanism, however, efficiency has metastasized over the past century into the principle virtue, not just for machines but for all life forms as well. We have undergone a kind of mechanomorphism, turning all life into machines and then judging and changing life utilizing the mechanistic value of efficiency. As noted, this view of animals as machines is the fundamental ideological underpinning of the animal "factories." However, humanity itself has not escaped the efficiency mandate. The effort to make humans more efficient began in earnest over a century ago when the eugenics movement became accepted public policy in the United States and led to the sterilization of thousands of the "unfit." The cult of efficiency was further forced on humans in the years prior to World War I by the pioneering work of American mechanical engineer Frederick Winslow Taylor, who began a managerial revolution to make workers more efficient in the newly developed assembly line method of production.

Efficiency has become our number one unquestioned virtue. A large part of our public and personal lives is constructed around this cult. As a society we repeatedly urge efficient government, an efficient and productive workforce, efficient use of natural resources, and efficient use of human resources. We have all become multitaskers, using the best-selling minute-manager manuals for reference (surely *The Nanosecond Manager* will be a bestseller of the future).

As demonstrated by the creation of pig No. 6707, the cult of efficiency is leading to enormous crimes against life. The great philosopher Owen Barfield in his seminal work *Saving the Appearances* warned that "those who mistake efficiency for meaning inevitably end by loving compulsion." Now genetic engineers such as Pursel are literally remaking the genetic code of the world's animals and other life forms to make them more efficient. Humans are not to be spared, as indicated by the November 2003 report "A Survey of the Use of Biotechnology in U.S. Industry," with recommendations by the U.S. Department of Commerce and the National Science Foundation; altering the permanent genetic makeup of humanity to increase the "efficiency of performance" is now a top scientific priority. Even as the doctrine of efficiency is becoming the dictate for biotechnology, nanotechnologists tell us that they will soon be rebuilding all of matter, molecule by molecule, to make it more efficient.

As with the cult of objectivity, if the efficiency principle is applied to private life, it quickly turns into the ludicrous. Such an incongruity should not surprise us, for efficiency is a machine value, not a life value. Is a mother to treat her children efficiently, giving them minimum food, affection, and "quality time" for maximum good behavior or academic performance? Are we to treat our friends according to an efficiency calculation? Do we treat our beloved pets on an efficiency basis? Most pets produce nothing at all (except perhaps spoiled rugs and chewed baseball gloves), but we lavish on them our love and affection. In fact, all these relationships are based not on efficiency but on empathy and love. Yet the cult of efficiency has robbed much of our public life of the language of empathy. Thus the cold evil cruelties of the workplace, the slaughterhouse, and the research laboratory are detached from the values that could reform and heal them.

THE CULT OF COMPETITION

In 2004, President George W. Bush urged Congress to pass international trade legislation and issued a call for economic competitiveness: "In an economy where competition is global, our only chance is to take the world head on, to compete and win . . . we cannot flinch. Our people are winners . . . we need to compete and win to shape the world of the twenty-first century." Some critics asked what it really meant to win economically against other countries. Was it right to enthusiastically herald competition and victory that would result in increasing poverty, unemployment, and social unrest in the losing countries? However, most in the world of economics and the media continue to praise the call by a succession of presidents for economic competition. And the competition ethic does not apply only to economics. In *No Contest: The Case Against Competition*, educator Alfie Kohn observes that competition permeates virtually every aspect of our lives: "From the time the alarm clock rings until sleep overtakes us again, from the time we are toddlers until the day we die, we are busy struggling to outdo others. This is our posture at work and at school, on the playing field and back at home. It is the common denominator of American life."

How did competition become the common denominator of our lives? Once again, it is because an ideology has trickled down to become part of the public consciousness. Anthropology teaches us that competition was never, prior to modernity, the manner in which a society allocated scarce resources. As historian Marcel Mauss writes: "Nowhere in the uninfluenced primitive society do we find labor associated with the idea of competition." The idea of competition as the means of achieving economic survival and furthering one's self-interest is relatively recent. The eighteenth-century philosopher Francis Hutcheson was looking for rules of human behavior that would be analogous to the newly discovered laws of physics. He finally determined that the greatest motivator of life is self-interest, asserting that this ethic is to social life what gravity is to the physical universe.

In 1776 Adam Smith, Hutcheson's most notable pupil, published *The Wealth of Nations.* This book would become a gospel of the new competitive economics. Smith maintained that each individual freely pursuing his own selfish needs would, without intending to, contribute to the economic and moral good of all. He thus saw the market as an almost divine "invisible hand" that would magically turn selfish competition into unintentional altruism. Smith's teachings encouraged the growth of the industrial revolution, providing the "moral" basis for the development of the capitalist-industrial state. Today Smith's theories concerning self-interest, competition, and the market have evolved into a veritable faith in human secular salvation through a self-regulating market.

As with objectivity and efficiency, competition is a "cold" ethic. It is the ethic of isolation and annihilation, separating us one from the other in the blood sport of making a living and leading us to desire the annihilation of the competitive other. As we each relentlessly pursue our self-interest, we become ever more cold hearted and isolated, ever more autistic—the very prescription for a cold evil society. Psychoanalyst Nathan Ackerman gives a telling description of the pathology of competition: "The strife of competition reduces empathetic sympathy, distorts communication, and impairs the mutuality of support and sharing."

Morton Deutsch, perhaps the most well-known researcher in the psychology of competition, describes the mindset required of those mired in the cult of competition: "In a competitive relationship, one is disposed to . . . have a suspicious, hostile, exploitative attitude towards the other, to be psychologically closed to the other, to be aggressive and defensive towards the other, to seek advantage and superiority for self and disadvantage and inferiority for the other." The proliferation of this mindset in the competitive market system acts as a powerful disincentive to practicing the empathy and cooperation so essential to fighting factory farming and other cold evil activities.

Additionally, the fear that profits will be lost and that a business or a nation will lose in the global economic competition is used as the single primary justification for not regulating the exploitation of the environment, the workers, and of course the billions of animals in the factory system. The ethic of competition also completely devalues the virtue of cooperation. Anthropologists tell us that the secret to a society's longevity is the cooperation between its members and the cooperative relationship it has with the elements of nature. Again we experience this in the family circumstance. No parent would throw out a child because he failed to successfully compete in grades with a sibling. We do not eliminate our elders because they can no longer compete with us in strength or in earning power. We do not destroy one pet because it cannot compete in speed or size with another. Quite the contrary, parents teach sharing and cooperation in a family as the secret to happiness and mutual growth.

THE RELIGION OF PROGRESS

What unites the dogmas of reductionist science, efficiency, and competition is what can only be described as our collective secular religion. That is, of course, our belief in Progress. More than a half century ago, philosopher Richard M. Weaver, in *The Ethics of Rhetoric*, noted the central religious position that "Progress" has taken in the modern technological state: "'Progress' becomes the salvation man is placed on earth to work out; and just as there can be no achievement more important than salvation, so there can be no activity more justified in enlisting our sympathy and support than 'progress.'" Our faith in technological progress may be obvious, but I think it is more difficult, and not completely fanciful, to see that it has a governing Trinity. The secular "Cold Trinity" of Progress apes the Christian Holy Trinity in a tragicomic way: Science will let us know everything; Technology will let us do everything; the Market will let us buy everything.

In the new Trinity, Science takes the place of God the Father. Mysterious and unknowable to all but the cognoscenti, Science has its own objective, unemotional laws and rules, which define the universe. To find the Truth it has its own unwavering impersonal process (ritual), known as "the scientific method." Any statement that begins "Science tells us . . ." has the imprimatur of unquestioned Truth.

Technology plays the role of the incarnated God, the Son. Science incarnates in our daily lives as Technology. It is an admittedly inhuman, cold, mechanical incarnation, yet it manufactures miracles. Technology saves lives, allows us to fly and to speak to others who are thousands of miles away, and creates so many other everyday wonders. Our belief in the Father (Science) is bolstered by the acts of the Son (Technology), which appear to be devoted to making our lives a "heaven on earth." Technology also has its impersonal, unquestioned commandments based on its mechanical nature, the aforementioned "laws" of efficiency. Importantly, Technology takes on the mysterious nature of its progenitor, Science. After all, few of us understand how even the most basic technologies (telephone, television) actually work. So Technology is in this world but, at least to our consciousness, not wholly of this world. It is a kind of incarnated magic.

Our adoration of Technology, despite its dominance over our lives, is not with us at all times, nor does it fully motivate our daily lives. Although we do not understand our technologies, we soon tend to take them for granted, so an animating, ever-visiting third member of the Trinity is needed: the Holy Spirit (the Market). We wake every day, go to work, and make money—with a deep desire to buy. Just as in traditional theology the Holy Spirit gives us access to the Son, so too the Market gives us access to (the ability to purchase) Technology and brings it into our lives. It is this spirit of acquisition that brings us fully to the Trinity. The Market also takes on the numinous quality of Science and Technology. As noted, its "laws" of supply and demand and competition are unquestioned dogmas that control public policy in virtually every sphere of our national and global economic lives. They are laws to which almost all of our economists and politicians genuflect on a daily basis.

The Cold Trinity provides a powerful, though mostly unconscious, arsenal for the defense of cold evil. No matter what environmental horror or exploitation of animals or humans occurs, it can be rationalized through the Trinity, whereas complaints against cold evil are routinely condemned as heresies. The Trinity acts as a kind of implicit enclosure of the spirit, a spiritual cocoon, blocking society from any incursion against the cold and binding laws of Science, Technology, and the Market. Questioning any one part of the Trinity leads to immediate suspicion, the potential ouster from serious discussion, or loss of influence. Those "heretics" who would expose the cold evil inherent in this default religion of Progress risk ridicule as well as academic and social excommunication.

RELATIONSHIP AND HEALING

To halt practices such as factory farming and the other technologies of industrial production, we must learn to regularly practice heresy against the religion of Progress. It is not enough to attempt to halt industrial practices through legal or market persuasion. We must also address the consciousness that creates, promotes, and provides a rationale for these cold evils. Even as we file lawsuits, demonstrate against factory farms, or work for humane certification, we must also do public outreach and education to halt the spread of these dangerous dogmas of the industrial mind. We must reinfuse science with the qualitative experiences required for any holistic search for truth. Intuition and feeling provide a better handle for many truths about nature, animals, and ourselves than does reductionist, quantitative science. We must also refuse to elevate the mechanistic value of efficiency to the supreme value for life; instead we must value above all the ethic of empathy toward all living things. Similarly we must balance competition with cooperation, not only in our private lives but also in the form and content of our policy and public discourses. We must never allow the word *progress* to be used except in the context of the question, Progress toward what? Factory farms, the genetic engineering of animals, the destruction of nature, and the alteration of human nature are not progress; they are regressions into a less than human and humane future.

There is, of course, a metaphysical framing involved in this work. In the memorable words of ecotheologian Thomas Berry, our current economic and technological systems have turned all of nature "from a community of subjects into a collection of objects." To restore relationship and begin healing we must again treat the living kingdom as a community of subjects, each with its own meaning and destiny, its own eidos and telos. Living beings must never be treated as mere objects, commodities, or means of production. Moving toward this new moral community involves nothing less than replacing the infrastructure of cold evil practices such as factory farming with technologies and human systems that are responsive to our physical and spiritual needs along with the needs of the rest of the biotic community. Such a shift requires evolving a means of production and social organization for which we can truly take ethical responsibility. It is a daunting, even overwhelming task, but the alternative is to continue to live in a state of cold evil, complicit in the current system's crimes and distanced from relationship and healing with our fellow creatures and nature. This we can no longer do.

RENEWING HUSBANDRY

The Mechanization of Agriculture Is Fast Coming to an End

WENDELL BERRY

IN A CLASSIC SENSE, TO HUSBAND *means to use with care, to keep, to save, to make last, to conserve. The replacement of husbandry with the science and industry of agriculture has effectively reduced the number of landowners and the self-employed. It has transformed the United States from a country of many owners to a country of many employees. Can husbandry be renewed?*

❖

I remember well a summer morning in about 1950 when my father sent a hired man with a McCormick High Gear No. 9 mowing machine and a team of mules to the field I was mowing with our nearly new Farmall A. That memory is a landmark in my mind and my history. I had been born into the way of farming represented by the mule team, and I loved it. I knew irresistibly that the mules were good ones. They were stepping along beautifully at a rate of speed in fact only a little slower than mine. But now I saw them suddenly from the vantage point of the tractor, and I remember how fiercely I resented their slowness. I saw them as "in my way."

This is not an exceptional or a remarkably dramatic bit of history. I recite it to confirm that the industrialization of agriculture is a part of my familiar experience. I don't have the privilege of looking at it as an outsider.

We were mowing that morning, the teamster with his mules and I with the tractor, in the field behind the barn on my father's home place, where he and before him his father had been born, and where his father had died in February of 1946. The old way of farming was intact in my grandfather's mind until the day he died at eighty-two. He had worked mules all his life, understood them thoroughly, and loved the good ones passionately. He knew tractors only from a distance, he had seen only a few of them, and he rejected them out of hand because he thought, correctly, that they compacted the soil.

Even so, four years after his death his grandson's sudden resentment of the "slow" mule team foretold what history would bear out: the tractor would stay and the mules would go. Year after year, agriculture would be adapted more and more to the technology and the processes of industry and to the rule of industrial economics. This transformation occurred with astonishing speed because, by the measures it set for itself, it was wonderfully successful. It "saved labor," it conferred the prestige of modernity, and it was highly productive.

During the fourteen years after 1950 I was much away from home. I never entirely departed from farming or at least from thoughts of farming, and my affection for my homeland remained strong. In 1964 my family and I returned to Kentucky and settled on a hillside farm in my native community, where we have continued to live. Perhaps because I was a returned traveler intending to stay, I now saw the place more clearly than before. I saw it critically, too, for it was evident at once that the human life of the place, the life of the farms and the farming community, was in decline. The old self-sufficient way of farming was passing away. The economic prosperity that had visited the farmers briefly during World War II and for a few years afterward had ended. The little towns that once had been social and economic centers, thronged with country people on Saturdays and Saturday nights, were losing out to the bigger towns and the cities. The rural neighborhoods, once held together by common memories, common work, and the sharing of help, had begun to dissolve. There were no longer local markets for chickens or eggs or cream. The spring lamb industry, once a staple of the region, was gone. The tractors and other mechanical devices certainly were saving the labor of the farmers and farmhands who had moved away, but those who had stayed were working harder and longer than ever.

The effects of this process of industrialization have become so apparent, so numerous, so favorable to the agribusiness corporations, and so unfavorable to everything else, that by now the questions troubling me and a few others in the 1960s and 1970s are being asked everywhere. It has become increasingly clear that the way we farm affects the local community, and that the economy of the local community affects the way we farm; that the way we farm affects the health and integrity of the local ecosystem, and that the farm is intricately dependent, even economically, upon the health of the local ecosystem. We can no longer pretend that agriculture is a sort of economic machine with interchangeable parts, the same everywhere, determined by "market forces" and independent of everything else. We are not farming in a specialist capsule or a professionalist department; we are farming in the world, in a webwork of dependences and influences probably more intricate than we will ever understand. It has become clear, in short, that we have been running our fundamental economic enterprise by the wrong rules. We were wrong to assume that agriculture could be adequately defined by reductionist science and determinist economics.

It is no longer possible to deny that context exists and is an issue. If you can keep the context narrow enough (and the accounting period short enough), then the industrial criteria of labor saving and high productivity seem to work well. But the old rules of ecological coherence and of community life have remained in effect. The costs of ignoring them have accumulated, until now the boundaries of our reductive and mechanical explanations have collapsed. Their collapse reveals, plainly enough for all to see, the ecological and social damages they were meant to conceal. It will seem paradoxical to some that the national and global corporate economies have narrowed the context for thinking about agriculture, but it is merely the truth. Those large economies, in their understanding and in their accounting, have excluded any concern for the land and the people. Now, in the midst of so much unnecessary human and ecological damage, we are facing the necessity of a new start in agriculture.

The tractor's arrival had signaled, among other things, agriculture's shift from an almost exclusive dependence on free solar energy to a total dependence on costly fossil fuel. But in 1950, like most people at that time, I was years away from the first inkling of the limits of the supply of cheap fuel.

We had entered an era of limitlessness, or the illusion thereof, and this in itself is a sort of wonder. My grandfather lived a life of limits, both suffered and strictly observed, in a world of limits. I learned much of that world from him and others, and then I changed; I entered the world of labor-saving machines and of limitless cheap fossil fuel. It would take me years of reading, thought, and experience to learn again that in this world limits are not only inescapable but also indispensable.

Mechanical farming makes it easy to think mechanically about the land and its creatures. It makes it easy to think mechanically even about oneself, and the tirelessness of tractors brought a new depth of weariness into human experience, at a cost to health and family life that has not been fully accounted.

Once one's farm and one's thoughts have been sufficiently mechanized, industrial agriculture's focus on production, as opposed to maintenance or stewardship, becomes merely logical. And here the trouble completes itself. The almost exclusive emphasis on production permits the way of working to be determined, not by the nature and character of the farm in its ecosystem and in its human community, but rather by the national or the global economy and the available or affordable technology. The farm and all concerns not immediately associated with production have in effect disappeared from sight. The farmer too in effect has vanished. He is no longer working as an independent and loyal agent of his place, his family, and his community, but instead as the agent of an economy that is fundamentally adverse to him and to all that he ought to stand for.

The word *husbandry* is the name of a connection. In its original sense, it is the name of the work of a domestic man, a man who has accepted a bondage to the household. To husband is to use with care, to keep, to save, to make last, to conserve. Old usage tells us that there is a husbandry also of the land, of the soil, of the domestic plants and animals—obviously because of the importance of these things to the household. And there have been times, one of which is now, when some people have tried to practice a proper human husbandry of the nondomestic creatures in recognition of the dependence of our households and domestic life upon the wild world. Husbandry is the name of all the practices that sustain life by connecting us conservingly to our places and our world; it is the art of keeping tied all the strands in the living network that sustains us.

Most and perhaps all of industrial agriculture's manifest failures appear to be the result of an attempt to make the land produce without husbandry. The attempt to remake agriculture as a science and an industry has excluded from it the age-old husbandry, which was central and essential to it.

This effort had its initial and probably its most radical success in separating farming from the economy of subsistence. Through World War II, farm life in my region (and, I think, nearly everywhere) rested solidly upon the garden, dairy, poultry flock, and meat animals that fed the farm's family. Especially in hard times farm families, and their farms too, survived by means of their subsistence economy. The industrial program, on the contrary, suggested that it was "uneconomic" for a farm family to produce its own food; the effort and the land would be better applied to commercial production. The result is utterly strange in human experience: farm families that buy everything they eat at the store.

An intention to replace husbandry with science was made explicit in the renaming of disciplines in the colleges of agriculture. "Soil husbandry" became "soil science," and "animal husbandry" became "animal science." This change is worth lingering over because of what it tells us about our susceptibility to poppycock. Purporting to increase the sophistication of the humble art of farming, this change in fact brutally oversimplifies it.

"Soil science," as practiced by soil scientists, and even more as it has been handed down to farmers, has tended to treat the soil as a lifeless matrix in which "soil chemistry" takes place and "nutrients" are "made available." And this, in turn, has made farming increasingly shallow—literally so—in its understanding of the soil. The modern farm is understood as a surface on which various mechanical operations are performed, and to which various chemicals are applied. The undersurface reality of organisms and roots is mostly ignored.

"Soil husbandry" is a different kind of study, involving a different kind of mind. Soil husbandry leads, in the words of Sir Albert Howard, to understanding "health in soil, plant, animal, and man as one great subject." We apply the word *health* only to living creatures, and to soil husbandry a healthy soil is a wilderness, mostly unstudied and unknown, but teemingly alive. The soil is at once a living community of creatures and their habitat. The farm's husband, its family, its crops and animals, all are members of the soil community; all belong to the character and identity of the place. To rate the farm family merely as "labor" and its domestic plants and animals merely as "production" is thus an oversimplification, both radical and destructive.

Science is too simple a word to name the complex of relationships and connections that compose a healthy farm—a farm that is a full membership of the soil community. The husbandry of mere humans of course cannot be complex enough either. But husbandry always has understood that what is husbanded is ultimately a mystery. A farmer, as one of his farmer correspondents once wrote to Liberty Hyde Bailey, is "a dispenser of the 'Mysteries of God.'" The mothering instinct of animals, for example, is a mystery that husbandry must use and trust mostly without understanding. The husband, unlike the "manager" or the would-be objective scientist, belongs inherently to the complexity and the mystery that is to be husbanded, and so the husbanding mind is both careful and humble. Husbandry originates precautionary sayings like "Don't put all your eggs into one basket" and "Don't count your chickens before they hatch." It does not boast of technological feats that will "feed the world."

Husbandry, which is not replaceable by science, nevertheless uses science, and corrects it too. It is the more comprehensive discipline. To reduce husbandry to science, in practice, is to transform agricultural "wastes" into pollutants, and to subtract perennials and grazing animals from the rotation of crops. Without husbandry, the agriculture of science and industry has served too well the purpose of the industrial economy in reducing the number of landowners and the self-employed. It has transformed the United States from a country of many owners to a country of many employees.

Without husbandry, "soil science" too easily ignores the community of creatures that live in and from, that make and are made by, the soil. Similarly, "animal science" without husbandry forgets, almost as a requirement, the sympathy by which we recognize ourselves as fellow creatures of the animals. It forgets that animals are so called because we once believed them to be endowed with souls. Animal science has led us away from that belief or any such belief in the sanctity of animals. It has led us instead to the animal factory, which, like the concentration camp, is a vision of Hell. Animal husbandry, on the contrary, comes from and again leads to the psalmist's vision of good grass, good water, and the husbandry of God.

Agriculture must mediate between nature and the human community, with ties and obligations in both directions. To farm well requires an elaborate courtesy toward all creatures, animate and inanimate. It is sympathy that most appropriately enlarges the context of human work. Contexts become wrong by being too small— "too small, that is, to contain the scientist or the farmer or the farm family or the local ecosystem or the local community"—and this is crucial. "Out of context," as Wes Jackson has said, "the best minds do the worst damage."

Our recent focus upon productivity, genetic and technological uniformity, and global trade—all supported by supposedly limitless supplies of fuel, water, and soil—has obscured the necessity for local adaptation. But our circumstances are changing rapidly now, and this requirement will be forced upon us again by terrorism and other kinds of political violence, by chemical pollution, by increasing energy costs, by depleted soils, aquifers, and streams, and by the spread of exotic weeds, pests, and diseases. We are going to have to return to the old questions about local nature, local carrying capacities, and local needs. And we are going to have to resume the breeding of plants and animals to fit the region and the farm.

The same obsessions and extravagances that have caused us to ignore the issue of local adaptation have caused us to ignore the issue of form. These two issues are so closely related that it is difficult to talk about one without talking about the other. During the half century and more of our neglect of local adaptation, we have subjected our farms to a radical oversimplification of form. The diversified and reasonably self-sufficient farms of my region and of many other regions have been conglomerated into larger farms with larger fields, increasingly specialized, and subjected increasingly to the strict, unnatural linearity of the production line.

But the first requirement of a form is that it must be comprehensive; it must not leave out something that essentially belongs within it. The form of the farm must answer to the farmer's feeling for the place, its creatures, and its work. It is a never-ending effort of fitting together many diverse things. It must incorporate the life cycle and the fertility cycles of animals. It must bring crops and livestock into balance and mutual support. It must be a pattern on the ground and in the mind. It must be at once ecological, agricultural, economic, familial, and neighborly.

Soon the majority of the world's people will be living in cities. We are now obliged to think of so many people demanding the means of life from the land, to which they will no longer have a practical connection, and of which they will have little knowledge. We are obliged also to think of the consequences of any attempt to meet this demand by large-scale, expensive, petroleum-dependent technological schemes that will ignore local conditions and local needs. The problem of renewing husbandry, and the need to promote a general awareness of everybody's agricultural responsibilities, thus becomes urgent.

How can we restore a competent husbandry to the minds of the world's producers and consumers? This effort is already in progress on many farms and in many urban consumer groups scattered across our country and the world. But we must recognize too that this effort needs an authorizing focus and force that would grant it a new legitimacy, intellectual rigor, scientific respectability, and responsible teaching. There are many reasons to hope that our colleges of agriculture might supply this.

The effort of husbandry is partly scientific, but it is entirely cultural, and a cultural initiative can exist only by becoming personal. It will become increasingly clear, I believe, that agricultural scientists will need to work as indwelling members of agricultural communities or of consumer communities. It is not irrational to propose that a significant number of these scientists should be farmers, and so subject their scientific work, and that of their colleagues, to the influence of a farmer's practical circumstances. Along with the rest of us, they will need to accept all the imperatives of husbandry as the context of their work. We cannot keep things from falling apart in our society if they do not cohere in our minds and in our lives.

MAN, THE PARAGON OF ANIMALS?

Questioning Our Assumptions About Evolution

CHRISTOPHER MANES

OUR TREATMENT OF ANIMALS *is not simply cruel and inhumane: it reflects a deeply destructive culture in which animals are bred— and genetically engineered—into units of economic and social convenience. In the process, we destroy our own animal spirit, producing a creatureless mechanical society. To create meaningful change we must see animals and nature as our equals, rather than as ingredients for industrial "progress."*

❖

We are all familiar with the evolutionary tableau. It hovers there, visible to our thinking, an idea given graphic form in our minds, as much a part of our sense of self as childhood photographs. On the far left (the side from which we read and write texts), in some primordial sea floats a colony of single-celled creatures, protozoa huddled together as if conspiring about what is to follow. To their immediate right, more complicated but still rudimentary forms appear: a worm, an anemone, a jellyfish, a mollusk. Then, to fill this ocean of progress to the brim, a primitive fish swims into existence. Continuing to the right, poised between sea and land, an ungainly creature with a gaping mouth rears up on elongated fins to breathe its first gulp of air. It is succeeded by a salamander-like amphibian, with all four feet moving tentatively forward on dry ground. After that creeps a reptile, large and arrogant, seemingly aware that for a season it has dominion over the Earth. Farther to the right, however, a craftier animal, covered with fur and ambling on bearlike paws, takes its place: a protomammal. No bird appears at this point, or if it does, it is an insignificant pair of wings flying high above the mammal—an apparent digression from the orderly procession below.

Now the really interesting creatures make their appearance; the ones we have all been waiting for. First, a monkey and an ape, still on all fours but apparently straining to stand upright. That virtue, however, is reserved for the next in line, a primitive hominid, perhaps an australopithecine, still hirsute and a bit stooped. His successor, a *Homo erectus*, stands straighter and more confident as he lumbers into humanness: only his heavy-browed face gives his backwardness away. After that, a Neanderthal walks, often shown holding a club, perhaps to suggest he hasn't quite made it yet to the noble estate of civilized existence. And finally, on the far right, front and center, leading this zoomorphic parade of emerging forms is the being toward which this compressed history of life has been converging: taller than the rest and high browed, a fully erect *Homo sapiens* marches. With his back to the remainder of nature, he faces the blankness at the margin of the graphic, striding off into the invisible unknown with the self-assured gait of one who walks in the evolutionary limelight.

This graphic representation of evolution, which we have all seen in high school textbooks, is of course a crude simplification. It is a heuristic, meant to bring home a basic principle of a scientific theory rather than to capture the complex, subtle lineage of living forms on this planet. Nevertheless, the particular way our culture chooses to present evolutionary theory suggests an ethical and philosophical stance, if not in the makeup of the graphic itself, then at least in how it is used and understood by our culture at large.

Would it not be possible to make a graphic true to evolution theory in which, say, a greyhound occupies the coveted far right position? Dogs emerged more recently than humans. If the graphic is ordered chronologically, as it appears to be, then wouldn't this be a more perfect representation?

The incongruity of having a greyhound succeed a human in our alternate evolution highlights an important ambiguity in the tableau. Strictly speaking, the graphic represents only *human* evolution, not evolution in general, as any biologist would have already vehemently pointed out. But this unimpeachable, scientifically accurate objection neglects the way in which the graphic is actually used in our society. For a technological culture transfixed by the presumed supremacy of intellect over nature, human evolution *is* evolution for all intents and purposes. The emergence of *Homo sapiens* stands as a symbol for the entire saga of biological adaptation on this planet. Ask people to "draw" evolution and they will probably come up with something akin to our graphic, with a human being at the lead. Hasn't evolution always been "tending" toward humanity, our culture seems to insist, with a steady development in intellect, creativity, consciousness, or some other ambiguous quality that the struggle for survival has apparently lavished on human beings above all else? Even trained biologists use the term *lower life forms.*

In this way, a double meaning emerges: the representation has not only a scientific significance but a cultural life in which it embodies and reinforces the idea that the human species is the "goal" of evolution. No reputable biologist would condone such a notion, and yet it is undeniably part of our technological culture.

A truly accurate representation of evolution would have humans, greyhounds, slimeworts, and all other modern organic forms on the right, representing the present, each equally sharing in the unpredictable unfolding of evolution, with their ancestral forms off somewhere in the past, on the left, intermingling promiscuously in a wanton dance of life. But universal kinship is not what comes to mind when the word *evolution* is used in our culture.

We should ask: Why privilege brain size or bipedalism or any of the other traits of humanity in representing evolution? Couldn't we give the privileged position according to some other quality we see, rightly or wrongly, as central to understanding the evolutionary process? Thus, if we assumed the ordering principle of evolution is the development of fleetness of foot rather than intellect, a cheetah should be the first in line—running well ahead of the pack. If, instead, longevity is that special quality, then bristlecone pine trees would capture the privileged spot now held by a hominid. The list could be extended indefinitely depending on the characteristic being promoted, in essence giving each species its privileged moment as the capstone of evolution, and thus requiring as many representations as there are species on the planet. It would be Andy Warhol's fifteen minutes of fame played out on an evolutionary canvas.

The theory of evolution maintains that all living things, under the pressure of natural selection and domestication, have developed from past forms and are more or less related genealogically depending on the proximity of a common ancestor. This is to say that there is really no basis for putting any life form at the forefront of evolution: elephants are no more developed than toadstools, salmon are no less advanced than seagulls, cabbages have as much status in the scheme of life as kings. To be sure, we are more closely related genealogically to chimpanzees than to lichen, but that doesn't mean lichen lag behind either humans or chimpanzees in the history of life. Chimps and humans can make tools, but lichen photosynthesize and we can't; chimps and humans have high IQs, but lichen dissolve stones. The useless comparisons could continue indefinitely. Although it may bruise our species' ego to be likened to lichen, from an evolutionary perspective, we cannot produce any biologically aristocratic escutcheon to the contrary.

THE MONOLOGUE OF MAN

The popular representation of evolution has become a cultural icon for a purpose altogether at variance with the scientific theory. What it presents is a story, a narrative, with a fictionalized version of humanity: the character of "Man," or as John Muir called him, "Lord Man." We have turned evolution into the monologue of "Man."

The theme of this monologue is that "Man" is a distinct entity among all the other species of this planet. There is "Man" and then there is nature, the realm of "lower" forms, from which "Man" has emerged and separated himself. But this unique creature is not only superior to other life forms; he is their consummation, the goal toward which they have been striving during the past 3.5 billion years of organic history. "Man," so the story goes, is the aim of evolution, its telos. And therefore, this paragon of animals, this demigod of creation, has a sort of cosmic sanction bestowed upon his activities. "Man" is the principle behind the order of things, as Bacon argued, and his intellect with its devices can rightfully supplant the natural world and its unrefined denizens.

While evolutionary theory stands in exact contradiction to the superiority of humanity (and was vigorously denounced by religious authorities as a result), its representation has very much been captured by this idea. Thus a theory that demoted humanity from semi-divine status into the swelter of biological forms has strangely come to serve the purpose of promoting the biological and moral superiority of humanity. A biological category has become a moral imperative.

Each religion has its own way of dealing with evolutionary theory: rejecting it, accepting it, modifying it, retelling it. My point is to highlight the misuse of the fictionalized version of the theory as a metaphor for human existence, a metaphor many religions themselves embrace in placing humanity above the rest of animal creation. Moreover, the fictional character of "Man" no longer merely dwells in the story of evolution, but rather he has installed himself in all the institutions of our culture, including our religious institutions. "Man," as the morally superior center of the world, has banished the saintly view of animals, has marginalized the rest of creation, has monopolized the conversation about spirituality in a way early Christianity, Judaism, and Islam would not have understood—or at best deemed an expression of the ultimate sin of pride.

THE MARGINALIZATION OF ANIMALS

This narrative placing "Man" above and separate from the rest of the biotic community has had devastating impacts on the natural world and is reflected, most tellingly, in our treatment of animals. The most egregious abuse is that of the domesticated animals. As the pinnacle of evolution, we do not hesitate to artificially change the "evolution" of these animals, including the billions of cattle, pigs, and chickens used by humanity each year for food, by breeding them to accentuate the traits that suit our needs, or by genetic engineering. In this way, domesticated animals have become tragic symbols of the worst aspects of civilization. "The pathos of the over-fat pig, white rat stripped of nuance, and dog breeds with their congenital debilitations," suggests Paul Shepard, "signals to us an aspect of the human condition." We have projected these animals as inferior to ourselves and then turned them into physical representations of our own worse instincts.

Wild animals have also succumbed to the influence of humanity's "sovereignty." Wild animals have become spectacles in our culture. Millions of people visit zoos every year to see wild creatures, but the institution is a monument to the impossibility of such an encounter. Framed by the walls and other artificial props, isolated from interactions with other species, alienated from their habitat, zoo animals are mere simulacra of wild beasts, neither domesticated nor feral, but shadow puppets. Doug Peacock, an expert on grizzly bears, defines true wilderness as the place where something bigger than you can eat you. This is not the space of the zoo. We never meet the true gaze of a wild beast, either as predator or prey or mere neighbor, since all their actions have been rendered void. The relationship is one-dimensional: the visitor gawks, and the animals submit to being objects of observation.

Nature films, whose popularity has exploded in recent years just as the animals they depict disappear, produce a more subtle form of marginalization. Natural history documentaries of wild animals purport to show creatures interacting with their environment in a natural manner. We supposedly meet predator, prey, and biological curiosities in all their beauty and freedom. How can the camera lie after all? But the camera always lies when it comes to encountering the wild. As with zoo visitors, film viewers become pure observers of the wilderness spectacle, with nothing at stake except the observation of images moving across the screen. Aspects of an animal's life that have no interest to us, but which may dominate their existence, get edited out by people who understand that for such films to sell, they must cater to the desires of modern viewers with all their cultural biases. As a result, in the editing process, only images of the more spectacular events—chases, mating displays, mothers defending their young—make it to the screen. The verisimilitude of the representations tempts us to disregard that nature films are merely a patronizing version of the "Monologue of Man," works that show only certain views of the animals that "Man" finds of interest. As a way to encounter the wild, nature films inevitably fail through the very form they take, and we must not fool ourselves into accepting a human-edited image of a jaguar as a substitute for Jaguar. The former is a cultural artifact, no matter how meticulously accurate; the latter is a wild being filled with potential meaning and a fundamental challenge to the narrative of "Man."

REDISCOVERING THE ANIMAL

In *The Order of Things*, Michel Foucault argued that our modern view of humanity as the sovereign of all possible knowledge, ethics, and values is a recent invention, a result of the Enlightenment and the distinct way it arranged and categorized knowledge. What if, he wonders, the way we have come to understand the world were to change, perhaps in the wake of some monumental event, perhaps through the reevaluation of our values? Foucault concludes the book with this premonition:

> If those arrangements were to disappear as they appeared, if some event of which we can at the moment do no more than sense the possibility . . . were to cause them to crumble . . . then one can certainly wager that man would be erased, like a face drawn in sand at the edge of the sea.

Could it be that "Man" as we have understood him to be, as the zenith of evolution, as the biological and ethical centerpiece of nature and God, is an extravagant temporary fiction we can no longer afford, not only because he has wreaked havoc on the animal kingdom, but also because he has impoverished our soul? To change the Foucauldian stick figure "Man" has become, we require a new spiritual vision of animals. "In a wonderful and inexpressible way," wrote medieval philosopher John Scotus Erigena, "God is created in his creatures." The question we face, in a geography increasingly creatureless and artificial, an environment more and more derivative and mechanical, is, How can we again embody our spirituality in the living organic world of animals? For the power to refresh our spiritual insights as well as our misguided understanding of our biological evolution resides in our bestiaries, both the animals of nature and the animals of the mind. Our own religious history teems with the clamor of significant beasts that tradition, sheer neglect, and the narrative of "Man" have eclipsed from view. Since the rise of science, Western culture has undertaken the discovery and cataloging of the Earth's remarkable zoological diversity. Perhaps the time has come for us to embark upon a different though related journey of discovery, the rediscovery of the meaningful fauna that leads from the visible to the invisible, from knowledge to virtue—from the narrative of "Man" to our true humanity. Each of us needs to understand that each creature followed its own course oblivious to "me." And yet together they seem to make up an intelligible whole that concerns me in ways I have not even begun to fathom.

Part Two

MYTHS OF THE CAFO

INDUSTRIAL FOOD IS CHEAP

TRUTH

The retail prices of industrial meat, dairy, and egg products omit immense impacts on human health, the environment, and other shared public assets. These costs, known among economists as "externalities," include massive waste emissions with the potential to heat up the atmosphere, foul fisheries, pollute drinking water, spread disease, contaminate soils, and damage recreational areas. Citizens ultimately foot the bill with hundreds of billions of dollars in taxpayer subsidies, medical expenses, insurance premiums, declining property values, and mounting cleanup costs.

❖

Walk into any fast-food chain and you're likely to find a "value" meal: chicken nuggets or a cheeseburger and fries for a price almost too good to be true. For families struggling to make ends meet, a cheap meal may seem too tough to pass up. Indeed, animal factory farm promoters often point to America's bargain fast-food prices as proof that the system is working. The CAFO system, they argue, supplies affordable food to the masses. But this myth of cheap meat, dairy, and egg products revolves around mounting externalized social and ecological costs that never appear on restaurant receipts or grocery bills.

STAGGERING ENVIRONMENTAL BURDENS Environmental damages alone should put to rest any illusions that food produced in industrial animal factories is cheap. Soil and water have been poisoned through decades of applying synthetic fertilizers and pesticides to grow billions of tons of livestock feed. Water bodies have been contaminated with animal wastes. The atmosphere is filled with potent greenhouse gases such as carbon dioxide, methane, and nitrous oxide. The mitigation costs for these problems are enormous. But what is worse, this essential cleanup work of contaminated resources is, for the most part, not being done.

To cite just one example, agricultural runoff—particularly nitrogen and phosphorus from poultry and hog farms—is a major source of pollution in the Chesapeake Bay, a once-vital East Coast fishery, now with numerous species on the verge of collapse.[1] One study estimated the price tag for restoring the bay at $19 billion, of which $11 billion would go toward "nutrient reduction."[2] There are over 400 such dead zones throughout the world.[3]

HEALTH COSTS Industrial animal production brings profound health risks and costs to farmers, workers, and consumers. CAFO workers suffer from emissions associated with industrial farming, as do neighboring communities. Medical researchers have linked the country's intensive meat consumption to such serious human health maladies as heart disease, stroke, diabetes, and certain types of cancer.[4] Annual costs for just these diseases in the United States alone exceed $33 billion.[5] Antibiotic-resistant organisms ("superbugs") created by overuse of antibiotics in industrial meat and dairy production can increase human vulnerability to infection. One widely cited U.S. study estimated the total annual costs of antibiotic resistance at $30 billion.[6] Estimated U.S. annual costs associated with *E. coli* O157:H7, a bacteria derived primarily from animal manure, reach $405 million: $370 million for deaths, $30 million for medical care, and $5 million for lost productivity.[7]

All these associated health problems drive up the costs of social services and insurance premiums. They reduce productivity and increase employee sick days. They can also result in premature deaths, with incalculable costs for families and communities.

FARM COMMUNITIES The retail prices of cheap animal food products also fail to reflect industrial agriculture's ongoing dislocation of farm families and the steady shuttering of businesses in rural communities. According to Robert F. Kennedy Jr., the average industrial hog factory puts ten family farmers out of business, replacing high-quality agricultural jobs with three to four hourly wage workers in relatively low-paying and potentially dangerous jobs.[8] When small farmers fall on hard times, many local employers close their doors and, at worst, entire communities, towns, and regional food production and distribution webs disappear from the landscape.

GOVERNMENT SUBSIDIES Perverse government subsidies—both in the United States and Europe—provide billions of tax dollars to support industrial animal agriculture. Tufts University researchers estimate that in the United States alone, between 1997 and 2005 the industrial animal sector saved over $35 billion as a result of federal farm subsidies that lowered the price of the feed they purchased.[9] Similar savings were not available to many small and midsize farmers who were growing their own feed and raising livestock in diversified pasture-based systems. Throughout the 2002 U.S. farm bill, individual CAFO investors were also eligible to receive up to $450,000 for a five-year EQIP contract from the U.S. government to deal with animal wastes—allowing large operations with many investors to rake in a much greater sum. European Union agricultural subsidies also bolster industrial animal producers, providing $2.25 per dairy cow per day—25 cents more than what half the world's human population survives on.[10]

A LESS COSTLY ALTERNATIVE By contrast, many sustainable livestock operations address potential negative health and environmental impacts through their production methods. They produce less waste and forego dangerous chemicals and other additives. Grass-pastured meat and dairy products have been shown to be high in omega-3 and other fatty acids that have cancer-fighting properties.[11] Smaller farms also receive fewer and smaller federal subsidies. While sustainably produced foods may cost a bit more, many of their potential beneficial environmental and social impacts are already included in the price.

INDUSTRIAL FOOD IS EFFICIENT

TRUTH

Industrial food animal producers often proclaim that "bigger is better," ridiculing the "inefficiency" of small- or medium-size farms using low-impact technologies. CAFO operations, however, currently rely on heavily subsidized agriculture to produce feed, large infusions of capital to dominate markets, and lax enforcement of regulations to deal with waste disposal. Perverse incentives and market controls leverage an unfair competitive advantage over smaller producers and cloud a more holistic view of efficiency.

❖

Factory farms and CAFOs appear efficient only if we focus on the quantity of meat, milk, or eggs produced from each animal over a given period of time. But high *productivity* or domination of market share should not be confused with *efficiency*. When we measure the total cost per unit of production, or even the net profit per animal, a more sobering picture emerges. Confinement operations come with a heavy toll of external costs—inefficiencies that extend beyond the CAFO or feedlot. These hidden costs include subsidized grain discounts, unhealthy market control, depleted aquifers, polluted air and waterways, and concentrated surpluses of toxic feces and urine. The massive global acreage of monocrops that produce the corn, soybeans, and hay to feed livestock in confinement could arguably be more efficiently managed as smaller, diversified farms and pasture operations, along with protected wildlands.

REVERSE PROTEIN FACTORIES Animal factory farms achieve their efficiencies by substituting corn and soybeans and even wild fish for pasture grazing. To gain a pound of body weight, a broiler chicken must eat an average of 2.3 pounds of feed.[1] Hogs convert 5.9 pounds of feed into a pound of pork.[2] Cattle require 13 pounds of feed per pound of beef,[3] though some estimates range much higher. To supplement that feed, one-third of the world's ocean fish catch is ground up and added to rations for hogs, broiler chickens, and farmed fish.[4] The 2006 United Nations Food and Agriculture Organization report *Livestock's Long Shadow* summed it up this way: "In simple numeric terms, livestock actually detract more from total food supply than they provide. . . . In fact, livestock consume 77 million tons of protein contained in feedstuff that could potentially be used for human nutrition, whereas 58 million tons of protein are contained in food products that livestock supply."[5]

TOTAL RECALL The efficiency of slaughterhouse practices should also be called into question, as their incessant increases in speed, drive for profit, and huge scale have resulted in contamination and massive meat recalls. In the United States, between spring 2007 and spring 2009 alone, there were twenty-five recalls due to the virulent *E. coli* O157:H7 pathogen involving 44 million pounds of beef.[6] When all costs of research, prevention, and market losses are added up, over the last decade *E. coli* contamination has cost the beef industry an estimated $1.9 billion.[7]

MOUNTING WASTE The U.S. Department of Agriculture estimates that factory animal farms generate more than 500 million tons of waste per year—more than three times the amount produced by the country's human population.[8] On a small, diversified farm, much of this manure could be efficiently used for fertilizer. Instead, most CAFOs store waste in massive lagoons or dry waste piles with the potential to give off toxic fumes, leak, or overflow. Ground and surface water can be contaminated with bacteria and antibiotics; pesticides and hormones containing endocrine disruptors; or dangerously high levels of nitrogen, phosphorus, and other nutrients. Inconsistent enforcement of regulations has allowed CAFO waste disposal problems to escalate in many areas. Meanwhile, the environmental and health impacts of this pollution are rarely calculated as part of the narrow range of parameters that CAFO operators use to define efficiency.

GOVERNMENT SUBSIDIES Not only do CAFOs burden citizens with environmental and health costs, they also gorge themselves at the proverbial public trough. Thanks to U.S. government subsidies, between 1997 and 2005, factory farms saved an estimated $3.9 billion per year because they were able to purchase corn and soybeans at prices below what it cost to grow the crops.[9] Without these feed discounts, amounting to a 5 to 15 percent reduction in operating costs,[10] it is unlikely that many of these industrial factory farms could remain profitable. By contrast, many small farms that produce much of their own forage receive no government money. Yet they are expected somehow to match the efficiency claims of the large, subsidized megafactory farms. On this uneven playing field, CAFOs may falsely appear to "outcompete" their smaller, diversified counterparts.

ANTICOMPETITIVENESS Another issue clouding any meaningful discussions of efficiency is the lack of access to markets among many independent producers. Because CAFOs have direct relationships with meat packers (and are sometimes owned by them, or "vertically integrated"), they have preferred access to the decreasing number of slaughterhouses and distribution channels to process and market products. Many midsize or smaller independent producers have no such access and as a result must get big, develop separate distribution channels, or simply disappear.

INDUSTRIAL FOOD IS HEALTHY

TRUTH

Industrial animal food production heightens the risk of the spread of food-borne illnesses that afflict millions of Americans each year. Rates of heart disease, cancer, diabetes, and obesity—often related to excessive meat and dairy consumption—are at an all-time high. Respiratory diseases and outbreaks of illnesses are increasingly common among CAFO and slaughterhouse workers and spill over into neighboring communities and the public at large.

❖

The Centers for Disease Control and Prevention (CDC) estimate that contaminated meat- and poultry-related infections make up to 3 million people sick each year, killing at least 1,000—figures that are probably underreported.[1] Crammed into tight confinement areas in massive numbers, factory farm animals often become caked with their own feces. Animal waste is the primary source of infectious bacteria such as *E. coli* and *Salmonella*, which affect human populations through contaminated food and water.[2] Grain-intensive diets can also increase the bacterial and viral loads in confined animal wastes. As a result, CAFOs can become breeding grounds for diseases and pathogens.

DIETARY IMPACTS Americans consume more meat and poultry per capita today than ever before, part of a diet that is high in calories and rich in saturated fats. According to the Center for a Livable Future at Johns Hopkins University, meat and dairy foods contribute all of the cholesterol and are the primary source of saturated fat in the typical American diet.[3] Approximately two-thirds of Americans are overweight or obese, increasing their chances of developing breast, colon, pancreas, kidney, and other cancers. Obesity and high blood cholesterol levels are among the leading risk factors for heart disease. Both of these conditions are associated with heavy meat consumption. More directly, researchers have linked diets that include significant amounts of animal fat to an increased incidence of cardiovascular disease.

On the other hand, studies regularly show that vegetarians exhibit the lowest incidence of heart problems.[4] High intakes of fruits, vegetables, whole grains and Mediterranean dietary patterns (rich in plant-based foods and unsaturated fats) have been shown to reduce the incidence of chronic diseases and associated risk factors, including body mass index and obesity.[5]

CONTAMINATED FEED Animal feeding practices also raise important health concerns. Corn and soybeans, for example, have been shown to absorb dioxins, PCBs, and other potential human carcinogens through air pollution. Once fed to animals, these persistent compounds can be stored in animal fat reserves. These harmful pollutants can later move up the food chain when animal fats left over from slaughter are rendered and used again for animal feed. As fats are recycled in the animal feeding system, the result is a higher concentration of dioxins and PCBs in the animal fats consumed by people. Animal and plant fats, both of which can store dioxins and PCBs, can compose up to 8 percent of animal feed rations.[6]

WORKER HEALTH CAFO workers suffer from numerous medical conditions, including repetitive motion injuries and respiratory illness associated with poor air quality. Studies indicate that at least 25 percent of CAFO workers experience respiratory diseases such as chronic bronchitis and occupational asthma.[7] Slaughterhouse workers are also at risk for work-related health conditions. In early 2008, for example, an unknown neurological illness began afflicting employees at a factory run by Quality Pork Processors in Minnesota, which slaughters 1,900 pigs a day. The diseased workers suffered burning sensations and numbness as well as weakness in the arms and legs. All the victims worked at or near the "head table," using compressed air to dislodge pigs' brains from their skulls. Inhalation of microscopic pieces of pig brain is suspected to have caused the illness.[8] After a CDC investigation, this practice was discontinued.

COMMUNITY HEALTH CAFOs can put neighboring communities at risk of exposure to dangerous air and water contaminants. More than a million Americans, for example, take drinking water from groundwater contaminated by nitrogen-containing pollutants, mostly derived from agricultural fertilizers and animal waste applications.[9] Several studies have linked nitrates in the drinking water to birth defects, disruption of thyroid function, and various types of cancers.[10] Further, the use of antibiotics on livestock over sustained periods is widely acknowledged to increase the prevalence of antibiotic-resistant bacteria. Infections from these new "superbugs" are difficult to treat and increase human risk of disease.[11]

In a study of 226 North Carolina schools, children living within three miles of factory farms had significantly higher asthma rates and more asthma-related emergency room visits than children living more than three miles away.[12] A separate study found that people living close to intensive swine operations suffer more negative mood states (e.g., tension, depression, anger, reduced vigor, fatigue, and confusion) than control groups.[13] Exposure to hydrogen sulfide—given off by concentrated animal feeding operations—has been linked to neuropsychiatric abnormalities.[14]

Food production that is safe for the environment, humane to animals, and sound for workers and communities gives us the best chance for a food system that is safe and healthy for eaters and producers alike.

CAFOS ARE FARMS, NOT FACTORIES

TRUTH

Among many assertions put forth by industrial animal producers is that CAFOs are farming enterprises rather than industries. In terms of scale, levels of pollution emitted, and production characteristics, it's not too difficult to assert that CAFOs are in fact industrial entities and, as such, should be subject to industrial regulation of their air and water emissions and solid waste.

❖

Despite countless exposés and well-publicized CAFO-related meat recalls, many people still associate animal production with nostalgic images of family farming. It's no wonder. The industry invests considerable resources convincing the consuming public that all is wholesome and healthy down on the factory farm. Advertisements and brand imagery from meat, dairy, and egg industries show dairy cows grazing in pastures instead of mired knee-deep in mud and feces. Chickens appear in barnyard scenes diametrically opposed to the grim realities of 30,000 birds crammed in a broiler shed, or 130,000 hens in an egg-laying facility.

LOBBYING AGAINST REGULATION The CAFO industry lobbies mightily to have this agricultural qualification codified into laws and regulations. If granted status as agricultural enterprises, CAFOs in the United States can obtain certain immunities from Clean Air Act, Clean Water Act, and Superfund regulations. If considered industrial enterprises, however, they are subject to industrial regulation of their pollution and required to pay the cleanup costs of their operations. For decades, the CAFO industry has worked to receive exemptions from noxious odors, greenhouse gas emissions, and solid waste discharges. They have also strategically favored placement and concentration of operations in states and counties where economic development is desperately needed and environmental regulations are easily manipulated.

INDUSTRIAL-SCALE PRODUCTION In reality, CAFOs bear no resemblance to farms. By definition, a CAFO is a facility with 1,000 or more "animal units."[1] The scale of these massive factories makes them "production facilities" rather than farms. Smithfield's subsidiary Murphy-Brown, currently the largest hog producer in the United States and the world, brings 17 million hogs to market each year and employs 6,000 people to run its operation. Pilgrim's Pride, one of the biggest chicken producers, employs 48,000 people to process 45 million birds *per week*. Cal-Maine, the largest egg producer in the United States, sold 685 million dozen eggs in 2007 and keeps a flock of 23 million layers. Its empire includes 2 breeding facilities, 2 hatcheries, 16 feed mills, 29 shell egg production facilities, 19 pullet-growing facilities, and 28 processing/packing facilities. CAFO operators call their buildings "production facilities" and their animals "production units." Gone are the days of pastures, barns, field crops, and farm animals.

ASSEMBLY LINE PRODUCTION The livestock sector is dominated by "vertically integrated" conglomerates that specialize tasks into distinct segments that are often spread out across different parts of the country: feed production in one factory; breeding in another; "finishing," or fattening, in a separate facility; and processing or slaughtering in yet another. Hatcheries ship eggs and chicks across the continent; feed is shipped across the world. Farmers have become low-wage employees or "contract growers" that don't even own their animals. Hogs, turkeys, and dairy cows are products of artificial insemination—a highly controlled process by which a human operator goes down the line to arouse and/or inseminate female animals. Much of the industry functions on this assembly line model—whether it's female hogs being injected with semen, cows being milked by computerized machines, or cattle being systematically disassembled at the slaughterhouse. Instead of caring for sick or weak animals, CAFOs simply cull their vulnerable production units. The typical cull rate for dairy cattle in the United States is over 20 percent per year.[2] As in any other industry, if a machine or production material is substandard, it is simply replaced.

TOXIC EMISSIONS Rather than operating on a closed-system model—in which farms grow their own feed, recycle their animals' waste back into fertilizer, and act as responsible stewards of the land—CAFOs operate on an industrial model. Inputs come from off-site, and wastes are trucked back off-site. Livestock operations generate 75 percent of the ammonia emissions reported in the United States. Confined dairy cows, however, have been shown to generate five to ten times more ammonia than pasture-raised animals.[3]

Since the 1980s, U.S. farms have been required to report large emissions of ammonia and hydrogen sulfide from animal manure to the Environmental Protection Agency, and findings by the agency's scientists confirm that the gases pose a genuine health threat. But the EPA does not impose limits on releases; it merely requires that farms disclose emissions over a certain level. In the final days of the Bush administration, the EPA further relaxed regulations on air emissions and reporting. If not overturned, these rule changes would exclude big animal-feeding operations from reporting ammonia emissions.

In 2008, Minnesota attorney general Lori Swanson filed a still unsettled suit against Excel Dairy, a CAFO with 1,500 dairy cattle in Thief River Falls, Minnesota, for air emission violations.[4] Residents living nearby were evacuated from their homes because of extremely high hydrogen sulfide readings. Symptoms from such releases can include headache, nausea, vomiting, dizziness, diarrhea, coughing, and shortness of breath.

Does this sound like a healthy family farm or an industry with a toxic emission problem?

CAFOS ARE GOOD FOR RURAL COMMUNITIES

TRUTH

CAFO operators entice rural communities with promises of skilled jobs and economic development opportunities. Preferred targets are regions up against years of persistent poverty. But hopes of economic revival are often accompanied by harsher realities. Members of CAFO communities frequently complain about losing control of their lives because of stench and pollution. They often can't sit outside and enjoy their backyards or decks, plan birthday parties, enjoy recreational areas, fish in their local streams, or even visit loved ones in cemeteries.

❖

The arrival of industrial agriculture in a rural region often forebodes a downturn in quality of life, particularly when heavy concentrations of animals are involved. Civic participation declines. Public health can deteriorate. A "CAFO-friendly" rural community can soon find itself unattractive to other economic development opportunities. Tragically, the decision to rely on CAFOs as a primary path toward economic development may be difficult for a community to reverse in the long term.[1]

LOW-WAGE HAZARDOUS WORK   By design, a CAFO uses as little labor as possible. Those jobs that are created pay relatively low wages. Not all CAFO jobs offer medical benefits despite frequent exposure to hazardous conditions inside barns and processing facilities. The slaughterhouse industry also brings potential health risks to workers in communities across the globe. According to a 2008 series in the *Charlotte Observer*, "The Cruelest Cuts," human costs of the ever-faster-paced slaughterhouse industry are rising in communities across North Carolina and South Carolina, where chicken and turkey production and processing are highly concentrated.[2] Poultry workers can reportedly make as many as 20,000 cutting motions in a single shift.[3] Many suffer chronic nerve and muscle damage, are maimed by machines, or are poisoned by toxic chemicals. Repetitive tasks can leave their hands wracked with pain or missing fingers. Such emotional and physical stress can radiate throughout an entire community.

ECONOMIC OUTSOURCING One would think that the establishment of a new industry in an area would at least have a positive "multiplier effect" on the regional economy, as the purchase of goods and services benefits local businesses. Studies consistently show, however, that CAFOs don't necessarily infuse a great deal of money into local communities—not even in the short term. Since many CAFOs are vertically integrated (owning hatcheries, feed mills, production, and even slaughter facilities), they often purchase within their own organization rather than from local suppliers. Building materials, equipment, feed, and feeder animals are sourced from the cheapest outside supplier rather than from a local business. The same applies to labor. The work is so physically, mentally, and economically demanding that many of those employed in confinement operations, feed mills, and slaughterhouses turn out to be recent immigrants to communities, particularly Hispanics, and increasingly other ethnic minorities such as Hmong and Sudanese. This can add to heightened tensions in communities where CAFOs operate.

DECLINING TAX AND PROPERTY VALUES Unless a CAFO generates more tax revenues than it consumes over time, it will eventually burden the coffers of local governments. Egregious air and water emissions may reduce opportunities for development in other economic sectors. The cost of infrastructure upkeep for road maintenance and water treatment in the region can begin to mount. As the value of surrounding residences declines, tax revenues from properties may plummet, further draining administrative budgets. A 1999 study estimated the average decline in land values within a three-mile

radius from each CAFO in Missouri at $2.68 million.[4] The Union of
Concerned Scientists extrapolated that figure to include the 9,900
CAFOs in the United States. The total drop in U.S. land values due
to industrial concentrated animal production was estimated at $26
billion.[5]

Ultimately, even the corporate contract operations may be forced
to leave rural communities in the United States and Canada. Labor
and investment costs are far lower in other countries of the world
where giant multinational corporations operate today, and where
environmental concerns, labor issues, and animal welfare regulations
are far less developed. People of many other countries are even more
desperate for economic opportunities than are communities across
rural America. If and when CAFO operations leave North America,
rural communities may be left with enormous messes to clean up.

HEALTHY FARMS, HEALTHY COMMUNITIES Locally based food
and farming networks are arguably the best way to rebuild local
communities and restore the American farmer's chances for a better
future. The challenge before us, however, is that following decades of
consolidation and industrialization of the animal food sector, rural
processing capacities and distribution networks have been gutted
and are in desperate need of rebuilding. Billions of dollars have been
invested in a grain-based CAFO food system. Yet demand for sustainably and locally produced meats, eggs, and milk in many regions
is growing faster than the numbers of farmers able to supply them.
Grass-based, free-range, and pastured livestock and poultry present
excellent opportunities for family farmers transitioning out of intensive feed grain production. Public concerns about health, food safety,
and inhumane growing conditions will continue to speed expansion
of these community-friendly production methods.

INDUSTRIAL FOOD BENEFITS THE ENVIRONMENT AND WILDLIFE

TRUTH

Even though industrial animal feeding operations are intensively concentrated, their impacts radiate across the entire landscape, with devastating effects on surrounding ecosystems and wildlife. Throughout the world, hundreds of millions of acres of grasslands, wetlands, and forestlands have been converted to produce feed for confined livestock. Far from benefiting the environment and wildlife, global-scale industrial animal food production poses one of the most dire threats to the natural world.

❖

The demand for industrial feeds, primarily corn and soybeans, has decimated biodiversity in the midwestern United States, plowing up grasslands, draining and replumbing wetlands and stream systems, and pushing many native plant and animal species to the verge of extinction. Nutrient runoff from midwestern feed grain fields each year flows through the Mississippi River drainage and into the Gulf of Mexico, contributing to an 8,000-square-mile oxygen-starved dead zone that smothers sea life.

AN ENORMOUS ENVIRONMENTAL FOOTPRINT The massive environmental footprint of industrial animal food production includes far more than the impact of factory farms. In the United States, alone, roughly two-thirds of public, private, and tribal lands are used for agriculture, either in grazing, haying, or row cropping—much of that to grow livestock feed.[1] Growers annually apply billions of pounds of chemical fertilizer and tens of millions of pounds of pesticides to those fields, contributing to soil erosion, water pollution problems, and wildlife habitat destruction. Each year in the United States, some 670 million birds are exposed to pesticides, with 10 percent dying from the exposure.[2]

This is not just a North American issue. For the past ten years, the leading cause of deforestation in the Amazon has been conversion of rainforest to industrial soybean plantations—primarily for CAFO production in Brazil or for export to industrial animal operations in China and Europe. But rainforest destruction for feed crop and pasture conversion is occurring at an even faster pace in other Latin American countries.[3] Nearly 60 percent of the world's freshwater resources are diverted for agriculture, of which at least a third goes to food animal production.

According to the United Nations Food and Agriculture Organization, the world's livestock contribute 18 percent of all annual greenhouse gas emissions. But a recent report from the World Watch Institute estimates that the livestock sector could be responsible for as much as 50 percent of all climate-changing emissions—making it the most critical influential factor in global warming.[4]

RIVERS OF WASTE Livestock-induced water pollution is increasingly a global problem with the huge volumes of contaminated waste produced wherever food animals are raised, milked, and slaughtered. This waste can become fugitive, leaching from overapplication on farmland, overflowing or leaking from lagoons and holding ponds, volatilizing in the atmosphere, and devastating wildlife habitats and the rest of the environment. Hog, chicken, and cattle waste has polluted 35,000 miles of rivers in 22 states and significantly contaminated groundwater in 17 states, according to a U.S. Environmental Protection Agency report.[5] The results of large spills can be catastrophic. In August 2005, for example, a lagoon collapsed at a western New York dairy, sending 3 million gallons of waste into the Black River. As many as 250,000 fish were killed, and residents of Watertown had to suspend their use of the river as a water supply and recreation area.[6]

Waste can also contain persistent substances that affect wildlife. Cattle, for example, can be given ear implants that provide a slow release of trenbolone, an anabolic steroid that causes cattle to bulk up. But not all the trenbolone is metabolized. A German study showed that 10 percent of the steroid passed right through the animals.[7] Water sampled downstream from a Nebraska feedlot revealed steroid levels four times as high as the water taken upstream. Male fathead minnows living in that downstream area exhibited low testosterone levels and undersized heads.[8]

"DAMAGE CONTROL" The U.S. Department of Agriculture's Animal Damage Control (ADC) program was established in 1931 to eradicate and control wildlife considered detrimental to the country's western ranching industry. In 1997, under pressure from advocates for wildlife, the federal government gave the ADC both a new name—Wildlife Services—and a new motto—"Living with Wildlife."[9] To protect livestock from predators, an estimated 100,000 coyotes, bobcats, bears, wolves, and mountain lions are killed each year by USDA's Wildlife Services.[10] Tragically, most of the cattle raised for food production on ranches in the western United States eventually end their days in crowded, feces-encrusted feedlots.

OCEAN IMPACTS The oceans have simultaneously become dumping grounds for agricultural wastes and food sources for cattle rations. Dead zones, caused when nutrients such as fertilizers from feed production and animal wastes overwhelm an aquatic environment, are multiplying around the world at a rapid pace. Also alarming is the amount of wild fish that is currently fed to confinement animals. Consider that an estimated 17 percent of the global wild fish catch goes to feed the world's chickens and hogs.

The great challenge of this century will be to develop food production systems that meet the needs of the human population and that accommodate and even benefit from wild nature and a healthy environment.

INDUSTRIAL FOOD CAN
FEED THE WORLD

T R U T H

Feeding the entire world a diet emphasizing industrial meat and other animal products could exponentially increase world hunger by diverting much of our crop-producing capacity into growing feed for animals. It could also greatly reduce or eliminate traditional diets of grains, legumes, and native fruits and vegetables, and ultimately lead to devastating nutritional diseases and environmental problems.

❖

By the turn of the twenty-first century, the world's 800 million hungry people were outnumbered by 1 billion people who were overweight.[1] The increasing adoption of the Western diet, with its emphasis on animal food products (often high in saturated fats), is contributing to this global nutritional conundrum. Massive amounts of grain are diverted to fatten livestock rather than to feed the undernourished. Yet poverty-stricken people cannot afford to purchase meat and other luxury foods that have emerged as the core of the modern industrial agricultural diet.

FOOD VERSUS FEED Exporting the Western model of industrial meat production significantly widens the hunger gap between the world's wealthiest and poorest residents. Not only does an expansion of meat production divert more land and resources from feeding people to fattening animals, it also involves a transition away from traditional staple cropping systems toward grain and soybean monocultures for export. In a world of plenty, the poor often find themselves even further deprived of their farming heritage, lacking access to land or the financial resources to buy into factory farming's new world food order.

In the United States, 157 million tons of cereals, legumes, and vegetable protein are fed to livestock to produce just 28 million tons of animal protein in the form of meat.[2] In contrast, an acre of cereal crops can produce five times more protein than an acre used for meat production. Using land in developing countries to create an animal-intensive food chain has resulted in a food security crisis and misery for hundreds of millions of people.

According to author Jeremy Rifkin, the human consequences of the shift from food to feed production were dramatically illus-trated during the Ethiopian famine in 1984. While locals starved, Ethiopia exported linseed cake, cottonseed cake, and rapeseed meal to European livestock producers. Despite this history, millions of acres of land in the developing world are still being used for export feed production. Tragically, 80 percent of the world's hungry children live in countries with grain surpluses that are fed to animals for con-sumption by the affluent.[3]

EXPORTING THE WESTERN DIET Whether intentional or not, the forces of agribusiness are promoting the animal product–inten-sive Western diet around the world at the expense of traditional foods. Multinational corporations that supply the seeds, chemicals, and cattle and also control the slaughterhouses and the marketing and distribution of beef are eagerly promoting grain-fed livestock. A nation's prestige becomes linked with its ability to "climb the protein ladder." Chicken and egg consumption are at the lower rungs. As their economies grow, nations climb to pork, dairy products, grass-fed beef, and ultimately to grain-fed beef.[4] U.S. fast-food chains have opened restaurants in more than 120 countries. In China alone, pork consumption is growing dramatically, with the equivalent of over 1 million hogs slaughtered each day to meet the country's surging demand for meat.

Many experts argue that while the Western diet is pulling people away from traditional foods, it cannot possibly feed the entire world. According to Professor Vaclav Smil of the University of Manitoba: "Extension of the affluent world's carnivorousness to the rest of the global population is . . . impossible with current crop yields and feeding practices.[75] Feeding the entire world a Western diet that emphasizes meat, dairy, eggs, and other luxury products, says Professor David Pimentel of Cornell University, would require over 6 billion acres of agricultural land—67 percent more than presently under cultivation.[6] Not only can the Earth not provide enough arable land to support a spike in meat and animal food consumption, it can't sustain the environmental damage that would be inflicted on the world's air, water, soil, and ocean resources as a result. The industrial meat model simply will not scale up to feed the entire world a Western diet in its present form.

As people grapple with global dietary and nutritional ironies, it is also important not to reduce the issue to an oversimplified choice between a meat-based and a vegetarian diet. A significant reduction in an animal product–intensive diet is arguably in the long-term best interests of the planet. But the overall issue is complex. Studies show, for example, that sustainably raised, locally procured animal product–inclusive diets can compare favorably in environmental impacts to heavily processed, long-distance transported, plant-based diets. These shifts in diet and production will take place over a long period of transition and will not be distributed equally across the landscape, as regions are climatically suited for certain types of food production.

What we are not yet sure of is how to produce regionally diversified, nutritionally balanced diets that are sustainable over the long term. Certainly we can and must do better.

CAFO MANURE IS A BENIGN RESOURCE

Confining more animals whose wastes cannot safely be absorbed by the surrounding land, watershed, and atmosphere is detrimental, if not illegal. CAFO wastes (including fish farms) can contain a slurry of toxins, including viruses, infectious bacteria, antibiotics, heavy metals, and oxygen-depleting nutrients that run off the land, contaminate groundwater and aquatic systems, and pollute the atmosphere.

❖

According to one estimate, if the amount of confined livestock and poultry waste produced in the United States each year were packed in boxcars, they would track around the world fourteen times.[1] To offer just a few more comparisons, a new hog plant in Utah will produce more animal waste than all the human sewage created by the city of Los Angeles; California's 1,600 Central Valley dairies churn out more waste than a city of 21 million people; and the 600 million chickens living on the Delmarva Peninsula near Washington, DC, generate as much nitrogen as a city of almost 500,000 people.[2] The key difference is that while human waste is treated in plants that must meet rigorous processing standards, the management and disposal of most animal wastes are poorly regulated.

TOXIC STORAGE "LAGOONS" Lagoon storage and sprayfield applications on land are two common methods of dealing with CAFO wastes. Neither is problem-free. Spraying liquid manure onto croplands can spread viruses, bacteria, antibiotics, metals (such as zinc, arsenic, copper, and selenium),[3] nitrogen, phosphorus, and other compounds that run off the land, contaminate the groundwater, travel through subterranean field drains (tiles), and pollute the atmosphere. Spraying more animal waste than the surrounding land can safely absorb is common. When lagoons burst, develop leaks, or are overwhelmed by flood events, as often happens, millions of gallons of manure reach waterways and spread microbes that can cause gastroenteritis, fevers, kidney failure, and death. One bacteria, *Pfiesteria piscicida*, produces a powerful toxin that has been responsible for massive fish kills in waters polluted by hog manure.

HARMFUL GASES According to the Pew Commission on Industrial Farm Animal Production:

> Decomposing manure produces at least 160 different gases, of which hydrogen sulfide (H_2S), ammonia, carbon dioxide, methane, and carbon monoxide are the most pervasive. These gases may seep from pits under the building or they may be released by bacterial action in the urine and feces on the confinement house floor. Possibly the most dangerous gas common to industrial food animal production (IFAP) facilities is hydrogen sulfide. It can be released rapidly when the liquid manure slurry is agitated, an operation commonly performed to suspend solids so that pits can be emptied by pumping. During agitation, hydrogen sulfide levels can soar within seconds from the usual ambient levels of less than 5 ppm to lethal levels of over 500 ppm. Animals and workers have died or become seriously ill in swine industrial farm animal production (IFAP) facilities when hydrogen sulfide has risen from agitated manure in pits under the building. Hydrogen sulfide exposure is most hazardous when the manure pits are located beneath the houses, but an acutely toxic environment can result if gases from outside storage facilities backflow into a building (due to inadequate gas traps or other design faults) or if a worker enters a confined storage structure where gases have accumulated.[4]

AIRBORNE POLLUTION For people living anywhere near these animal factories, the stench can be horrific: smells like rotten eggs and rancid butter are commonly reported. But this is just a beginning. Airborne toxicity travels long distances. Ammonia can be carried more than 300 miles through the air before being dumped back onto the ground or into the water, where it has the potency to cause algal blooms and fish kills.[5]

PATHOGEN AND ANTIBIOTIC TRANSFER CAFO manure also frequently carries pathogens such as *Salmonella, E. coli, Cryptosporidium*, and fecal coliform, which can be 10 to 100 times more concentrated than in human waste. In fact, more than forty diseases can be transferred to humans through manure. Furthermore, if humans get sick from one of the diseases in CAFO manure, our antibiotics may no longer be able to cure us. Antibiotics are regularly administered to most CAFO animals in "subtherapeutic" doses—regardless of whether there is a medical need. Constant exposure to antibiotics, has, in turn, created new generations of disease pathogens resistant to the very antibiotics we invented to fight them. A significant percentage of those antibiotics are later discharged in animal waste and can seep into aquifers, creeks, rivers, and lakes with potential consequences along the way.

FOUL WATERS According to the Pew Commission on Industrial Farm Animal Production, over 1 million Americans are estimated to take their drinking water from groundwater that shows moderate or severe contamination with nitrogen-containing pollutants, mostly owing to the heavy use of agricultural fertilizers and high rates of land application of animal waste.

Wendell Berry eloquently described the difference between traditional diversified farms and CAFOs: "Once plants and animals were raised together on the same farm—which therefore neither produced unmanageable surpluses of manure, to be wasted and to pollute the water supply, nor depended on such quantities of commercial fertilizer. The genius of American farm experts is very well demonstrated here: they can take a solution and divide it neatly into two problems."[6]

Part Three

INSIDE THE CAFO

INTRODUCTION

What the Industry Doesn't Want Us to Know

So much of agriculture takes place at vast distances from eaters that it is fairly safe to say most Americans don't really know where their food comes from. This is especially true with the CAFO industry, which for decades has granted journalists, activists, and the concerned public only occasional access to the confinement operations where meat, egg, and dairy production takes place. CAFO lobbyists have aggressively resisted any attempts at transparency regulations that would require full disclosure about where and how animals are raised and exactly what is contained in the end products. How safe or humane can factory-farmed foods be if producers don't want us to know the details of their production?

On the heels of Eric Schlosser's *Fast Food Nation*, Michael Pollan's groundbreaking *New York Times* essay "Power Steer" launched a revolution in food journalism by exposing the inner workings of the feedlot industry. Pollan purchased a steer from a stockyard, and followed its short life cycle: from a cow-calf ranching operation, to a midwestern feedlot, and finally to a Kansas slaughterhouse killing floor. He offers readers a reality check on what we actually feed the industrial animals we eat. Young beef cows typically start their lives grazing on pastures and eating grass, a diet they naturally ruminate. But to speed the fattening process and fill the industrial food pipelines with beef products, industrial feedlots implant cows with growth hormones and substitute feed corn for pasture. The corn-intensive diet and hormones cause the cows to gain weight rapidly but also make them sick. To prevent outbreaks of disease caused by their overly acidified stomachs and the crammed and filthy conditions of the feedlot, cows are routinely administered antibiotics. Hormone residues end up in the meat, and antibiotics leach into the environment through manure, setting off a chain reaction with the microbial world. In the end, Pollan questions whether we can possibly be healthier for the chemical and corn-fed bulk of the all-American power steer.

In 1950, the United States had 3 million hog farms, most of them small-scale and family-run. By 2000, that number had dwindled to 80,000. Today, more than 80 percent of the nation's hogs come from operations that raise more than 5,000 hogs a year.[1] States like Iowa and North Carolina have arguably sacrificed the well-being of entire rural counties in favor of large industrial swine operations by turning a blind eye as their waterways were heavily polluted and their communities devastated by stench. As Jeff Tietz reports, one of the principal corporations driving that explosive growth was Smithfield Foods. Under its founder, Joseph Luter III, Smithfield became the most powerful hog-producing corporation in the world, slaughtering 27 million hogs per year. But the production of 6 billion pounds of "the other white meat" comes with an incredible price tag: lakes of manure so concentrated it might be classified as toxic waste.

With 30 million beef cattle and 100 million hogs slaughtered each year in the United States, it might come as a surprise that chickens dominate the modern industrial food chain. Over 9 billion "broiler" chickens are raised and slaughtered each year in the United States. On average, Americans consume 87 pounds of chicken per year—three times the amount of poultry eaten in the 1960s (per capita beef consumption is at 66 pounds and pork at 51 pounds).[2] But as former slaughterhouse worker Steve Striffler explains, it's not just the chickens themselves that suffer intolerably. The sheer speed and monotony of the task requires almost unimaginable mental and physical endurance just to survive a single shift on the disassembly line.

We may think of the CAFO as a late-twentieth-century construct. However, Anne Mendelson writes that confinement dairies emerged in the nineteenth century alongside whiskey distilleries in America's growing urban centers. These so-called swill milk dairies were established to make a profitable commodity out of the acidic wastes of alcohol production. But the feed made the cows unhealthy, the milk ill tasting, and consumers sick too. All the while, milk was touted as essential for children and healthful for all. Demand kept rising, as did production, and eventually the primary issue became how to squeeze more milk out of a cow. The rest of the story follows the arc of industrialization. Modern dairy cows can still be fed distillers' grains (by-products of modern ethanol production), but the latest high-output diet is driven by corn and soybeans. Following decades of genetic selection and the use of hormones, antibiotics, and industrial feed rations, dairy cows produce staggering volumes of milk, but at a very steep price. Cows are suffering numerous stomach and hoof ailments related to diet and these factorylike conditions, while independent dairy farmers are struggling to stay afloat in a market that is literally drowning in cheap milk.

The retail sector also shoulders a responsibility for shaping industrial animal production, writes longtime industry journalist Steve Bjerklie. By pressuring producers to keep costs as low as possible, food retailers squeezed most of the margins out of milk, meat, and egg production, forcing a thirty-year wave of consolidation and concentration that has ravaged rural communities and created a precarious food system. In the end, if we want an environmentally sound and fair animal products industry, we consumers are going to have to find ways to pay for it.

Even the modern aquaculture industry has adopted the pitfalls of the CAFO model—antibiotics, intensive concentrations of animals and waste, and a high-protein diet—writes Ken Stier and Emmett Hopkins. Salmon, for example, are carnivorous and need to eat wild fish to bulk up fast and remain healthy. Estimates show that it takes up to 5 pounds of wild fish to produce 1 pound of farmed salmon.[3] Meanwhile, fish wastes and uneaten feed smother the seafloor beneath these farms, generating bacteria that consume oxygen vital to shellfish and other bottom-dwelling sea creatures. In the end, it can be argued that many of today's fish and shrimp farms function as floating CAFOs.

POWER STEER

On the Trail of Industrial Beef

MICHAEL POLLAN

AFTER SPENDING ITS FIRST SIX MONTHS *grazing on pastures, a cow arrives at the feedlot to face the cold efficiencies of industrial weight gain. The transformation from grass-fed calf to power steer will be driven mostly by a corn-based feed ration that may be supplemented with synthetic growth hormones, antibiotics, feather meal, pig and fish protein, and even chicken manure. Feedlot beef appears cheap until the total costs of industrial production are tallied.*

❖

Garden City, Kansas, missed out on the suburban building boom of the postwar years. What it got instead were sprawling subdivisions of cattle. These feedlots—the nation's first—began rising on the high plains of western Kansas in the 1950s, and by now developments catering to cows are far more common here than developments catering to people.

Poky Feeders, population 37,000. Cattle pens stretch to the horizon, each one home to 150 animals standing dully or lying around in a grayish mud that it eventually dawns on you isn't mud at all. The pens line a network of unpaved roads that loop around vast waste lagoons on their way to the feedlot's beating heart: a chugging, silvery feed mill that soars like an industrial cathedral over this teeming metropolis of meat.

I traveled to Poky early in January with the slightly improbable notion of visiting one particular resident: a young black steer that I'd met in the fall on a ranch in Vale, South Dakota. The steer, in fact, belonged to me. I'd purchased him as an eight-month-old calf from the Blair brothers, Ed and Rich, for $598. I was paying Poky Feeders $1.60 a day for his room, board, and meds and hoped to sell him at a profit after he was fattened.

This is the biography of my cow.

EARLY DAYS ON GREEN PASTURES

The Blair Brothers Ranch occupies 11,500 acres of short-grass prairie a few miles outside Sturgis, South Dakota, directly in the shadow of Bear Butte. In November, when I visited, the turf forms a luxuriant pelt of grass oscillating yellow and gold in the constant wind and sprinkled with perambulating black dots: Angus cows and calves grazing. Ed and Rich Blair run what's called a "cow-calf" operation, the first stage of beef production, and the stage least changed by the modern industrialization of meat. Although four giant meatpacking companies (Tyson, Cargill, JBS Swift, and National Beef) now slaughter and market more than 80 percent of the beef cattle born in this country, that concentration represents the narrow end of a funnel that starts out as wide as the Great Plains.

Calving season begins in late winter, a succession of subzero nights spent yanking breeched babies out of their bellowing mothers. In April comes the first spring roundup to work the newborn calves (branding, vaccination, castration); then more roundups in early summer to inseminate the cows ($15 mail-order straws of elite bull semen have pretty much put the resident stud out of work); and weaning in the fall. If all goes well, your herd of 850 cattle has increased to 1,600 by the end of the year.

My steer spent his first six months in these lush pastures alongside his mother, No. 9,534. His father was a registered Angus named GAR Precision 1,680, a bull distinguished by the size and marbling of his offspring's rib-eye steaks. Born last March 13 in a birthing shed across the road, No. 534 was turned out on pasture with his mother as soon as the 80-pound calf stood up and began nursing. After a few weeks, the calf began supplementing his mother's milk by nibbling on a salad bar of mostly native grasses: western wheatgrass, little bluestem, green needlegrass.

Although the modern cattle industry all but ignores it, the recip-
rocal relationship between cows and grass is one of nature's underap-
preciated wonders. For the grasses, the cow maintains their habitat
by preventing trees and shrubs from gaining a foothold; the animal
also spreads grass seed, planting it with its hooves and fertilizing
it. In exchange for these services, the grasses offer the ruminants a
plentiful, exclusive meal. For cows, sheep, and other grazers have the
unique ability to convert grass—which single-stomached creatures
like us can't digest—into high-quality protein. They can do this
because they possess a rumen, a 45-gallon fermentation tank in which
a resident population of bacteria turns grass into metabolically useful
organic acids and protein.

This is an excellent system for all concerned: for the grasses, for
the animals, and for us. What's more, growing meat on grass can
make superb ecological sense: so long as the rancher practices rotational grazing, it is a sustainable, solar-powered system for producing
food on land too arid or hilly to grow anything else.

ON TO THE INDUSTRIAL FOOD CHAIN

So if this system is so ideal, why is it that my cow hasn't tasted a blade
of grass since October? Speed, in a word. Cows raised on grass simply
take longer to reach slaughter weight than cows raised on a richer
diet, and the modern meat industry has devoted itself to shortening
a beef calf's allotted time on Earth. "In my grandfather's day, steers
were 4 or 5 years old at slaughter," explained Rich Blair. "In the fif-
ties, when my father was ranching, it was 2 or 3. Now we get there at
14 to 16 months." Fast food indeed. What gets a beef calf from 80 to
1,200 pounds in 14 months are enormous quantities of corn, protein
supplements—and drugs, including growth hormones. These "efficiencies," all of which come at a price, have transformed raising cattle
into a high-volume, low-margin business. Not everybody is convinced
that this is progress. "Hell," Ed Blair told me, "my dad made more
money on 250 head than we do on 850."

In early October, a few weeks before I met him, No. 534 was
weaned from his mother. Weaning is perhaps the most traumatic
time on a ranch for animals and ranchers alike; cows separated from

their calves will mope and bellow for days, and the calves themselves, stressed by the change in circumstance and diet, are prone to get sick. On many ranches, weaned calves go directly from the pasture to the sale barn, where they're sold at auction, by the pound, to feedlots. The Blairs prefer to own their steers straight through to slaughter and to keep them on the ranch for a couple of months of "backgrounding" before sending them on the 500-mile trip to Poky Feeders. Think of backgrounding as prep school for feedlot life: the animals are confined in a pen, "bunk broken"—taught to eat from a trough—and gradually accustomed to eating a new, unnatural diet of grain.

It was in the backgrounding pen that I first met No. 534 on an unseasonably warm afternoon in November. I'd told the Blairs I wanted to follow one of their steers through the life cycle; Ed suggested I might as well buy a steer, if I wanted to really understand the daunting economics of modern ranching. Ed and Rich told me what to look for: a broad, straight back and thick hindquarters. Basically, you want a strong frame on which to hang a lot of meat. Almost as soon as I started surveying the 90 or so steers in the pen, No. 534 moseyed up to the railing and made eye contact. He had a wide, stout frame and was brockle faced—he had three distinctive white blazes.

Rich said he would calculate the total amount I owed the next time No. 534 got weighed, but that the price would be $98 a hundredweight for an animal of this quality. He would then bill me for all expenses (feed, shots, et cetera) and, beginning in January, start passing on the weekly "hotel charges" from Poky Feeders. In June we'd find out from the packing plant how well my investment had panned out: I would receive a payment for No. 534 based on his carcass weight, plus a premium if he earned a USDA grade of choice or prime.

FROM GRASS TO "HOT RATIONS"

My second morning on the ranch, I helped Troy Hadrick, Ed's son-in-law and a ranch hand, feed the steers in the backgrounding pen. Hadrick and I squeezed into the heated cab of a huge swivel-hipped tractor hooked up to a feed mixer: basically, a dump truck with a giant screw through the middle to blend ingredients. First stop was a hopper filled with Rumensin, a powerful antibiotic that No. 534 will consume with his feed every day for the rest of his life. Calves have no need of regular medication while on grass, but as soon as they're placed in the backgrounding pen, they're apt to get sick. Why? The stress of weaning is a factor, but the main culprit is the feed. The shift to a "hot ration" of grain can so disturb the cow's digestive process— its rumen, in particular—that it can kill the animal if not managed carefully and accompanied by antibiotics.

After we'd scooped the ingredients into the hopper and turned on the mixer, Hadrick deftly sidled the tractor alongside the pen and flipped a switch to release a dusty tan stream of feed in a long, even line. No. 534 was one of the first animals to belly up to the rail for breakfast. He was heftier than his pen mates and, I decided, sparkier too. That morning, Hadrick and I gave each calf 6 pounds of corn mixed with 7 pounds of ground alfalfa hay and ¼ pound of Rumensin. Soon after my visit, this ration would be cranked up to 14 pounds of corn and 6 pounds of hay. It would add 2½ pounds every day to No. 534.

As fall turned into winter, Hadrick sent me regular e-mail messages apprising me of my steer's progress. On November 13 he weighed 650 pounds; by Christmas he was up to 798, making him the seventh-heaviest steer in his pen, an achievement in which I, idiotically, took a measure of pride. Between November 13 and January 4, the day he boarded the truck for Kansas, No. 534 put away 706 pounds of corn and 336 pounds of alfalfa hay, bringing his total living expenses for that period to $61.13. I was into this deal now for $659.

THE BOVINE METROPOLIS

To travel from the ranch to the feedlot, as No. 534 and I both did (in separate vehicles) the first week in January, feels a lot like going from the country to the big city. Indeed, a cattle feedlot is a kind of city, populated by as many as 100,000 animals. It is very much a premodern city, however—crowded, filthy, and stinking, with open sewers, unpaved roads, and choking air.

I started my tour at the feed mill, the yard's thundering hub, where three meals a day for 37,000 animals are designed and mixed by computer. A million pounds of feed pass through the mill each day.

Every hour of every day, a tractor-trailer pulls up to disgorge another 25 tons of corn. Around the other side of the mill, tanker trucks back up to silo-shaped tanks, into which they pump thousands of gallons of liquefied fat and protein supplement. In a shed attached to the mill sit vats of liquid vitamins and synthetic estrogen; next to these are pallets stacked with 50-pound sacks of Rumensin and tylosin, another antibiotic. Along with alfalfa hay and corn silage for roughage, all these ingredients are blended and then piped into the dump trucks that keep Poky's 8½ miles of trough filled.

The feed mill's great din is made by two giant steel rollers turning against each other twelve hours a day, crushing steamed corn kernels into flakes. This was the only feed ingredient I tasted, and it wasn't half bad; not as crisp as Kellogg's, but with a cornier flavor. I passed, however, on the protein supplement, a sticky brown goop consisting of molasses and urea.

Corn is a mainstay of livestock diets because there is no other feed quite as cheap or plentiful, thanks to federal subsidies and—until the recent ethanol boom—ever-growing surpluses. The rise of the modern factory farm is a direct result of these surpluses, which soared in the years following World War II, when petrochemical fertilizers came into widespread use. Ever since, the USDA's policy has been to help farmers dispose of surplus corn by passing as much of it as possible through the digestive tracts of food animals, converting it into protein. Compared with grass or hay, corn is a compact and portable foodstuff, making it possible to feed tens of thousands of animals on small plots of land. Without cheap corn, the modern urbanization of livestock would probably never have occurred.

We have come to think of "corn-fed" as some kind of old-fashioned virtue; we shouldn't. Granted, a corn-fed cow develops well-marbled flesh, giving it a taste and texture American consumers have learned to like. Yet this meat is demonstrably less healthy to eat, since it contains more saturated fat. A recent study in the *European Journal of Clinical Nutrition* found that the meat of grass-fed livestock not only had substantially less fat than grain-fed meat but that the type of fats found in grass-fed meat were much healthier. Grass-fed meat has more omega-3 fatty acids and fewer omega-6 fatty acids, which are believed to promote heart disease; it also contains beta-carotene and

CLA (conjugated linoleic acids), another "good" fat. A growing body of research suggests that many of the health problems associated with eating beef are really problems with corn-fed beef. In the same way that ruminants have not evolved to eat grain, humans may not be well adapted to eating grain-fed animals. Yet the USDA's grading system continues to reward marbling—that is, intramuscular fat—and thus the feeding of corn to cows.

The economic logic behind corn is unassailable, and on a factory farm, there is no other kind. Calories are calories, and corn remains the cheapest, most convenient source of calories. Of course the identical industrial logic—protein is protein—led to the feeding of rendered cow parts back to cows, a practice the Food and Drug Administration (FDA) banned in 1997 after scientists realized it was spreading mad cow disease.

Make that mostly banned. The FDA's rules against feeding ruminant protein to ruminants make exceptions for "blood products" (even though they contain protein) and fat. Indeed, my steer has probably dined on beef tallow recycled from the very slaughterhouse he's heading to in June. "Fat is fat," the feedlot manager shrugged when I raised an eyebrow.

FDA rules still permit feedlots to feed nonruminant animal protein to cows. (Feather meal is an accepted cattle feed, as are pig and fish protein and chicken manure.) Some public health advocates worry that since the bovine meat and bone meal that cows used to eat is now being fed to chickens, pigs, and fish, infectious prions (proteins implicated in the transfer of mad cow disease) could find their way back into cattle when they eat the protein of the animals that have been eating them. To close this biological loophole, the FDA is now considering tightening its feed rules.

Until mad cow disease, remarkably few people in the cattle business, let alone the general public, comprehended the strange semicircular food chain that industrial agriculture had devised for cattle (and, in turn, for us). When I mentioned to Rich Blair that I'd been surprised to learn that cows were eating cows, he said, "To tell the truth, it was kind of a shock to me too." Yet even today, ranchers don't ask many questions about feedlot menus. Not that the answers are so easy to come by. When I asked Poky's feedlot manager what exactly was in the protein supplement, he couldn't say. "When we buy supplement, the supplier says it's 40 percent protein, but they don't specify beyond that." When I called the supplier, it wouldn't divulge all its "proprietary ingredients" but promised that animal parts weren't among them. Protein is pretty much still protein.

Compared with ground-up cow bones, corn seems positively wholesome. Yet it wreaks considerable havoc on bovine digestion. During my day at Poky, I spent an hour or two driving around the yard with Dr. Mel Metzen, the staff veterinarian. Metzen, a 1997 graduate of Kansas State's vet school, oversees a team of eight cowboys who spend their days riding the yard, spotting sick cows, and bringing them in for treatment. A great many of these cows' health problems can be traced to their diet. "They're born to eat forage," Metzen said, "and we're making them eat grain."

Perhaps the most serious thing that can go wrong with a ruminant on corn is feedlot bloat. The rumen is always producing copious amounts of gas, which is normally expelled by belching during rumination. But when the diet contains too much starch and too little roughage, rumination all but stops, and a layer of foamy slime that can trap gas forms in the rumen. The rumen inflates like a balloon, pressing against the animal's lungs. Unless action is promptly taken to relieve the pressure (usually by forcing a hose down the animal's esophagus), the cow suffocates.

Cows rarely live on feedlot diets for more than six months, which might be about as much as their digestive systems can tolerate. "I don't know how long you could feed this ration before you'd see problems," Metzen said; another vet said that a sustained feedlot diet would eventually "blow out their livers" and kill them. As the acids eat away at the rumen wall, bacteria enter the bloodstream and collect in the liver. More than 13 percent of feedlot cattle are found at slaughter to have abscessed livers.

THE FEEDLOT'S LITTLE HELPER: ANTIBIOTICS

What keeps a feedlot animal healthy—or healthy enough—are antibiotics. Rumensin inhibits gas production in the rumen, helping to prevent bloat; tylosin reduces the incidence of liver infection. Most of the antibiotics sold in America end up in animal feed—a practice that, it is now generally acknowledged, leads directly to the evolution of new antibiotic-resistant "superbugs." In the debate over the use of antibiotics in agriculture, a distinction is usually made between clinical and nonclinical uses. Public health advocates don't object to treating sick animals with antibiotics; they just don't want to see the drugs lose their efficacy because factory farms are feeding them to healthy animals to promote growth. But the use of antibiotics in feed-lot cattle confounds the issue. Here the drugs are plainly being used to treat sick animals, yet the animals probably wouldn't be sick if not for what we feed them.

I asked Metzen what would happen if antibiotics were banned from cattle feed. "We just couldn't feed them as hard," he said. "Or we'd have a higher death loss." (Less than 3 percent of cattle die on the feedlot.) The price of beef would rise, he said, since the whole system would have to slow down.

"Hell, if you gave them lots of grass and space," he concluded dryly, "I wouldn't have a job."

Before heading over to Pen 43 for my reunion with No. 534, I stopped by the shed where recent arrivals receive their growth hormone implants. The calves are funneled into a chute, herded along by a ranch hand wielding an electric prod, then clutched in a restrainer just long enough for another hand to inject a slow-release pellet of Revlar, a synthetic estrogen, in the back of the ear. The Blairs' pen had not yet been implanted, and I was still struggling with the decision of whether to forgo what is virtually a universal practice in the cattle industry in the United States. (The use of growth-promoting hormone implants has been banned in the European Union.)

American regulators permit hormone implants on the grounds that no risk to human health has been proved, even though measurable hormone residues do turn up in the meat we eat. These contribute to the buildup of estrogenic compounds in the environment. Recent studies have also found elevated levels of synthetic growth hormones in feedlot wastes; these persistent chemicals eventually wind up in the waterways downstream of feedlots, where scientists have found fish exhibiting abnormal sex characteristics.

Implanting hormones in beef cattle is legal and financially irresistible: an implant costs $1.50 and adds between 40 and 50 pounds to the weight of a steer at slaughter, for a return of at least $25. That could easily make the difference between profit and loss on my investment in No. 534. Thinking like a parent, I like the idea of feeding my son hamburgers free of synthetic hormones. But thinking like a cattleman, there was really no decision to make.

Around lunchtime, Metzen and I finally arrived at No. 534's pen. My animal had put on a couple hundred pounds since we'd last met, and he looked it: thicker across the shoulders and round as a barrel through the middle. He carried himself more like a steer now than a calf, even though he was still less than a year old.

Poky is indeed a factory, transforming cheap raw materials into a less-cheap finished product, as fast as bovinely possible. Every day between now and his slaughter date in June, No. 534 will convert 32 pounds of feed (25 of them corn) into another 3½ pounds of flesh. Yet the factory metaphor obscures as much as it reveals about the creature that stood before me. For this steer was not a machine in a factory but an animal in a web of relationships that linked him to certain other animals, plants, and microbes, as well as to the Earth. And one of those other animals is us. The unnaturally rich diet of corn that has compromised No. 534's health is fattening his flesh in a way that in turn may compromise the health of the humans who will eat him. The antibiotics he's consuming with his corn were at that very moment selecting, in his gut and wherever else in the environment they wind up, for bacteria that could someday infect us and resist the drugs we depend on.

I thought about the deep pile of manure that No. 534 and I were standing in. We don't know much about the hormones in it—where they will end up or what they might do once they get there—but we do know something about the bacteria. One particularly lethal bug most probably resided in the manure beneath my feet. *Escherichia coli* O157 is a relatively new strain of an intestinal bacteria (it was first isolated in the 1980s) that is common in feedlot cattle, more than half of whom carry it in their guts. Ingesting as few as ten of these microbes can cause a fatal infection.

Most of the microbes that reside in the gut of a cow and find their way into our food get killed off by the acids in our stomachs, since the cow microbes originally adapted to live in a neutral-pH environment. But the digestive tract of the modern feedlot cow is closer in acidity to our own, and in this new, man-made environment, acid-resistant strains of *E. coli* O157 have developed that can survive our stomach acids—and go on to kill us. By acidifying a cow's gut with corn, we have broken down one of our food chain's barriers to infection. Yet this process can be reversed: James Russell, a USDA microbiologist, has discovered that switching a cow's diet from corn to hay in the final days before slaughter reduces the population of *E. coli* O157 in its manure by as much as 70 percent. Such a change, however, is considered wildly impractical by the cattle industry.

So much comes back to corn, this cheap, heavily subsidized feed that turns out in so many ways to be not cheap at all. For if you follow the corn from this bunk back to the fields where it grows, you will find an 80-million-acre monoculture that consumes more chemical herbicide and fertilizer than any other crop. Keep going and you can trace the nitrogen runoff from that crop all the way down the Mississippi into the Gulf of Mexico, where it has created (if that is the right word) a 8,000-square-mile "dead zone."

But you can go farther still, and follow the fertilizer needed to grow that corn all the way to the oil fields of the Persian Gulf. No. 534 started life as part of a food chain that derived all its energy from the sun; now that corn constitutes such an important link in his food chain, he is the product of an industrial system powered by fossil fuel. (And in turn, defended by the military—another uncounted cost of "cheap" food.) I asked David Pimentel, a Cornell ecologist who specializes in agriculture and energy, if it might be possible to calculate precisely how much oil it will take to grow my steer to slaughter weight. Assuming No. 534 continues to eat 25 pounds of corn a day and reaches a weight of 1,250 pounds, he will have consumed in his lifetime roughly 284 gallons of oil. We have succeeded in industrializing the beef calf, transforming what was once a solar-powered ruminant into the very last thing we need: another fossil-fuel machine.

THE LAST RIDE

Sometime in June, No. 534 will be ready for slaughter. Though only 14 months old, my steer will weigh more than 1,200 pounds and will move with the lumbering deliberateness of the obese. One morning, a cattle trailer from the National Beef plant in Liberal, Kansas, will pull in to Poky Feeders, drop a ramp, and load No. 534 along with thirty-five of his pen mates.

The National Beef plant is a sprawling gray-and-white complex in a neighborhood of trailer homes and tiny houses a notch up from shanty. These are, presumably, the homes of the Mexican and Asian immigrants who make up a large portion of the plant's workforce. The meat business has made southwestern Kansas an unexpectedly diverse corner of the country.

A few hours after the steers' arrival in the holding pens outside the factory, a plant worker will open a gate and herd No. 534 and his pen mates into an alley that makes a couple of turns before narrowing down to a single-file chute. The chute becomes a ramp that leads the animals up to a second-story platform and then disappears through a blue door. That door is as close to the kill floor as the plant managers were prepared to let me go. I could see whatever I wanted to farther on—the cold room where carcasses are graded, the food safety lab, the fabrication room where the carcasses are broken down into cuts—on the condition that I didn't take pictures or talk to employees. But the stunning, bleeding, and evisceration process was off-limits to a journalist, even a cattleman-journalist like myself.

What I know about what happens on the far side of the blue door comes mostly from Temple Grandin, who has been on the other side and, in fact, helped to design it. Grandin, an assistant professor of animal science at Colorado State, is one of the most influential people in the United States cattle industry. She has devoted herself to making cattle slaughter less stressful and therefore more humane by designing an ingenious series of cattle restraints, chutes, ramps, and stunning systems. Grandin is autistic, a condition she says has allowed her to see the world from the cow's point of view. The industry has embraced Grandin's work because animals under stress are not only more difficult to handle but also less valuable: panicked cows produce a surge of adrenaline that turns their meat dark and unappetizing. "Dark cutters," as they're called, sell at a deep discount.

Grandin designed the double-rail conveyor system in use at the National Beef plant; she has also audited the plant's killing process for McDonald's. Stories about cattle "waking up" after stunning only

to be skinned alive prompted McDonald's to audit its suppliers in
a program that is credited with substantial improvements since its
inception in 1999. Grandin says that in cattle slaughter "there is the
pre-McDonald's era and the post-McDonald's era—it's night and day."

Grandin recently described to me what will happen to No. 534
after he passes through the blue door:

> The animal goes into the chute single file. The sides are high
> enough so all he sees is the butt of the animal in front of him.
> As he walks through the chute, he passes over a metal bar,
> with his feet on either side. While he's straddling the bar, the
> ramp begins to decline at a 25-degree angle, and before he
> knows it, his feet are off the ground and he's being carried
> along on a conveyor belt. We put in a false floor so he can't look
> down and see he's off the ground. That would panic him. The
> conveyor is moving along at roughly the speed of a moving
> sidewalk. On a catwalk above stands the stunner. The stunner
> has a pneumatic-powered "gun" that fires a steel bolt about
> seven inches long and the diameter of a fat pencil. He leans
> over and puts it smack in the middle of the forehead. When it's
> done correctly, it will kill the animal on the first shot.

For a plant to pass a McDonald's audit, the stunner needs to
render animals "insensible" on the first shot 95 percent of the time.
A second shot is allowed, but should that one fail, the plant flunks.
At the line speeds at which meatpacking plants in the United States
operate—390 animals are slaughtered every hour at National, which
is not unusual—mistakes would seem inevitable, but Grandin insists
that only rarely does the process break down. Then:

> After the animal is shot while he's riding along, a worker
> wraps a chain around his foot and hooks it to an overhead trol-
> ley. Hanging upside down by one leg, he's carried by the trol-
> ley into the bleeding area, where the bleeder cuts his throat.
> Animal rights people say they're cutting live animals, but
> that's because there's a lot of reflex kicking.

This is one of the reasons a job at a slaughter plant is the most
dangerous in America. "What I look for is, Is the head dead?" Grandin

said. "It should be flopping like a rag, with the tongue hanging out. He'd better not be trying to hold it up—then you've got a live one on the rail." Just in case, Grandin said, "they have another hand stunner in the bleed area."

Much of what happens next—the dehiding of the animal, the tying off of its rectum before evisceration—is designed to keep the animal's feces from coming into contact with its meat. This is by no means easy to do, not when the animals enter the kill floor smeared with manure and 390 of them are eviscerated every hour. But since that manure is apt to contain lethal pathogens like *E. coli* O157, and since the process of grinding together hamburger from hundreds of different carcasses can easily spread those pathogens across millions of burgers, packing plants now spend millions on "food safety"— which is to say, on the problem of manure in meat.

Most of these efforts are reactive: it's accepted that the animals will enter the kill floor caked with feedlot manure that has been rendered lethal by the feedlot diet. Rather than try to alter that diet or keep the animals from living in their waste or slow the line speed—all changes regarded as impractical—the industry focuses on disinfecting the manure that will inevitably find its way into the meat. This is the purpose of irradiation (which the industry prefers to call "cold pasteurization"). It is also the reason that carcasses pass through a hot steam cabinet and get sprayed with an antimicrobial solution before being hung in the cooler at the National Beef plant.

It wasn't until after the carcasses emerged from the cooler, thirty-six hours later, that I was allowed to catch up with them, in the grading room. Two by two, the sides of beef traveled swiftly down the rails, six pairs every minute, to a station where two workers—one wielding a small power saw, the other a long knife—made a single 6-inch cut between the twelfth and thirteenth ribs, opening a window on the meat inside. The carcasses continued on to another station, where a USDA inspector holding a round blue stamp glanced at the exposed rib eye and stamped the carcass's creamy white fat once, twice, or— very rarely—three times: select, choice, prime.

The manager of the packing plant has offered to pull a box of steaks from No. 534 before his carcass disappears into the trackless stream of commodity beef fanning out to America's supermarkets and restaurants this June. From what I can see, the Blair brothers, with the help of Poky Feeders, are producing meat as good as any you can find in an American supermarket. And yet there's no reason to think this steak will taste any different from the other high-end industrial meat I've ever eaten.

I paid $598 for No. 534 in November; his living expenses from then until slaughter came to $61 on the ranch and $258 for 160 days at the feedlot (including implant), for a total investment of $917. With a carcass weight of 787 pounds and a grade at the upper end of choice, my projected profit is $27. It's a razor-thin margin, and it could easily vanish should the price of corn rise or No. 534 fail to make the predicted weight or grade—say, if he gets sick and goes off his feed. Without the corn, without the antibiotics, without the hormone implant, my brief career as a cattleman would end in failure. According to CattleFax, a market research firm, the return on an animal coming out of a feedlot has averaged just $3 per head over the last twenty years.

In fact, the system's reliance on cheap feed is being challenged as the push to increase ethanol production has created new demand for corn, driving up corn prices to record levels. The recent recession has pushed those prices back down, but only minimally and for a limited time. Corn prices are predicted to rise steadily throughout the next decade, forcing livestock producers to look for new sources of cheap feed. They won't have to look far. Already, ethanol by-products are being considered as an alternative source to corn—the distiller grains and solubles make for high-protein, cheap feed, especially for those feedlots operating close to ethanol plants.

THE GRASS-FED ALTERNATIVE

While waiting for my box of meat to arrive from Kansas, I've explored some alternatives to the industrial product. Nowadays you can find hormone- and antibiotic-free beef as well as organic beef, fed only grain grown without chemicals. This meat, which is often quite good, is typically produced using more grass and less grain (and so makes for healthier animals). Yet it doesn't fundamentally challenge the corn feedlot system, and I'm not sure that an "organic feedlot" isn't, ecologically speaking, an oxymoron. What I really wanted to taste is the sort of preindustrial beef my grandparents ate—from animals that have lived most of their full-length lives on grass.

I discovered that grass-fed meat is more expensive than supermarket beef. Whatever else you can say about industrial beef, it is remarkably cheap, and any argument for changing the system runs smack into the industry's populist arguments. Put the animals back on grass, it is said, and prices will soar; it takes too long to raise beef on grass, and there's not enough grass to raise them on, since the western rangelands aren't big enough to sustain America's 100 million head of cattle. And besides, Americans have learned to love corn-fed beef. Feedlot meat is also more consistent in both taste and supply and can be harvested twelve months a year. (Grass-fed cattle tend to be harvested in the fall, since they stop gaining weight over the winter, when the grasses go dormant.)

All of this is true. The economic logic behind the feedlot system is hard to refute. And yet so is the ecological logic behind a ruminant grazing on grass. Think what would happen if we restored a portion of the Corn Belt to the tallgrass prairie it once was and grazed cattle on it. No more petrochemical fertilizer, no more herbicide, no more nitrogen runoff. Yes, beef would probably be more expensive than it is now, but would that necessarily be a bad thing? Eating beef every day might not be such a smart idea anyway—for our health, for the environment. And how cheap, really, is cheap feedlot beef? Not cheap at all, when you add in the invisible costs: of antibiotic resistance, environmental degradation, heart disease, *E. coli* poisoning, corn subsidies, imported oil, and so on. All these are costs that grass-fed beef does not incur.

So how does grass-fed beef taste? Uneven, just as you might expect the meat of a nonindustrial animal to taste. One grass-fed tenderloin from Argentina that I sampled turned out to be the best steak I've ever eaten. But unless the meat is carefully aged, grass-fed beef can be tougher than feedlot beef—not surprisingly, since a grazing animal, which moves around in search of its food, develops more muscle and less fat. Yet even when the meat was tougher, its flavor, to my mind, was much more interesting. And specific, for the taste of every grass-fed animal is inflected by the place where it lived. Maybe it's just my imagination, but nowadays when I eat a feedlot steak, I can taste the corn and the fat, and I can see the view from No. 534's pen. I can't taste the oil, obviously, or the drugs, yet now I know they're there.

A considerably different picture comes to mind while chewing (and, okay, chewing) a grass-fed steak: a picture of a cow outside in a pasture eating the grass that has eaten the sunlight. Meat eating may have become an act riddled with moral and ethical ambiguities, but eating a steak at the end of a short, primordial food chain comprising nothing more than ruminants and grass and light is something I'm happy to do and defend. We are what we eat, it is often said, but of course that's only part of the story. We are what what we eat eats too.

BOSS HOG

The Rapid Rise of Industrial Swine

JEFF TIETZ

THE ANNUAL OUTPUT *of the world's most prolific industrial pork producer is not limited to billions of pounds of packaged meat from the slaughter of tens of millions of animals. The company also generates sufficient waste to destroy rivers, kill millions of fish, and severely impact the lives of residents in hundreds of rural communities. Now that Smithfield has conquered the U.S. swine industry, it is moving rapidly into Poland, Romania, and other hog-producing nations.*

❖

Smithfield Foods, the largest and most profitable pork processor in the world, killed 27 million hogs in 2007. That's a number worth considering. A slaughter-weight hog is 50 percent heavier than a person. The logistical challenge of processing that many pigs each year is roughly equivalent to butchering and boxing the entire human populations of New York, Los Angeles, Chicago, Houston, Philadelphia, Phoenix, San Antonio, San Diego, Dallas, San Jose, Detroit, Indianapolis, Jacksonville, San Francisco, Columbus, Austin, Memphis, Baltimore, Fort Worth, Charlotte, El Paso, Milwaukee, Seattle, Boston, Denver, Louisville, Washington, DC, Nashville, Las Vegas, Portland, Oklahoma City, and Tucson.

Smithfield Foods actually faces a more difficult task than transmogrifying the populations of America's thirty-two largest cities into edible packages of meat. Hogs produce three times more excrement than human beings do. The 500,000 pigs at a single Smithfield subsidiary in Utah generate more fecal matter each year than the 1.5 million inhabitants of Manhattan. The best estimates put Smithfield's total waste discharge at 26 million tons a year. That would fill four Yankee Stadiums. Even when divided among the many small pig production units that surround the company's slaughterhouses, that is not a containable amount. Smithfield's total sales in 2009 will reach an estimated $12 billion.[1] So prodigious is its fecal waste, however, that if the company treated its effluvia as big-city governments do—even if it came marginally close to that standard—it would lose money. Many of its contractors consequently allow great volumes of waste to run out of their slope-floored barns and sit blithely in the open, untreated, where the elements break it down and gravity pulls it into groundwater and river systems. Smithfield avows a culture of environmental responsibility, but ostentatious pollution is a linchpin of its business model.

A lot of pig shit is one thing; a lot of highly toxic pig shit is another. The excrement of Smithfield hogs is hardly even pig shit: it would be more accurate to compare it to industrial waste than to organic manure. The reason it is so toxic is Smithfield's efficiency. In 2008, the company produced 7 billion pounds of pork.[2] That's a remarkable achievement, a prolificacy unimagined two decades ago, and the only way to do it is to raise pigs in astonishing, unprecedented concentrations.

Smithfield's pigs live by the hundreds or thousands in warehouselike barns, in rows of wall-to-wall pens. There is no sunlight, straw, fresh air, or earth. Sows are artificially inseminated and fed and delivered of their piglets in cages too small to turn around in. Forty fully grown 250-pound male hogs often occupy a pen the size of a tiny apartment. In such internment, hogs with even minor open wounds are vulnerable to cannibalism. Slatted openings in the concrete floors allow excrement to fall into a catchment pit under the pens, but numerous things besides excrement can wind up in the pits: afterbirths, old batteries, piglets accidentally crushed by their mothers, broken bottles of insecticide, antibiotic syringes, stillborn pigs—anything small enough to fit through the foot-wide pipes that drain the pits. The pipes remain closed until enough sewage accumulates in the pits to create good expulsion pressure; then the pipes are opened and everything bursts out into a large holding pond.

The temperature inside hog houses can exceed 90 degrees. The air, at times saturated almost to the point of precipitation with gases from shit and chemicals, can be lethal to the pigs. Enormous exhaust fans run twenty-four hours a day. The fans function like the ventilators of terminal patients: if they break down for any length of time, pigs start dying.

From Smithfield's point of view, the problem with this lifestyle is immunological. Taken together, the immobility, poisonous air, and constant terror of confinement badly damage the pigs' immune systems. They become susceptible to infection, and in such dense quarters microbes or parasites or fungi, once established in one pig, will rush spritelike through the whole population. Accordingly, factory farm pigs are doused with insecticides and infused with a large range of antibiotics and vaccines. Without these compounds—oxytetracycline, Draxxin, ceftiofur, tiamulin—diseases would likely kill them. Thus the pigs remain in a state of dying until they're slaughtered. When a pig nearly ready to be slaughtered grows ill, workers sometimes shoot it up with as many drugs as necessary to get it to the slaughterhouse under its own power. As long as the pig remains ambulatory, it can be legally killed and sold as meat.

The drugs and chemicals Smithfield administers to its pigs, of course, exit its hog houses in pig shit. Industrial pig waste contains a host of pernicious substances: ammonia, hydrogen sulfide, cyanide, phosphates, nitrates, and heavy metals. The waste also nurses more than 100 microbial pathogens that cause illness in humans, including salmonella, cryptosporidia, streptococci, and giardia. Each gram of hog shit can carry up to 100 million fecal coliform bacteria.

Smithfield's largest holding ponds—the company calls them lagoons—cover 120,000 square feet. The area around a single slaughterhouse can encompass hundreds of lagoons, some of which are 30 feet deep. Even light rains can cause lagoons to overflow; major floods have transformed entire counties into pig-shit bayous. To alleviate swelling lagoons, workers sometimes pump the shit out of them and spray it on surrounding fields, which results in what the industry daintily refers to as "overapplication." This will turn hundreds of acres—thousands of football fields—into shallow mud puddles of pig shit. Tree branches will drip with pig shit.

Many pig farm lagoons have polyethylene liners, which can be punctured by rocks in the ground, allowing shit to seep beneath the liners and spread and ferment. Gases from the fermentation inflate the liner like a hot-air balloon and rise in an expanding, accelerating bubble that forces thousands of tons of feces out of the lagoon in all directions.

The lagoons themselves are so viscous and venomous that it is often impossible to save people who fall into them. A few years ago, a truck driver in Oklahoma was transferring pig shit to a Smithfield lagoon when he and his truck went over the side. It took almost three weeks to recover his body. In 1992, when a worker making repairs to a lagoon in Minnesota began to choke to death on the fumes, a coworker dived in after him, and they died the same death. On another occasion, a worker who was repairing a lagoon in Michigan was overcome by the fumes and fell in. His fifteen-year-old nephew dived in to save him but was overcome; the worker's cousin went in to save the teenager but was overcome; the worker's older brother dived in to save them but was overcome; and then the worker's father dived in. They all died in pig shit.

The chairman of Smithfield Foods, Joseph Luter III, is a funny, jowly, canny, barbarous guy who lives in a multimillion-dollar condo on Park Avenue in Manhattan and conveys himself about the planet in a corporate jet and a private yacht. At seventy, he is unrepentant in the face of criticism. He describes himself as a "tough man in a tough business" and his factories as wholly legitimate products of the American free market. He can be sardonic; he likes to mock his critics and rivals. "The animal rights people," he once said, "want to impose a vegetarian's society on the U.S. Most vegetarians I know are neurotic." When the Environmental Protection Agency (EPA) cited Smithfield for thousands of violations of the Clean Water Act, Luter responded by comparing what he claimed were the number of violations the company could theoretically have been charged with (2.5 million, by his calculation) to the number of documented violations up to that point (74). "A very, very small percent," he said.

Luter grew up butchering hogs in his father's slaughterhouse in the town of Smithfield, Virginia. When he took over the family business forty years ago, it was a local, marginally profitable meatpacking operation. Under Luter, Smithfield was soon making enough money to begin purchasing neighboring meat packers. From the beginning, Luter thought amorally and monopolistically. He bought out his local competition until he completely dominated the regional pork processing market, but he was dissatisfied. The company was still buying most of its hogs from independent farmers, and Luter wanted to control every stage of production, from cage birth to mechanized dismemberment and distribution.

So Luter devised a new kind of contract. Smithfield would own the living hogs; its contractors would raise them and be responsible for disposing of their shit and, should they die before slaughter, their corpses. This arrangement made it impossible for small hog farmers to survive—those who could not handle thousands and thousands of pigs were driven out of business. "It was a simple matter of economic power," says Eric Tabor, chief of staff for Iowa's attorney general.

Smithfield's expansion was unique in the history of the industry: Between 1990 and 2005, it grew by more than 1,000 percent. In 1997 it was the nation's seventh-largest pork producer; by 1999 it was the largest. Smithfield now kills one of every four pigs sold commercially in the United States. As Smithfield expanded, it consolidated its farms, clustering millions of fattening hogs around its slaughterhouses.

Under Luter, the company was becoming a great pollution machine: Smithfield was suddenly generating unheard-of amounts of pig shit adulterated with drugs and chemicals. According to the EPA, Smithfield's largest farm-slaughterhouse operation—in Tar Heel, North Carolina—dumps more waste into the nation's water each year than all but three other manufacturing facilities.

Luter likes to tell this story: An old man and his grandson are walking in a cemetery. They see a tombstone that reads: HERE LIES CHARLES W. JOHNSON, A MAN WHO HAD NO ENEMIES. "Gee, Granddad," the boy says, "that man must have been a great man. He had no enemies."

"Son," the grandfather replies, "if a man didn't have any enemies, he didn't do a damn thing with his life."

If Luter were to set this story in Ivy Hill Cemetery, in Smithfield, while he was growing up there, the branches of the cemetery's trees would be bent with the weight of dozens of buzzards. The waste stream from the Luters' meatpacking plant, with its thickening agents of pig innards and dead fish, flowed nearby. Inflicting indignity on the deceased is an ancient way of making enemies. In 2005, before he retired as CEO of Smithfield Foods, Joseph Luter took home $10,802,134. He held $19,296,000 in unexercised stock options.

One day in the fall of 2006, a retired Marine Corps colonel and environmental activist named Rick Dove, the former riverkeeper of North Carolina's Neuse River, arranged to have me flown over Smithfield's operation in North Carolina. Dove hires private planes to document regulatory violations from the air. He is a focused guy of seventy; it is hard for him to talk about corporate hog farming without becoming angry. After he got out of the Marine Corps in 1987, he became a commercial fisherman, which he had wanted to do since he was a kid. He was successful, and his son went into business with him. Then factory hog farming arrived and killed the fish and both Dove and his son got seriously ill.

Dove and other activists provide the only effective oversight of corporate hog farming in the region. The industry has long made big campaign contributions to politicians responsible for regulating hog farms. In 1995, while Smithfield was trying to persuade the state of Virginia to reduce a large regulatory fine, Joseph Luter gave $100,000 to then-governor George Allen's political action committee. In 1998, hog operators in North Carolina spent $1 million to help defeat state legislators who wanted to phase out open-pit lagoons. The state has rarely had enough inspectors to ensure that hog farms are complying with environmental regulations.

The airport Dove uses, in New Bern, North Carolina, is tiny; the plane he uses, a 1975 Cessna single-prop, looks tiny even in the tiny airport. We arrived early on a lightly cloudy day. From the parking lot, we walked unnoticed across the noiseless tarmac to the plane. The pilot, Joe Corby, was waiting for us. Corby was considerably older than I'd expected him to be. The Cessna's cabin had four cracked yellow linoleum seats. It looked like the interior of a 1975 VW bug; possibly it had more dials.

"I have a GPS," Dove said to Corby as we got in, "so I can kinda guide you."

"Oh you *do*!" Corby said. "Well, OK."

We took off. "Bunch of turkey buzzards," Dove said, looking out the window. "They're big."

"Don't wanna hit them," Corby said. "They would be . . . very destructive."

We climbed to 2,000 feet and headed toward the densest multitude of hogs in the world. The landscape at first was unsuspiciously pastoral—fields planted in corn or soybeans or cotton, tree lines staking creeks, a few unincorporated villages of prefab houses. Then we arrived at the global locus of hog farming, and the countryside turned into an immense subdivision for pigs. Hog farms that contract with Smithfield differ in dimension but are otherwise very similar: parallel rows of six, eight, or twelve one-story hog houses, some holding many thousands of hogs, all backing onto a single large lagoon. The lagoons are not brown. Bacterial activity turns them pink. The pink comes in two shades: dark or Pepto-Bismol—vile, freaky colors in the middle of green farmland.

From the plane, Smithfield's farms replicated one another as far as I could see in every direction. Visibility was about four miles. I counted the lagoons. There were 103. That worked out to at least 50,000 hogs per square mile. You could fly for an hour, Dove said, and you would see nothing but lagoons and hog houses, with little towns of modular homes and a few family farms pinioned amid them.

Each lagoon was surrounded by large fields. Pollution control at Smithfield consists of spraying the pig shit from the lagoons onto the fields. The idea is borrowed from the past: the small hog farmers that Smithfield drove out of business fertilized their crops with manure. Smithfield says this is what it does—its crops gratefully ingest every ounce of its pig shit, creating a zero-discharge system. "If you manage your fields correctly, there should be no runoff, no pollution," says Dennis Treacy, Smithfield's vice president of environmental affairs. "If you're getting runoff, you're doing something wrong."

The environmental scientists who have studied this system say that Smithfield is doing something wrong. So do former and current officials at the North Carolina Department of Environment and Natural Resources, a former director of the North Carolina Department of Health and Human Services, officials at the EPA, and every person I talked to who lived near a lagoon.

Smithfield doesn't grow nearly enough crops to absorb all of its pig shit. The company raises so many pigs in so little space that it has to import the majority of their feed. In 2009, North Carolina had 10 million hogs.[3] Its farmers imported 124,000 metric tons of nitrogen and 29,000 tons of phosphorus for use in hog feed. The hogs ate the feed and then nutritiously shit out 101,000 metric tons of nitrogen and 22,700 metric tons of phosphorus. That kind of nutrient injection into an ecosystem creates what Dan Whittle, a former senior policy associate with the Department of Environment and Natural Resources, calls a "massive imbalance." Well before hogs reached their current population in North Carolina, three hog-raising counties were generating more nitrogen, and eighteen were generating more phosphorus, than all the crops in the state could assimilate.

Few human food crops can withstand the nutrient loads in industrial pig shit, so Smithfield's contract farmers plant a lot of hay, which is extremely nitrate-tolerant. In 1992, when the number of hogs in North Carolina was escalating wildly, so much hay was planted to deal with the fresh volumes of pig shit that the market for hay collapsed. The high-potency nitric acid in hog lagoon hay often sickens livestock. For a while, former governor Jim Hunt—a recipient of pork sector campaign money—was feeding hog farm hay to his cows. Locals say it made the cows queasy and irritable, and they kicked Hunt repeatedly, seemingly in revenge. It's a popular tale in hog country.

When you fly over eastern North Carolina, you notice right away that springs and streams and swamplands and small lakes are everywhere. You are looking down at a pluvial coastal plain, grooved and tilted toward the sea. The sandy coastal soil is highly permeable, and the water table lies just three feet beneath the surface. Smithfield's sprayfields almost always incline toward creeks or creek-fed swamps. Climate, geology, and topography rinse and drain the sprayfields thoroughly.

Many studies have documented the harm caused by hog waste runoff. One showed pig shit raising the level of nitrogen and phosphorus in a receiving river as much as sixfold. Corporate hog farms in North Carolina are situated almost exclusively in the Cape Fear and Neuse River basins. Nine of the rivers and creeks in those basins have been classified by the state as either "negatively impacted" or environmentally "impaired."

On our way back to the New Bern airport, we passed over a curiosity: perfectly vertical fountains of shit-mist. Smithfield's contractors, Dove said, were spraying the contents of their lagoons straight up into the air. What seemed like an inexplicably inefficient irrigation method, he said, was actually a disposal technique. Lofted and atomized, the gossamer pig shit is blown clear of the farms.

Open-pit lagoons emit hundreds of volatile gases into the atmosphere: methane, carbon dioxide, hydrogen sulfide. A single lagoon releases many millions of bacteria into the air per day, some resistant to human antibiotics. Hog farms in North Carolina also discharge 300 tons of nitrogen every day as ammonia gas, much of which falls back to earth, stimulating algal eruptions that asphyxiate lakes and streams.

In 1995, a woman downwind from a corporate hog farm in Olivia, Minnesota, called a poison control center and described her symptoms. "Ma'am," the poison control officer told her, "the only symptoms of hydrogen sulfide poisoning you're not experiencing are seizures, convulsions and death. Leave the area immediately."

People who breathe the air emanating from hog lagoons get bronchitis, diarrhea, and nose bleeds; they suffer from mood disturbances, headaches, asthma, eye and throat irritation, and heart palpitations. Lagoon odors have been shown to suppress immune function: inhaling the particulate waste of hogs with compromised immune systems compromises human immune systems. In eastern North Carolina, virtually everyone lives close to a lagoon.

To wholly appreciate what this agglomeration of hog production does to the people who live near it, you have to appreciate the smell of industrial-strength pig shit. The ascending stench can nauseate pilots at 3,000 feet. On the day we flew over Smithfield's farms, there was little wind to stir up the lagoons or carry the stink, and because it had been dry, the lagoon managers weren't spraying very frequently. It was the best of times. We could smell the farms from the air, but the mephitic scent was intermittent and not particularly strong.

To get a really good whiff, I drove down a narrow country road of white sand and walked up to a Smithfield lagoon. At the end of the road stood a tractor and spray rig. The fetid white carcass of a hog lay on its back in a dumpster known as a "dead box." Flies covered the hog's snout. Its hooves looked like high heels. Millions of factory farm hogs—one study puts it at 10 percent—die before they make it to the killing floor. Some are taken to rendering plants, where they are propelled through meat grinders and then fed cannibalistically back to living hogs. Others are dumped into big open pits called "dead holes." The borders of many hog farms are littered with pig corpses and bleached pig bones. The bears and buzzards of eastern North Carolina are said to be lazy and fat.

No one seemed to be around. It was quiet except for the gigantic exhaust fans affixed to the six hog houses. There was an unwholesome tang in the air, but there was no wind and it wasn't hot, so I couldn't smell the lagoon itself. I walked the few hundred yards over to it. It was covered with a thick film; its edge was a narrow beach of big black flies. Here, its odor was leaking out. I took a deep breath. *Concentrated manure* was my predictable first thought, but I was fighting an impulse to vomit even as I was thinking it. I've smelled stronger odors in my life, but nothing so insidiously and instantaneously nauseating. It took my mind a second or two to get through the odor's first coat. The smell at its core had a frightening, uniquely enriched putridity, both deep-sweet and high-sour. I backed away and returned to the car, but I remained sick—it was a shivery, retchy kind of nausea—for a good five minutes. That's apparently characteristic of industrial pig shit: It keeps making you sick for a good while after you've stopped smelling it. It's an unduly invasive, adhesive smell. Your whole body reacts to it. It's as if a substance has entered your stomach. A little while later I was driving and I caught a crosswind stench, and from the moment it hit me a timer in my body started ticking: you can only remain functional in that smell for so long. The memory of it makes you gag.

If the temperature and wind aren't right and the lagoon managers are spraying, people in hog country can't hang their laundry or sit on their porches or mow their lawns. Epidemiological studies show that those who live near hog lagoons suffer from abnormally high levels of depression, tension, anger, fatigue, and confusion. "We are used to farm odors," one local farmer told me. "These are not farm odors."

The stink literally knocks people down: they walk out of the house to get something in the yard and become so nauseated they collapse.

That has happened to Julian and Charlotte Savage, an elderly couple whose farmland now abuts a Smithfield sprayfield—one of several meant to absorb the shit of 50,000 hogs. The Savages live in a small kit house. Sitting in the kitchen, Charlotte told me that she once saw Julian collapse in the yard and ran out and threw a coat over his head and dragged him back inside. Before Smithfield arrived, Julian's family had farmed the land for the better part of a century. He raised tobacco, corn, wheat, turkeys, and chickens. Now he has respiratory problems and rarely goes outside.

Behind the house, a creek bordering the sprayfield flows into a swamp; the Savages have seen hog waste running right into the creek. Once, during a flood, they found pig shit six inches deep pooled around their house. They had to drain it by digging trenches, which took three weeks. Charlotte has noticed that nitrogen fallout keeps the trees around the house a deep synthetic green. There is a big buzzard population.

The Savages said they could keep the pig shit smell out of their house by shutting the doors and windows, but I thought the walls reeked faintly. They had a windbreak—an 80-foot-wide strip of forest—between their house and the fields. They knew people who didn't, though, and when the smell was bad, those people quickly shut their windows and doors like everyone else, but their coffee and spaghetti and carrots still tasted like pig shit.

The Savages have had what seemed to be hog shit in their bathwater. Their well water, which was clean before Smithfield arrived, is now suspect. "I try not to drink it," Charlotte said. "We mostly just drink drinks, soda and things." While we talked, Julian spent most of the time on the living room couch; his lungs were particularly bad that day. Then he came into the kitchen. Among other things, he said: *I can't breathe it, it'll put you on the ground; you can't walk, you fall down; you breathe you gon' die; you go out and smell it one time and your ass is gone; it's not funny to be around it. It's not funny, honey.* He could have said all this tragicomically, with a thin smile, but he cried the whole time.

Smithfield is not just a virtuosic polluter; it is also a theatrical one. Its lagoons are historically prone to failure. In North Carolina alone they have spilled, in a span of four years, 2 million gallons of shit into the Cape Fear River, 1.5 million gallons into its Persimmon Branch, 1 million gallons into the Trent River, and 200,000 gallons into Turkey Creek. In Virginia, Smithfield was fined $12.6 million in 1997 for 6,900 violations of the Clean Water Act—the third-largest civil penalty ever levied under the act by the EPA. It amounted to .035 percent of Smithfield's annual sales.

A river that receives copious waste from a confinement hog farm begins to die quickly. Toxins and microbes can kill plants and animals outright; the pig shit itself consumes available oxygen and suffocates fish and aquatic animals; and the transported nutrients foment deoxygenating algal blooms. The Pagan River runs by Smithfield's original plant and headquarters in Virginia, which served as Joseph Luter's staging ground for his assault on the pork-raising and pork-processing industries. For decades, before a spate of regulations, the Pagan had no living marsh grass, a paltry and poisonous population of fish and shellfish, and a half foot of noxious black mud lining its bed. The hulls of boats winched up out of the river bore inch-thick coats of greasy muck.

In North Carolina, an abundance of pig waste from Smithfield's farms makes its way into the Neuse River. In a five-day span in 2003, more than 4 million fish in the river died. In 2004, an estimated 15 million fish died. In 2009, over 100 million died. The largest recorded fish kill in the history of the United States, which had a death toll of over 1 billion, occurred in the Neuse in 1991. Studies have consistently implicated nutrient overload as the cause of all these deaths. Research conducted between 2001 and 2006 showed a 500 percent increase in the river's ammonia content. Pig waste runoff from the Neuse and other rivers has badly damaged the Albemarle-Pamlico Sound, which is almost as big as the Chesapeake Bay and provides half the nursery grounds used by fish in the eastern Atlantic.

The biggest spill in the history of corporate hog farming happened in 1995. The dike of a 120,000-square-foot lagoon owned by a Smithfield competitor ruptured, releasing 25.8 million gallons of effluent into the headwaters of the New River in North Carolina. It was the biggest environmental spill in United States history, more than twice as big as the *Exxon Valdez* oil spill six years earlier. The sludge was so caustic it reportedly burned your skin if you touched it, and so dense it took almost two months to make its way 16 miles downstream to the ocean. Over 1 million fish died.

It's hard to conceive of fish kills on this scale. The 1995 kill began with turbulence in one small part of the water: fish writhing and dying. It then spread in patches along the length of the river. In two hours, dead and dying fish were mounded wherever the river's contours slowed the current. Within a day, they were covering the riverbanks and coagulating the water. Buoyant dead eyes and scales and white bellies scintillated up and down the river out of sight—more fish than the river seemed capable of holding. The air above the water was chaotic with scavenging birds. There were far more fish than the birds could eat.

Spills aren't the worst thing that can happen to virulent pig excrement lying exposed in fields and lagoons. Hurricanes are worse. In 1999, Hurricane Floyd washed 120,000,000 gallons of unsheltered hog waste into the Tar, Neuse, Roanoke, Pamlico, New, and Cape Fear rivers. Many of the pig shit lagoons of eastern North Carolina were underwater. Satellite photographs show a dark brown tide closing over the region's waterways, converging on the Albemarle-Pamlico Sound and feeding itself out to sea in a long, well-defined channel. Very little freshwater marine life remained behind. Feces contaminated beaches; people encountered drowned pigs miles from their cages. A picture taken at the time shows a shark eating a dead pig three miles off the North Carolina coast.

Industrial hog farming fosters another kind of environmental havoc: outbreaks of *Pfiesteria piscicida*, a multiform microbe that has killed hundreds of millions of fish and harmed dozens of people. When nutrient-rich waste like pig shit floods waterways and precipitates algal blooms, fish arrive in large congregations to eat the algae, and this convergence of life attracts a lethal form of *Pfiesteria*.

Pfiesteria is invisible and odorless—you know it by the trail of dead. It kills fish by perforating their skin and eating their tissues and blood cells. Afflicted fish appear to dissolve. After the 1995 spill, *Pfiesteria* attacked and killed several million fish. *Pfiesteria* also consumes human blood cells: fishermen developed widening lesions on their hands and arms. People found that at least one of *Pfiesteria's* toxins could take flight: breathing the air above the harrowed water caused severe respiratory difficulty, memory loss, headaches, blurry vision, and logical impairment. Some fishermen couldn't find their way home. Others had trouble speaking in complete sentences. Laboratory workers exposed to *Pfiesteria* lost the ability to dial phones and solve simple math problems; they forgot their own names. Recovering from *Pfiesteria's* pulmonary and nervous system damage could take days, weeks, months, or years.

Smithfield is no longer able to disfigure watersheds quite so obviously as in the past; it can no longer expand and flatten small pig farms quite so easily. In some places, new slaughterhouses are required to meet expensive waste disposal requirements. Several state legislatures have passed laws prohibiting or limiting the ownership of small farms by pork processors. North Carolina, where pigs now outnumber people, has passed a moratorium on new hog facilities and has prevailed upon Smithfield to fund research into alternative waste disposal technologies. Politicians in South Carolina, having taken a good look at their neighbor's coastal plain, have pronounced the company unwelcome in the state. A few of Smithfield's recent acquisition deals have come under federal and state scrutiny.

These efforts, of course, come comically late. Confinement hog operations control at least 75 percent of the market. Smithfield's dominance is hardly at risk: Twenty-six percent of the pork processed in this country is Smithfield pork.[4] The company's expansion does not seem to be slowing down: From 2004 to 2006, Smithfield's annual sales grew by $1.5 billion. In 2006, the company opened a $100 million processing plant in North Carolina. In September of that year, Smithfield announced that it would be merging with Premium Standard Farms, the nation's second-largest hog grower and sixth-largest pork processor. The acquisition was completed in 2007; Smithfield now manufactures more pork than the next five largest pork producers in the nation combined.

As it grew, the company sought to present itself as an innovator of environmental technology. In 2003, Smithfield announced that it was investing $20 million in a program to turn its pig shit in Utah into clean-burning alternative fuel. It founded Smithfield Bioenergy, LLC, and built a biodiesel facility in Texas.[5]

"We're paying a lot of attention to energy right now," the Smithfield vice president, Dennis Treacy, said of the green energy initiatives. "We've come such a long way." The company had undergone a "complete cultural shift on environmental matters." In 2007, though, Smithfield Bioenergy still hadn't turned a profit, and Smithfield dissolved it.[6]

Nothing could have altered the physical reality of Smithfield Foods itself. "All of a sudden we have this 800-pound gorilla in the pork industry," *Successful Farming* magazine warned—nine years ago. There is simply no regulatory solution to the millions of tons of searingly fetid effluvium that confinement hog farms discharge and aerosolize on a daily basis. Smithfield alone has sixteen operations in twelve states. Fixing the problem completely would bankrupt the company. According to Dr. Michael Mallin, a marine scientist at the University of North Carolina at Wilmington who has researched the effects of corporate farming on water quality, the volumes of concentrated pig waste produced by industrial hog farms are plainly not containable in small areas. The land, he says, "just can't absorb everything that comes out of the barns." From the moment that Smithfield attained its current size, its waste disposal problem became conventionally insoluble.

Joe Luter, like his pig shit waste, has an innate aversion to being restrained in any way. Ever since American regulators and lawmakers started forcing Smithfield to spend more money on waste treatment and attempting to limit the company's expansion, Luter has been looking to do business elsewhere. In recent years, his gaze has fallen on the lucrative and unregulated markets of Poland and Romania.

In 1999, with the help of politicians eager for capital investment, Luter bought a state-owned company called Animex, one of Poland's biggest hog processors. He then began acquiring huge moribund Communist-era hog farms and converting them into concentrated feeding operations. Pork prices in Poland were low, so Smithfield's sweeping expansion didn't make strict economic sense, except that it had the virtue of pushing small hog farmers toward bankruptcy.

By 2003, Animex was running six subsidiary companies and seven processing plants, selling nine brands of meat and taking in $338 million annually. By 2008, 600,000 Polish hog farmers had lost their livelihoods.

The usual violations occurred. Near one of Smithfield's largest plants, in Byszkowo, an enormous pool of frozen pig shit, pumped into a lagoon in winter, melted and ran into two nearby lakes. The lake water turned brown, residents in local villages got skin rashes and eye infections, and the stench made it hard to eat. A 2004 Helsinki Commission report found that Smithfield's pollution throughout Poland was damaging the country's ecosystems. Overapplication was endemic.[7] Farmers without permits were piping liquid pig shit directly into watersheds that replenish the Baltic Sea.

As Smithfield was subduing Poland, it was moving into Romania. A former U.S. ambassador ushered the company's executives into the offices of the president and prime minister. Smithfield made large cash contributions to the Romanian government. Its lobbying firm opened an office in Bucharest.

Romanian peasants had been raising hogs on the land for hundreds of years. Small farmers produced 75 percent of the country's pork. Then Smithfield established itself and began extinguishing household farms at an average rate of 100,000 per year. Within five years of the company's arrival, 90 percent of the independent hog market was gone, and Smithfield was Romania's largest pork producer. Its facilities foul Romanian air, water, and soil. Residents shut their windows and doors against the smell.

Three thousand miles away, in West Africa, a novel product has begun appearing in local hog markets: frozen packets of pig offal from Poland and Romania. The packets, whose export is subsidized by the European Union, cost far less than fresh pork. Liberian and Ivorian and Guinean farmers are discovering that they cannot compete with scrap viscera from Smithfield's newest pig factories.

WATCHING THE CHICKENS PASS BY

The Grueling Monotony of the Disassembly Line

STEVE STRIFFLER

WORK ON THE POULTRY DISASSEMBLY LINES, *where birds are processed every few seconds, is a demanding and dangerous occupation. In a single shift a worker can make thousands of repetitive cuts or movements. But although much has been written about the physical pain of slaughterhouse work, the mental anguish of making it through a single shift can be equally harrowing.*

❖

There is no shortage of eye-catching and often horrific stories when it comes to the meat industries. The deaths of some two dozen workers in a 1991 fire at an Imperial Foods chicken processing plant is perhaps the most tragic case, but it is by no means isolated. However, in my two summers working on the production line at Tyson while conducting research for a book, there were no horror stories of the type that make the evening news. To be sure, safety regulations and standards designed to protect both workers and consumers were routinely broken or ignored in the poultry plants where I worked. But what impressed me most about the strange world of poultry processing was the unbearable weight of routine. The oppressiveness of routine work is very difficult to convey. Yet it defines factory life and is perhaps the most devastating part of work in the poultry industry. Minute by minute, hour by hour, day by day, month by month, year by year, one of the most basic features of life—work—becomes an unbearable and unwinnable struggle against the clock. In fact, the more one struggles, the worse it is. The first complaint that virtually all workers point to—before wages, working conditions, and supervisors—is the intolerable monotony. As one worker explained:

> It's something that is impossible to describe. You worked here, so you understand. It's weird, but for three or four days a week, at some point during the day, I honestly feel like I will not make it through the day . . . that I will not possibly make it to break. Most of the time I think about something else, or play a game with myself. I try to make the best cuts, or see how fast I can work, or see how little I can do and still get the job done, or see if I can do it with one hand, something, anything. But at some point during the day these little tricks don't work and I feel like I am going to have a panic attack. I look at the clock. Then I start to think about every movement I make. Once you start to think you are finished. It's like if you think about breathing, you can't breathe. I feel like I am going to scream. The clock does not move. I swear it goes backward! You know what I am saying. I even tell God that if he lets me make it to break I will never come back. I promise myself I will quit. And I am totally serious.
>
> I have been playing this game for ten years! I come back every day. For ten years I have been torturing myself, spending the best years of my life in this ugly building, without windows, watching the chickens pass by, doing the same exact thing. I honestly don't know why I do it. The money of course. And once I leave the plant I somehow forget how awful it was and here I am the next day. I can't explain it. I suppose I am so relieved when I leave the plant that I forget how bad it was.[1]

Routine does not simply mess with your mind; it destroys your body. Not all workers are affected in the same way or to the same extent, but if you spend more than a year on the line—doing the exact same series of motions over and over again—it is certain that your fingers, wrists, hands, arms, shoulders, or back will feel the effects. A few more years and the damage may be irreparable. Almost all of the line workers I met had serious wrist problems. Many had undergone surgery and more than a few were permanently debilitated.[2] A 2005 report on the meat and poultry industries from Human Rights Watch put it this way:

> Nearly every worker interviewed for this report bore physical signs of a serious injury suffered from working in a meat or poultry plant. Automated lines carrying dead animals and their parts for disassembly move too fast for worker safety. Repeating thousands of cutting motions during each work shift puts enormous traumatic stress on workers' hands, wrists, arms, shoulders, and backs. They often work in close quarters, creating additional dangers for themselves and coworkers. They often receive little training and are not always given the safety equipment they need. They are often forced to work long overtime hours under pain of dismissal if they refuse. Meat and poultry industry employers set up the workplaces and practices that create these dangers, but they treat the resulting mayhem as a normal, natural part of the production process, not as what it is—repeated violations of international human rights standards.[3]

As one worker I worked with points out, the pain can cause even more anguish because "as soon as I start hanging chickens I feel fine. It's like that is all my muscles know how to do. I am in constant pain when I am not at work. My hands hurt so bad sometimes that I cannot make dinner or hold my child. When I wake up in the morning it takes my hands and arms thirty minutes to wake up."[4]

In other cases, the work provides no relief: "This is the fifth or sixth job [in the plant] I have had. After a year in one job I can't do it anymore. Something starts to hurt so bad that I can't do the job. If I complain enough, they usually switch me, but not always to something better."[5]

The industry's response is that workers develop repetitive motion disorders and other injuries when they fail to follow proper procedures. If workers would just use tools properly, maintain good posture, and do their exercises, they would experience no pain or injuries. Such statements would be comical if the consequences were not so tragic. Further, the company's stance can be perverse. On one memorable occasion, Michael, our supervisor, conducted a routine "training session" on ergonomics. Because the supervisors could not afford to stop the line, Michael was to read "the lesson" while the workers continued to work and the machines drowned out his voice. Each worker was to then sign a sheet of paper confirming that he or she had received the lesson. "I sign," one worker quipped, "because I do receive a lesson. I learn how little Tyson cares about us."

On this particular occasion, Arturo challenged Michael in full view of the other workers, suggesting that if the instruction was to have any meaning, he had to stop the line and gather the workers in a quiet place for the lesson. Michael, embarrassed, reluctantly stopped the line, moved the workers into the hallway, and read a single sheet of paper with about ten points. Arturo insisted that I translate, since, as he pointed out, there was little point in conducting a lesson in a language that the majority of workers could not understand. (Even with the translation, four of the workers from Southeast Asia were left completely out of the loop.) The ten points were all straightforward enough. Workers should use their legs, not backs, to lift heavy objects; they should stand close enough, and at the right height, when sorting chicken on the conveyor belt; and so on.

Hoping to avoid discussion, Michael ignored the last line of the lesson, "Ask the workers if they have any questions," which I blurted out in Spanish before he could send us back to work. The women line workers responded by approaching Michael with a ferociousness that caught everyone off guard. The scene must have looked a bit odd from a distance. Eight or nine Mexican and Salvadoran women, all over forty-five and standing about five feet tall, were berating their bewildered six-foot-three, twenty-two-year-old supervisor. Looking at Michael with serious determination, Maria began, "Tell him we know how to do our jobs. But we are too short and need stools so we can be at the correct height." Ana chimed in: "Tell him I agree with the lesson. We shouldn't reach as far as we do. It hurts our backs. But if you are by yourself, you have to reach [all the way across the conveyor belt]. The problem is we don't have enough workers at each station." Feeling momentarily empowered, Blanca quickly added: "I can barely move my wrists when I get home because I am doing the job of two people. We don't need a lesson, we need more workers. Tell him to come work and see what it is like."

I translated as quickly as possible. The women were serious, but they were also enjoying the moment. Things were how they should be. Michael was a kid receiving a tongue-lashing from women who were old enough to be his mother. Winking at me, Isabel said, "Tell the boy we know how to do our jobs and that he needs to start doing his." As we well knew, Michael *was* doing his job. That was the problem. Looking for an exit, Michael panicked and dug himself in even deeper: "Tell them if they hurt, they should go to the nurse." There was hardly a sorer subject than the ineffective company nurse. All workers in the group started to laugh dismissively. To make sure he got the message, Maria scoffed, "When we go to the nurse, she just gives us Advil and tells us to go back to work." She lifts her arms. "Look at my wrists. Do you think Advil is the answer?" And with that, the workers decided that the discussion was over and returned to work.

The production line and factory rhythm give work an unbearable routine that places mental and physical strain on workers of all ages, genders, and nationalities. There is no escaping it. Unfortunately, the weight of routine does not end at work. When I first began at Tyson, I had this naïve idea that the one virtue of working in a factory was that once I left work I would be free. Little did I know.

I worked the second shift, arriving around 2:30 p.m. to set up the production lines. I would then lift bags of flour for the next eight hours, enjoy two half-hour breaks, prepare the lines for the cleaning crew, and finally get out of the plant sometime after 12:30 a.m. (often after 1:00 a.m.). Exhausted, I would first shower and then wind down by having a beer and watching some late-night TV before hitting the sack. Rarely did I get to bed before 2:30, and I often fell asleep in front of the TV. I slept well but frequently woke up in the middle of the night with the sensation that my hands were so bloated they were going to explode. This is what you get when you clench bags of flour all day long. Around 9:00 or 10:00 a.m. I would wake up in time to do it all over again. Free time? I had trouble finding the time, let alone energy, to shop, exercise, or even do something as simple as get a haircut.

Yet my situation was much easier than that of the other workers. My stint in the factory was temporary, a fact that was not only comforting but also allowed me to postpone or ignore "life" in ways that most workers could not. I had no family, few commitments, and no financial problems. I came home to a quiet apartment and had the luxury of vegging out. No other worker could do that. Most had families, and many worked another job. Some even additionally worked the night shift in our plant. As one worker recounted:

> I am always tired. The worst part is that since I work the second shift I am rarely around my children or wife. When I am home I am usually asleep. I get home at one in the morning. My wife works the first shift so when I return she is asleep. We cannot both work the same shift because someone has to be with the kids. When I wake up in the morning she is already at work and I have to get the kids ready for school. Something always goes wrong. One can't find his shoe. Another lost this or that. It's a circus. I get them to school, come home, sleep a little bit more before I get ready for work. I go to work and my wife is leaving. She gets home in time to be with the kids in the afternoon. Sometimes there is a little time when the kids are alone. We don't like that because something could happen, but it is no more than an hour and the oldest is now thirteen. I see my wife on Sunday. We joke that it is a good thing we don't want more kids because we don't see each other enough to make them![6]

The sad irony is that although working in a factory imposes a routine on daily life, it is not one that makes it possible to have a "normal" life. Even the mundane tasks of daily living—shopping for groceries, putting children to bed, intimate moments with a spouse—become difficult to accomplish. It is hard to tell which is more overwhelming: the oppressive routine at work or the inability to establish a viable routine beyond the factory gate.

THE MILK OF HUMAN UNKINDNESS

Industrialization and the Supercow

ANNE MENDELSON

BY WRINGING THE LAST POSSIBLE DROP *from dairy cows, confinement operations turn one of the world's oldest foods into a mockery of what milk can be. The process began two centuries ago, when newly rising demand for fresh milk put dairy farming on the path toward industrial-scale production that treats the biological limits of lactating mothers as an inconvenient obstacle.*

❖

Raise your hand if you know what's wrong with this sentence: "Last year I visited a farm and met a seventeen-year-old dairy cow named Sarah."

Anyone familiar with modern dairying will spot the blooper at once. There *are* no seventeen-year-old cows on today's commercial dairy farms, and not all that many *seven*-year-old cows. Under favorable conditions, a healthy cow can live out a natural span of around twenty years. As it is, the farms supplying milk for your breakfast cereal are likely to send most members of the herd off to the hamburger plant within three or four years of their first lactation at about age two.

Sarah, you see, belonged not to a commercial dairy but to a tiny New Jersey farmstead cheese-making operation run along highly unconventional lines by an iconoclast named Jonathan White, who once declared his intention of "setting back the dairy industry 100 years"—to a time, that is, when a cow her age was nothing special. How did we get from there to here?

FRESH MILK: A HISTORICAL NEWCOMER

Trade in fresh milk is only about two centuries old. Historically, the natural fate of milk freshly drawn from the udder when animals came into milk during the warm months was to be swiftly colonized by neighborhood bacteria. The kinds that changed lactose (milk sugar) into lactic acid enjoyed a certain competitive advantage— which is why people in dairying regions from Africa to England usually consumed milk in the form of simple fresh cheeses or soured products resembling today's yogurt or cultured buttermilk. "Sweet" milk is not only more perishable than soured, but less digestible by the huge majority of the human race that has some degree of lactose intolerance.

Among the few scattered lactose-tolerant groups, one from north-western Europe and the British Isles was destined to exercise vast influence on diets throughout the world. Shortly after 1800, people from these regions and their colonies became intensely fixated on unsoured milk drunk fresh from their favorite dairy animal, the cow. An urban market specifically for fresh milk began to take shape, bolstered by vaguely scientific theories that in a few generations would make it a nearly mandatory part of everyone's diet, especially children's. Entrepreneurial visionaries suddenly glimpsed the possibility of selling fresh milk for drinking *at a higher profit than in any other form.*

By about 1830, a huge demand for fresh milk existed in the major northeastern American cities. But getting milk there meant getting *cows* there. In earlier times, individual sellers had often driven a cow or goat about the streets and milked a few cups' worth into a customer's bowl or pot, or hawked milk from pails. Cows in the city were a more dubious proposition now—but many profit seekers started herding dozens or hundreds of them into crowded, filthy milking sheds next to breweries or distilleries and buying up the mash wastes for fodder. For more than a generation this shameless practice sickened or killed great numbers of cows and provoked horrified outcries from public health advocates who saw the watery, bluish, ill-tasting "swill milk" doing the same to people.

A better alternative arrived in the 1840s, when country milk started reaching cities in sealed cans via rail or steamboat transport. Small though they look today, the East Coast operations begun during this era in areas like Orange County, New York, enabled tens of thousands of city dwellers to take up milk drinking as a relatively safe, affordable daily habit—now perceived, however, as necessity, not habit. (Medical opinion now unanimously considered fresh milk for drinking indispensable for children and healthful for everyone else.) Within a few decades after the Civil War, a continuous country-to-city pipeline materialized throughout much of the country with the aid of temperature control (mostly through ice cooling) and expanding railway systems.

At just the same time, farmers and distributors were hailing the advent of "scientific" dairying, which would expand the milk supply even further. The question that dwarfed all others for many people was *how to get more milk out of a cow.*

THE REDESIGNED COW

Larger yields per animal are no new goal. But it wasn't until well into the twentieth century that farmers had the tools to make the dream a reality. No one could have foreseen the costs at which it would be achieved, from chronic national milk surpluses cutting into farm profits to chronic illnesses cutting short the lives of the nation's dairy cows—and chronic air pollution in some cities on the fringes of the vast confined operations that now account for the bulk of American milk production.

It wasn't supposed to be this way. Before about 1950, the application of Mendelian genetics to cow breeding and chemical analysis to milk had seemed to promise infinitely expanding yields with no clouds on the horizon.

Dairyists had long known that some cows have the gift of converting comparatively more of what they eat and drink into making milk and comparatively less into maintaining their own body weight. Such animals were the foundation of various "dairy breeds" that became recognized during the nineteenth century and still exist today. Let's take the examples of "Bessy"—fictitious—and "Ellen"—all too real.

Bessy is the pretty little animal Will Belton presents to his cousin

Clara Amedroz in a charming episode of Anthony Trollope's 1866 novel *The Belton Estate.* "Her eyes were mild, and soft, and bright. Her legs were like the legs of a deer . . . and in her whole gait and demeanour" she "almost tempted one to regard her as the far-off descendant of the elk or the antelope." Her breed was what we'd now call "Jersey." Such cows then weighed only about six or seven hundred pounds. How much milk might she have given on average? Probably somewhat less than the 28 quarts a day (about 56 pounds) recorded for one especially productive cow over a six-week period in George Dodd's 1856 survey *The Food of London.*

Ellen, or officially "Beecher Arlinda Ellen," mirrors an age when dairy cows are less likely to evoke thoughts of deer and antelope than of ruminant SUVs. A Holstein-Friesian who at maturity weighed 1,750 pounds, in 1975 she set the dairy world on fire by pumping out a daily average of 152.5 pounds (more than 76 quarts) over a year's lactation. This feat has since been surpassed several times, always by members of the same breed. The triumph of scientific breeding for heritable milking qualities helped boost the total amount of milk produced by the nation's cows from 120 billion to roughly 190 billion pounds between 1960 and 2008, at the same time that the number of dairy cows shrank from about 18 million to 8.5 million. In other words, average yield per cow is about two and a half times what it was less than fifty years ago.

Breeding, however, wasn't the only factor. The increase also reflects a drastic revolution in feeding practices.

Like human mothers, some lactating cows produce more milk and some less, with higher-yielding animals usually eating more to compensate for what they're channeling into milk secretion. In unimproved animals like Bessy, the balance between calories taken in and calories put into lactating is largely stable and self-regulating. Genetic selection for abnormally high yields complicates the picture. It means that the best cows are always in a sort of metabolic race against "negative energy balance"—in plain English, inadequate calorie intake. Feeding them has become an intricate puzzle.

In 1866 Bessy undoubtedly ate what cows were meant to digest: grass, perhaps supplemented with hay if she was still in milk when winter arrived. Just as surely, in 1975 Ellen ate rations bolstered with "concentrate," mostly meaning corn and soybeans. Such "high-energy" feeds tend to stimulate milk production. Unfortunately, cows can eat only so much grain- or soy-based concentrate—not an element of normal ruminant diet—without getting sick.

THROWAWAY COWS

It may now be less of a mystery why seventeen-year-old dairy cows are as rare in 2010 as hundred-year-old humans were in 1910.

Already pushed by genetic manipulation to the threshold of negative energy balance, the members of modern dairy herds are systematically maintained on computer-monitored rations meant to steer a razor-thin line between stimulating high production and triggering serious illnesses. A typical formula would include varying amounts of chopped hay, cornstalk or other silage, corn or cornmeal, ground soybeans or cottonseed, and beet pulp or molasses, not to mention chemical buffers like sodium bicarbonate, dicalcium phosphate, or powdered lime to counter a condition known as "ruminal acidosis."

Ruminal acidosis in a nutshell is a dangerous fall in the normal pH of the rumen, or first stomach chamber, where trillions of bacteria start breaking down the fiber in grass or hay. The usual cause is too much concentrate in the feed, which alters the normal balance of different bacterial species and can increase ruminal acidity until the walls of the rumen become ulcerated.

Nobody knows how many American dairy cows suffer repeated bouts of subacute or acute ruminal acidosis. The unhappy animals often lose their appetite, which pushes them further toward the slippery slope of negative energy balance. They may try to slake a constant thirst by drinking more water, which means more (though of course thinner) milk. As the condition progresses, the ulcerated ruminal walls release infectious bacteria that often travel to the liver and cause abscesses, or generate by-products that migrate to the interior of the hooves and cause a painful foot inflammation called laminitis. (This condition probably was the reason that the "downer cows" surreptitiously filmed by the Humane Society at a California slaughtering plant early in 2008 had to be goaded onto their feet by electric shock.) In addition, lowered ruminal pH encourages the growth of *E. coli* bacteria, which can survive through the entire digestive tract (ending up in manure and fertilizer made from it) and often include the virulent O157:H7 strain.

The quest for more milk also leaves modern herds perennially riddled with mastitis (inflammation of the udder). Any of half a dozen organisms can cause this condition, which may have visible symptoms like swollen, painful teats or in subclinical cases may be detectable only through rising numbers of "somatic cells"—chiefly, white blood cells—shed by a cow's system into her milk. To battle mastitis, farmers must constantly test the somatic cell count of milk, identify affected cows, and dose them with antibiotics. The financial cost is enormous, since milk from animals under treatment must by law be dumped until no antibiotic residues remain.

Skyrocketing milk yields per cow have gone hand in hand with plummeting life expectancy, chiefly through mastitis, ruminal acidosis, and laminitis. Not surprisingly, these diseases disproportionately affect the already most stressed animals: the high producers. As if this weren't enough, since the mid-1990s many farmers have been making high-producing cows even higher producing through injections of the hormone bovine somatotropin (BST), also known as bovine growth hormone (BGH). All the "Breed, Feed, and Exceed" factors together add up to sheer physical burnout for many cows over the age of five or six.

THE FARMER'S DILEMMA

Has stressing out cows made life easier for farmers? Far from it. Every year, thousands of the remaining U.S. dairy farmers—today there may be about 75,000, compared with 648,000 in 1970—abandon the struggle to make a living producing a food that everybody else takes for granted without understanding the first thing about it. In fact, most dairy farmers who supply the fresh fluid milk market are sinking under their own "negative energy balance": the widening disparity between production costs per unit of milk produced and the prices guaranteed to them under the U.S. government's convoluted federal milk marketing order system. The gap between the market price and actual unit costs runs to 35 or 40 percent in some of the Northeastern states. Shaving every cent from production costs is not an option but a life-or-death imperative.

Dairy farming used to be the most labor-intensive form of agriculture. Today, however, it is incredibly capital-intensive. (Not that labor requirements have gone away despite desperate attempts to mechanize everything.) It requires staggering capital investments, along with high outlays on upkeep, for necessities like milking machines, pipeline collection systems, and refrigerated bulk tanks. During the twentieth century, farmers kept hoping that larger herds and other economies of scale would make all this expensive hardware (and software, as special dairy management and record-keeping programs became indispensable) pay for itself. "Small" farms went from about 8 or 10 cows to 50 or 60 and—by century's end—to 90 or 100 cows. Of course the amount of land required for pasturage increased in proportion. So did the amount of effort needed to maintain it, especially with 1,500-pound Holstein-Friesians. Besides, dairy experts were singing the praises of "total mixed rations" (TMRs) with formulated amounts of hay and high-energy concentrates, either premixed by the farmer or bought from a supplier. Farmers might start out using TMRs in conjunction with pasture grazing, but as time went on, many of them started seeing grazing as a headache and confined feeding systems as the smoothest way to go.

Then disaster struck for farmers—or most of them—in the old dairying regions of the Northeast and upper Midwest. From the mid-1980s on, the focus of dairying began to shift to huge operations in the Pacific Coast and Rocky Mountain states. Unlike third- or fourth-generation farms back East, these were new, amply capitalized start-up factory farms unhampered by the design of Grandpa's barn or the distance between two hayfields. They could commit wholly to economies of scale that older farmers had only struggled to make half-feasible.

Today in California or Colorado, a dairy farm—or anyhow, agricultural engineering center—may milk 15,000 or 18,000 cows— or anyhow, bovine assembly-line components with the drawback of being alive. The majority of the new farms are confined feeding operations. The animals may be tied up in stalls and directly milked on the spot, or allowed somewhat freer movement within the barn and moved to and from a milking parlor. Because of their great numbers—it's difficult to pasture herds of more than several hundred animals under effective supervision—they never graze on real pasture while lactating, though in some herds dubbed "organic" they may have limited access to an open-air area. Almost without exception, they are Holstein-Friesians descended from a handful of sires with records of high-producing daughters. (Some industry observers consider the terrible narrowing of the Holstein-Friesian gene pool a genetic train wreck waiting to happen.)

The scale of the big western farms is such that in California's San Joaquin Valley, dairy farmers are locked in angry controversies with local health authorities over chronic air pollution from the methane and ammonia given off by ruminal bacteria and belched by the animals as they chew the cud. Mastitis, ruminal acidosis, and laminitis claim thousands of cows after their first or second lactation without anybody much noticing.

And if you think all this is just some regional fluke unrelated to your eating habits, think again. By sheer colossal volume, the new western behemoths have reached the holy grail that has frustrated everyone else for generations—production costs for fresh (make that "fresh") fluid milk low enough to be recouped by sales under the system of federal price guarantees.

It is cheaper to produce, truck, and distribute California or Colorado milk for retail sale in many states east of the Mississippi than it is for local farmers to get their own milk to consumers. In a desperate game of catch-up, some eastern and midwestern dairy farmers are trying to construct their own versions of confined feeding factory farms in relatively isolated neighborhoods—almost guaranteed better chances of survival than the small and middle-size holdouts that haven't already been killed by soaring property taxes and real estate values in the orbit of cities.

Today not just naïve outsiders but hardheaded experts consider the American dairy industry a deeply troubled giant on the verge of toppling under its own crazy weight. You don't have to be a malicious enemy of our national farm heritage to think that the collapse can't come too soon.

SIZE MATTERS

The Meat Industry and
the Corruption of Darwinian Economics

STEVE BJERKLIE

THE SURVIVAL-OF-THE-FITTEST STRUGGLE *in the meat industry has resulted in decades of increasing corporate concentration that punishes independent producers. The commodity meat industry has adopted the values and assembly-line approaches of mass manufacturing to cut costs and maximize returns on dwindling profit margins. In an age that requires the reinvigoration of diverse locally adapted food production systems, markets are dominated by just a handful of retailers and meatpacking corporations.*

❖

The years following World War II were especially good ones for the beef industry in California. The state's surging population provided abundant can't-miss markets, and the mild climate allowed cattle to flourish in all but the hottest desert regions and highest mountain ranges. Cattle dotted California's golden landscape like sprinkles of confetti on cashmere. The state's beef industry in the 1950s and early 1960s was one of the largest in the country. Iowa, the leading U.S. beef state then, raised more cattle, but most of them were shipped to packinghouses in Chicago. The cattle raised in Texas, Kansas, Oklahoma, Nebraska, and Colorado were mostly shipped north, too. Only California had a large homegrown beef packing and processing industry to accommodate locally grown cattle. Meat companies could be found in nearly every midsize and larger community in the state.

The period was also a boom time for supermarkets. The onrush of the postwar middle class in Southern California allowed several independent grocery chains to flourish in Los Angeles and its booming suburbs, but in the northern half of the state the supermarket business continued to be controlled by two chains, Lucky Markets and Safeway, with the latter the more powerful. Indeed, Safeway bought in such volume that it could determine California market prices for a wide assortment of perishable foods, including beef.

Safeway made the beef market according to a simple scheme: on a given day of the week, sellers from all the major beef packers in California got together on a conference call with Safeway's beef buyer, who told the packers what price Safeway would be paying that week. The telephone conference call was new technology, and to the sellers it must have seemed as if they were being included in a highly sophisticated negotiation. In fact, Safeway bought its beef the way beef had been bought and sold on the market since the nineteenth century: an offer, an acceptance, a deal. The packers knew they had little choice, because no other supermarket in the state had the clout to give them a better price. But no matter how stingy its offer, Safeway made sure its beef suppliers made at least a little money—just not too much. Bankrupt meat companies were no good to Safeway.

Then one day in the early 1960s, Safeway's buyer informed the intently listening sellers on the weekly conference call that the supermarket had decided it was going to do business with an upstart company called Iowa Beef Packers, whose processing plant was located in Dennison, Iowa. This made no sense at all to the California beef men: wouldn't Safeway have to truck its beef from this new midwestern outfit across thousands of miles? Yes, it would—but Iowa Beef Packers had a new way of doing things. It didn't ship carcasses, as virtually every other packer in the United States did at the time; it shipped vacuum-packaged pieces of carcasses, called primals. Safeway didn't have to contend with waste from shanks, spinal columns, and other unwanted, unsellable carcass parts. Moreover, out on the prairie, Iowa Beef Packers didn't have to pay Chicago-scale labor wages. Buying from Iowa Beef, even though it was two time zones away, would save Safeway hundreds of thousands of dollars a week.

The day Safeway's buyer told all of this to the California beef sellers was the beginning of the end of California's beef packing industry.

By 1980, only a few struggling packers survived in Los Angeles, in the Vernon area; Harris Ranch Beef survived, too, out in the San Joaquin Valley, by focusing on the export market. But now even the Los Angeles beef packers are gone. Harris Ranch continues, as do a few other packers, but they're like the last operating businesses in a ghost town.

It was also the day that cemented the modern structure of the meat industry, in which retailers (and, in subsequent years, fast-food chains), not packers and processors, are in control. By keeping a controlling downward pressure on price, the retailers ensured that the only way packers could survive was to run their abattoirs according to what's called in the industry "economies of scale"—a formula that the late Robert Peterson, who was the longtime chairman of Iowa Beef Packers, soon to be known as IBP, once boiled down to these simple words: "runnin' volume." With the retailers pushing down from the top, the packers make profits in fractions of a cent. The only way to show real dollars on the bottom line is to process enormous numbers of livestock in ever-larger packing plants.

Not that there ever was much money to be made in beef to begin with. The general rule of thumb that has applied to the meat industry as a whole since the 1960s is that meat processors—those companies that manufacture ground meat, hamburger patties, hot dogs, sausage, prepared meals, jerky, lunch meats, and the like—operate on about a 2 percent profit margin. Packers—companies that slaughter livestock and process the carcasses first into "sides" and then into smaller primals and even smaller suprimal cuts (which are sold to processors and supermarkets)—operate on a profit margin of 1 percent. The profits tend to come in cycles, however: When livestock prices are low but consumer demand is high, packers and processors make good money. When livestock prices are high and consumer demand is low, as it was in the spring of 2008, packers and processors lose money, sometimes lots of it.

Supermarket and fast-food chains can usually protect themselves from such cycles by focusing on other areas of their businesses, but the meat industry must struggle in the face of climatic, economic, and political forces mostly beyond its control. Weather, for example: Drought conditions disrupted Florida's large cattle business in 2007.

The long drought in the Intermountain West, which lasted from the mid-1990s through 2006, pushed more cattle farther north, where winter conditions come into play.

The U.S. beef industry, which exports about 10 percent of its production, can also be buffeted by changes in global demand and political alliances. When the European Union ruled in 1986 that it would no longer accept imported beef that came from cattle fed growth-promoting hormones, the bottom dropped out of the market for U.S. organ meats and sweetbreads (the thymus gland and pancreas of calves), which American beef companies had been shipping to Europe in volume because such products are all but impossible to sell to U.S. consumers. China's ability to render cattle hides into leather cheaply has taken away another domestic market for U.S. packers. And in 2008, record high prices for corn and other feed grains, driven upward by the U.S. government's pro-ethanol policy, not only squeezed packers between increasing prices for livestock and shrinking demand due to a downward-sliding economy but forced cattlemen by the hundreds to get out of the business. In 2009, for the first time in many years, no one in the beef chain, from ranchers to cattle feeders to beef packers to processors to retailers, made money on beef.

In simple schematic terms, economic forces of inexorable power have pushed meat companies into a survival-of-the-biggest corruption of Darwinian economics. In any capitalist economy, the buyer wants to pay less and the seller wants to gain more, which often works well for all concerned when the forces pushing against each other are more or less equal, because compromise is the only route to agreement. But in the American food industry's economy, the power is overwhelmingly in the hands of the retailers and fast-food merchants. There are two reasons for this: (1) they have gone through a consolidation of their own, growing into larger and larger chains with enormous buying power; and (2) the supermarkets and fast-food outlets are the closest links in the chain to the consumer, who is, perhaps without quite knowing it, the final authority in this sequence. A small handful of supermarket chains basically control prices in the food market—those prices, that is, that aren't already controlled by Wal-Mart, which in 2001 became the largest-volume food retailer in the United States. The big meat companies, which have grown larger because their cus-

tomers have grown larger even as the overall number of those customers has decreased, basically have no one else to sell to. The retailers
and fast-food chains know that.

The meat industry, its customers, and its livestock suppliers have
since World War II essentially pushed the production, marketing,
and sale of meat, which is, after all, a biological product, into an
industrial model. Thus the meat you buy from a large supermarket
chain or from a fast-food outlet is no longer a simple farming product.
It is a commodity, as soulless as copper or scrap iron, and made so
by economic forces that require it to be a commodity rather than a
specialty product. In turn, the packers naturally put price pressure
on the livestock producers that supply the packers with animals for
meat. The producers respond by using production practices that load
on the weight (because livestock are sold by weight) as quickly as
possible, such as feedlots. Ranchers and cattlemen talk in terms of
yield and feed efficiency. What they're really talking about is their
cost of production relative to how quickly an animal is heavy enough
to bring to market. The longer a producer such as a cattleman or hog
farmer must feed an animal to build it up to market weight, the more
expensive that animal is to the producer. In beef, grass-fed cattle gain
weight steadily but slowly compared with animals that are "finished,"
to use the industry's word for it, for the last three to four months of
their lives in feedlots on fattening feed grains.

There are exceptions. Among supermarket chains, Whole Foods
is famous for figuring out a scheme to buy a substantial portion of its
produce and meat from smaller local suppliers close to its stores. But
even Whole Foods, which is equally famous for its sky-high prices
compared with mainstream supermarket prices, is vulnerable to price
pressure. It buys grass-fed beef from Uruguay, for example, because
it is substantially cheaper than domestically produced grass-fed beef.
Even so, in the grand scheme of food retailing in the United States,
Whole Foods, the largest player by far among its direct competitors, is
master of only a tiny sliver of the overall food market.

When asked about the economy they participate in, which is a
kind of indentured servitude, meat packers and processors tend to
shrug: they don't have the power to change it. "If we could make
money running a smaller plant and selling just to local supermarkets,

we would," one packer who does big business with large retailers and fast-food chains told me. "But there aren't very many local independent supermarkets anymore; everything's a chain. If you want to sell to them, you have to sell at the volumes the chains need. Same thing with McDonald's. It's not your local McDonald's that buys your ground beef, it's a buying office somewhere that's buying ground beef on price from an approved list of suppliers, and they buy it in huge quantities. Small companies simply can't participate in that economy."

Bill Marler, a partner at Marler Clark in Seattle, is an attorney who has successfully sued meat companies on several occasions for damages caused by *E. coli* adulterations and infections. "When you're talking about causes and liabilities of pathogenic contamination, the retailers get a pass, and that's something no one really knows about," he said in July 2008. "I would love to be able to sue Wal-Mart and Costco for failing to monitor the safety records of their suppliers, but there's no way for me to do it because there's no requirement for them to monitor those records. So without that liability, they can push and push and push their suppliers on price, because the suppliers are the ones holding the bag."

The buying power and the high-volume demands of the mainstream supermarkets and fast-food chains, and the pressure this power creates on meat companies to operate at ever-higher and ever-faster volumes to make money in a commodity business, aren't the only economic forces that have hammered and molded the meat industry into its present shape. Another is the cost of federal regulation. All U.S. meat companies that sell products across state borders must operate under federal meat inspection regulations managed by the U.S. Department of Agriculture's Food Safety and Inspection Service. While the actual cost of inspection is borne by the taxpayers, because it is deemed a public benefit (unlike USDA meat grading, which is paid for by the industry, because grading facilitates market activity), the cost of meeting inspection regulations must be borne by the meat companies themselves.

That cost has become increasingly expensive, especially since 1993 with the watershed outbreak of *E. coli* O157:H7. The source of the outbreak was traced to undercooked hamburgers served by Jack in the Box restaurants in the Seattle area, and these burgers killed four children and sickened hundreds of other children and adults. The tragedy led to an overhaul of the old system of inspection, which dates back to passage of the Federal Meat Inspection Act of 1906. Without quite throwing out the old way of doing things, the Food Safety and Inspection Service embraced, with encouragement from the industry, a protocol known by its acronym, HACCP (pronounced "hassip"), which stands for hazard analysis critical control points. HACCP requires a meat plant to determine which points in its production line are the most at risk for bacterial and other forms of contamination of the meat, and then to monitor those points, correcting them as needed.

In a packinghouse, the key critical control points are located in what's called the "kill floor," where livestock are slaughtered, drained of blood, the hides removed, and the carcasses cleaned of internal organs. Pathogenic bacteria can arrive on the hides of animals, in their stomachs, and in many other ways. Controlling those pathogens is enormously expensive: a highly strange but efficient machine that washes the mud and manure off of hides before the hides are removed from the carcasses, a kind of macabre car wash, costs in excess of a million dollars, for example. No small company can afford that, because it isn't the kind of expense that can be passed on to customers. Steam vacuum systems to lift and remove pathogens from outside carcass fat, pathogen-killing organic acid washes, electronic vision systems to detect contaminants: all these are expensive to install and operate. The "test and hold" protocol that some of the major ground beef processors have embraced, which involves testing every production lot for pathogens and not releasing the lot for distribution until test results are returned, ties up valuable inventory, an expense that only the best-funded packers can bear.

Buffeted by such strong economic winds, the meat industry huddles for protection. The U.S. beef industry is now dominated by three companies: Tyson Foods, which bought IBP in 2001; Cargill; and JBS Swift, which purchased the beef operations of Smithfield Foods in October 2008. JBS Swift, owned by Brazil's JBS S.A., is currently the largest meat company in the world. Collectively, the three top beef companies control about 75 percent of the beef slaughter capacity in the United States and significant portions of the market in other beef countries, including Brazil and Australia. Concentration in the pork and poultry industries is not quite as limited but is still narrow. The big will get bigger as long as it makes economic sense for them to do so—and as long as a complacent Justice Department believes no anti-trust obstacles need be employed.

Remember, too, that Americans pay less per capita for food than just about any nation in the world—and with the exception of successful high-end niche marketers such as Whole Foods, we've demonstrated time and again that we're not interested in paying more for food than we already do. Ultimately, then, the true sculptor of the shape of American agriculture, including agriculture's meat production complex, is the consumer. If Americans want a food industry that's polished with the values of sustainability, environmentalism, and humane handling of livestock; that includes a return to family farming; that emphasizes the small and local as opposed to the huge and distant; that employs local rather than imported workforces; that gives up the impersonal and industrial for the friendly and biological—then Americans must be willing to pay for it.

California's once-diverse beef packing industry, which had supported hundreds of small ranchers and thousands of packing plant employees and had been a mainstay industry in dozens of rural communities across the state, began to sink inexorably from sight after a single decision was made in a supermarket chain's buying office. That decision was made according to economic formula: what's most efficient is best. The formula won't change. But the definition of "efficiency" can.

FLOATING HOG FARMS

Industrial Aquaculture Is Spoiling the Aquatic Commons?

KEN STIER AND EMMETT HOPKINS

ON THE HEELS OF INDUSTRIAL AGRICULTURE'S *"Green Revolution," international development advocates began promoting fish farming as an alternative food source. The "Blue Revolution," they argued, would solve the global hunger crisis without deleterious impacts. But as the aquaculture industry has developed, so too have its side effects: water pollution, declining wild fish populations, habitat degradation, and inefficient use of resources. In fact, many industrial fish and shrimp farms resemble floating CAFOs.*

❖

Imagine a hog farm floating out at sea. Hundreds of thousands of animals crammed together on the open ocean, heaps of waste riddled with feces and antibiotics drifting off with the current. With certain types of aquaculture, this imaginary scene is not far from reality. What many eaters may not realize as they dine on grilled farmed salmon or pen-raised, pan-seared tuna is that modern aquaculture's ecological impacts are potentially tantamount to the destruction caused by land-based factory farms.

Critics claim that industrially farmed fish are a decadent luxury that comes with grave ecological costs to our oceans. Rather than supplementing—and maybe even eventually replacing—wild fisheries as the seafood of choice, some segments of the aquaculture industry may actually be polluting the oceans, disabling fishing communities, and abetting the collapse of the world's fisheries.

Meanwhile, the $78 billion aquaculture industry[1] insists that it is becoming more ecologically friendly and that there is every reason to continue enjoying tasty farmed salmon along with the growing array of species it is learning to farm.

Getting to the truth of the matter is of immense importance to the future of ocean fisheries. That's because 50 percent of the seafood we eat—more than 60 million tons per year—comes from aquaculture,[2] and we are becoming ever more dependent on farmed fish as we heedlessly continue overfishing. Without a major course correction, all major fish stocks could be commercially depleted to less than 90 percent of their historical levels by midcentury.

EGREGIOUS EXCRETIONS: POLLUTION AND ECOSYSTEM DEGRADATION

Of the collateral problems created by industrial-scale aquaculture, waste disposal is perhaps the most revolting. Like CAFOs on land, fish farms concentrate immense amounts of feces in relatively small areas. Fish excrement and excess feed result in the release of nitrogen, phosphorus, and chemical residues into the open ocean.[3] A recent report by the Worldwatch Institute, a globally focused research organization based in Washington, DC, equates the fecal matter from a 200,000-fish operation to the sewage from a city of 20,000 to 60,000 people.[4] The eutrophication caused by such massive waste streams can cause shellfish contamination, toxic algal blooms, and loss of biodiversity.

What's more, cramped living conditions make fish vulnerable to disease. To compensate, fish farmers apply antibiotics, delicing compounds, and other medicines.[5] A 2005 UN FAO report estimated that approximately 150 pounds of antibiotics are applied per acre of farmed salmon harvested in the United States.[6] When pens are placed in the open ocean, these chemicals drift into the greater environment and can be ingested by other organisms.[7] Health experts worry that the persistent use of low-level antibiotics is prompting the growth of antibiotic-resistant bacteria that may pose later health threats to humans.[8]

Several studies have also shown farmed fish to be laced with toxic polychlorinated biphenyls (PCBs),[9] which bioaccumulate and move up the food chain as larger fish eat smaller ones. Laboratory tests commissioned by the Environmental Working Group in 2003 found that the average farmed salmon has 16 times the PCBs found in wild salmon, 4 times the levels found in beef, and 3.4 times the levels found in other seafood.[10] These PCB studies may make fish consumers think twice about buying farmed salmon.

Farmed fish—with their increased prevalence of disease—also pose a risk to wild populations. In 1995, the southern oceans were hit by a massive herpes virus epidemic that originated near tuna ranches south of Australia. The virus spread at a rate of 30 kilometers a day, affecting at least 10 percent of the sardine population[11] and sparking a mass starvation of gannets, penguins, and other seabirds. Although the epidemic has not been traced definitively to tuna farms, some marine scientists point to the industry as the cause.[12] In the United States, a neurological disorder called whirling disease is reported to have spread from farmed to wild trout in more than twenty northeastern and western states[13] since it was first detected in the 1950s.[14] In 2008, multiple outbreaks of infectious salmon anemia (ISA) hit Chilean salmon farms. According to Juan Carlos Cárdenas, director of the Chilean nongovernmental organization Ecoceanos, the virus can spread at a rate of 1 percent of a caged population per day and was able to extend 1,200 miles in southern Chile in a single year.[15]

When ISA first appeared in 2008, many offshore aquaculture companies moved their production farms farther south in Chile, into waters still unaffected by the disease. Instead of lessening the problem, however, the industry actually extended ISA's reach into the southern waters. Industry source Intrafish projected that Chile's 2009 salmon output could decline by as much as 87 percent—a drop from 279,000 metric tons in 2008 to between 37,000 and 67,000 metric tons.[16] Despite efforts to address the crisis, Chilean salmon stocks have been devastated, and the world's food supply will be affected. Before the outbreak, Chile was second only to Norway in farmed salmon production and was the largest exporter to the United States. As a result of the Chilean crisis, an 18 percent shortfall in the global harvest of farmed Atlantic salmon is predicted for 2009, and perhaps 2010 as well.[17]

EFFECTS ON WILD BIODIVERSITY:
INFERIOR GENETICS AND THIRSTY FISH

Disease is not the only thing escaping fish farms. The fish themselves often break loose. Roughly 2 million salmon escape into the North Atlantic each year,[18] practically making wild salmon a minority in the open ocean. In Norway alone, between 250,000 and 650,000 salmon escape each year, and a full third of the salmon spawning in coastal rivers are of escaped origin.[19] The escapes have been a major concern for wild salmon, whose genetics are downgraded when they interbreed with genetically inferior farmed salmon. For a population already facing numerous barriers—such as overfishing and destruction of spawning habitat—the last thing wild salmon need is an infusion of genes that will make them more docile and less able to survive on their journeys from birth to reproduction. By allowing fish to escape, open-cage aquaculture is working against the long-term health of ocean ecosystems, which depend on a diversity of robust wild genetic populations.

It's not just wild fish that are thrown out of balance by aquaculture operations. Many factory fish farms can also pose risks to land-based ecosystems. Some aquaculture systems lean heavily on freshwater resources. Intensive carp and tilapia production uses over 20 gallons of freshwater per pound of meat.[20] Shrimp farms use even more freshwater.[21] Like the feedlots in Kansas or the hog buildings in North Carolina, these thirsty fish farms are draining local aquifers and consequently jeopardizing the ecosystems and human settlements that rely on freshwater. The U.S. Geological Survey estimates that aquaculture draws 3,700 million gallons of freshwater each day from American soils and surface waters.[22] Consequences of this water-chugging industry can be seen in the United States and around the world.

In the Ranot region of Thailand, an influx of shrimp ponds in the late 1980s reportedly caused the average groundwater level to fall by more than 12 feet over three years.[23] When aquaculture businesses and locals compete for natural resources, the locals—both humans and ecosystems—often lose. In addition to indirect competition for water, ecosystems and animals in fish farming regions have also been hit by more direct harm.

Throughout Asia and South America, the farmed shrimp industry has been responsible for the clearing of coastal ecosystems—mangrove forests in particular—to make space for aquaculture.[24] This deforestation leaves locals who depend on the mangrove forests for harvesting wild crabs and shellfish without food, and can also trigger erosion and coral reef damage.

Death, wounding, and harassment of local fauna has also been a problem at some aquaculture facilities—caused either by intentional attack or by inadvertent problems such as net entanglement or depletion of wild fish resources that nourish many marine animals.[25] Even if marine mammals, birds, and fish aren't directly engaged by aquaculture personnel, it is becoming increasingly likely that their fates will be influenced by this growing industry. As the industry expands, so too does its appetite for fish meal to feed the caged fish. And with the market for fish meal booming, we see the general depletion of the smaller fish species that are vital for the ocean's ecosystems. These are the previously abundant fish that support commercially valuable wild fish, marine mammals, and seabirds.

A FISH-EAT-FISH WORLD: REVERSE PROTEIN FACTORIES

In her book *Diet for a Small Planet*, Frances Moore Lappé argued almost 40 years ago that grain-fed cattle were essentially "reverse protein factories" because they required many more pounds of plant protein to produce a pound of flesh. A similar dynamic exists in the global aquaculture industry, especially as it strains to satisfy our voracious appetite for top-of-the-food-chain carnivorous fish such as salmon, tuna, and shrimp.

"Aquaculture's current heavy reliance on wild fish for feed carries substantial ecological risks," says Roz Naylor, a leading scholar on the subject at Stanford University's Center for Environmental Science and Policy. "And unless alternatives become commercially viable at a large scale, some key pelagic fisheries could be pushed over the edge of sustainability, thus reducing food sources for many other species in the marine food chain."[26]

The aquaculture industry took off as wild fishing captures stagnated. Since 1970, it has grown by almost 9 percent per year to satisfy a global demand that has nearly doubled in that time, thus making it the fastest-growing food group.[27]

But there is a catch to this stunning human achievement. It takes a lot of other inputs, mainly other, "lesser" fish—also known as "reduction" or "forage" fish—to create the kind of fish we prefer to eat directly. These smaller pelagic fish are processed into fish meal and oil and then mixed with other ingredients to create pellets that are fed to penned-in fish. While the average ratio of wild fish input to farmed fish output has finally dropped to below 1 for the overall industry, many farmed fish still require far more than their weight in wild fish. For instance, it takes roughly 5 pounds of the smaller pelagic fish (open-seas species like anchovies, mackerel, and herring) to create 1 pound of Atlantic salmon.[28]

Industry and publicly funded research has significantly enhanced this efficiency—while reducing the percentage of fish and oil content in aquafeeds. "I would say cost, the sustainability of resources . . . and human health concerns have been driving researchers to find replacements for fish meal and fish oil . . . and we are doing this to the greatest extent possible," says David Higgs, a Canadian government fish nutritionist who works closely with British Columbia's $450 million salmon industry.[29] (Reducing the fish content reduces the bioaccumulation of PCBs, which helps the industry's public image.) But these improvements have been offset by the industry's explosive growth. The salmon industry, the largest aquaculture sector, has made modest reductions in the amount of wild fish required to produce one unit of salmon in recent years, but total industry production has grown by a substantially greater percent.

There are more worrisome trends, such as the rapid expansion of other species now being farmed that have even higher fish feed requirements. Ranched tuna, for instance, dine on live pelagic fish, but it takes about 20 pounds of such inputs to get 1 pound of tuna ready for a sushi bar near you.[30] (Tuna are ranched—corralled from the wild and then fed in anchored pens—because despite prodigious efforts, especially by Japan, no one has been able to raise them from eggs.)

"The problem is we've gone straight to the top; we are essentially, as some argue, farming tigers when we raise tuna or striped bass or cod," argues Brian Halweil, a senior researcher at the Worldwatch Institute. "We need to start from the ground up and encourage farming of shellfish, which are the basic building blocks of a healthy coastal ecosystem, and from there move upwards to fish that eat algae, and *then* to fish that eat other fish. But putting all our attention on things like tuna and cod, while it may be incredibly profitable, is also very destructive from an ecological point of view."[31]

Although environmentalists and industry dispute whether current harvesting is done at sustainable levels, there is no doubt that the global fish stock is a finite resource, and there is no end in sight for the growing demand. A staggering 37 percent of all marine fish catch is now ground into feed, up from 7.7 percent in 1948, according to 2006 research from the University of British Columbia Fisheries Centre.[32] Much of that goes to China, where 70 percent of the world's fish farming takes place.[33]

It may be a surprise that much of the global production of fish meal and fish oil goes to the livestock industry, mostly pigs and poultry. Aquaculture, however, has recently become the top consumer of fish meal and fish oil, its use rising dramatically from 10 percent in 1988 to over 60 percent in 2009.[34] This share continues to rise, especially because, as fish meal prices have risen, the livestock industry has been quicker to substitute vegetable proteins than has the aquaculture industry. If current trends continue unabated, demand for fish oil will outstrip supply within a decade, and the same could happen for fish meal by 2050, says Naylor. These trends are reflected in rising fish meal prices as the wild fish used to produce fish meal become ever more scarce.

Wild fish stocks are further depleted by the aquaculture industry's practice of tapping wild fisheries as seed for farmed populations. In parts of Asia, fish farmers bring young wild fish inland to stock lakes. Similarly, industrial shrimp operations use wild larvae to build their cultivated supplies.[35] The use of wild seed stock—in concert with fish meal as feed—raises serious doubts about the viability of aquaculture as a solution to overharvesting of wild fish.

POOR MAN'S FISH: FOOD SECURITY AND FISHING COMMUNITIES

If international development agencies originally envisioned fish farming as an antidote to world hunger, they were mistaken to think that this antidote would come without costs. Ironically, the industry has done great damage to some small-scale fishermen and aboriginal peoples, encroaching on their traditional areas and competing for wild fish stocks. In the village of Ao Goong in southern Thailand, when shrimp ponds moved in alongside the local community, the villagers' lives changed dramatically. Waste materials from the shrimp ponds—dumped both on land and in the ocean—killed the wild shrimp the villagers had subsisted on, poisoned their coconut trees, and tainted their well water.[36] The traditional local economy and way of life were ruined by the arrival of irresponsibly managed commercial aquaculture.

In Bangladesh, the district of Khulna has also seen the destruction caused by shrimp farmers. Despite the institution of a shrimp-free zone, shrimp traders colluded with government officials to reject the zoning and destroy existing agricultural fields to make way for shrimp ponds. The conflict has taken a physical toll on the residents as well. Women have been sexually abused by shrimp farm employees, and over a hundred villagers have died in the struggle against aquaculture's takeover of land.[37] Similar stories can be told in other fishing communities around the world.

More broadly, fish farms are creating a scarcity of affordable seafood for the world's poor. The reliance on wild fish to fuel the aquaculture industry presents food security dilemmas for developing countries. World Wildlife Fund—Germany has been investigating whether the recent surge in illegal emigration from West Africa to Europe is related to the deterioration of local fishing conditions. And in Peru, which hosts the world's largest anchovy industry, many locals are living in poverty and showing signs of fish protein deficiencies. Peru exports over 2 million tons of fish each year,[38] mostly anchovies for fish meal to fuel aquaculture in China and elsewhere.[39] As an increasing share of these small fishes is fed into aquaculture, the foundation for healthy wild fisheries erodes away and there is less available for those who might benefit from wild fish as a key direct source of protein.

Instead of offering an alternative to wild fish—and allowing wild fisheries to rebound from decades of overfishing—aquaculture is often undermining the very foundation of marine ecosystems. Some marine scientists are now concerned that the Antarctic krill population is at risk. Krill, a fundamental building block for many large marine species, including whales and penguins, has already been in decline owing to global warming. But now krill harvesting companies are scooping up massive amounts of the invertebrate animals to be used as fish farm feed and health supplements. According to the Antarctic Krill Conservation Project, the factory trawler *Saga Sea*— operated by Norwegian multinational corporation Aker ASA—is able to continuously vacuum millions of krill.[40] Other firms are eyeing similar technology. Although the harvesting companies estimate that 400–500 million tons of krill remain, the British Antarctic Survey puts the number at only 110 million tons.[41] The legal catch limit is 4 million tons,[42] and new suction harvesting techniques will allow the industry to more easily meet this target. "Whales, penguins, seals, albatrosses and petrels—all those creatures we think are absolute icons of Antarctica—depend on krill," said Richard Page, a marine reserves expert with Greenpeace International. "It's part of the global commons, and one of the most pristine environments on Earth."[43]

AN ALTERNATIVE APPROACH: TRADITIONAL AQUACULTURE AND SUSTAINABLE SYSTEMS

In contrast to today's farmed salmon and tuna, the fish species at the core of the millennia-long tradition of fish farming in Asia and parts of Africa—catfish, carp, and milkfish—actually require less weight in fish inputs than the weight ultimately harvested because they are herbivorous or even omnivorous. To traditional fish farmers, the idea of feeding several times more pounds of fish meal to get one pound back would seem sheer folly. "Ultimately that is really where the solution is—to cut back on these carnivorous species and turn our attention to these plant-eating ones," says U. Rashid Sumaila, a renowned expert at the University of British Columbia. "Whether we are willing to do that is another thing, but that's the fundamental solution."[44]

The earliest known fish farming dates back to China, where raised carp have fed people for millennia. Small inland carp ponds often existed alongside farms; waste from adjoining pig or duck pens would feed the carp, and several times a year the rich bottom soil from the ponds would be reapplied to neighboring fields as fertilizer.

This system continued until the Tang Dynasty, when a linguistic fluke precipitated the evolution of traditional aquaculture. Legend has it that a close similarity between the emperor's name and the word for carp prompted many farmers to trade carp for other fish species, not wanting to risk associating the emperor with a farmed fish. Thus the Chinese polyculture system—raising many types of fish together— was born.[45]

Even today, China's traditional pond systems continue to be some of the most productive freshwater fisheries in the world. Part of their secret is the near elimination of the concept of waste: one species' waste becomes another species' food. Many of today's industrial aquaculture systems allow unused nutrients to attract bacteria, insects, and birds—depleting nutrients available for the fish. In these operations, untapped wastes create ecological nightmares.

In contrast, in the traditional Chinese closed-loop pond system, each fish species fits into a particular niche, resulting in a balanced community. Silver carp and tilapia feed on phytoplankton; bighead carp graze on zooplankton; grass carp, Wuchang fish, and common carp eat green fodder; common carp, black carp, and mud carp forage in sediments at the bottom of the pond. From China to India to Thailand, this balanced approach to fish farming continues to feed many rural dwellers without the unintended consequences of modern aquaculture.[46]

The traditional pond model has inspired some twenty-first-century fish farmers to aim for more technologically complex versions of its nutrient cycling. Entrepreneurs and academics have been looking at various ways to cycle nutrients: sending fish waste to nearby agriculture fields; using fish as wastewater treatment; or growing vegetables hydroponically on top of fish ponds. Forward-looking aquaculture models are also pursuing new strategies to treat, recycle, and recirculate freshwater for inland aquaculture. But when governments fail to put a price on water use or to adequately regulate it, profit-oriented aquaculture companies have little incentive to save water, stop the escape of waste and fish into the wild, or provide adequate buffers between their fish and other water sources.

Recognizing the need for industry to move toward these more sustainable practices, the World Wildlife Fund (WWF) has spurred efforts to craft voluntary industry standards aimed at minimizing or eliminating the main environmental risks. WWF has been facilitating a multistakeholder dialogue process including producers, buyers, and various nongovernmental organizations since 2004. "This is a major priority for us," says Jose Villalon, who heads WWF's recently expanded aquaculture team. Standards will yield certifications; the first two—covering tilapia and pangasius (catfish)—have progressed through a public comment period. The draft standards provide specific targets for site location, water quality, antibiotic use, feed efficiency, and fair labor practices for the farmed tilapia industry. Standards for other species are proving more contentious, with shrimp and salmon not expected until 2010 at the earliest.

In the meantime, the meaning of sustainability is a movable metric shaped largely by restaurants, where 70 percent of seafood consumed in the United States is eaten.[47] "As chefs, we need to celebrate diversity in the oceans so that we are not relying too heavily on any one species," avows Peter Hoffman, owner of Manhattan's Savoy Restaurant and a board member of the 1,000-strong Chefs Collaborative, an organization committed to "educating chefs about the sustainability of the seafood they purchase and serve." That's partly a creative challenge, making tilapia, for instance, taste as interesting as seared ahi. As we move to herbivorous fish like catfish, tilapia, and carp, and to bivalves like oysters, mussels, and scallops, we eliminate the reverse protein problem.

Going down the food chain means no real diminution in health benefits but can reap significant ecological pluses. This calculus may already be helping to regenerate the dimmed luster of the modest shellfish, including the oyster, which is the subject of reseeding campaigns from Long Island Sound to Washington State's Puget Sound, where it has been most successful. Not only are oysters, along with other mollusks, good for you—oysters are freakishly high in zinc, needed to create testosterone—they feed themselves.

And by being able to thrive even in slightly polluted water, oysters also provide an invaluable ecological service; a single adult oyster can filter 50 gallons of water a day. When Jamestown founder John Smith first sailed into the pristine Chesapeake Bay four hundred years ago, he had to navigate around oyster reefs 20 feet high and miles long

that were effectively filtering the entire estuary—the country's largest—every few days, according to Rowan Jacobsen, the author of *A
Geography of Oysters: The Connoisseur's Guide to Oyster Eating in
North America.* "If we can get oysters to historic levels, they can make
a huge difference," Jacobsen says. But his dream of a return to the
oyster's golden age in the late nineteenth century—when 100 million
pounds of oysters were harvested from the Chesapeake every year, in
contrast to today's 250,000-pound haul—is a long way off. To most
diners, salmon and shrimp are still the seafood treats of choice.

Part Four

THE LOSS
OF DIVERSITY

INTRODUCTION

Extinction Is Forever

For millennia, agriculturalists have diminished native biodiversity from the world around them to repopulate landscapes with desirable species. In the case of livestock, humans selected species from the abundance of their wild surroundings, protected them from predation, provided a constant food supply, and slowly domesticated them to their advantage. Poultry descended from jungle fowl, cattle from the ancient grazing aurochs, pigs from feral herds that roamed the oak savannas. Today's domesticated animals are the only living representatives of those wild lineages.

Even as agriculture spread across the world, domestication remained somewhat localized. Livestock were carefully bred to perform well in regional conditions, whether cold or hot, highland or lowland, arid or humid. The rise of industrial agriculture and concentrated animal feeding operations in the twentieth century, however, brought with it a heightened assault on that diversity. The CAFO model, which is predicated on species uniformity, maximum output, and intensive confinement, is radically transforming the food production landscape. Industrial selection has led to tragic losses of diversity on many levels: in the numbers of livestock breeds in favor today and the essential genetic heritage they may be able to provide to present and future agriculturalists; in the number of farmers on the land; and in the staggering number of native species and biodiversity disappearing from landscapes where agriculture takes place.

Out of the numerous traditional animal breeds still in favor a half century ago, the world's food supply has become increasingly dependent on a handful of highly engineered breeds: the Holstein dairy cow, the Large White pig, the egg-laying White Leghorn, and the White Cornish Cross broiler chicken. By pushing the limits of rapid growth and productivity—in dairy cows, broilers and layers, and hogs—industrial breeders are creating animals that suffer from weak bone development and other chronic maladies. "Bad things happen when an animal is bred for a single trait," writes Temple Grandin, an animal behavior expert at Colorado State University. "Nature will give you a nasty surprise."[1]

Scientists warn that just as mid-nineteenth-century Irish farmers were devastated by the vulnerability of a single potato variety, future diseases could ravage uniform populations of domesticated livestock. The consequences could mean not only massive food shortages, but rapidly mutating diseases capable of devastating animals and spreading to the human population as well. Experts stress that our best insurance against such a catastrophe is an abundant and genetically diverse pool of breeds with enough resilient traits to withstand numerous shocks and adversity in regional settings. Yet that insurance is fragile. A 2007 United Nations Food and Agriculture Organization study reported that at least one livestock breed had become extinct each month over the preceding seven years.[2] Twenty percent of the world's breeds of cattle, goats, pigs, horses, and poultry are currently at risk of extinction.[3] With each extinction, genetic characteristics disappear. It is this very diversity of traditional livestock breeds that could one day prove invaluable to agriculturalists attempting to adapt to climate fluctuations, new and virulent livestock diseases, and other unknown challenges.

The farming population is also shrinking, losing diversity as well as the food production skills formerly passed from generation to generation. As we entered the twenty-first century, 330 U.S. farmers were leaving their land every week, according to the agricultural organization Farm Aid. Today, there are 5 million fewer farms in the U.S. than there were in the 1930s. Half of all U.S. farmers are between the ages of forty-five and sixty-five, while only 6 percent of all farmers are under the age of thirty-five. This trend is appearing in other parts of the world as well.

Many agribusinesses are also vertically integrated, meaning they control all stages of the products they market—"from semen to cellophane." Vertically integrated companies own the animals from birth (or artificial insemination) all the way to the processing and marketing of milk and meat. For decades, independent farming organizations have been protesting and petitioning for antitrust enforcement laws against market concentration and "captive supply" chains, which allow corporations that slaughter and distribute products to own the animals they are processing as well.[4]

In standard economic theory, a market stops being competitive when the four largest players control over 40 percent—what is known as a "four-firm concentration ratio" (CR4) of 40. According to University of Missouri rural sociologists Mary K. Hendrickson and William Heffernan, nearly every sector of U.S. livestock production is dominated by the top four producers, including the following: beef packers, CR4 = 83.5 percent; pork packers, CR4 = 66 percent; broiler chickens, CR4 = 58.5 percent; turkeys, CR4 = 55 percent; soybean crushing, CR4 = 80 percent.[5]

With the disappearance of a family farming tradition and independent food production capacities, the lifelong skills so necessary for regional food and farming systems also vanish. Family farmers are some of our best stewards of traditional animal breeds and heirloom plant varieties. Small family farmers typically live on or near their farms and strive to preserve the surrounding environment for future generations. Since these farmers have a vested interest in their communities, they are more likely to use sustainable farming techniques to protect natural resources and human health—including animals ideally suited and locally adapted to their particular environments. We face a revolution of no small proportions in how our food and fiber will be produced. Our society will determine, through public policies and purchasing habits, through farming practices and markets, what kinds of landscapes we support and what level of species diversity remains on them. The science is clear. The only path toward resilience and adaptability must honor and protect diversity in all of its forms. We can only hope efforts spearheaded by organizations dedicated to the conservation of livestock diversity, such as the American Livestock Breeds Conservancy, Slow Food's "Ark of Taste," and others, can speed these efforts worldwide. Extinction is forever.

OLD MACDONALD HAD DIVERSITY

The Role of Traditional Breeds in a Dynamic Agricultural Future

DONALD E. BIXBY

AGRICULTURE DEPENDS ON GENETIC DIVERSITY *for its stability, yet in 2007 the United Nations Food and Agriculture Organization estimated that at least one livestock breed per month had become extinct since the turn of the twenty-first century. The fundamental difference between agricultural and other biological systems is the widespread human selection involved in agriculture. Habitats within agriculture are essentially the result of human activity, and the diversity of those habitats must be protected to ensure the long-term survival of genetic diversity in domestic animals and plants.*

❖

For over 10,000 years, domesticated animals have been essential to human society, filling a wide array of human needs, including food, fiber, draft power, land management, protection, and transportation. Domestic livestock are also deeply engrained in human culture, and are often the first animals we learn about as the subject of nursery rhymes and children's stories. Livestock have always been integral to farming systems, and today they are essential to current efforts to diversify agriculture.

The uses of livestock can be roughly divided into two categories: animal products and animal services. The most widely recognized animal product is food—meat, eggs, and dairy products. As a complement to cultivated food crops, livestock can be raised in regions poorly suited to row crops, and they can transform forage nutrients unavailable to humans into high-quality foods for human consumption. Rather than competing with plant production for human foods, foraging livestock can supplement food crop production, as long as they are appropriately managed.

Other animal products include high-quality natural fibers such as wool, cashmere, mohair, and feathers. These natural fibers remain in high demand since they have qualities unequaled by synthetic fiber. Leather is an important animal product for clothing, furniture, and other uses. Manure is the most widely used fertilizer in the world and provides essential soil nutrients not found in synthetic fertilizers. And because animals are mobile, they can be moved around a farm to deposit the manure where it is needed.

Animal services such as grazing, brush clearing, power, and pest control are less well known to the current agricultural generation, even less so to the general public, and therefore merit additional consideration. These services are often the only practical complement or alternative to the use of chemicals, fossil fuels, and machinery. Further, well-managed livestock production systems have a positive environmental impact by reducing erosion, increasing plant diversity, and protecting grasslands from invasion by woody scrub growth.

Grasses and other types of forages are part of a biological system that developed under the pressure of grazing. Grazing must be continued to sustain and to maintain the plant diversity of natural grasslands, although it has recently come under intense scrutiny as the effects of a century of overgrazing in the American West are being recognized. Overgrazing rapidly degrades natural resources, while well-managed grazing can enhance grassland environments. Managed forage production is an excellent method for healing and recovering abused and damaged land. Much of the marginal farmland now in use could be taken out of row crop production and put into permanent or semipermanent forage crops. This decrease in row crops would reduce water runoff and soil erosion and allow the reestablishment of organic material and carbon sequestration within the soil. Research has shown, and the growing market has underscored, the increased value of the enhanced nutrition and flavor of grass-produced animal products.

Goats, sheep, and some breeds of cattle are good browsers, consuming saplings, shrubs, and other woody plants, as well as rapidly growing pest plants such as leafy spurge, blackberry, kudzu, poison ivy, and other tenacious invaders. Goats are being used to reduce the risk of fire by consuming brush and decreasing fuel load buildup. Hogs can be used as self-motivated bulldozers to clear land for cultivation, to glean fields after harvest, or to turn over compost or manure pack in readiness for use.

Draft power and transportation are other important services provided by cattle, horses, donkeys, and mules. Globally, oxen are the most widely used draft animals, though horses are far more common in America. More people are coming to appreciate the versatility, usefulness, and economy of animal power, particularly given the rising cost of fossil fuel. Draft animals are used in selective logging because of the minimal environmental damage they impart to the soil and the remaining trees.

Interest is growing in the use of livestock as part of integrated pest management systems. Swine and poultry work well to control pests in gardens and orchards. Before the introduction of heavy pesticide use in fruit production, sheep were often pastured in orchards; with organic production they can again be used for grass and weed control. St. Croix sheep are now being grazed in organic macadamia nut plantations in Hawaii, and Southdown sheep are grazed in Christmas tree plantations in Vermont and in California vineyards. Using animal services is doubly beneficial—the services are in themselves positive, and they replace expensive or potentially detrimental inputs such as chemical pesticides or fossil fuels—while the animals are also producing marketable food and fiber products.

When the value of animal service is understood, the complicated and rewarding interconnections between humans and livestock become more obvious. Agricultural systems that utilize the complex interrelationships of people, livestock, and specific environments to the fullest extent are also the ones that benefit most from the availability of traditional breeds of livestock and poultry.

THE IMPORTANCE OF GENETIC DIVERSITY

Genetic diversity within a species is the presence of a large number of genetic variants for each of its characteristics. This variability allows the species to adapt to changes by selection for the most successful variant. A variant for long hair, for example, would better adapt to a cold climate than a variant for short hair. A population that is genetically uniform may be exquisitely suited to a particular environment, but specialization frequently results in an inability to meet the challenges imposed by any change in the environment or in selection goals. A truly uniform population has no reserve of options for change.

The global importance of genetic diversity is widely recognized as it relates to wildness—rainforests, wetlands, tidal marshes, and prairies. Diversity of habitats, species, and genes allows evolution to continue apace and makes possible the constant adaptations to slight or marked changes in the environment that are necessary for interacting life forms to continue living and functioning together. Similarly, agriculture depends on genetic diversity for its stability. The fundamental difference between agricultural and other biological systems is the widespread human selection involved. Habitats within agriculture are essentially the result of human activity, and the diversity of such habitats must be protected to ensure the long-term survival of genetic diversity in domestic animals and plants.

The accomplishments of modern agriculture have been made possible through the selection and use of genetic diversity in animals and plants from around the world, coupled with various modern technologies. Future selection of different characteristics and development of new breeds are completely dependent on the presence of genetic variation within existing populations. While livestock breeders in North America have historically imported the genetic diversity they needed, much of that diversity has now been extinguished. We can no longer assume that someone else will have the genetic resources we need for the future. Stewardship of existing genetic resources must become a priority.

Genetic variation in domestic animals is manifested in different ways than in wild animals, owing largely to the impact of human selection. Most of the ancestral wild relatives are extinct, and domesticated animals are the only living representatives of some historic lineages. Domesticated animals are thus a critical component of the total biodiversity of life on Earth.

The primary taxonomic unit of variation in domestic animals is the breed, a classification that roughly coincides with the subspecies in wild animals. A breed is a group of animals that may be readily distinguished from other members of the species and when bred to one another reproduce this distinguishing type (i.e., like begets like). Breeds are created by geographic or political isolation coupled with selection by humans and the environment to concentrate characteristics of the population. It is important to realize that more than external physical qualities define a breed. Breeds are also defined by specific complex behaviors and other heritable traits. All of these characteristics, collectively known as the "phenotype," are not easily attributed to specific identifiable genes. Rather they are the result of unique gene configurations and combinations developed through generations of reproductive selection and isolation.

Beginning in the 1700s, the formal organization of breeds through the use of flock, herd, or stud books codified the genetic isolation of breeds. Since livestock breeds were developed to be different from one another and have been maintained in isolation from one another, they are identifiable packages of distinct genetic content and configuration. The number of breeds and the numbers of animals within the breeds are good indicators of the status of genetic diversity within each livestock species.

GENETIC EROSION IN NORTH AMERICAN LIVESTOCK

The status of genetic diversity can best be understood through an appreciation of breed population dynamics. Breeds are the units of most significant genetic variation in domestic animals and are also the units about which information is most readily available. When a breed declines in numbers, specific genes as well as specific gene combinations within the breed become less common, and certain genes and gene combinations will cease to exist within the breed. If the breed becomes extinct, then both the specific genes as well as gene combinations in that breed are lost to the species as a whole.

Genetic erosion by breed reduction or extinction can be counteracted by timely action, but effective conservation efforts can only be implemented if breed status is understood. A complete evaluation of livestock breeds includes an inventory of the number of breeds per

species and the number of animals per breed. Equally important is
the genetic breadth of the breed, the number of parents for each suc-
cessive generation.

The number of breeds within a species is a useful indicator of
the diversity available to the species. The domination of a livestock
species by a single breed or a few breeds is a recent phenomenon. For
example, the Holstein breed exceeds all other cattle breeds in the
quantity of milk produced per cow and is now the dominant dairy
breed around the world. The popularity and prevalence of this breed
has come at the expense of most other dairy breeds, several of which
are threatened with extinction. Yet the Holstein is a specialized animal dependent on high-quality feed and intensive management. Its
advantages decline under lower-input systems, where other breeds
may be more efficient.

Swine provide another example of reduced diversity as a result of
the loss of entire breeds and the selection of all breeds for the same characteristics—thus deleting some unique characteristics of the species.
While the most significant and obvious genetic loss is total extinction,
genetic dilution through the combination of breeds may also remove
unique genetic combinations and decreases the integrity of the original
genetic package available to the species. The introduction of Australian
Illawarra and Red and White Holstein genetics into the American Milking Shorthorn breed to increase milk production has threatened the loss
of unique genetic combinations within the breed, and the pre-Illawarra
strain of Milking Shorthorn is now extremely rare. Fortunately, the
value of the grazing characteristics of the breed for grass-based production and the identification of valuable and unique milk characteristics
have focused attention on these original or "native" animals.

THE AGRICULTURAL CONTEXT
OF GENETIC EROSION

Rapid genetic erosion is occurring in all the livestock species of North
America. Over 150 breeds are in decline or in danger of extinction.
C. M. A. Baker and C. Manwell assert: "It is often assumed that the
spread or decline of a breed is solely or mainly because of its relative
merit. In fact, a complicated web of interacting socio-economic rea-

sons is involved, and merit or lack thereof may make a relatively small contribution."[1] The web of factors is readily observed in American agriculture today: uniform industrial selection, substitution of non-renewable resources for animals' natural abilities, devaluation of the purebred, consolidation of the livestock resources, and attitudes favoring standardization. These factors apply generally to all livestock species and directly or indirectly have led to loss of genetic diversity.

Traditionally, many breeds were utilized, and they all served more than one purpose. Current selection has generally been concentrated on a single breed or type for each animal product. As a result, a single breed or a very few breeds have become dominant. These highly selected populations are known as industrial breeds. The high production levels of industrial stocks are not to be disparaged, however. Industrial livestock provide most of the animal products in our diet. At the same time, these incredibly successful animals are functioning in a very recently developed, expensive, and specialized environment, one that is unique in agricultural history.

Uniform Industrial Selection

New technologies eliminate geographical limits to the reproduction of animals. Artificial insemination, embryo transfer, and cloning have the potential to reproduce the most productive individuals many times over their natural capacity. As fewer and fewer animals are used for breeding, the genetic base of the breed is narrowed with every generation. The drive toward uniformity has become a problem at the species level. Not only are individuals in a breed increasingly uniform, but all commercial breeds within a species are being selected toward the highest-producing types.

Substitution of Nonrenewable Resources for Natural Abilities

Industrial selection largely ignores the innate abilities of livestock now made redundant through substitution of capital, energy, and other inputs. The breeds that are climate adapted, show strong maternal instincts, and thrive under extensive husbandry are not relevant to current intensive industrial production systems and have generally been cast aside. Modern agriculture has used a variety of inputs to support and expand production levels. Animal feed now consists of high-energy grain and protein supplements. These feeds are frequently coupled with additives and growth enhancers. Single-purpose, high-tech housing for industrial production has removed the need for climate adaptation. Intensive husbandry creates an increased need for veterinary support and monitoring of health status owing to the concentration of large numbers of animals. Increased management is also required for successful reproduction and includes fertility enhancement, birthing assistance, and the hand rearing of young.

Devaluation of the Purebred

"Hybrid vigor" is the performance boost attained through crossing distantly related parents. Also called *heterosis*, hybrid vigor is the foundation of modern commercial livestock production. It is now assumed that the crossbred will outperform the purebred. In the rush to utilize crossbreeding, however, the necessity to maintain genetically distinct parent breeds has been widely ignored. If all breeds become uniform, through selection or through crossbreeding, the potential benefits of hybrid vigor will be greatly diminished. Decreasing emphasis on purebred stock has also resulted in a diminished appreciation of the art of livestock breeding and the host of associated skills that are also in danger of being lost.

Consolidation of Livestock Resources

Since World War II, all agricultural resources, including livestock, have become consolidated into fewer units of larger size. Genetic resources have also been concentrated, and many nonindustrial stocks have been lost. While we have enjoyed an abundance of cheap and varied foods as a benefit of modern production and distribution systems, there have also been significant unanticipated consequences. The increasing size and specialization of agricultural operations have meant the separation of livestock production from food crop and forage production. Livestock are now considered an end product only, rather than an integral part of a diversified agricultural system.

Much of our food is produced by a few international conglomerates. The consolidation of breeding, production, and processing has encouraged a move toward the selection of animals that are uniform, interchangeable units. The impact on breeds has been tremendous. Those breeds that perform best under industrial conditions have been further modified to excel when given additional resource inputs. The vast majority of our food-producing animals are selected only for industrial conditions. Consolidation has meant a reduction in the number of decision makers in agriculture. In contrast, the history of agriculture is the result of the genius of millions of creative and skilled individuals.

Attitudes Favoring Standardization

Inseparable from these trends are the attitudes that support them, attitudes that favor increased uniformity of animals and management systems. In its acceptance of uniform, high-input livestock production systems, livestock agriculture may inadvertently destroy the very base of its own success—genetic diversity.

The single system favored by industrial producers is the use of intensive management for maximized output. Concentrated and intensive animal farming has been assumed to be the only modern way to produce livestock and the single system believed to be appropriate for all climates and geographies for the entire future of society. Research has been narrowly focused, and the answers generated are likewise narrow. With fewer decision makers, the results tend to be more widely implemented and fostered than the original questions and assumptions would warrant. As a result, agricultural systems become more similar, and choices of acceptable genetic resources also become increasingly narrow.

During the last fifty years, for example, there has been virtually no research on the production of livestock on low-input, forage-based systems. This lower-cost production system is a potential option for many farmers, but the research to support its implementation remains to be done. If the assumptions that undergird modern agriculture—such as the continued availability of cheap energy—were to change, it is reasonable to expect that the animals necessary in future agriculture would be different from those functioning well today. It is for this reason that the rare breeds need to be kept intact as *functional and viable genetic units* that can be used in the future.

CONSERVATION OF GENETIC DIVERSITY

Livestock genetic diversity, as represented by a wide variety of genetically distinct breeds, must be conserved to meet six societal needs:

food security, economic opportunity, environmental stewardship, scientific knowledge, cultural and historical preservation, and ethical responsibility.

Food Security

The very fabric of American society depends on a secure food supply, which assumes a continuation of domestic agriculture. At risk is the genetic breadth required to produce an array of foods, in a variety of climates, and utilizing a variety of systems. Genetic diversity is also the basis for responding to future environmental challenges such as global warming, evolving pests and diseases, and availability of energy. Along with market demand and human needs, these challenges are profoundly unpredictable. The necessity of genetic diversity in food crops is well illustrated by the Irish potato famine of the 1840s, caused by a blight to which the genetically uniform Irish potato crop was not resistant. The blight destroyed potatoes for five years with staggering social consequences—the dislocation or death of millions of people. Luckily there were potato varieties in the Americas that were resistant to the blight.

Examples of such disasters for livestock are also compelling. Parasite control in sheep has been a universal management problem. Modern parasiticides have eliminated the need to select for parasite resistance, but suddenly the literature is documenting sheep parasites with complete resistance to current drugs. Gulf Coast sheep and Caribbean Hair sheep show remarkable genetic parasite resistance—an adaptation to the heat, humidity, and parasite loads of their native habitats. Epidemics of foot and mouth disease and avian influenza are recent disease scares that could challenge the genetic uniformity of our industrial stocks. An old adage warns against putting all your eggs in one basket. A genetically uniform livestock and/or crop base does just this. Diversity is essential for long-term food security.

Economic Opportunity

The value of breed conservation and genetic diversity lies in long-term economic potential. Many breeds yield high-value products such as naturally colored wool, free-range poultry products, grass-fed meat, and unusual cheeses. Rare breeds may also be a foundation for development of domestic industries to serve markets that now rely on imports. For example, we now import almost all the sheep's milk cheeses, such as feta and Roquefort, and over 10 percent of the lamb consumed in the United States.

Unique genetic combinations in endangered breeds—particularly those that are distantly related to commercial stocks—must be conserved if these opportunities are to be protected. Breeds that are rare today may carry traits that will be of commercial importance tomorrow. Not long ago St. Croix, Barbados Blackbelly, and other hair sheep were considered oddities, but with the decline in the wool support system, these breeds become sought after as meat producers without the necessity of shearing and marketing wool. Genetic conservation makes possible the development of new breeds such as Senepol cattle (a blend of N'dama and Red Poll) and Katahdin sheep (developed from a foundation of genetics contributed by Wiltshire Horn, Gulf Coast, and Caribbean Hair sheep).

Environmental Stewardship

Agriculture is the chief human interaction with the environment. Maintaining genetic resources allows for the adaptation of agriculture to environmental changes; improves the environmental sustainability of agricultural production; and substitutes livestock services and products for the environmentally and economically costly use of chemicals, energy, and other inputs. Increasingly these alternatives make economic as well as environmental sense.

In addition, properly managed grazing of livestock can be used to recover diversity in damaged habitats, such as restored strip mines, wetlands, woodlands, and prairies, as well as in the recovery of abused and eroded crop and range lands. Grazing is essential to the long-term health of grasslands, which cover more global land surface that any other ecosystems. Grasslands are an important collector of solar energy and are essential in global recycling systems for energy, water, minerals, and oxygen. Given the extinction of many wild herbivores, their domestic counterparts are of great ecological importance.

Scientific Knowledge

A full understanding of the animal kingdom requires the protection of maximum genetic diversity. Many rare breeds are biologically unusual and provide opportunities to study adaptation, disease and parasite resistance, reproduction differences, and feed utilization under a variety of forage systems. The Ossabaw Island hog is a research model for non-insulin-dependent diabetes and cardiovascular diseases. Myotonic goats are a similar model for human myotonia congenita.

Cultural and Historical Preservation

Historic breeds of livestock are the result of human creativity and culture, worthy of being protected along with complex artifacts such as language, works of art, and technological innovations. Solutions to contemporary problems are often found in records of the past. Many traditional livestock husbandry techniques retain their usefulness today, but the common wisdom of the past is no longer valued or taught in institutions of higher education. Our responsibility to future generations requires us to pass on as complete an agricultural record as possible, giving farmers the opportunity to learn from past generations the uses of heritage breeds, which have been the basis for American agriculture.

Ethical Responsibility

Stewardship of the Earth includes not only the myriad species of wild creatures, plants, and habitats but also the domestic animals and plants that are part of the biological web of life. Those who appreciate the role of livestock in conserving the environment and in providing services, companionship, food, and other products believe that domestic animals have a right to continued existence, as do wild species. Human beings have a particular obligation to protect the domestic species that have been our partners for millennia of coevolution and interdependence.

SQUEEZED TO THE LAST DROP

The Loss of Family Farms

TOM PHILPOTT

FOUR MULTINATIONAL COMPANIES *control over 70 percent of fluid milk sales in the United States: Land O'Lakes, Foremost Farms, Dairy Farmers of America, and Dean Foods. Consolidation has forced many small- and medium-size dairy farms around the country into a corner: go into debt to get bigger, sell out to developers, or try to survive in a market flooded with cheap industrial milk.*

❖

In 2005, dairy giant Dean Foods shuttered a milk-processing facility in Wilkesboro, a town at the eastern edge of North Carolina's Appalachian Mountains. Dean processes 35 percent of the fluid milk in the United States and Canada—roughly equal to the market share of its three biggest rivals combined. In my area of western North Carolina, Dean processes 100 percent of the fluid milk. Since there were no other USDA-approved processing plants around, the few remaining dairy farmers in the mountains faced a stark choice: pay to have their milk hauled an additional 55 miles to Winston-Salem, where Dean ran another plant, or exit the business.

In the tiny mountain town of Bethel, North Carolina—45 miles west of Wilkesboro—one such farmer took the second option, closing a 50-cow operation he had started in 1959. When he started his farm, Bethel had around a dozen dairy farms. Today it has none.

When I think of consolidation in the food industry—fewer and fewer companies controlling more and more production—I think of that small farm in Bethel.

SQUEEZED TO THE LAST DROP

In many ways, that small Bethel dairy farm embodied what many of us think of as sustainable agriculture. The cows there fed on ample, lush pasture in the temperate months, and on hay and corn grown on the farm in winter. The farmer rejected growth hormones and used antibiotics only on sick animals, not as a prophylactic. And rather than letting manure fester in a lagoon, he spread it back on the pasture, fertilizing the next season's grass and feed crops.

And the farm enjoyed broad support within the community. I was among the ranks of people, probably four or five per day, who would show up at the milk house in the afternoon with empty jugs to buy rich, raw milk—delicious on its own, but even more wonderful in coffee or transformed into yogurt and cheese.

We did so illicitly. Under North Carolina law, unpasteurized milk can only be sold to consumers as animal feed; that's why I'm withholding the farmer's name. He charged us twice what he got per gallon from the processor, and we would have paid more.

Our support provided a nice income stream, but not enough to pay his bills. As in most localities throughout the United States, demand for local, delicious, responsibly grown food is growing briskly in western North Carolina. Yet only a limited number of people are willing to drive out of their way, bring their own containers, ignore hysterical warnings against raw milk, and defy the law just to support a local dairy. The path of least resistance leads to the supermarket.

So the farmer still relied on Dean Foods for a steady paycheck. He still needed to have his milk trucked away to a facility run by the nation's largest dairy processor, where it would be mixed indiscriminately with milk from much larger, less pasture-based farms, pasteurized, homogenized, bottled, and sent to supermarkets throughout the Southeast.

To market their milk, farmers, not the processor, pay the trucking costs. When the Wilkesboro facility closed, farmers suddenly had to bankroll a trip more than twice as long as before. Around the same time, gas prices were surging, meaning that the farmer not only had to pay for 55 additional miles, but each mile became more expensive, making the operation no longer profitable.

We had growing demand for locally and sustainably produced milk and a farmer willing to supply it, but what could have been a thriving enterprise plunged into an abyss.

THE ILLUSION OF CHOICE

While the nation's dairymen face dwindling options for their milk, American consumers face a similar dearth of choice at the grocery store. Consolidation has made it hard for farmers and consumers alike to avoid participating in the industrial food system. As small farms like the Bethel dairy die off, Americans inevitably have to buy their milk products from anonymous refrigerators at the grocery store.

Walking down the dairy aisle of the supermarket, dozens of distinct brand names pop out at us: Morning Glory, Golden Guernsey, Heritage, Lactaid, New England Creamery, Country Fresh, Alta Dena, Berkeley Farms, Meadow Gold, Shenandoah's Pride, Horizon. We may think we have dozens of cute, independent dairy labels to choose from, but when we drill down to the source, a handful of industry giants emerge.

Just four multinational companies control over 70 percent of fluid milk sales in the United States: Land O'Lakes, Foremost Farms, Dairy Farmers of America, and Dean Foods.[1] Their shareholders cash in while small dairy farmers struggle to make ends meet. Needless to say, premium paychecks reward executives for maximizing profits for the corporation, not for ensuring healthy milk, happy farmers, or safe, sustainable farming practices.

An overview of the leading milk companies gives a sense of just how huge the dairy industry has become and just how little choice American consumers have. Land O'Lakes—America's top butter supplier—has combined forces over the years with Cenex and Purina Mills. Land O'Lakes reported $159.6 million in profits in 2008.[2] As of 2009, Dairy Farmers of America was producing close to 30 percent of the U.S. milk supply, with $11.7 billion of sales in 2008, while in 2007 DFA ranked twenty-ninth on *Fortune* magazine's list of the thirty-five largest U.S. private companies.[3]

Dean Foods—the same company that controls the market in Bethel, North Carolina—sits atop the U.S. dairy pyramid, dominating milk sales across the country. Shoppers can find Dean Foods' milk packaged within an array of seemingly independent labels: Adohr Farms, Alta Dena, Borden, Meadow Gold, Nature's Pride, Shenandoah's Pride, Sealtest, and dozens more. The company also owns Horizon Organic Milk and soymilk maker WhiteWave. This industry giant raked in $131 million dollars of profit in 2007.[4] And while more than 100 dairy farmers throughout America go out of business every week—like the Bethel dairy farmer—Gregg L. Engles, the 51-year-old CEO of Dean Foods, made over $9,600,000 in 2008.[5]

THE HUGE GET BIGGER

Corporate takeover of the supply chain is not limited to the milk sector. The same conditions faced by small dairy farmers prevail through most of the U.S. food industry. Like most of the orange juice it produces, the U.S. food system is highly concentrated. University of Missouri researchers Mary Hendrickson and William Heffernan track market consolidation among food companies. Their April 2007 report tells a stark story.[6]

At the time of the Missouri study, just four companies—Tyson, Cargill, Swift & Co., and National Beef Packing—were slaughtering 83.5 percent of cows. In late 2007, Brazilian beef-backing giant JBS barreled into the market, snapping up Swift. Within months, JBS had bought the beef operations of pork giant Smithfield Foods, which had been the fifth-largest packer. Today, the Big four—Tyson, JBS Swift, Cargill, and National Beef—control well more than 80 percent of the market.

In hogs and chickens, the big are getting bigger too. In 2001, the top four companies (at the time, Smithfield, Tyson, Swift & Co., and Cargill) killed 59 percent of hogs. By 2008, that number had risen to 64 percent, although JBS had taken over Swift & Co. For chickens, just two companies—Tyson and Pilgrim's Pride—were killing 47 percent of birds. The top four companies controlled 58.5 percent of the market, up from 50 percent in 2000.

The Obama administration has vowed to take a harder line on agriculture consolidation than its predecessors. Yet in October 2009, it approved JBS's buyout of Pilgrim's Pride.[7] That deal left two companies—JBS and Tyson—with large positions in the Big Three of the supermarket meat case: beef, chicken, and pork.[8]

As these few companies engulf market share, they gain increasing power to dictate terms to growers. In meat processing, the companies wield a second weapon: captive herds. Smithfield, for example, is not only the nation's dominant hog processor. In addition to slaughtering 27 million hogs per year, the behemoth also raises over 20 million hogs of its own (not including the 220,000 hogs it produces internationally)—more than any other operation by a factor of three.[9] It also controls a huge portion of the hogs it slaughters indirectly, through contracts with large-scale growers.

Pork giants Tyson and Cargill also keep large captive herds and buy most of the rest of the hogs they slaughter under contract. They use their market might to squeeze prices, giving small, independent growers two options. They can get bigger, in hopes of making up in volume what they're losing in price; or they can shut down. The result has been a nearly wholesale obliteration of small hog farms and an explosion in the size and geographical concentration of operations.

Iowa, the nation's leading hog-producing state, tells the story. According to the Iowa Pork Producers Association, the total number of hog farms plunged from more than 59,000 in 1978 to around 10,000 in 2002, an 83 percent drop. Over the same time span, the total number of hogs raised per year jumped from 19.9 million to 26.7 million. That means the average number of pigs per farm soared from 250 to more than 1,500. And production, which had been broadly distributed across the state, shifted to just a few counties.[10] North Carolina, the nation's number two hog state, shows similar trends.[11]

Conventional vegetable farmers also face tightly consolidated markets. Power to influence vegetable prices rests with a few large middlemen selling to huge buyers like supermarkets and fast-food chains. Just five companies, led by Wal-Mart, control nearly half of U.S. supermarket sales, Hendrickson and Heffernan report. Because of the regionally fragmented nature of the industry, that number understates the situation. In any given region, three or four supermarket chains typically dominate sales, with Wal-Mart usually taking the number 2 or number 3 spot.

If you're a farmer with, say, 100 acres of tomatoes in Florida, you take the price the big buyers are offering or watch your crop wither as buyers look south to Mexico for a willing seller.

THE NOT-SO-FREE MARKET

How did a few corporations gain such dominance over food production and retailing? One response is: people want cheap food, and the market gave it to them. If low cost is the main goal of food production, consolidation makes sense. Big operations gain economies of scale. You can't argue with the results—even with prices going up, the United States has the world's cheapest food as a percentage of income.

But that reasoning is naïve. Agricultural markets don't operate freely; they're manipulated as a matter of course. As feedlot and slaughterhouse interests gained economic might, they also began to wield extraordinary political leverage. Local and state governments have been notoriously lax in forcing feedlot operations to clean up their considerable environmental messes.[12] Authorities have also historically looked away from the industry's brazen violations of labor code.[13] Indeed, labor conditions in our corporate slaughterhouses have gotten so grim that Human Rights Watch recently saw fit to issue a scathing report.[14] The ability to abuse the environment and labor with near impunity acts as a de facto subsidy, allowing industry giants to keep costs down as they gobble market share.

After fifty years of such trends, merely ending feed crop subsidies and forcing agribusiness giants to clean up their messes won't rebuild more benign food production networks. Throughout most of the nation, local food infrastructure has withered away, and the few remaining small farmers aren't making enough spare cash to make the necessary investments.[15]

To undo the damage of a half century of increasing consolidation, we'll need to commit public funding to rebuilding that infrastructure—along with a vigorous dash of real antitrust enforcement. Only if we throw our support behind small farms can we hope that one day thousands of thriving family dairies and small milk processors in North Carolina will force industry giants like Dean Foods to shutter their windows.

ASSAULT ON NATURE

CAFOs and Biodiversity Loss

GEORGE WUERTHNER

PROPONENTS OF INDUSTRIAL AGRICULTURE *often argue that the intensification of food production helps to protect the world's imperiled biodiversity. But the facts show a sad and disconcerting story. The CAFO system has devastating impacts on native habitats and wildlife, including the blanketing of feed crop monocultures across global landscapes, the dewatering of aquatic systems, and the loss of species along with valuable ecosystem processes such as pollination, predation, water filtration, and carbon sequestration.*

❖

Biodiversity, simply put, is a contraction of two words—biological diversity. Though most people tend to think of biodiversity as simply the sheer number of plants or animals in a given area, the concern of scientists goes well beyond just the presence or absence of species. Biological diversity refers to both the variety and the number of organisms, with the emphasis on native species. A field full of exotic species from another continent, for example, might increase the number of organisms but would also likely come at the expense of native habitat and wildlife, thereby resulting in a decrease in biodiversity.

The definition of biodiversity also includes the interactions between living organisms at four levels of organization—genetic, population, species, and landscape. To preserve biodiversity, the major ecological influences and processes that maintain species and their habitat must be protected and maintained. For instance, wolves are top-down predators that shape the behavior and number of other animals, thus exerting a defining influence that goes beyond their presence as a species. If you have only a few wolves occupying a given landscape, but not enough to exert a significant ecological influence on prey species, such a situation would represent a loss of biodiversity.

Generally speaking, agriculture of any kind typically diminishes biodiversity. Agriculture's main goal is to funnel the vast majority of solar energy and local resources into a few selected species—whether plant or animal. Such ecological simplification can occur only at the expense of native species. And when we exchange cattle for the diverse native fauna of the Great Plains that once included bison, elk, pronghorn, deer, prairie dog, sage grouse, and a lengthy list of other species, the result is a simplification of the ecosystem. The reduction of native biodiversity is measured not only in terms of species loss, but in the loss of genetic diversity, landscape diversity, and ecological processes as well. You cannot channel the vast majority of a region's plant biomass into an exotic species like cattle or sheep without significantly compromising the existence of many native species. Something has to give.

Furthermore, native species and healthy ecosystems provide a broad range of what are termed "environmental services," such as pollination, natural pest control, water filtration, carbon sequestration, and the cycling of nutrients in soils. If a landscape's biodiversity is simplified and its natural processes are interrupted or eliminated, many of these ecological services are either lost or severely restricted in scope.

MONOCULTURES AND GRAZING

Factory farming and CAFO production greatly contribute to these losses because of their unhealthy and unwieldy reliance on land for grazing and feed production. Estimates from satellite imagery suggest that 28 percent of the Earth's surface is now used for crop and livestock production. Some 41 percent of this area is intensively farmed with heavy machinery and chemicals, at a huge expense to native biodiversity.[1] To produce grain, hay, or other forage crops, the naturally diverse native plant and animal communities are typically replaced with a single monocrop that is often drenched in chemical pesticides and harvest-boosting fertilizers. Since monocropping occurs across hundreds of millions of acres, the ecological effects are substantial. Once-diversified landscapes are radically simplified.

While it's difficult to determine how much of any crop is pumped into concentrated animal feeding operations as opposed to small- and medium-size diversified farms and ranches, the total impact of animal agriculture of any kind is significant. Consider these statistics. Globally, production of livestock feed occupies one-third of the Earth's arable land.[2] Over the past ten years, vast areas of the Amazon Basin have been burned for conversion to industrial soybean plantations to produce feed for Brazilian feedlots and CAFOs, as well as for export to feeding operations in Europe and Asia. U.S. farmland production is even more skewed toward livestock feed.

In 2008, U.S. farmers, primarily in the Midwest, planted 87 million acres to feeder corn.[3] Part of that acreage figure was due to the increasing demand for corn created by ethanol, but the bulk of the acreage is used for animal feed. By comparison, farmers planted only an average of 370,000 acres across the entire country for fresh market sweet corn, the plant we consume directly for corn on the cob, canning, and other uses.[4] To give some comparison, Montana, the fourth-largest state in the nation, occupies 93 million acres. Imagine nothing but corn stretching east and west across Montana's 550 miles and north and south by 300 miles. This is a huge area to be plowed up and planted to an exotic grass crop that requires vast inputs of water, pesticides, and fertilizer to sustain.

Similarly the acreage devoted to soybeans is enormous. According to the U.S. Department of Agriculture (USDA), 74.5 million acres were planted to soybeans in 2008.[5] And despite the popularity of tofu and other soy-based food products, less than 2 percent of the soybean crop is used for production of food for direct human consumption. Most of the annual soybean crop goes to animal feed.

Alfalfa hay is yet another significant crop for concentrated livestock production, primarily dairy cows and beef cattle. In the United States, approximately 59 million acres are planted to alfalfa hay annually.[6] The state of Oregon comprises roughly 60 million acres. Though serving slightly better as wildlife habitat than a row crop like corn or soybeans, alfalfa hayfields still result in a net loss in native biodiversity. Alfalfa hay replaces native vegetation, often requires excessive amounts of fertilizers, and is cut or mowed frequently, destroying even its temporal value as hiding and nesting cover for many wildlife species.

Taken together, these three animal feed crops cover a minimum area of over 200 million acres in the United States alone. To put the landscape use of animal feed versus food production into perspective, the amount of land used to grow the top ten fresh vegetables in the United States (asparagus, broccoli, carrots, cauliflower, celery, head lettuce, honeydew melons, onions, sweet corn, and tomatoes) totals about 1 million acres.[7] Consider also that as much as 22 percent of all wheat grown in the United States ultimately ends up as animal feed, rather than in food products like bread or cereal consumed directly by humans.[8]

Where formerly an acre of grassland or forest may have supported thousands of native plants and animals, including insects, the typical livestock feed operation is dominated by one or two exotic species. The loss of native plant species has major consequences for other dependent forms of life. Aspen and balsam poplar, for instance, are common tree species across the Northern Tier states from Maine to Minnesota. In many parts of this region, these native trees have been cut down and replaced with corn, hay, and other field crops for livestock production. Yet there are 7 species of giant silk moths, 77 species of nocturnal moths, 7 species of sphinx moths, and 10 species of butterflies known to use aspen and poplar for larval development alone. That's more than 100 species of butterflies and moths! A list of all insects, microorganisms, birds, mammals, and other life associated with just aspen and poplar would likely number in the thousands.

If you fly or drive across Iowa, Illinois, Ohio, Missouri, and other midwestern states, you'll pass mile after mile of corn and/or soybean fields. Growing these crops has led to the near-extirpation of native plant communities like the tallgrass prairie.[9] Less than 4 percent of the native tallgrass prairie remains, and in some states like Iowa, tallgrass prairie is functionally extinct, with less than 0.1 percent of its original habitat remaining. "Clean" farming has eliminated the surrounding natural vegetation such as woodlots, fenceline strips, wetlands, and other natural areas that in the past supported native species with the agricultural matrix.

Agriculture, including livestock production and crop production combined, is the number one source for species endangerment in the United States,[10] and this tally would be higher if we add in the species that are negatively impacted by exotic species, many of which increase because of habitat modification by agricultural production.

WATER RESOURCES

Agricultural production also negatively impacts aquatic ecosystems and biodiversity. Agriculture is the largest user of U.S. water resources, with concentrated animal feeding operations the largest per capita consumer of water. The primary mission of most western reservoirs is to store water for irrigated agriculture. Even in California, which grows the bulk of the nation's vegetables and fruits, the state's largest use of irrigation water by acreage is for irrigated alfalfa hay production. Although production requirements vary between regions and individual operations and times of year, it is clear that meat and other animal food products are extremely water-intensive compared with grains and other foods, not just to irrigate feed crops, but also to hydrate livestock, move waste in CAFO facilities, and service slaughterhouse disassembly lines.

The environmental impacts associated with dams and reservoirs, such as barriers to salmon migration and changes in water flows and flooding, are just one indirect impact on biodiversity from factory farming operations. Add to this the direct dewatering of rivers for hay and other forage crop production, along with the loss of groundwater supplies by excessive pumping—particularly of the Ogallala Aquifer—for irrigated feed crops, dairies, hog CAFOs, feedlots, and processing facilities throughout arid regions from Texas and the southwest to South Dakota. It's easy to see why some argue that livestock production is the leading cause of water degradation.[11] The disappearance of native fish, amphibians, mollusks, and aquatic insects as a result of livestock production is significant.

More than four-fifths of the western United States' native fish populations are either listed or candidates for listing under the Endangered Species Act. For many of these species, habitat change due to water loss or degradation resulting from livestock production operations is a dominant cause of population decline. The dewatering of Montana's Big Hole River to irrigate forage crops for cattle is, for instance, one of the prime factors in the near extinction of the Montana grayling.

The negative effect on fish of such a river's being drawn down to a trickle is easy enough to comprehend, but other times the cause-and-effect relationships are subtle and indirect. For example, Colorado River dams created for irrigation storage subsequently used for livestock forage crops have significantly changed natural flood regimes and flows. These changes are responsible for the decline of native fish species, including the humpback chub, the bonytail chub, the roundtail chub, the razorback sucker, and the Colorado squawfish.

PUBLIC LANDS RANCHING

Unbeknownst to many people, a sizable portion of the United States public domain is leased to private ranching livestock operations. The typical public lands livestock grazing permittee runs what is known as a "cow-calf" operation. That is, a cow and calf are grazed for all or a portion of the year on public lands, then shipped to a feedlot for fattening before slaughter and processing. Thus public lands grazing operations are a major contributor to CAFO-type feeding ventures, since nearly all the animals that are grazed on public lands ultimately wind up in feedlots.

More than 260 million acres of western public lands managed by the Bureau of Land Management and U.S. Forest Service, as well as smaller amounts of land operated by the Fish and Wildlife Service and even some national park units, are leased in "allotments" for livestock grazing. (For comparison, the entire state of Vermont occupies 6 million acres.) Ranchers pay $1.35 per animal unit month (AUM)—virtually pennies a day—to feed and house a 1,000-pound cow and her calf. You couldn't feed a hamster for what ranchers pay U.S. taxpayers for the privilege of grazing their animals on public lands.

The acreage available to U.S. ranchers is larger than the combined area of all the eastern seaboard states from Maine to Florida, with Missouri thrown in for good measure. Though the low cost paid by ranchers for grazing privileges is a direct subsidy to these government welfare ranchers, the ultimate price is lost biodiversity—something difficult, if not impossible, to ever recover.

Since the majority of these lands are arid and rugged, their productivity is low and vegetation is sparse. Livestock grazing has led to even greater productivity losses, major soil erosion, and detrimental changes in native plant communities. In the arid western United States, it can take up to 250 acres of land to support a single cow for a year compared with an animal that can subsist on a couple of acres of pasture in the moist, humid East. As a consequence of this low productivity, the negative impacts of any grazing operation are magnified.

For instance, up to 90 percent of the annual forage on many grazing allotments may be allotted to domestic livestock. You can't put that much grass into the belly of a cow without impacting native animals, from elk to ground squirrels. The mere presence of livestock negatively impacts native wildlife. Many species, including elk and pronghorn, are socially displaced by the presence of livestock. They are pushed into habitats that are often less productive and suffer accordingly.

Beyond forage competition, cattle evolved in moist woodlands in Eurasia, and they tend to congregate in habitats that are similar to their evolutionary past—namely the narrow strip of green riparian woodlands along rivers and streams. In the process, they consume many of the plants and trample and compress the moist soils, damaging these fragile green corridors. Since at least 80 percent of all species in the West depend on these riparian habitats for water, food, and shelter, the loss and damage to these areas by livestock take a direct toll on many wildlife species. Everything from red bats to the Southwest willow flycatcher depends on riparian areas, and has suffered steep declines because of the loss of riparian habitat.

Excessive and poorly timed hoof compaction of riparian soils, which are natural water-holding sponges, increases downstream flooding in spring, often with serious damage to human habitation, while it also simultaneously reduces late-season flows. Hooves can also tear apart stream banks, creating wider, but shallower streams that are less suitable for fish.

Another cost of public lands livestock grazing is predator and "pest" control. Taxpayers fund the killing of coyotes, wolves, bears, mountain lions, and other wildlife that may prey on livestock. Hundreds of thousands of animals are killed annually. Endangered species like wolves are killed to protect private livestock that are grazing on public lands. So-called pests are poisoned by government animal control agents. Wildlife like prairie dogs (which are candidates for listing under the Endangered Species Act) are regularly poisoned on public lands because ranchers consider them forage competitors with their livestock.

Trampling of soil crusts, plus the alteration of native plant communities by selective grazing pressure has led to major invasion of exotic weeds. The changes in plants have hurt many native species. For instance, many native butterflies and bees, which depend on specific native flowers that have been replaced by exotic species, are in steep decline. Exotic plant invasions have had other effects as well.

Cheatgrass, an exotic favored by livestock grazing, is an annual that burns very well. The widespread invasion of cheatgrass facilitated by domestic livestock grazing has led to increased fire frequency in many grasslands. These fires are burning out the native vegetation, creating even better conditions for the growth of more cheatgrass.

BIODIVERSITY FOR NATURE, FOOD FOR PEOPLE

Many, though not all, of these environmental impacts and the subsequent loss of biodiversity would be reduced or avoided altogether with a shift to smaller, diversified farms, along with a reduction, if not outright elimination, of meat consumption. Rather than grow hundreds of millions of acres of feed for livestock, we should shift the focus toward producing food for *people*. Such changes in consumption and production would contribute to a huge decrease in the environmental impacts of animal agriculture. By preserving wildlands and biodiversity in and around farmlands, we will protect not only ecosystems that are invaluable to the survival of myriad species of flora and fauna, but ecosystems that are also crucial to the very success and ultimate survival of future generations.

Consequences of Diversity Loss

❖ ❖ ❖

The industrialization of food production has imparted and continues to impart devastating harm to the world's agricultural and biological diversity. These losses are not limited to the decline of traditional livestock breeds but also include the vanishing of family farmers and dismantling of local and regional production capabilities. The following short essays outline some of these tragic consequences.

Narrowing of Poultry Breeds

There are predominantly two types of food-producing chickens—egg layers and meat birds, or "broilers." Until the twentieth century, dozens of breeds were prized for both meat and egg production. Today's industrial chickens, in contrast, have been engineered for very specific characteristics. Laying hens, predominantly the White Leghorn and to a lesser extent the Rhode Island Red, are bred for egg output and the ability to endure the confinement of battery cages. Broiler chickens, mainly the Cornish Cross, reach slaughter weight in just seven weeks and have been bred for optimal breast size, the ability to be plucked in industrial-grade machines, appetite, and astoundingly rapid weight gain.

In the 1920s, more than sixty breeds of chickens were raised on farms across the United States. Today the industry is reliant on just two or three industrial composite hybrids. This domination of commercial egg and meat production by just two breeds is a testament to advances in modern technologies and industrial farming. But it is also a grave concern to scientists, farmers, animal conservationists, and others around the globe. The vast genetic heritage of traditional poultry breeds is being lost in a short amount of time.

U.S. animal scientists report that commercial chickens have been so narrowly bred that they are missing more than half of the genetic diversity native to the species. Researchers such as Purdue University professor Bill Muir warn that these genetic deficits leave them vulnerable to new diseases.[1] Commercially bred hens suffer from calcium deficiency and weak bones, reports doctor of animal science Temple Grandin. And the broiler chicken has been so overselected for rapid growth that its bone physiology is totally abnormal, often resulting in lameness.[2]

Poultry, by far, have become the world's favored animal food, with nearly 10 billion produced each year in the United States alone. Noncommercial breeds and wild birds should be safeguarded for their own sake. Interbreeding traditional species with commercial lines might also help to protect the industry in the long run.

Traditional Versus Industrial Beef and Dairy Cattle

At least 800 breeds of cattle are recognized worldwide. Traditionally, cattle were raised for a triple purpose: meat, milk, and labor (and, of course, leather). Animal husbandry developed around a foundation of highly diverse cattle breeds adapting to a vast range of grazing and climatic conditions, with different temperaments, varying resistance to diseases, and distinct qualities of meat, milk, fat, and muscle.

Modern dairy breeds are changing rapidly. In the United States, over 80 percent of the registered pure-bred dairy cattle are a single breed—the black-and-white Holstein. Together with more active grazers like Jerseys, Ayrshires, Guernseys, and Brown Swiss, just five breeds make up almost all of the country's milking herds. While the Holstein is known for its prolific lactation in modern confinement systems, that success rests largely on the availability of large amounts of feed, veterinary support, and replacement stock.

Increasingly the Holstein is being crossed with traditional dairy breeds throughout the world, including the massive Ankole cattle of Uganda. And as the Holstein begins to take over the global dairy industry, some scientists worry about a loss of genetic diversity. According to University of Minnesota professor Les Hansen, 30 percent of all existing Holstein genes today are traceable to just two bulls, one born in 1962 and one born in 1965. Although both bulls are dead, their genes live on in modern dairy cattle.[1]

Dairy cows must become pregnant during the year to continue milking. Only half their calves will be female; millions of males are destined for slaughter, either as veal or feedlot beef. To be used for meat, the male calves must be a suitable crossbreed for grain fattening, so there is increasing consolidation between milk and beef producers.

In the past, the large number of beef cattle breeds—and the genetic diversity they possess—has been a cornerstone of success for the beef industry, allowing producers to respond to changing market demands. Today, however, 60 percent of the beef cattle in the United States are Angus, Hereford, or Simmental. Although so far diversity has been conserved because of the broad range of habitats in which beef cattle are raised, the accessibility of markets, and decentralized approaches to selection, this genetic resilience could change if we are not diligent.

Traditional Swine and Lean Hogs

The majority of the pig breeds we know today are believed to be descended from the Eurasian wild boar (*Sus scrofa scrofa*). Archaeological evidence from the Middle East indicates domestication of the pig occurred as early as 9,000 years ago, though it may have begun even earlier in China. Fast growth, large litter sizes, early maturity, and efficient feed-to-meat conversion were among the many traits that early farmers took advantage of when domesticating pigs.

As pigs spread across Asia, Europe, and Africa, they became indicative of settled rather than nomadic or migratory farming communities. The reason was simply that pigs are difficult to herd and move for long distances. When the Spanish conquistadors brought pigs to North America, the escapees quickly inhabited the oak-savanna grasslands throughout the country. Many of these pigs descended from the ancient European and Mediterranean breeds that evolved in the unique ecological conditions of France and Spain. As the pigs adapted to the conditions of new lands, farmers developed numerous breeds, including the Arkansas Razorback, Mississippi Mulefoot, Piney Woods Rooter, Choctaw, and the saltwater-tolerant Ossabaw.

In the 1930s, fifteen breeds of pigs were raised for the U.S. market. Today, at least six of these are extinct. The Hampshire, Yorkshire, and Duroc breeds provide 75 percent of the genetics for modern commercial production.

With the rise of animal factory hog production after the 1980s, the number of small family hog farms has plummeted. The animals themselves have also undergone a dramatic restructuring. The modern industrial hog is a feat of efficiency engineering. The narrow gene pool now preferred produces "lean hogs" with significantly less body fat and what many would argue is far less flavor. Leaner hogs have less resilience for the cold winter temperatures, so they are now kept indoors in temperature-controlled environments and no longer graze. Artificial insemination ensures relative genetic consistency, and (with the exception of a number of European Union countries) antibiotics are heavily used to promote growth and prevent disease in industrial breeds.

Demise of the Family Farmer

For centuries, the family farm served as the backbone of agriculture in rural areas throughout the world. Healthy rural communities depended on farm families, who labored full-time on land they cared for and managed, and who practiced sound animal husbandry. Today, the average U.S. farmer is fifty-five years old. People under thirty-five are increasingly reluctant to enter the profession. CAFOs are now producing much of the animal foods sold in the United States and increasingly in other traditional farming societies, such as Poland, Romania, Brazil, and Mexico.

In particular, markets for pork, poultry, and eggs are controlled by a small number of very large corporations, primarily through the practice of "vertical integration." These corporations own the animals from birth through processing, and also have substantial holdings in marketing, distribution, or grain supplies. While farmers go heavily into debt erecting factory buildings, the large integrators dictate the rest—from breeds to feed rations to slaughter weights, all in the name of output and uniformity. Though they don't own the animals, the farmers are usually responsible for disposing of the vast amounts of animal waste and are on the hook for fatalities.

This practice of ownership of the animals by the processors, also referred to as "captive supply," skews the ability to set prices toward the vertically integrated corporations rather than independent producers. Farmers who join the CAFO industry often become nothing more than subcontractors on the animal factory production line. Today, for example, poultry farmers raising birds under contract with corporations are no longer referred to as farmers, but as "contract growers."[1]

There are many Americans eager to begin farming, given the right opportunities and circumstances. One of the fastest-growing segments is in organic and grass-fed livestock production. The infrastructure investment for these operations is often affordable, and direct-marketing opportunities can make such farming more profitable, productive, and better in many other ways. What is lacking is a coordinated effort to ensure that we'll have plenty of productive and secure farming families for subsequent generations.

Loss of Individual Farms

In the United States, and increasingly in other parts of the world, livestock production has changed dramatically from family-based, small-scale, relatively independent farms to larger industrial operations more tightly aligned across the production and distribution chains.

The problem with applying the industrial economic model to agriculture is the nature of farming itself. Farms are not factories. Farms are embedded within biological systems. A healthy farm has natural diversity rather than factory-like precision and specialization. A healthy farm exhibits complex communities of plant and animal species instead of oversimplified monocultures. And finally, a healthy farm is scaled according to what the land can resiliently sustain, not drawing too excessively from local water supplies, or overwhelming the surrounding area with wastes that can't be safely applied as fertilizers or tolerated by neighbors.

According to the Union of Concerned Scientists, several factors have contributed to the rapid expansion of the CAFO industry: (1) subsidy programs that have allowed large producers to lower operating costs by buying discounted grains; (2) innovations in breeding that produce animals tailored to harsh confinement conditions; (3) increasing use of antibiotics to thwart disease; (4) the ability of CAFOs to avoid costs of safe manure treatment and handling; (5) lack of enforcement of existing antitrust and environmental regulations; (6) the domination of markets through contracts and ownership; and (7) the disregard of the negative effects of concentrated production on people living near the facilities.[1]

Between 1980 and 2000, the percentage of U.S. livestock produced from large operations rather than smaller farms increased dramatically across all sectors.[2] The trend toward consolidation in poultry, dairy, and beef feedlot operations actually started much earlier than that, but the concentration of industrial pork production accelerated during that time. Between 1982 and 2006, the number of U.S. hog operations fell by a factor of almost 10, from just under 500,000 to about 60,000.[3] However, the number of swine has remained about the same over that time period, demonstrating that the increased size of an operation was not required to meet the rising demand for pork products. The big are getting bigger and the small are simply disappearing. It's happening all over the world.

Part Five

HIDDEN COSTS
OF CAFOS

INTRODUCTION

Economists Have Forgotten How to Add

No matter how you slice it, industrial meat, egg, and dairy production comes at a heavy cost to society—a price not reflected at our checkout counters. While it can be argued that large-scale industrial animal agriculture has had its successes in boosting world food production, the essays in this section reveal that the hidden costs of that system can no longer be ignored. Like chickens that have flown the coop, many unforeseen consequences of CAFO production are now coming home to roost. These costs enter our lives in unexpected avenues: in waterways, through air particulate pollution, via taxpayer-funded subsidy programs, in the food chain, through underground drainage networks across farm country, or as tears in the very fabric of our democracy.

In *CAFOs Uncovered: The Untold Costs of Confined Animal Feeding Operations,* Doug Gurian-Sherman of the Union of Concerned Scientists attempts to document and quantify these hidden costs, which include (1) a major manure disposal problem unless ample cropland is available nearby; (2) odors that disrupt quality of life and lower property values for nearby homeowners; (3) the loss of independent medium- and small-scale farms; (4) ballooning taxpayer subsidies; and (5) the spread of pathogens and disease.[1]

At stake are what public interest attorney and conservation crusader Robert Kennedy Jr. has characterized as violations of the commons: not just of common resources, but of our values, natural heritage, and the very process of governance. For over a decade, Kennedy and the activist organization he founded, the Waterkeeper Alliance—comprised of regional Riverkeeper and Baykeeper organizations—have been waging a campaign to hold CAFO operators accountable for their devastating impacts on water quality. This campaign includes the vital commitment to the full enforcement of the U.S. Clean Water Act.

In *Fast Food Nation*, Eric Schlosser dropped a huge question mark on the wholesomeness of the all-American meat-intensive diet, connecting the dots between food-borne illness and industrial meat production:

> The medical literature on the causes of food poisoning is full of euphemisms and dry scientific terms: coliform levels, aerobic plate counts, sorbitol, MacConkey agar, and so on. Behind them lies a simple explanation for why eating a hamburger can now make you seriously ill: There is shit in the meat.[2]

Indeed, thanks to the presence of feces in the meat supply, outbreaks of *E. coli* O157:H7 and salmonella are increasingly common, and it seems barely a week or a month goes by in the United States without the news of some massive recall of industrial meat. Each year more transmissible disease agents appear in our industrial animal food production system.[3] Pharmaceutical companies invest huge amounts of money developing vaccines against future viral outbreaks potentially originating in CAFOs, while the meat industry resists tighter regulation and testing. As Schlosser points out, although meatpacking companies don't want to make people sick, they also don't want to be held liable for contamination. Until significant changes in meatpacking oversight occur, recalls will continue to be an unfortunate part of the business plan.

Hot dogs, apple pie, and democratic freedoms are part of the American way of life that so many of us take for granted. Anthropologist Kendall Thu agrees that there is much to be learned about a society from its food production systems. But what he has learned may not be so appetizing. CAFOs, writes Thu, are threatening our very democratic freedoms. It starts with simple violations in rural communities, where oppressive odors can make being outside unbearable for residents, and where emissions of toxic compounds pollute air and waterways. From there, the CAFO industry has infringed on the right to free speech in many U.S. states with laws that make it illegal to photograph a feedlot or to disparage an agricultural enterprise. In the end, we have an industrial agriculture complex holding hostage the rural communities and some of the very democratic processes we hold dear.

Instead of making the CAFO industry pay the costs of cleaning up its own toxic violations of the air and waterways, many of our public policies are perversely set up to actually "pay the polluters." By following the trail of taxpayer subsidies, farm bill programs, and government regulations used to prop up the industrial animal production machine, attorney Martha Noble exposes a world of collusion between big government, regulatory agencies, and industrial agribusiness. These government programs include money for subsidized feed production, toxic cleanup, manure lagoon construction, and methane digester technologies, as well as precious research dollars that drive the industry forward rather than develop viable alternative production methods. The real losers are small family farmers and workers, rural communities, consumers, and, of course, taxpayers.

Decades ago, our favorite cuts of meat were processed before our eyes by the local butcher—today, rarely so. Christopher Cook journeys into the modern-day jungle of the meatpacking industry. As the amount of meat Americans consume continues to set records, the consolidation of the processing industry puts increasing pressure on slaughterhouse workers to keep up with the demand on a daily basis. Nearly a century removed from Upton Sinclair's meatpacking exposé, *The Jungle*, Cook still finds an industry with a steep human price and a world of cruel cuts. What's more, the consolidation of the slaughterhouse industry into a smaller number of ever-larger facilities that increasingly favor contract producers to the exclusion of independent farmers makes further cuts at a landscape of diverse and fair markets. Without access to nearby facilities to process their animals, many independent producers have no access to distribution and marketing, even if their products are cost-competitive. Such consolidation can hurt farmers and consumers alike.

Anna Lappé writes about a potentially more illusive but equally concerning hidden cost of CAFO production: the enormous contribution of animal food production to global warming and climate change. More than all transportation impacts combined, the domestic livestock we depend on for food are emitting heat-trapping gases into the atmosphere—through digestion, the decomposition of manure, transportation, crop fertilization, and a global dietary shift to meat and animal product–intensive diets. We are literally heating up the planet by the way we put food on our tables.

FROM FARMS TO FACTORIES

Pillaging the Commons

ROBERT F. KENNEDY JR.

EXTREME AIR AND WATER POLLUTION *from factory farms is a by-product of the CAFO industry's economic and political clout. Animal factory corporations harvest profits by undermining democracy, weakening—and routinely violating—air and water laws, and destroying rural quality of life. Relying on outdated laws and business-friendly politicians, the CAFO industry creates a toxic waste stream comparable to those of heavy industry and big cities, without comparable regulation.*

❖

A rtful propaganda by industrial meat producers has succeeded in persuading most Americans that our meat and dairy products still come from bucolic family farms. In reality the vast majority of America's meat and produce are controlled by a handful of ruthless monopolies that house animals in industrial warehouses where they are treated with unspeakable and unnecessary cruelty. These meat factories destroy family farms and rural communities and produce vast amounts of dangerous pollutants that are contaminating America's most treasured landscapes and waterways.

In North Carolina today, hogs produce more fecal waste than the human population. But while human waste must be treated, hog waste is simply dumped into the environment. Giant warehouse facilities shoehorn 100,000 sows into tiny cages where they endure bleak and tortured lives without sunlight, rooting opportunities, straw bedding, or the social interactions that might give them some joy or dignity. Concrete culverts collect and channel their putrefying waste into 10-acre, open-air pits three stories deep. Noxious vapors choke surrounding communities and endanger the health of neighbors, destroying property values and civic life. Billions of gallons of hog feces ooze into America's rivers from these facilities, killing fish and putting fishermen out of business. The festering effluent has given birth to lethal outbreaks of harmful algae and bacteria that thrive in nutrient polluted waterways, including *Pfiesteria piscicida*, a toxic microbe that causes massive fish kills. Scientists strongly suspect *Pfiesteria* causes brain damage and respiratory illness in humans who touch infected fish or water.

Beef and dairy cattle, poultry, hogs, and sheep and the facilities that house them are doused with toxic pesticides, and the herds are fed antibiotics and hormones necessary to keep confined animals alive and growing. Residues from those chemical wastes saturate our waterways, fostering the growth of antibiotic-resistant superbacteria.

These new industrial techniques have allowed a few giant multinational corporations to put a million American chicken farmers and most of America's independent hog farmers out of production and to gain control of our precious landscapes and food supplies. In North Carolina, 27,000 independent hog farmers have abandoned that business in recent years to be replaced by 2,200 factories—1,600 of which are owned or operated by a single company, Smithfield Foods. In this way, America's rural communities are being shattered, and our landscapes are being occupied by giant corporations who have demonstrated little concern for our national values or welfare. They are driving the final nail into the coffin of Thomas Jefferson's vision of an American democracy rooted in tens of thousands of independent freeholds owned by family farmers—each with a stake in the system. They are undermining America's national security by putting our food supply in the hands of a few ruthless corporations rather than millions of American citizens.

Family farms are replaced by stinking factories, manned by a miniscule and itinerant workforce paid slave wages for performing some of the most unpleasant and dangerous jobs in America. The market dominance by corporate meat factories is not built on greater efficiencies, but on the ability to pollute and get away with it. The whole illegal system runs on massive political contributions by billionaire agriculture barons who must evade laws that prohibit Americans from polluting our air and water. They rely on this political clout to undermine the market, reap huge government subsidies, and pollute. If existing environmental laws were enforced against them, these multinationals simply couldn't compete in the marketplace with traditional family farmers.

Waterkeeper Alliance has been on the front lines fighting corporate takeover of American food production since our first day in business in 1999. In January 2006 we settled a case with Smithfield Foods, the nation's largest hog producer, forcing the company to clean up 275 meat factories in North Carolina. Our historic settlement put industrial meat producers across the country on notice they will have to meet a higher standard of performance. Most importantly, this settlement has, for the first time, forced the factory meat industry to closely monitor its pollution and its impact on surrounding waterbodies and groundwater. The Smithfield agreement set the stage for the next phase of Waterkeeper Alliance's Pure Farms/Pure Water campaign to civilize the industrial meat industry. It's time that the agroindustry either figures out how to produce meat without poisoning our drinking water and destroying our fisheries and communities, or get out of the food business.

But reforming the system is as much about personal choices as it is about winning our environmental campaigns. A growing number of America's consumers are coming to recognize what great chefs have long known; the best-quality meat comes from good animal husbandry.

Americans can still find networks of family farmers who raise their animals to range free on grass pastures using natural feeds without steroids, subtherapeutic antibiotics, or artificial growth promotants. These farmers treat their animals with dignity and respect and bring tasty, premium-quality meat to customers while practicing the highest standards of husbandry and environmental stewardship. They give the rest of us an opportunity to do right by eating well.

When we demand the highest-quality food, Americans promote our farmers, our democracy, our children's health, and national security. Waterkeepers works with traditional farmers, ranchers, and fishermen across the country who share our vision for a sustainable American food production—grown by farmers who earn a living wage and contribute directly to the economic, environmental, and political health of our nation.

For these reasons we are heartened by the proliferation of organic food markets and products. Organic sections are migrating from gourmet to mainstream supermarkets. A growing number of chefs and restaurateurs—who represent the vanguard of our thinking on food—are converting to sustainable foods. Retail sales of organic foods were $10.4 billion in 2003, and by 2008 sales had grown to $22.9 billion, even in the midst of an economic downturn. That's still a small piece of the $550 billion retail food market, but organic sales have maintained an impressive growth rate of 17 to 20 percent per year (against only 2 to 3 percent growth for the rest of the industry). Americans know good food when they taste it, and choose sustainability even when it costs more.

There is a large chorus of united voices of farmers, fishermen, chefs, and consumers who are standing up for good-tasting foods and American values. Sustainable food tastes better. It is more nutritious and safer for you, your family, and the environment.

BAD MEAT

Deregulation Makes Eating a High-Risk Behavior

ERIC SCHLOSSER

THOUSANDS OF AMERICANS *are sickened every year by dangerous pathogens in meat—yet the politically connected meat industry resists regulation and evades liability. Despite recurring outbreaks of disease and massive recalls of contaminated meat, the USDA—responsible for both ensuring meat safety and expanding meat sales—allows contaminated beef on supermarket shelves and lacks critical enforcement powers. Getting the risk out of eating meat means getting the meat industry out of the regulatory process.*

❖

The Bush administration and its Republican allies in Congress allowed the meatpacking industry to gain control of the nation's food safety system, much as the airline industry was given responsibility for airport security in the years leading up to the September 11 attacks. The deregulation of food safety makes about as much sense as the deregulation of air safety. Anyone who eats meat these days should be deeply concerned about what our meatpacking companies now have the freedom to sell.

At the heart of the food safety debate is the issue of microbial testing. Consumer advocates argue that the federal government should be testing meat for dangerous pathogens and imposing tough penalties on companies that repeatedly fail those tests. The meatpacking industry, which has been battling new food safety measures for almost a century, strongly disagrees. In 1985 a panel appointed by the National Academy of Sciences warned that the nation's meat inspection system was obsolete. At the time, USDA inspectors relied solely on visual and olfactory clues to detect tainted meat. After the Jack in the Box outbreak in 1993, the Clinton administration announced that it would begin random testing for *E. coli* O157:H7 in ground beef. The meatpacking industry promptly sued the USDA in federal court to block such tests.

E. coli O157:H7, the pathogen involved in the Jack in the Box outbreak and dozens of recalls since then, can cause severe illness or death, especially among children, the elderly, and people who are immunosuppressed. It is a bug that often preys on the vulnerable and the weak. The Centers for Disease Control and Prevention (CDC) estimate that about 73,000 Americans are sickened by *E. coli* O157:H7 every year. An additional 37,000 are sickened by other dangerous strains of *E. coli* also linked to ground beef. At a slaughterhouse, these pathogens are spread when manure or stomach contents get splattered on the meat.

The USDA won the 1993 lawsuit, began random testing for *E. coli* O157:H7, and introduced a "science-based" inspection system in 1996 that requires various microbial tests by meatpacking companies and by the government. The new system, however, has been so weakened by industry opposition and legal challenges that it now may be less effective than the old one. Under the Hazard Analysis and Critical Control Points plans that now regulate production at meatpacking plants, many food safety tasks have been shifted from USDA inspectors to company employees.

In return for such concessions, the USDA gained the power to test for salmonella and to shut down plants that repeatedly failed those tests. Salmonella is spread primarily by fecal material, and its presence in ground beef suggests that other dangerous pathogens may be present as well. In November 1999, the USDA shut down a meatpacking plant for repeatedly failing salmonella tests. The Texas company operating the plant, Supreme Beef Processors, happened to be one of the leading suppliers of ground beef to the National School Lunch Program. With strong backing from the meatpacking industry, Supreme Beef sued the USDA, eventually won the lawsuit, and succeeded in December 2001 in overturning the USDA's salmonella limits. About 1.4 million Americans are sickened by salmonella every year, and the CDC has linked a nasty, antibiotic-resistant strain of the bug to ground beef. Nevertheless, it is now perfectly legal to sell ground beef that is thoroughly contaminated with salmonella—and sell it with the USDA's seal of approval.

America's food safety system has been expertly designed not to protect the public health, but rather to protect the meatpacking industry from liability. For decades, the industry has received abundant help in this effort from the Republican Party, which has thwarted congressional efforts to expand the USDA's food safety authority. According to the Center for Responsive Politics, during the 2000 presidential campaign, meat and livestock interests gave about $23,000 to Al Gore and about $600,000 to George W. Bush. The money was well spent. Dale Moore—who served as chief of staff at the Department of Agriculture throughout the Bush administration—was previously the chief lobbyist for the National Cattlemen's Beef Association. Elizabeth Johnson, appointed by Bush to be a senior adviser at the USDA, had worked as the associate director for food policy at the cattlemen's group. Mary Waters, Bush's choice for USDA assistant secretary for congressional relations, assumed the post after working as legislative counsel for ConAgra Foods.

It would be an understatement to say that the Bush administration was friendly toward the big meat packers. During congressional testimony, Elsa Murano, USDA chief food safety advocate from 2001 until 2004, claimed that her agency did not need the power to order a recall of contaminated meat. Nor did it need, she said, any new authority to shut down ground beef plants because of salmonella contamination.

The meatpacking companies don't want any of their customers to get sick. But they don't want to be held liable for illnesses either, or to spend more money on preventing outbreaks. The exemplary food safety system now in place at Jack in the Box increases the cost of the fast food chain's ground beef by about one penny per pound. The other major hamburger chains also require that their suppliers provide meat largely free of dangerous pathogens—and that requirement has not yet driven the meatpacking industry into bankruptcy.

Food will never be perfectly sterile and germ-free, and we shouldn't expect it to be. But a handful of simple regulatory changes could greatly reduce the risk of being sickened by something you eat. The USDA should immediately be given the authority to demand the recall of contaminated meat and to impose civil fines on meatpacking companies. Limits should be placed on the amounts of disease-causing bugs that meat can legally contain.

Above all, our food safety system should be guided by common sense. Companies that produce clean meat should be allowed to sell it; those that produce dirty meat shouldn't. The Republican Party's alliance with the big meat packers has never reflected widespread public support. The issue of food safety isn't like abortion or gun control, with passionate and fundamentally opposing views held by millions of American voters. When most people learn how the meatpacking industry operates, they're appalled. The outrage crosses party lines. Democrat or Republican, you still have to eat.

No reform, however, will prove as important and effective as the creation of an independent food safety agency with tough enforcement powers. The USDA has a dual and conflicting mandate. It's supposed to promote the sale of American meat—and to protect consumers from unsafe meat. As long as the USDA has that dual role, consumers must be extremely careful about where they purchase beef, how they handle it, and how well they cook it. While many Americans fret about the risks of terrorism, a much more immediate threat comes from the all-American meal. Until fundamental changes are made in our food safety system, enjoying your hamburgers medium-rare will remain a form of high-risk behavior.

CAFOS ARE IN EVERYONE'S BACKYARD

Industrial Agriculture, Democracy, and the Future

KENDALL THU

MUCH HAS BEEN WRITTEN *about the deterioration of communities and degradation of the environment due to industrial animal agriculture. Less is said about how a highly centralized animal products industry directly tears away at the fabric of the democratic process. For years, the CAFO industry has been working in the courts and with elected officials and agencies to immunize itself from government regulation, from photographic documentation, and even from freedom of speech.*

❖

From the hunting and gathering !Kung Bushmen of the Kalahari Desert and intensive agricultural Maya and Aztec civilizations, to the plantations of the American South and feudal landholders of western Europe, to our contemporary industrialized hog factories in Canada and the United States, we can impart a basic anthropological lesson. The ways in which food is gathered, grown, and distributed fundamentally shape human societies. Throughout the prehistoric, historic, and contemporary record of human adaptation, a reasonably clear pattern is discernible—as the food system becomes more centralized, so too do political, economic, and even religious systems. Contrary to what we might hear about the role of agriculture, it can be argued that today's rapid centralization of ownership and control over land and food does not necessarily free the remainder of society from tilling the soil to pursue affluence. Rather, it alienates and oppresses a society's inhabitants. And the current global concentration of agricultural production, processing, and distribution into fewer hands portends a future of increasing human struggle and conflict.

Just ask neighbors of an industrial hog operation in rural Saskatchewan or North Carolina about their experiences. In vivid detail they will describe their diminished quality of life; the impairment of surface and groundwater; the horrific odor, the social upheaval and divisions among neighbors, friends, and family members; and the displacement of family farmers and rural decay. They will tell you about the inequitable burden placed on impoverished rural neighborhoods and communities of color; concerns over health problems from airborne emissions; intimidation by local officials and industry representatives; and the collusion between industry, government, and research institutions. Each of these areas is in itself worthy of attention. Taken together, they paint a compelling picture of a fundamental pathology undermining the core infrastructure of society.

The proliferation of industrial hog production facilities and the concentration of swine ownership into fewer hands parallel technological changes. The most notable is the shift from pasture-based and open-lot production to total animal confinement, beginning in the early 1970s. Confinement production does supply an advantage to hog producers in temperate regions by providing an antidote to harsh weather conditions that impede growth rates and time to market. When hogs expend a larger proportion of their nutrients in the form of energy to protect themselves from the cold or to shed pounds in oppressive heat, their feed-to-meat conversion rates decline. Enclosed production units also allow for stricter control of feed rationing and reproduction. Yet these and other efficiencies do not come without dramatic consequences.

A wide variety of environmental and public health problems have emerged as a result of the industrialization of livestock production.[1] Surface and groundwater contamination occurs from the huge volumes of manure produced. In contrast to the solid manure generated in open-air hog production, confined animal production brings the storage and management of manure in a liquid form that is much more concentrated and mobile. Swine produce over twice as much manure per day as humans do, and the biological oxygen demand (BOD) of undiluted hog waste is 160 times greater than that of raw human municipal sewage. What's more, huge volumes of antibiotics fed to livestock, primarily as growth promotants in feed, are largely excreted in the liquid manure. Consequently, antibiotics, as well as antibiotic-resistant bacteria, join the nitrogen, phosphorus, heavy metals, and other swine manure constituents that find their way into, and degrade, surface and ground waters. The problem has become so pronounced in the United States that the Environmental Protection Agency (EPA) is now legally required to develop new regulations to issue discharge permits for large-scale animal production facilities comparable to the types of permits typically issued to urban factories.

In revisions to the federal Clean Water Act originally promulgated in 1972, new rules concerning livestock operations were issued in December 2002. These rules specify the primary problem as coming from large livestock operations, in part because large operations are more likely than smaller operations to have an insufficient land base for utilizing manure nutrients. Solid manure that was once widely distributed as fertilizer for large numbers of sustainable farm systems in a given region has been transformed into an unmanageable liquid industrial pollutant contaminating the water and air.

Anyone who has spent even a little time on farms clearly understands that some type of odor is inherent to the agricultural environment. However, concentrating hundreds of thousands of gallons of liquid manure in one area is anything but natural and can have a devastating effect on the quality of life for neighboring farmers and other rural residents. Some 160 volatile organic compounds are emitted from liquid hog manure, and their odiferous character can offend even the most seasoned farmer or rural resident. Industrial production facilities housing thousands of swine come with storage facilities holding hundreds of thousands, even millions, of gallons of liquid manure. Large exhaust fans dot the exterior walls of these facilities, testifying to the fact that the interior ambient environment is not particularly healthy, so particulates and gases are forced outside. Fully a third of the people working inside these facilities will develop one or more chronic respiratory problems in direct response to exposure to gas and dust mixtures.[2] Compounds such as hydrogen sulfide and ammonia, blended with dusts and endotoxins, create problems for neighbors, particularly when large volumes of manure are stored in liquid form.

Neighbors of industrial swine production operations frequently share common views, values, expectations, and experiences concerning country living. Their lives revolve around centrally cherished values of family, friends, home, and faith. The ability to express these values through activities at their homes is centrally important to their quality of life. The encroachment of a factory livestock facility near their homes and properties strips them of the freedom and independence associated with outdoor living. Ultimately, that loss of freedom gives way to a sense of violation and infringement as even the most basic activities—backyard barbecues, visits by friends and family— are taken away. Children and grandchildren cannot experience the unfettered joy of outdoor life in the country—jumping on the trampoline, bicycling, playing in the pool, picking flowers and playing with bugs in the yard, and inviting friends over to play. Parents become upset when their children are affected by odors, which in turn has a ripple effect creating frustration, anger, and family tensions.

The homes of these families are no longer an extension of, nor a means for, enjoying the outdoors. Instead, their homes become a barrier against an outdoors that harbors an intrusive stench. The odors disrupt more than an itemized list of events on a calendar; they take away the most basic elements of their lives and offer them no control in return. This lack of control is the consequence of so-called state right-to-farm laws that originated in the 1960s and have now been enacted in all fifty states.[3] These laws were originally intended to protect family farmers from urban encroachment and nuisance lawsuits from new neighbors who do not understand normal farm operations. In recent years, however, the industry has successfully staked claim to these laws by cloaking CAFOs in laws that prevent county government or zoning boards from developing siting restrictions. In short, local communities and neighborhoods that know most about their local environment are stripped of the power to make decisions about CAFOs. Recent public health research shows that neighbors of large-scale swine operations are at elevated risk for health problems.[4] Neighbors appear to be experiencing elevated rates of health symptoms related to the upper respiratory tract. Symptoms such as excess coughing, wheezing, chest tightness, dizziness, and shortness of breath appear more frequently among neighbors of large-scale swine operations as compared with other groups in rural areas. Results indicate that neighbors may be experiencing clusters of symptoms similar to the well-documented toxic or inflammatory respiratory effects among factory farm workers exposed to gases and related conditions.

With the mounting evidence of negative social, economic, environmental, and public health consequences of industrial scale livestock production, the natural question is, *Why?* Why not simply approach our government representatives, explain the problem by showing them the scientific research coupled with local experiences of neighbors, and have them make changes? After all, representative democratic free governments are supposed to exist to protect individual rights and ensure that the public interest is being served. This lack of effective government action in the face of the litany of problems associated with industrialized agriculture demonstrates that the most fundamental violation is not the air, water, or even the decay of rural communities. Most problematic is the erosion of freedom and democracy via the centralization of political power that follows from industry consolidation. How can we fix water quality, air quality, economic decay, rural community social upheaval, and rural health if we lose our freedom of speech and find a tightening noose around channels of access to government, scientific research, and the courts? Deeply disturbing efforts to thwart regulation, stymie independent agricultural research, muzzle public criticism of industrial livestock facilities, and force independent family farmers to pay the government for messages about their occupation that they do not agree with signal tendencies not of freedom and democracy, but of autocracy and authoritarianism.

In 1996, famed U.S. talk show host Oprah Winfrey invited vegetarian activist Howard Lyman on her show to discuss mad cow disease and the livestock industry. The show's content suggested the possibility that mad cow disease could spread from cows to humans. To audience applause, an effervescent Oprah proclaimed: "It has just stopped me from eating another burger!" The show—what Oprah probably viewed as just another day at the office—turned out to be a major legal battle brought against her by the Texas cattle industry. The plaintiffs, Texas Beef Producers, contended that Oprah and her guests spoke disparagingly about beef, which had a significant effect on consumer confidence resulting in considerable financial losses for the industry. No doubt Oprah was unaware that Texas, like twelve other U.S. states, had passed "veggie libel laws" that prohibit people from speaking disparagingly about agriculture. A representative example can be seen in South Dakota's law, which defines *disparagement* as follows:

> Disparagement: *dissemination in any manner* to the public of any information that the disseminator knows to be false and that states or implies that an agricultural food product is not safe for consumption by the public or that generally accepted agricultural and management practices make agricultural food products unsafe for consumption by the public.[5]

Oprah Winfrey ultimately prevailed in her case. But what may seem an innocuous and inconspicuous law actually represents a bold frontal attack on the fundamental core of the First Amendment of the U.S. Constitution: freedom of speech. U.S. citizens in these states are supposed to not talk publicly about food safety and to accept the state's proposition that there are "generally accepted agricultural and management practices" that will protect them. Aside from the glaringly obvious constitutional affront, who ultimately gets to decide what constitutes "generally accepted agricultural and management practices"? I have a hunch that neighbors of industrial-scale livestock operations are not the first line of industry experts outlining what is "generally accepted."

In and of themselves, veggie libel laws are reason for concern. Unfortunately, they are not isolated events, but rather part of an emerging pattern of attempts to preemptively curtail free speech over problems of industrialized agriculture. For example, in 2002, agricultural industry lobbyists in Illinois tried to get the state legislature to make illegal any attempt to photograph confined animal production facilities. This was a direct response to images produced by animal welfare groups showing deplorable living conditions for livestock. In 2003, Texas lawmakers proposed that bringing a camera into a slaughterhouse should be a Class B misdemeanor, while Missouri legislators sought felony charges for photographing or videotaping "any aspect of an animal facility."[6] Although both of these efforts ultimately failed, the CAFO industry has continually pressed for similar protections ultimately designed to keep citizens in the dark about what goes on behind the closed doors of industrial animal production and slaughter operations.

Examples abound of political interference with attempts to environmentally regulate CAFOs. In 2003, the U.S. General Accounting Office (GAO) issued a report assessing the EPA's handling of its regulatory program for CAFOs.[7] After reviewing all regional EPA offices, the report concluded that large CAFOs were escaping oversight via regulatory exemptions. Consequently, many of the CAFOs that the EPA itself believed were polluting the nation's waterways were going unchecked. The GAO recommended increased oversight of the EPA program for CAFOs. In fact, just the opposite has occurred. The potentially effective regulations for CAFOs promulgated under the Clinton administration were summarily gutted by an industry-allied Bush regime. High-ranking EPA enforcement officials (who later resigned in protest) pointed out that Vice President Dick Cheney ordered the EPA director of civil enforcement to halt enforcement action against certain CAFOs.[8] Again in 2004, the EPA buckled to industry pressure when it proposed and eventually enacted a "Safe Harbor Agreement" for CAFOs that emit known pollutants into the air. Rather than regulate known emissions such as hydrogen sulfide, ammonia, volatile organic compounds, and dust particulate matter, the EPA granted amnesty to any CAFO operator who signed up to help it develop an emissions monitoring method. When it comes to toxic air emissions, CAFOs were essentially given a get-out-of-jail-free card. And the EPA, charged with protecting the citizen health, became little more than an enabler for polluters.

Problems of suppression also extend to scientific research, both in government-funded programs and in land grant universities. Since science is supposed to provide the foundation for public policy decisions, agency action, and legal adjudication, it is critically important that researchers be allowed the unfettered freedom to conduct their work and freely present their results. But not even research institutions have survived the reach of the industrial food cartel. Suppression of research studies unfavorable to agribusiness has been underway for decades. In the early 1940s, the anthropologist Walter

Goldschmidt began examining the effects of industrialized agriculture in the Central Valley of California. His work was sponsored by the Bureau of Agricultural Economics in the U.S. Department of Agriculture. Professor Goldschmidt painstakingly compared two similar towns that differed in the extent to which they were surrounded by smaller independent farms versus larger corporate-owned operations. Goldschmidt found that the town surrounded by smaller independent farms had less poverty, more churches, more civic activity, a better standard of living, more schools, more public recreation facilities, and more democratic governance. Thirty years later, in 1972, he provided congressional testimony to a Senate subcommittee on the role of giant corporations in the American and world economies:

> I was ordered [in early 1940s] by my bureau chief in Washington not to undertake the second phase of the study. He did so in response to a buildup of pressure from politically powerful circles. These same sources of influence would have, as a matter of fact, prevented the publication of the report itself, had it not been for . . . the actions of the late Senator Murray of Montana. I was told, Mr. Senator and gentlemen, that the official manuscript of the study was literally in the file drawer of the desk occupied by Clinton Anderson, then the Secretary of Agriculture, and that it was released to Senator Murray only upon his agreement that there would be no mention anywhere in the published report of the Department of Agriculture. I could regale this committee beyond its endurance with stories about this public pressure—as, for instance, our small research team being vilified on the radio each noon, as we ate our lunch . . . by the newscaster sponsored by the Associated Farmers of California.[9]

The bureau sponsoring Goldschmidt's work was dismantled.

Many independent family farmers in the United States are also discovering the very real consequences of oppression by a centralized agricultural system. Farmers throughout the country are forced to pay "tribute" to a centralized commodity organization when they market their products. In the pork industry, hog producers are required under the federal Pork Production, Research, and Consumer Education Act of 1985 to pay 40 cents out of every $100 of value when hogs are sold, known as the pork checkoff. Among the ostensible purposes of the money is the promotion of pork to U.S. consumers. Many family hog farmers in the United States, however, disagree with the advertising and public ideology created by these moneys. For example, they oppose the promotion of pork as the "other white meat" because it may discourage the sale of bacon and ham. Or they contend that family farmers end up paying for messages that promote the sale of brand name meats by large-scale integrators as opposed to their own family farm–produced meats. Each year, in fact, hog producers are essentially taxed some $50–$60 million in checkoff funds that are used to created and promote messages that may serve the interests of one segment of the industry over the other.

A legal challenge to this system was brought in 2001 by the Campaign for Family Farms (CFF), an advocacy organization consisting of four subgroups, including a substantial number of family hog farmers. CFF sought an end to the checkoff program on the grounds that it was unconstitutional under the First Amendment, as it essentially forced family hog producers to pay for messages they did not believe in or agree with. The case involved the CFF on one side against an opposition of *both* the Michigan Pork Producers (a state commodity organization funded, in part, by pork checkoff funds) *and* the U.S. Department of Agriculture. In other words, a branch of the federal government, the USDA, purposefully blurred the distinction between private industry and public governance by allying itself with the pork checkoff program. The federal government intentionally forced farmers to contribute to a state-run campaign that promoted messages to the general public that were counter to family farm interests. In October 2002, a U.S. district court judge ruled as follows:

> In days of low return on agricultural [sic], the decision of an individual farmer to devote funds to uses other than generic advertising is very important. Indeed, the frustration of some farmers is likely to only mount when those funds are used to pay for competitors' advertising, thereby depriving the farmer of the ability to pay for either niche advertising or non-advertising essentials (such as feed for 29 livestock). This is true regardless of whether objecting farmers are correct in their economic

analysis that the assessments and speech do not sufficiently further their own particular interests. In short, whether this speech is considered on either philosophical, political or commercial grounds, it involves a kind of outrage which Jefferson loathed. The government has been made tyrannical by forcing men and women to pay for messages they detest. Such a system is at the bottom unconstitutional and rotten. For these reasons, the Court concludes that the mandated system of Pork Act assessments is unconstitutional since it violates the Cross-Plaintiffs' rights of free speech and association.[10]

In an alarming reversal, the U.S. Supreme Court overturned this decision in 2005 by ruling that advertisements supported by checkoff funds were actually government speech and therefore not susceptible to First Amendment challenges. In other words, the government can require family farmers to pay taxes on their hogs *and* use that money to speak against their interests. And there's nothing they can do about it.

The general public needs to know about the larger contexts of these local and regional struggles, if only to grasp a basic civic reality. Maintaining an equitable and sustainable food system is fundamental to ensuring a democratic society. Fixing the problem in any one neighborhood's backyard should not mean chasing large-scale agricultural interests away to another neighborhood, another region, another province, or another part of the world. Rather, addressing the litany of problems brought about by facilities such as intensive livestock operations requires courageous and constant vigilance across the political landscape. Without it, we all become subservient to the political tyranny and wasteland created by industrial-scale agriculture.

But there is something greater at work here that is alarming and mobilizing citizens across the country and into Canada. Citizen groups and coalitions to fight CAFO injustices have formed from California to North Carolina, from rural Manitoba to the Texas ranges. For example, the Concerned Citizens of Tillery (CCT), a community-based organization formed in 1978 in rural North Carolina, led the state's first local intensive livestock ordinance and successfully helped champion the implementation of a statewide moratorium on the construction of new CAFOs in 1997. A statewide coalition of CAFO neighbors in Illinois proclaimed themselves the Illinois Citizens for Clean Air and Water (ICCAW). In spring 2008, ICCAW began taking back the rights assured them under the Clean Water Act by filing a formal petition with the U.S. EPA. The petition, similar to others filed through the Midwest, asked that the state's authority to issue permits and monitor CAFOs be removed because the Illinois EPA didn't even know where CAFOs were located, let alone monitor them as required under federal law. Similar promising stories are sprouting up across the country as residents increasingly recognize that these injustices are not just a rural problem. This erosion of freedoms and basic rights is not limited to rural Kentucky, Arkansas, North Carolina, Iowa, and other places with high concentrations of industrial animal agriculture. It is a degradation of rights and protections for all citizens. CAFOs are in everyone's backyard.

PAYING THE POLLUTERS

Animal Factories Feast on Taxpayer Subsidies

MARTHA NOBLE

THE CAFO SECTOR SPIN MACHINE, *including the world's largest meat and poultry packers, claims that CAFOs are "economically efficient" without mentioning the billions of dollars plucked each year from the public purse or the costs inflicted by pollution on others. The truth is that public funds are handed to CAFOs for building infrastructure, pollution control facilities and equipment, subsidized energy costs and feed grains, and precious USDA-sponsored research.*

❖

Rural residents, rural communities, public drinking water treatment facilities, and many others struggle with the flood of water and air pollutants coming from industrialized animal factories. One would think that the federal and state governments would discourage this model of production—but the opposite is true. The world's largest meat, poultry, and dairy processors have tapped into a bonanza of public subsidies. The industry receives grants, cost-share for capital construction, federal and state research dollars, tax credits, and other public funds to underwrite its proliferation—often in the guise of "conservation" and "pollution control."

Every year, according to the Union of Concerned Scientists, U.S. taxpayers shell out at least $7 billion to subsidize or clean up after CAFOs, with an additional $4.1 billion spent over the years to control leaking manure storage facilities.[1] Controlling animal factory waste and emissions to protect air and water quality and the public health should be a cost of doing business. But instead of applying a "polluter pays" principle to CAFOs, the animal factory sector has used its political clout to fashion publicly funded "pay the polluter" schemes. Perversely, the bigger the pollution problem posed by a large-scale animal factory, the more likely it is to rake in large amounts of public funding. Public dollars from federal, state, and local government coffers underwrite ever-larger animal factories with ever-growing pollutant streams. The result is what Brother David Andrews, former executive director of the National Catholic Rural Life Conference, has termed a "fecal flood."

Despite the industry's spin, CAFOs are not the only way to raise livestock and poultry. Thousands of farmers and ranchers integrate crop production, pastures, or forages with livestock and poultry to balance nutrients within their operations and minimize off-farm pollution through conservation practices and land management. By remaining a reasonable size and raising feed locally, they avoid some of the skyrocketing costs for energy, constructed infrastructure, and other features of industrialized animal agriculture.[2] Yet these sustainable producers, who must compete with factory farms for market share, receive comparatively little or no public funding for their sound management decisions.

FARM BILL SUBSIDIES: FROM FEED TO FECES

Passed every five to seven years by the federal government, the farm bill is the single largest source of public subsidies to animal factories. The animal factory sector has floated atop a sea of cheap corn, soybeans, and other feeds subsidized by the farm bill's commodity programs. Tufts University's Global Development and Environment Institute estimates that between 1997 and 2005, the industrial animal sector saved over $35 billion because farm program subsidies lowered the price of purchased feed.[3] Small and midsize farmers who grew their own feed grains and raised livestock in diversified systems received modest program benefits, but most farmers and ranchers who raised livestock on grass-based pasture systems received no such commodity subsidies.

The "implicit subsidy" of cheap market feed prices gives the

greatest advantage to industrial livestock production, with huge operations using purchased feeds. Among the biggest winners in this system are the meat and poultry companies that dominate the market.
The Tufts research estimates, for example, that between 1997 and
2005, Tyson Foods, which controlled over 20 percent of the chicken
market, received an implicit subsidy of $2.6 billion because of low-
priced feed. Smithfield Foods, which held over 30 percent of the pork
market, received $2.54 billion over that same period.

The Environmental Quality Incentives Program (EQIP), the major
farm bill conservation program for agricultural "working land," has
become another deep funding pool for CAFOs. Prior to the farm bill
reauthorization in 2002, EQIP funds were primarily focused on helping small livestock operators develop safer ways to handle waste. But
in 2002, the industry used its political influence to turn EQIP into a
publicly funded cash cow to pay the costs for CAFO infrastructure in
the name of environmental compliance. Restrictions were removed on
paying for large-scale waste lagoons, animal waste spraying systems,
and other waste facilities. The payment limit for a five-year EQIP contract was raised from $50,000 to $450,000. Moreover, that amount
could be paid to each investor in a CAFO, so that larger operations
can get many times the nominal payment limit. USDA's Natural
Resources Conservation Service (NRCS), the agency that implements
EQIP, shifted its priorities from the most cost-efficient applications to
those applicants with the greatest pollution potential. Since 2002, the
farm bill has essentially expended hundreds of millions of taxpayer
dollars to increase the overall amount of CAFO waste in communities
around the country. In many states, NRCS even established special
funding pools to ensure that CAFOs could get EQIP dollars, even if
the end result was net environmental degradation.

The Union of Concerned Scientists has reported that CAFOs
received an estimated $100 million per year in EQIP funding in
2002–2006, with the amount rising to $125 million in 2007. A more
recent study by the Campaign for Family Farms and the Environment
(CFFE) estimates that 1,000 dairy and hog CAFOs have received $35
million per year from EQIP funding since 2002, with an additional
unknown amount going to industrial poultry, beef cattle, aquaculture, and other animal operations.[4] The USDA claims that it cannot

determine the exact amount of EQIP funding provided to CAFOs. This is hard to believe, given that the agency has established separate EQIP funding pools for CAFOs. In addition, although CAFO operators must sign contracts that specify the practices being funded under EQIP, Congress has prohibited the release of individual information based on privacy concerns. Congress did not prohibit aggregation of funding data, but the USDA has consistently refused to make comprehensive, accurate aggregated CAFO data available. The public deserves better accountability from the USDA for this use of public funds, which can result in net degradation of our air and water resources.

Alarmingly, the recently passed 2008 farm bill is poised to provide even greater EQIP subsidies for animal factories. Over $7.3 billion in EQIP funding has been authorized for fiscal years 2008 through 2012, a large portion of which is targeted to fund factory farms. In addition to general funding from EQIP, CAFOs will benefit from a new EQIP Air Quality Initiative with a total of $150 million. In many states, this EQIP funding is being targeted to large-scale CAFOs. The 2008 farm bill lowered EQIP program payment limits to $300,000 over six years but carved out an exception for EQIP contracts with "special environmental significance," which can receive up to $450,000 over six years. The higher funding level is for "technologies" that will result in "significant environmental improvement." In other words, the largest factory farms, designed to generate and release the highest level of pollutants, can line up for the largest EQIP payments for publicly funded add-ons such as methane digesters and waste lagoon covers.

SUBSIDIZED WATER CONTAMINATION

In many states, EQIP funds, federal Clean Water Act funds, and other public dollars are used to underwrite the transportation of poultry litter away from areas with high concentrations of CAFOs.[5] In 2004, the NRCS in Alabama established an EQIP-funded poultry litter redistribution program to pay for the transportation of poultry litter out of nutrient-saturated areas. But there is no limit on new or expanding CAFOs in these nutrient-saturated areas. Rather than focusing on incentives to reintegrate crop, livestock, and poultry production on individual farms, the program ultimately provides a public funding stream that facilitates locating even more poultry CAFOs in watersheds already overburdened with high levels of nutrient pollution. Using poultry litter to replace synthetic fertilizer has its merits. But, as noted by a consultant on Alabama poultry waste, most of the poultry litter is applied to fields based on its nitrogen content. This can lead to a buildup of soil phosphorus and increase the risk of phosphorus runoff into waterways. What's more, the rules limiting poultry litter application in winter and wet weather (according to nutrient management plans), or requiring cover during storage, are not strictly enforced.[6] Without these safeguards, transporting poultry litter may ultimately result in transferring water pollution problems from CAFOs to other areas.

On the Delmarva Peninsula (Delaware, Maryland, and Virginia) of the Chesapeake Bay region, over 600 million broiler chickens are raised each year, generating over 2 billion pounds of poultry CAFO waste. Both EQIP funding and state funds have subsidized the transport of some of this waste away from areas with high levels of soil nutrients to other areas in the region. Although the nutrients in this poultry litter may have benefits, even if nutrient levels are controlled there is a major complication. Industrial poultry litter contains other pollutants, including heavy metals, pharmaceuticals, and pathogens. Researchers at Johns Hopkins University have identified arsenic in poultry litter as a particular pollutant of concern. Poultry growers regularly add arsenicals to feed to prevent parasitic infections and promote growth. Most of the arsenic is excreted by the animals and appears in poultry litter in a form that can be readily leached from soil and move into surface and groundwater. Arsenic can also be absorbed from the soil by many plants. Arsenic is recognized as a human health threat associated with a wide array of diseases and with human birth defects.[7] In the long run, publicly funded poultry litter transportation could result in spreading arsenic contamination throughout the Chesapeake Bay region.

Despite the billions of EQIP dollars flowing to CAFOs, there is no assurance that the end result will be a net gain for environmental improvement. Prohibitions on the release of information and poor record keeping by NRCS prevent the public from knowing what tax-payer dollars are being used for, or the environmental outcomes of that funding. The likely result is a net increase in CAFO air and water pollution, with the public continuing to pay a high bill for CAFO construction.

STATE FUNDING

In addition to federal subsidies, large-scale animal factories have been scoring significant direct funding streams from state govern-ments. One glaring example is an award of a total of $155,723 in public funding to Fair Oaks Dairy, an Indiana CAFO with more than 32,000 cows, to defray the costs of building methane digesters, which produce electricity from gases in manure. In 2002, this single operation received $95,723 from the U.S. government, $30,000 from the Indiana Department of Commerce's energy policy division, and another $30,000 in matching funds from the state for a methane digester.[8] Although the owners of the dairy control significant assets in the confined dairy industry and Fair Oaks is the largest dairy east of the Mississippi River, this conglomerate can still draw on the public purse to pay for profit-making ventures on its dairy farm.

Another example of state CAFO funding is a dairy owned by the Timothy den Dulk family in Ravenna, Michigan, which received $1 million from the Michigan Public Service Commission for a meth-ane digester. In 2006, this dairy was reported to have 4,000 cows producing about 155 million pounds of manure annually. Timothy den Dulk's assets included shares in dairy farms that milk approxi-mately 30,000 cows in California, New Mexico, Michigan, Ohio, and Indiana as well as dairy heifer operations with almost 60,000 cows in five other states. Just one of these operations, Quality Milk Sales, Inc., in New Mexico, produced about 350 loads of milk per day with $600,000,000 in yearly sales. Despite these resources, this well-heeled dairy received taxpayer dollars to pay for energy-producing methane digesters that will further offset the operation's costs. In addition, not surprisingly, two den Dulk family members joined with Michael McCloskey, the co-owner of Fair Oaks Dairy, to form the Fair Oaks

Farm Supply Company, which raked in over $900,000 in USDA commodity program subsidies from 2002 through 2006.[9]

ATTRACTING FOREIGN CAFO INVESTORS

Subsidies for CAFOs can also be folded into the structure of unlikely programs. One of these is the federal government's EB-5 investment visa program. Under provisions for immigration to rural areas under EB-5, a foreign resident investor or group of foreign investors who provide at least $500,000 in a new commercial business or a restructured or expanding business in a rural area in the United States is eligible to jump to the head of the line for a permanent U.S. resident visa ("green card"). This privilege is retained if the investment generates five direct or indirect jobs. The EB-5 program also includes regional centers, which focus on establishing certain types of enterprises.

The EB-5 program has a checkered history with regard to CAFOs. There is no requirement that the EB-5-funded enterprises protect or improve the environment and the public health of the community in which they are located. In addition, EB-5 allows passive investment, which can increase absentee ownership in rural areas.[10] In Iowa, an EB-5 regional center is focused on attracting young farm families from Europe to establish dairy operations on farms of 40 to 80 acres with between 250 and 500 cows—large dairies but not megadairies.[11] In contrast, the Center for Rural Affairs found that the EB-5 regional center in South Dakota focuses on CAFO megadairies funded by passive investment. The center found that the South Dakota EB-5 program had funded at least nine megadairies, with at least 1,700 cows at an estimated cost of $6.8 million per megadairy.[12]

Among the critics of the South Dakota EB-5 program is Bill DuBois, a resident of Marshall, Minnesota, who has pointed out that the influx of EB-5 investment capital has spurred an advance of megadairy factories in South Dakota that threatens small dairy producers and attracts large taxpayer subsidies. DuBois is a member of I-29ers for Quality of Life, which opposes the proliferation of industrialized dairies. The group has found that these big dairies get public subsidies for roads, infrastructure, and other needs. In addition, I-29ers for Quality of Life estimates that the megadairies' manure-handling operations have been underwritten by as much as 90 percent with public money.[13]

AGENCIES BETRAYING THE PUBLIC TRUST

One of the largest indirect subsidies provided to the CAFO industry is the acquiescence of federal, state, and local governments in allowing the industry to shift the costs of controlling waste to surrounding residents and communities in the form of polluted air and water resources and decreased public health. Foot dragging on effective enforcement at the federal level is chronic. The U.S. Environmental Protection Agency (EPA) implemented a revised Clean Water Act regulation for CAFOs in 2003, after being under a court order to do so since 1997. The regulation was successfully challenged by environmental groups in 2005, in part because important information about the nutrient management plan for manure and other CAFO waste could be kept from the public.[14] In response, in 2008 the EPA approved an even weaker regulation that allows large-scale CAFOs to self-certify that they do not intend to discharge pollutants. The public receives no notice of these self-certifications, and there is no required inspection of the CAFO by a regulatory agency. Moreover, a CAFO can have waste spills from many separate sources on the CAFO and recertify each time that its problems have been addressed.[15] The Michigan Department of Environmental Quality's public comments on this EPA regulation correctly observed that the regulation "appears to have been advanced by the lobbyists for the factory farms as a self-serving means of exempting factory farms from regulation, contrary to any other sector regulated by the Clean Water Act."[16]

The EPA has also avoided enforcement against CAFOs for violations of air pollution laws. Pending a study of CAFO air emissions, the EPA has entered into an agreement allowing thousands of large-scale CAFOs to avoid meeting Clean Air Act requirements as well as the requirements of the Comprehensive Environmental Response, Compensation and Liability Act (CERCLA) and the Emergency Planning and Community Right-to-Know Act (EPCRA) for reporting air emissions of hazardous substances. The study is not scheduled for completion until late 2010, and regulations will likely not be reimposed until 2012.[17] Overall, the EPA has ducked effective CAFO regulation, ignoring its legal duty to protect the public health and environment from CAFO pollution.

Congress is aware of the EPA's inaction but has yet to require effective agency regulation. In September 2008, the U.S. House of Representatives Committee on Energy and Commerce held a hearing on a CAFO report submitted by the Government Accountability Office, an investigative arm of Congress. The report, entitled *Concentrated Animal Feeding Operations: EPA Needs More Information and a Clearly Defined Strategy to Protect Air and Water Quality*, concludes that the EPA has not yet assessed the extent to which CAFO air and water pollution is harming human health and the environment because the agency has failed to obtain key data on the amount of pollutants that CAFOs are discharging. Neither the EPA nor the USDA could provide reliable, comprehensive data on the number, location, and size of CAFOs that have been issued permits and the amount of discharges released.[18]

At the state level, the CAFO industry has successfully lobbied many state legislatures to preempt local planning and public health regulations that could limit the concentration, size, and siting of CAFOs, moving the control of zoning from counties to the state level. But then these states fail to enforce the pollution control laws and leave local residents waiting days for the agencies to respond to complaints of CAFO air and water pollution. Untimely investigation and ineffective monitoring of CAFO pollution gives many state agencies the cover to contend that they have no evidence of CAFO violations.

With few exceptions, state environmental regulators allow CAFOs to repeatedly violate water and air pollution regulations with nothing more than a slap on the hand. Regulatory foot dragging is the norm, and action rarely happens unless a life-threatening situation arises or a citizens' group tries to enforce state and federal laws. For example, in June 2008, several families living near the Excel megadairy in northwest Minnesota had to flee as their homes were enveloped with toxic levels of hydrogen sulfide emitted from the dairy's waste lagoon. State health officials had recommended that residents leave because the hydrogen sulfide concentration levels exceeded 200 times the state air quality standard. But this evacuation need never have happened. The state attorney general and the Minnesota Pollution Control Agency, in announcing that they were jointly suing the dairy, also indicated that the Excel Dairy had repeatedly violated state air quality standards, environmental protection laws, and feedlot operating permits.[19] Local residents had complained for years that the dairy's fumes were causing headaches and nausea. Effective state monitoring and strict, swift enforcement of regulations—rather than a "polluter is always right" policy—could have put Excel Dairy on notice that it could not impose the burden of its toxic liability on the local community. But even more outrageous, months after the evacuation of residents and a declaration by the Minnesota state toxicologist that hydrogen sulfide levels in homes near the megadairy were still dangerously high, the Minnesota Pollution Control Agency continued to negotiate pollution control measures with the megadairy owner. Rather than clamp down and close the polluting dairy, state officials told local residents it was up to them to decide whether to abandon their homes as negotiation over cleanup of manure basins dragged into 2009.[20]

Many states actually facilitate CAFO proliferation. For years, North Carolina has recognized that the thousands of open waste lagoons and the effluent sprayfields of large-scale hog CAFOs in the state impose significant burdens on the state's public health and its environment. The state has had a moratorium on the establishment of new hog CAFOs since 1997. But the moratorium was not imposed until North Carolina became the second-largest hog producer in the country, with over 10 million hogs in the eastern part of the state. The moratorium applies only to new hog CAFOs. Existing CAFOs continue to use inadequate waste-handling systems, to rebuild them, and to even expand existing operations with substandard waste-handling systems.

In 2000, the state of North Carolina entered into an agreement with Smithfield Foods, the world's largest pork processor, which contracts with hundreds of hog CAFOs. Under the agreement, over $17.1 million was expended for research on alternatives to the hog waste lagoons and sprayfields that cover the state's coastal plain. In 2006, North Carolina State University researchers released a report identifying five alternative waste-handling systems that could reduce ammonia emissions and pathogens from hog CAFOs and significantly decrease public health and environmental risks. These alternative technologies were more expensive than the open cesspits and sprayfields, but estimates were that the hog industry in the state would shrink only about 12 percent if it paid to adopt the technology—a reasonable adjustment to protect the state's public health and environment.

Smithfield and the hog CAFO industry, however, simply said no to these alternatives. Instead, in 2007, the state legislature adopted a voluntary Lagoon Conversion Program under which the public is to pay polluting CAFOs up to 90 percent of the costs for adopting less-polluting alternatives to open waste cesspits and open-air spraying of hog waste.[21]

So far, the message from federal and state legislatures and regulatory agencies to sustainable farmers and ranchers, rural residents, and communities is clear. CAFOs can violate environmental laws with impunity and routinely impose public health hazards on surrounding populations, while neighboring residents and communities must bear the costs of coping with the pollution or pony up with the rest of us to pay the polluters, even for measures that actually increase the CAFO fecal flood. Meanwhile, the factory farm sector trumpets its "economic efficiency" while collecting billions of dollars in public subsidies at all levels of government, and every year livestock and poultry CAFOs grow larger and more concentrated. Sustainable farmers and ranchers are left to compete on an uneven playing field against some of the world's largest corporations and their allies.

SLICED AND DICED

The Labor You Eat

CHRISTOPHER D. COOK

AMERICA'S SUPPOSEDLY "CHEAP" MEAT SUPPLY *relies on cheap labor—but the costs to this largely immigrant workforce are astronomical. With declining union power, real wages have shrunk and workers are routinely denied bathroom breaks and health care. Employees are commonly wounded on high-speed assembly lines, suffering carpal tunnel and other disabling injuries. Long isolated, workers are taking these food sweatshops to court and joining with unions and community groups to resist the "killing line."*

❖

From the sprawling parking lot at the end of a road named Harms Way (named, presumably, for company cofounder Dennis Harms), the Premium Standard Foods plant, a subsidiary of Smithfield Foods, in Milan, Missouri, has an immaculate, information-age look. At the closely guarded entrance checkpoint, workers punch in by slipping their hands into a fingerprint identification machine. Next to the front door, a sign reads: ON THE JOB SAFETY BEGINS HERE.

Mexican men in cowboy hats stream through the checkpoint as if they're crossing another border. In the parking lot, a school bus idles in the biting January cold, slowly filling with workers awaiting their nightly ride home to disheveled company housing. Few of the men speak much English, but many, their arms bandaged and in slings, speak the universal language of pain.

Behind the factory's polished front, assembly lines churn 7,100 pigs into packaged product each day. It's not America's biggest meatpacking plant, but it is brutally efficient. José, a rib cutter, works with three others slicing rib plates into 14,200 pieces a day—3,550 cuts per person. "It's very tough," he says. "We usually take about three seconds for each rib, sometimes ten seconds if there's a lot of fat."[1]

The workers here, mostly impoverished transplants from Mexico and elsewhere, don't last much longer than the pigs. "Every week there are new workers, and every week others leave," says José. "In two weeks, I have seen about two hundred people leave." They leave, says José, because the company keeps speeding up the assembly line. To protect its narrow profit margins, the firm pushes the line to—and often beyond—the human breaking point.

There's little time for bathroom breaks. "When they were giving us the orientations, they told us to use the bathroom before work because they would not give us permission to go during work," says José. "We have four people working, and if one went to the bathroom, we would only have three to do the same amount of work. We would be making the others work even harder."

Emma, a packing line worker from El Paso, says she was denied bathroom trips even when she had morning sickness. Her supervisor told her to vomit in the garbage can next to the assembly line, she claims.

There is also little time for medical care. Sergio Rivera felt stabs of pain in his first few days at Premium. "My hand hurt, I went to the nurse, and she put me back on the line in ten minutes," he says. Local doctor Shane Bankus, a chiropractor in Milan, about a mile away from the Premium plant, says such treatment is the norm. The injured meat factory workers he sees "have got to get back to work, no matter how badly it hurts, which reaggravates it," says Bankus. Adding to the injuries, he says, most of the migrant workers "don't get any health insurance, because they want to send money home." José feels pulses of pain when he closes his fist. But when asked if he visits the company doctor, José says, "No, because the company told us if we went to the company doctor we would have to pay. None of the migrants have health insurance. It costs too much money."

Welcome to the rural jungle—not unlike Upton Sinclair's bleak depiction a century ago—where a new generation of immigrant meat packers toil in a grim, bloody world far away from sanitized supermarket aisles. It is a world fraught with peril: nearly 20 percent of meatpacking workers—often uninsured and frequently undocumented—suffer injuries requiring medical attention. While factories are cleaner and safer today, "it's still a deadly and dangerous industry," says Robyn Robbins, assistant director of the Occupational Safety and Health Office of the United Food and Commercial Workers International Union.

With meat consumption near record levels—the United States produced 91.2 billion pounds of red meat and poultry in 2007, roughly 230 pounds for every American consumer[2]—the meatpacking industry maintains brutal conditions by importing economically desperate immigrant workers. Turnover is higher than ever—up to 200 percent in some plants—because of grueling conditions and the precarious employment of undocumented workers.

In this high-volume, low-profit-margin industry, faster lines are the primary path to profits, explains anthropologist Mark Grey, who has studied meatpacking communities for more than a decade. "That's how they make money—jamming lots and lots of animals through the plant—and that's where your cumulative trauma problems come in." Nearly 12 percent of meat packers succumb to cumulative trauma injuries, such as carpal tunnel and tendonitis, according to the Bureau of Labor Statistics. This is thirty-seven times the average rate for all industries.

In a macabre, medieval scene, workers hack frantically at fast-moving carcasses while standing in pools of blood, fat, and chunks of abscess. Their knives, dulled from stabbing meat every three seconds or so, sometimes slice into the wrong piece of flesh—their coworker just a couple of feet away. Back injuries are common from slipping on the greasy floors. But the biggest risk is the mundane: the steady, ceaseless cutting—of heads, necks, knuckles, legs, organs, stomachs. Cutting a mind-numbing train of animal parts flying down the line at dizzying speeds: thousands of cuts per day, about three seconds per piece of meat.

Meatpacking was once a solid, if gritty, step toward the American middle-class dream. Before the union upheaval of the mid-1980s—symbolized by labor's crushing defeat in the Hormel meat packers' strike—unionized workers reported earning upward of $30,000 in a year.[3] In the 1970s, packing firms relocated to the rural High Plains, moving slaughterhouses closer to feedlots and escaping the unions and higher wages of Chicago, Kansas City, and other midwestern cities, according to historian Jimmy M. Skaggs.[4] By the late 1980s, immigrant refugees—many of them "products of failed American foreign policy maneuvers and plundered economies"[5]—were flocking to rural midwestern packing towns for dangerous, low-paid work that most white Americans simply won't do.

Now the predominantly nonunion industry cycles through a constant supply of destitute migrants for whom $6 to $9 an hour seems like a godsend. Meat packers' real wages have declined by $5.74 per hour since 1981, according to Bureau of Labor Statistics data using 1998 dollars. Yet the people keep coming, and the conditions and turnover persist, largely the result of weakened unions and a virtually limitless reserve supply of immigrant laborers.

By the 1990s, it had become common industry practice to import workers through border-state labor recruiters who, for a fee, deliver busloads of Mexicans and Central American immigrants to plants throughout the Midwest, according to Mark Grey, professor of anthropology at the University of Northern Iowa and director of the Iowa Center of Immigrant Leadership and Integration Reform. Many are undocumented and are prey to all manner of workplace abuse and widespread racist scapegoating. In 1998 the U.S. General Accounting Office found that 25 percent of meatpacking workers in Nebraska and Iowa are undocumented immigrants.[6] The situation is similar in poultry: A 1998 survey by the U.S. Department of Labor showed that 30 percent of chicken processors conduct long-distance recruitment. National Chicken Council vice president Bill Roenigk confirms that about 50 percent of the industry's 245,000 workers are immigrants.

A BLUR OF CHICKENS

Even speedier than the slaughtered pig or cow, the dead chicken may be the fastest animal in North America. From "catchers," to "hangers," to "evisc" (short for evisceration), the processing of roughly 9 billion chickens each year—meeting increased demands for cheap, versatile meals and slimmer hips—rests on low wages and treacherous speed. The typical poultry factory can, in a single eight-hour shift, turn 144,000 birds into packages of "RTC" ("ready to cook") chicken.

Amid clouds of ammonia and fecal matter carrying salmonella and other harmful bacteria, immigrant chicken catchers wade into 100-degree holding pens bustling with frantic, desperate birds. Dodging sharp beaks and claws, the catchers grasp the birds by their feet—generally snaring about 8,000 chickens a day—and hurl them into cages destined for the processing plant. Many catchers fall prey to cuts, eye infections, and respiratory ailments—not to mention enduring the constant urination of terrified chickens. At the factory, "hangers" attach the feet of up to 50 birds a minute (more than 20,000 a day) into metal shackles so that a razor-sharp wire just down the line can lop off the dangling heads efficiently. Rotator cuff and other repetitive motion injuries are widespread among hangers.[7]

After being scalded in huge vats of hot water to enable rapid plucking, the birds blast down the line to the evisceration section. Here, while most plants now gut chickens by machine, some workers perform "evisc" by hand—twisting and pulling the innards from 35 or more chickens a minute. In some plants, workers make up to 100 evisceration cuts a minute. Farther down the line, workers in "debone" stand shoulder-to-shoulder, slicing and chopping their way through joints, tendons, and tough gristle to produce the most popular chicken part on the market—boneless chicken breasts. The process here "slows" to 20 or 30 hard twisting motions a minute. Scissors and knives quickly dull, and workers routinely lacerate themselves or their neighbors when blades slip off the slimy carcasses. Disabling carpal tunnel syndrome and other repetitive stress disorders are common.

As annual chicken consumption has soared from 40 pounds per person in 1970 to 75 pounds today, the government has allowed industry to crank up assembly line speeds. According to research by attorney Marc Linder, corroborated by government documents, the poultry industry lobbied President Reagan's USDA to increase factory line speeds from an already blinding 70 birds per minute to today's astounding rate of 91 per minute. (The mere fact that the U.S. Department of Agriculture sets line speeds should be disconcerting, as the agency's mission is to spur food production, not to protect workers' safety.)

ers. Students and other concerned citizens boycott shoe and clothing companies whose products come from sweatshops—but what about the sweatshops that produce our food?

Despite astronomical injury rates that have generally increased along with faster lines, government agencies have made no effort to reduce factory speed limits. For profit-minded corporations with low profit margins, there is little economic incentive to slow the disassembly process—unless companies decide it is worth it to reduce injuries and workers' compensation costs, and to retain a stable workforce. But there has been no evidence of such forward thinking.

The food industry, including the farm labor sector, profits not only from cheap, highly exploited labor, but also from the remarkably modest expectations of immigrant workers who are accustomed to the lowest of wages, the toughest work, and spare living conditions. It may sound degrading or cliché, but what many immigrant workers demand—when they demand anything at all—is quite basic and humble by American standards. As José, the rib cutter for Premium Standard Foods put it: "If they paid a little more money and ran the line a little slower, the people wouldn't leave. I wouldn't leave."

But anthropologist Mark Grey and other critics, including the United Food and Commercial Workers, contend that meatpacking firms prefer short-term, destabilized workers so they can cut injury costs and beat back union organizing efforts. A migrant and immigrant workforce, says Grey, also enables companies to "pass along a lot of costs," such as unemployment and disability payments, to the workers' home country.

"Instead of dealing with the wages, working conditions, and injury rates, [meatpacking firms] are just trying to find new ways to cycle through new workers," says Grey. "Ultimately, their concern is not about a stable workforce but maintaining a transient workforce." And migrant they are. José the rib cutter, like Sergio Rivera, planned to leave in search of better work.

DIET FOR A HOT PLANET

Livestock and Climate Change

ANNA LAPPÉ

FROM THE ENERGY-INTENSIVE *production of feed to the razing of rainforests for cropland, animal food production is heating up the planet. According to the United Nations Food and Agriculture Organization (FAO), the livestock industry accounts for 18 percent of the human-caused climate change effect. This is more than the total emissions of the entire global transportation sector combined. It's time we look at the climate crisis on our plates.*

❖

In 1971, my mother, Frances Moore Lappé, hit on a powerful insight. Despite Malthusian predictions of imminent global famine, the planet was producing—and still produces—more than enough food to feed the world and its growing population. Hunger, she argued, is caused not by a scarcity of food, but by a scarcity of democracy. For my mother, one of the most powerful symbols of that lack of democracy was the squandering of abundance by taking land fit for growing food for humans and converting it into land used for raising feed for livestock. She summarized these findings in her seminal book *Diet for a Small Planet*, arguing for a plant-based food system that optimizes nature's abundance.[1]

Since *Diet for a Small Planet* was first published in 1971, we've seen the expansion of this feedlot system throughout the United States and overseas. Today, CAFOs in the United States produce more than half of our food animals and 65 percent of the animal waste.[2] The largest U.S. meat companies, Tyson and Smithfield among them, are moving overseas, expanding into China, Poland, Romania, and other emerging markets.[3] While we've long been aware of the environmental and human toll of this method of livestock production, we now know there's a mammoth climate change toll as well.

Scientific consensus has confirmed that increasing levels of human-caused releases of greenhouse gases in the atmosphere are trapping more and more heat, leading not just to global warming, but to global climate chaos: more extremes of droughts and floods; more weather-related disasters, including tornados and hurricanes. When asked to picture the climate-change perpetrators, many would still conjure images of industrial smokestacks or oil-thirsty jet planes before they'd picture pork chops, even though livestock production accounts for 18 percent of the human-caused climate change effect.[4] That's more than the emissions from the global transportation sector, including all planes, trains, and automobiles.

Livestock production contributes not just to the tally of carbon dioxide, but also to other more potent greenhouse gases, including methane and nitrous oxide, which pack, respectively, 23 and 296 times the global warming punch of carbon dioxide.[5] And although the livestock sector is responsible for just 9 percent of human-made carbon dioxide emissions, it is associated with 37 percent of methane emissions and 65 percent of nitrous oxide emissions.[6]

These emissions become exponentially more important in light of the sheer number of domestic livestock being raised on the planet. In 1965, 8 billion livestock animals were alive at any given moment, and 10 billion were slaughtered every year. Today, thanks in part to CAFOs that have spurred faster growth and shorter life spans, 20 billion livestock animals are alive at any one time, and more than 56 billion are slaughtered annually.[7] If global predictions are accurate, and if livestock production doubles by 2050, we could have ten times as many livestock animals roaming the planet as we do humans. (Keep in mind, these figures don't even include all the aquatic animals we eat too.)

This livestock boom has been driven, in part, by the growing demand for a Western meat-based diet. Until as recently as the 1970s, diets with significant calories from meat and dairy were reserved for the industrialized world. But between 1970 and 2002, per capita meat consumption in developing countries almost tripled, from 25 pounds to 64 pounds per person a year.[8] In the past decade alone, per capita meat consumption in China has doubled.[9] (While this is extraordinary growth, developing countries' 64 pounds doesn't hold a candle to the 222 pounds per capita consumed in the United States.)[10] If these trends hold, the United Nations estimates that global meat production will more than double from 229 million tons in 2000 to 465 million tons in 2050.[11] So consider the climate change consequences of the livestock industry detailed here—then double them.

Where do these impacts come from? Let's begin at the beginning, with the basics of ruminant digestion. Globally, a significant segment of methane emissions from livestock production comes from the enteric fermentation of ruminants. (The United Nations estimates the total emissions at 86 million metric tons annually, equivalent to the total emissions of Sweden and Norway combined.) Ruminants, such as cattle, buffalo, sheep, and goats, process their feed through microbial, or "enteric" fermentation in their rumen. This fermentation produces methane that is released by the animals, mainly through their noses and, to a lesser degree, their tailpipes. While this process is what allows ruminants to digest fibrous grasses that we humans cannot, it adds to livestock's extraordinary climate change toll.

In addition, in confined feedlots, livestock produce such volumes of manure that the waste can't be cycled back through the system as fertilizer. There's simply too much of it. Many CAFOs are also often geographically distant from feed production anyway, further complicating the ability to cycle waste back onto fields of feed. Instead, manure becomes greenhouse gas–emitting waste, stored as liquid or slurry in lagoons, ponds, tanks, or pits. Along with their noxious fumes and health impacts, these lagoons break down waste with bacteria, producing the unfortunate by-products of methane and other gases, including ammonia and hydrogen sulfide. With the increasing number of CAFOs, and the size of their animal populations, the manure management crisis is only getting worse. Today, the United States has the dubious honor of being the leading producer of methane emissions from liquid manure lagoons, mainly from our large-scale pig operations.[12] Over the past fifteen years, methane emissions from pig and dairy manure in the United States increased by 37 percent and 50 percent, respectively.[13]

FEED CROPS AND THE FERTILIZER FACTOR

Thirty-three percent of the planet's arable land is dedicated to growing feed crops, which are energy-intensive to raise.[14] Indeed, half of all the energy used in intensive animal production is used in the production of feed, from the manufacturing of fertilizers to the planting, harvesting, processing, and transportation of the feed.[15] In addition, feed crops like corn are a significant source of nitrous oxide emissions in part because of the widespread overuse of synthetic fertilizer. In the United States and Canada, half of all fertilizer is used on feed crops.[16] In the United Kingdom, the total is nearly 70 percent.[17] When nitrogen fertilizer is applied to soils, it breaks down under anaerobic conditions, releasing nitrous oxide, a potent greenhouse gas. These emissions are all the more stunning when you learn how much fertilizer goes to waste: in the United States, as much as half of all nitrogen fertilizer applied on cornfields is lost through volatization, leaching, and runoff.[18]

Fertilizer production itself is extremely energy-intensive. Though nitrogen gas is prevalent in the atmosphere, it takes significant energy to bind it into usable nitrogen fertilizer. In China, the world's largest producer and consumer of grain, synthetic nitrogen fertilizer is produced by coal-fired power plants. Every year, fertilizer production there releases 14.3 million tons of carbon dioxide—a quarter of the world's total emissions from fertilizer production.[19]

Fertilizers have an additional toll. Just as most feed is produced far from where the crops are consumed, fertilizer inputs are often produced or mined far from where they're applied. The United States, for instance, is now a net importer of fertilizer inputs, with 62 percent of our nitrogen and 88 percent of potash coming from imports in 2006.[20] More than half our imports in 2007 came from just four countries: Canada, Russia, Belarus, and Morocco.[21]

Keep in mind another inherent inefficiency of feedlot meat. Feedlot cattle need as much as 16 pounds of grain and soy to give us 1 pound of meat—more than triple the needed feed for poultry. Journalist Paul Roberts argues that the "true" conversion ratio is even higher: factor in the inedible parts of the cow, such as bones and hide, he says, and it "takes a full 20 pounds of grain to make a single pound of beef," compared with 3.5 pounds for chickens and 7.3 pounds for pigs.[22]

TRANSPORTATION IMPACTS

CAFOs are also responsible for the emissions from transporting not only feed to factory farms, but also the live animals to feedlots, then to slaughter, then the meat to the distribution centers and on to the stores to sell it to us consumers: a circuitous path indeed. And we're schlepping a lot of it. In 2007, the United States exported 1.4 billion pounds of beef and veal (5.4 percent of our total production)[23] and imported 3.1 billion pounds of the same.[24] Globally, the international trade in meat is accelerating. Take Brazil, for example. As recently as the late 1990s, Brazil wasn't even on the map as a major global meat exporter. Today, the country is among the world's largest exporters[25] and is second only to the United States in beef and veal production.[26]

LAND USE CHANGES:
DEFORESTATION AND COMPACTION

Another significant climate change impact comes from pressures on land from livestock, both for feed production and for grazing, with emissions caused by deforestation, overgrazing, compaction, and erosion. Poorly managed, compacted soils have been found to increase nitrous oxide emissions.[27] In fact, global livestock production is the single largest user of land on the planet.[28] According to the Intergovernmental Panel on Climate Change, 17.4 percent of the world's total greenhouse gas emissions derive from land use changes, including tearing down forests to make way for livestock grazing and feed production.[29] As I mentioned earlier, 33 percent of arable land is dedicated to raising feed crops,[30] and an additional 26 percent of the ice-free terrestrial surface of the planet is used for grazing.[31] In the Amazon alone, 70 percent of previously forested land has been transformed into pasture; much of the rest is now in feed crops.[32] By cutting down forests to make space for livestock and their feed, we are removing valuable carbon sinks that would otherwise help mitigate global carbon emissions.

As awareness of the significant role of livestock in emissions grows, the debate heats up about whether technological fixes can solve the problem—or whether we need deeper changes in eating and farming habits. To curb emissions, the livestock industry is promoting hasty remedies, ones that don't fundamentally change the system. Methane digesters on manure lagoons, for instance, can capture some of the gases, which can then be used to generate heat and electricity. Others in the livestock sector are tinkering with low-methane feeds,[33] "flatulence inoculations,"[34] and creative breeding programs.

But environmentalists are concerned that government subsidies for these so-called fixes actually incentivize CAFOs, when the truly sustainable solution requires shifting away from this production system entirely. And while one or more of these technological responses might somewhat reduce livestock emissions, we already know that we need a drastic reduction from the sector even to maintain emissions at current levels. This level of reduction simply cannot be achieved with mere tinkering. We need to simultaneously limit the growth of livestock production and shift the production we engage in toward sustainable approaches, including getting ruminants like cattle back to the land eating the grass they evolved on.

PUTTING THE COWS OUT TO PASTURE

While certainly much more research is needed to understand the complexity of the life cycles of livestock, we know some things for sure. Well-managed cattle on pasture can decrease emissions from soil degradation as well as from the reduced need for synthetic fertilizers. Livestock raised on pasture generate fewer fossil fuel emissions, because the animals themselves take care of the fertilizing and harvesting of most of their feed. And while some studies have shown that cows eating grass can belch more than cows eating grain, other studies have found that cattle rotated through paddocks with fresh, green grasses can produce up to 20 percent less methane than those that are not regularly rotated.[35] What's more, studies indicate that grass-lands—especially richly fertilized grasslands—can sequester carbon quantities comparable to those of forested lands.[36] Research is needed to further examine how pasture-based systems could generate less methane and promote the carbon sequestration potential of grazing lands.[37]

While we need more research, we don't need to wait for greater scientific consensus. We already know the fundamentals of how to raise animals with less of an environmental toll, and we already know the seriousness of the climate change impact of industrial production. We also know that livestock can have a vital place in sustainable food systems, as they do in small-scale farms, particularly in the global South, where livestock can provide a critical source of muscle, milk, and manure for fertilizer. Simple technologies used on small-scale farms can also convert manure into biogas, a cost-effective way to power homes and fuel stoves and decrease the demand on forests for firewood. While livestock can play a part of holistic farming systems, current trends of expanding large-scale production are unfortunately taking us in the opposite direction, away from sustainability.

PERSONAL RESPONSIBILITY, MOVING FORWARD

By eschewing or significantly reducing our meat consumption, we're helping to reduce emissions from livestock production. In one study of American diets, researchers Gidon Eshel and Pamela Martin found that reducing calories from animal sources by just 20 percent, and replacing them with vegetarian options, was the carbon-saving equiv-alent of a typical American trading in a gas-guzzling American car for a Prius.[38] For those of us who choose not to give up meat entirely, we can certainly cut back—a move that can significantly lower our ecological foodprint. In one analysis comparing energy used in meat production versus legumes, for instance, Claude Aubert, from the Agricultural Engineers' College of Higher Education, estimated that beef production contributes twenty to thirty times more to climate change than the production of the same amount of protein in the form of legumes.[39]

If we choose to consume meat and dairy, we can make the choice to support grass-fed and organic systems, which can have much lower emissions than feedlot production. Consider, for instance, that raising organic corn can require one-third less energy per acre so, by one estimate, we could save 64 gallons of fossil fuel per acre of corn simply by switching to organic production. In the case of organic meat production, this would translate into big energy savings.[40] (Life cycle analyses comparing grass-fed and conventional livestock systems to date have come to varied conclusions about the precise greenhouse gas savings of organic or pasture-based systems versus CAFOs, in part because of which aspects of production are included—or excluded—from analysis.)

In 1971, my mother was considered a heretic for writing *Diet for a Small Planet*, and daring to suggest that we humans could survive, indeed thrive, without meat. She told me that she remembers the National Cattlemen's Beef Association even hired a team of nutritionists to prove her vegetarian recipes inedible. Despite these protestations, her nutritional argument—that we can get more than enough protein from plant-based sources—turned out to be solid guidance for our health and for the environment. Along with the ecological and social costs of feedlot meat and dairy that my mother enumerated, we now know there is another cost as well: the climate. Today, choosing to eat less, or no, feedlot meat and dairy is not just a diet for a small planet, it's a diet for one that's getting hotter, too.

Part Six

TECHNOLOGICAL TAKEOVER

INTRODUCTION

From Farms to High-Tech

Technologies are overtaking CAFO production at nearly every level. Scientists are continually attempting to drive the system faster: developing drugs to battle diseases from stress and overcrowding; breeding and genetically engineering animals that can be grown and processed in less time and more passively tolerate artificial confinement; eliminating human labor from all aspects of production.

The predicament we face in applying industrial remedies to the challenges of agriculture is that so often we end up with a "technofix": a technological approach that seems to solve one problem but ultimately creates a cascading effect of unforeseen consequences. One oft-cited example is the Green Revolution, championed in the latter half of the twentieth century to increase global grain yields through plant breeding and the aggressive use of agrochemical fertilizers and pesticides and vast water and energy resources. Although the yields and advances of the Green Revolution were remarkable at the time, the unanticipated problems that this industrial farming approach created in terms of soil erosion, environmental contamination, biodiversity loss, and aquifer depletion have created a false sense of continual progress. In the short term, humanity averted large-scale famine and our population expanded, but arguably at extreme environmental, social, and economic costs.

Most technological approaches fail to address the Achilles heel of the CAFO industry: that of massive scale. When something goes wrong in a CAFO—the outbreak of a new disease or pathogen, for example—it can race through a population very quickly. In massive processing facilities comingling products such as ground meats or milk from widespread sources, pathogens can be distributed throughout the human food supply nearly as quickly. Relying on expensive technological solutions in the name of food safety or efficiency also often leads to greater concentrations of animals to pay for them. "Every time the industry comes up with a solution to a problem," writes animal behaviorist Dr. Temple Grandin, "the solution ends up costing so much to implement that the industry has to intensify production—raise more pigs—to remain afloat."[1]

Technologies geared to boost production eventually hurt small- and medium-size producers by flooding the market with cheap products. The only producers able to survive a low-margin market are those that can afford to spread their fixed costs around very substantial "animal units."

From the cloning of farm animals for food, fiber, and pharmaceutical production, to the genetic engineering of farmed fish and livestock, to the use of radioactive materials and other techniques to render unhealthy food "safe," the industry and its research arms are attempting to keep the CAFO system alive at all costs. Many of these techniques remain untested for long-term consequences. Instead, concerned citizens as well as eaters are expected to have faith in this brave new technology-intensive food system. The primary assumption is that industrial production offers the only real and practical solution for modern food needs given population demands.

Despite mixed rulings from the U.S. Department of Agriculture and the Food and Drug Administration on the safety of cloning technologies, foods from genetically cloned animals are already entering the marketplace: through rendered downer animals, the milk supply, the sale of semen from cattle cloning companies, the production of drugs for human use, and other avenues. Whether we like them or not, whether we want them or not, whether they've been properly tested or not, cloned animals are entering the food chain. Once introduced in the broader environment, cloned foods will become increasingly difficult to isolate from the food supply and from the farming world.

In 2008, the vegetarian activist group People for the Ethical Treatment of Animals (PETA) offered a $1 million reward for the commercial production of "in vitro" chicken. The contest winner must produce—by June 30, 2012—a faux meat that tastes indistinguishable from chicken. It must be approved by all requisite health agencies and be manufactured in significant quantities to be sold in at least ten states. But the biggest challenge of all? The flesh will be "vat meat," produced in a laboratory rather than from a living, breathing chicken.

Among PETA's largely vegetarian membership, the announcement was highly controversial. But its link to the organization's mission was clear. More than 40 billion chickens, pigs, cows, and fish are raised and slaughtered in the United States each year for food, many in horrific ways. Could in vitro meat production alleviate tremendous suffering? While this "high concept" idea might seem borrowed from a science fiction movie, "specialized tissue engineering" is, in fact, a serious pursuit and could one day contribute synthesized animal products to the food supply. In 2008, an international symposium was held in Norway to report on the progress being made to fabricate muscle tissue on an industrial scale. Does this sound appetizing or desirable?

We don't have to look far to see the future of industrial animal production. Featherless chickens that don't need plucking, with genetically shortened beaks so they can't angrily peck away at a neighbor. Or, eventually, extra-plump, omega-3-rich chicken breasts grown in petri dishes requiring no animals at all.

High-tech factory methods aren't the only way to raise animals. By the same token, alternative approaches don't have to be void of technology or innovation. The alternative to the CAFO system, however, does require more hands-on livestock handling, along with careful observation of how new technologies influence animal behavior and impact the broader environment. Management must be involved. Even the best staff training can be overturned by managers who are desensitized to suffering or overly focused on profitability and efficiency. A marriage of appropriate technology, proper scale, healthy production, and real animal welfare standards is not only possible but is clearly necessary to restore balance to a rapidly industrializing food system.

ANTIBIOTIC DRUG ABUSE

CAFOs Are Squandering Vital Human Medicines

LEO HORRIGAN, JAY GRAHAM, AND SHAWN MCKENZIE

ANTIBIOTICS HAVE BEEN CALLED *the "health care miracle of the last 500 years." However, the rampant use of antibiotics as growth promoters in industrial food animal production has put this health care miracle at risk. In North Carolina alone, the estimated volume of antibiotics used to make food animals grow faster exceeds all U.S. use of antibiotics for human medicine. The result is an ever-increasing prevalence of antibiotic-resistant strains of disease-causing organisms that erode the effectiveness of antibiotics in curing disease in humans.*

❖

Alexander Fleming, the scientist who discovered penicillin in 1928, later predicted that inappropriate use of such an antibiotic could lead to the development of resistance by the disease-causing organisms. "The time may come," Fleming said, "when penicillin can be bought by anyone in the shops. Then there is the danger that the ignorant man may easily underdose himself and, by exposing his disease-causing organisms to nonlethal quantities of the drug, make them resistant."[1] Even in the early years of the antibiotic age, some scientists understood that antimicrobials (a broader term than antibiotics that includes antivirals and antifungals in both natural and synthetic forms) are a generally irreplaceable resource for humankind—in fact, one that could be squandered if used indiscriminately or unwisely.

Antibiotics serve as a critical defense in the fight against numerous infectious organisms that can cause widespread disease and death in humans. The methods that now predominate in industrial food animal production (IFAP)—applying constant "subtherapeutic"[2] doses of antibiotics to the billions of food animals produced each year—facilitate the rapid emergence of antibiotic-resistant strains of disease-causing organisms (e.g., bacteria, often referred to as microbes or pathogens) and compromise the ability of medicine to treat disease. Such inappropriate practices must end.

THE RISE OF ANTIBIOTIC THERAPY

The discovery of antibiotics is considered to be among the most important milestones in the history of the public health field. Penicillin, the first antibiotic developed as a medicine, was once hailed as a "miracle drug" because it was so effective in fighting diseases that had long plagued humanity. Antibiotics have been such a successful cure for many infectious diseases that today it is difficult to imagine that in 1900 the three leading causes of death in the United States were pneumonia, tuberculosis (TB), and diarrheal diseases—and that these diseases caused more than 30 percent of all deaths.[3] In fact, in the first decade of the twentieth century, more than 40 percent of all deaths among people ages five to forty-four were caused by infectious diseases, with tuberculosis accounting for more than 25 percent.[4]

Antibiotics became widely available in the 1940s, and by the 1970s only 3 percent of people in these age groups were dying from infectious diseases, owing in large part to effective antibiotic therapy.[5] The World Health Organization (WHO) has referred to the existence and continued effectiveness of antibiotics as the "health care miracle of the last 500 years."[6]

ANTIBIOTIC USE IN INDUSTRIAL FOOD ANIMAL PRODUCTION

No doubt Alexander Fleming would be incensed to discover the methods used today in industrial food animal production. Giving antibiotics to animals in low doses has been found to accelerate growth by making the conversion of feed to weight gain more efficient. As a result, antibiotics are used routinely and on a massive scale in IFAP. In North Carolina alone, the volume of antibiotics used as a feed supplement has been estimated to exceed all U.S. antibiotic use in human medicine.[7] These practices have serious consequences. In addition to productivity changes, using antibiotics at subtherapeutic levels in IFAP also promotes the rise of *resistant* strains of disease-causing organisms. If antibiotic pressure is sustained, even at low levels, those resistant strains of disease-causing organisms have an edge over non-resistant strains when it comes to reproduction and spread.

Through evolutionary adaptation, disease-causing organisms (e.g., *E. coli*) almost always develop resistance to substances that humans exploit to kill them. In other words, they acquire the ability to thwart the toxicity of medicines designed to control them. The widespread and routine use of antibiotic drugs accelerates this evolutionary process, to the point where the declining effectiveness of antibiotics is now considered a serious public health crisis, expressed in the rising incidence of drug-resistant infections.

Recent studies in the Netherlands,[8] Ontario,[9] and in Iowa[10] found the same strain of methicillin-resistant *Staphylococcus aureus* (MRSA) present in both pigs and the people who regularly tend to those pigs, suggesting the disease was transmitted from animal to human. It has been estimated that MRSA killed more than 18,000 people in U.S. hospitals in 2005,[11] more than died from AIDS. Until recently, MRSA research was mostly focused on health care–associated infections (which have been estimated to account for about 85 percent of MRSA infections),[12] but so-called community-acquired infections—including those associated with agriculture—are beginning to attract more attention.

While discussion of the issue of declining effectiveness of antibiotics often centers on the importance of ensuring the proper use of antibiotics in human medicine, the fact is that 60 to 80 percent of antibiotic use in the United States is accounted for by IFAP's use of antibiotics as growth promoters.[13] A relatively small percentage of antibiotic use in IFAP is to treat sick animals, although the exact percentage is unknown because industry is not required to report these data. Much of what is needed for therapeutic purposes is the direct result of the

IFAP practice of severely crowding large numbers of food animals into small, unsanitary spaces—thereby increasing the chance that diseases will spread through their populations—and feeding animals an unnatural diet (e.g., raising cattle on grains instead of grass). While it has been recognized that crowding, inadequate housing, and unsanitary conditions facilitate the spread of infectious disease in human populations,[14] this knowledge has not been transferred to industrial food animal production.

RESERVOIRS OF RESISTANCE

Exacerbating the problem of using antibiotics for food animal growth promotion is the fact that disease-causing organisms can share genes that encode resistance to antibiotics, helping to spur a rapid evolution toward a resistant form. This gene sharing can even occur across different species. Evidence of shared resistance genes has been detected in fecal bacteria found in consumer meat products.[15]

Moreover, researchers often focus on specific patterns of resistance in selected disease-causing organisms—a "one bug, one drug" definition of the problem.[16] But this definition discounts the fact that it is the *community* of genetic resources—what can be called "reservoirs of resistance"—that determines the rate and propagation of resistance.[17] A reservoir of resistance refers to bacteria, both disease-causing and non-disease-causing, that are resistant to antibiotics. These bacteria can carry the genetic material (resistance genes) that may eventually be transferred to an organism that can cause disease in humans. The disease would then be more difficult to treat because of its antibiotic resistance. The large quantities of antibiotics given to food animals are likely creating a "pressure" that fundamentally alters biotic ecosystems, speeding the spread of resistance with few safeguards separating the animals that host these bacteria from the humans who consume the animals.

From a public health perspective, it clearly makes good sense to remove antibiotics from IFAP practices. When antibiotics are not used in food animal production, resistance in disease-causing organisms tends to decrease significantly.[18]

BENEFITS VERSUS RISKS

Recent studies call into question the assumed economic benefits of using antibiotics in animal feeds. Historically, economic gains from using antibiotics to promote growth have been thought to justify the expense of the drugs. Two large-scale studies—one with poultry and one with swine—found that the economic benefits were minuscule to nonexistent, and that the same financial benefits could instead be achieved by improving cleanliness in animal houses.[19] Even when improvements from growth-promoting antibiotics have been observed, their benefits are completely offset if costs from increased resistance are considered: loss of disease treatment options, increased health care costs, infections that are more severe and persist for longer. These costs are usually "externalized" to the larger society and not "internalized" or captured in the price of the meat.

Industry trade groups argue that using antibiotics in food animal production does not pose a threat to public health.[20] But numerous studies support a strong link between the introduction of antibiotics into animal feeds and an increased prevalence of drug-resistant organisms isolated from food animals. Those resistant strains of disease-causing organisms can pose public health threats through food routes and environmental routes.

In the United States and Europe, antibiotic-resistant disease-causing organisms are highly prevalent in meat and poultry products, including organisms that are resistant to the broad-spectrum antibiotics penicillin, tetracycline, and erythromycin.[21] Animals supplied antibiotics in their feed contain a higher prevalence of multidrug-resistant *E. coli* than animals produced on organic farms without exposure to antibiotics,[22] and the same disparity shows up when one compares the foods produced by these two styles of production.[23]

Waste disposal is the major source of antibiotic-resistant disease-causing organisms entering the environment from IFAP facilities. Each year, confined food animals produce an estimated 335 million tons of waste (dry weight),[24] more than forty times the mass of human biosolids generated by publicly owned treatment works (7.6 million tons in 2005). In contrast to regulation of human biosolids, there are no specific requirements for reducing the concentrations of disease-causing organisms in animal waste before it is disposed of, usually on croplands—even though levels of disease-causing organisms, as well as antibiotic-resistant disease-causing organisms, are often higher than in human feces.[25]

Moreover, resistant *E. coli* and resistance genes have been detected in groundwater sources for drinking water sampled near hog farms in North Carolina, Maryland, and Iowa.[26] Groundwater provides drinking water for more than 97 percent of rural U.S. populations. In addition, antibiotics used in IFAP are regularly found in surface waters at low levels.[27]

Resistant disease-causing organisms can also travel through the air from IFAP facilities. At swine facilities using ventilation systems, resistant disease-causing organisms in the air have been detected as far away as 30 meters upwind and 150 meters downwind.[28]

Farm workers and people living near IFAP facilities are at greatest risk for suffering the adverse effects of antibiotic use in agriculture. Studies have documented their elevated risk of carrying antibiotic-resistant disease-causing organisms.[29]

THE ETHICS OF ANTIBIOTIC USE

The obverse of antibiotic resistance is antibiotic effectiveness, which can be thought of as a resource that might well be finite and nonrenewable. Once a disease-causing organism develops resistance to an antibiotic, it may not be possible to restore its effectiveness. Declining antibiotic effectiveness can be equated with resource extraction.[30] As antibiotics are increasingly understood in this way, their use for nontherapeutic purposes becomes ethically dubious at best. If antibiotic effectiveness can be "exhausted" by nontherapeutic use, can society justify expending a large percentage of this precious resource for the sake of growth promotion in food animals? The very notion of antibiotic effectiveness as a natural resource is a new concept, so it is not surprising that there has been very little public discussion about the ethical implications of depleting this resource for nonessential purposes.

POLICY CHANGE

In 2003, the American Public Health Association (APHA) said that "the emerging scientific consensus is that antibiotics given to food animals contribute to antibiotic resistance transmitted to humans." APHA, the world's largest public health organization, also remarked that "an estimated 25–75 percent of feed antibiotics pass unchanged into manure waste."[31]

For its part, the World Health Organization (WHO) has recommended that "in the absence of a public health safety evaluation, [governments should] terminate or rapidly phase out the use of antimicrobials for growth promotion if they are also used for treatment of humans."[32]

For an industry that has become accustomed to using antibiotics as growth promoters, the idea of stopping this practice might seem daunting. But consider the case of Denmark, which in 1999 banned the use of antibiotics as growth promoters. In 2002, WHO reported that

the termination of antimicrobial growth promoters in Denmark has dramatically reduced the food animal reservoir of enterococci resistant to these growth promoters, and therefore reduced a reservoir of genetic determinants (resistance genes) that encode antimicrobial resistance to several clinically important antimicrobial agents in humans.[33]

WHO also reported that there were no significant differences in the health of the animals or the bottom line of the producers. The European Union has followed suit with a ban on growth promoters that took effect in 2006.

The Pew Commission on Industrial Farm Animal Production recommended that the United States "phase out and ban use of antimicrobials for nontherapeutic (i.e., growth-promoting) use in food animals." It also called for no "new approvals of antimicrobials for nontherapeutic uses in animals," and for investigating those already approved.[34]

THE TRAGEDY OF THE MEDICAL COMMONS

Antibiotics can best be viewed as a part of "the commons"—like air, water, and soil—in the sense that they are derived (in most cases) from naturally occurring substances produced by organisms as a defense against other organisms. The for-profit pharmaceutical companies, however, are largely controlling this particular "commons" as they manufacture antibiotics for various uses, including growth promotion in animal agriculture. A crucial human health benefit is being compromised for the sake of an economic benefit—slightly lower costs in producing meat—and one that might well be illusory.

In a sense, our animal agriculture industry has become a stand-in for the "ignorant man" that Alexander Fleming warned against. The industry is underdosing animals with antibiotics—some of them medically important ones—allowing resistance to develop more rapidly among disease-causing organisms.

Efforts to phase out the use of medically important antibiotics in agriculture are a step in the right direction, but the problem of antibiotic resistance caused by agriculture should be viewed as symptomatic of a larger problem—the unsustainable nature of an industrial model in food animal production. While in the short term, steps can be taken to mitigate the harm done by this practice—such as improved monitoring of antibiotic use and surveillance to track the spread of antibiotic resistance—the long-term solution is to move away from the industrial model entirely.

The misuse of antibiotics is only one of myriad problems that are *inherent* in industrial food animal production, but it is among the problems that present an acute and immediate risk to human health. The issue calls for bold and comprehensive policy change that can be guided by science but driven by an informed public. A failure to act will allow the "ignorant man" to continue to threaten our health.

FRANKEN FOOD

Livestock Cloning and the Quest for Industrial Perfection

REBECCA SPECTOR

CALL IT LIVESTOCK EUGENICS: *the meat industry is cloning geneti-cally "superior" animals for human consumption. Cloning repre-sents a dangerous new level of species manipulation, threatens biodiversity, and increases the susceptibility of homogeneous herds to disease. Despite food safety risks such as hormonal imbalances and added bacterial contamination, the FDA claims that food from cloned animals is safe and has allowed the sale of these products in the food chain without labeling.*

❖

Imagine endless packages of identically marbled prime-grade beef, lined up neatly on your supermarket shelves. Scott Simplot, chair-man of Boise, Idaho–based J.R. Simplot Company, imagines a day when such top-quality cuts are common and even better steaks are possible. "There is nothing like a great, memorable steak," says Simplot, "and we decided that we have to figure out a way to re-create that."[1] The fact that identical replicated steaks would, by virtue of their perpetual uniformity, be neither great nor memorable seems to be lost in Simplot's vision of perfect homogeneity.

The search to create better animals through chemistry doesn't end with Simplot's perfect T-bone. How about milk that's 50 percent higher in protein? Or bacon that's high in healthy omega-3 fatty acids? These are some of the purported goals of biotech companies that want to bring you meat and dairy products from cloned animals, whether you like it or not.

While the biotech industry likes to tout these potential benefits of animal cloning—which, by the way, are still only laboratory experiments—it rarely speaks about the process of cloning and its abhorrent effects on animals, or its potential food safety concerns. It's no wonder why the industry is masking the process. People don't want to know that the perfect steak they are eating comes from a grossly enlarged, possibly deformed, cow that's been pumped up with hormones and antibiotics since birth.

HELLO DOLLY: A TRAGEDY IN THE MAKING

Since a sheep named Dolly made headlines in 1996 when she became the first successfully cloned mammal, a public debate has swirled around the issues and implications of her very existence. Much of that discourse has shed more heat than light on the issue of cloning, with the result being that the public is confused, feels misled, and has become increasingly concerned about what's in its food.

In 2008, the U.S. Food and Drug Administration (FDA) released a report claiming that meat and dairy products from cloned animals are safe to eat, thus opening the gateway for the commercial sale of milk and meat from animal clones.[2] Because the FDA is not requiring that food from cloned animals be labeled, the agency's findings also result in consumers' unknowingly purchasing these novel foods.

Soon after her birth, Dolly became the poster child for biotechnology companies hoping to exploit cloned livestock for commercial production of meat, dairy products, pharmaceuticals, and body parts for xenotransplantation—a process of growing organs in animals and harvesting them for human use. When Ian Wilmut, the British embryologist who cloned Dolly, appeared before Congress, he was hailed as "a latter day Galileo," and the cloning was likened to Newton's discovery of gravity.

Ignored in the hype and hoopla over Dolly was the appallingly high failure rate inherent in all animal cloning. Cloning failures stem from frequent spontaneous abortions of cloned fetuses, the massive deformities in many clones, and the premature death and other health problems suffered by many clones that survive gestation. In fact, Dolly herself succumbed to a progressive lung disease called ovine pulmonary adenocarcinoma. She was euthanized in 2003, at the age of six—approximately midway through her expected life span.[3] Oddly enough, sheep were the only species of cloned animals that the FDA declined to approve for use in food, ostensibly because the agency had "insufficient information" on the health status of cloned sheep other than poor Dolly.

Still, companies wishing to profit from cloned livestock have convinced the FDA that foods derived from clones are safe to consume—and the FDA is allowing these novel food products on the market without any long-term testing or labeling. According to its 2008 report, the FDA considers that edible products derived from adult or healthy juvenile clones "pose no additional food consumption risks" when compared with conventional counterparts.[4] This finding however, is prevaricated by the recognition that cloned animals tend to be less healthy and have a lower survival rate, particularly in the early stages of development. The report's conclusion is further contingent on the assumption that animals demonstrating health problems associated with cloning "are not expected to pass inspection and would not be allowed into the food supply."[5] Essentially, the FDA's findings assume that products from unhealthy animals (which are recognized to be more prevalent among cloned livestock) can and will be effectively screened out and removed before entering the food system.

THE DEVIL IS IN THE DETAILS: THE CLONING PROCESS

Though biotechnology companies would like us to believe that animal cloning is simply "another tool in the toolbox" of assisted reproductive technologies, the truth is that animal cloning represents a fundamental change in our relationship with animals. For the first time, humans are acting as wholesale creators of genetic "replicas" of existing animals. The result will be a dramatic increase in animal suffering, a cruelty that is likely to grow as cloning becomes a widespread commercial venture.

The process used for cloning animals is somatic cell nuclear transfer (SCNT), which entails transferring the genetic material from a cell of an existing animal, typically a mature donor, into an egg cell that has had its genetic material removed. The egg, if it can be induced to begin and sustain cell division, is then implanted in the uterus of a surrogate, or "host" mother. Many mistakenly refer to a cloned offspring as an "identical twin" of its donor parent, because it shares the same genetic makeup. This characterization, however, is dangerously misleading. The way a clone's genes are expressed can differ markedly from the donor's gene expression.[6] Professor of molecular biomedical sciences Jorge Piedrahita, whose 2003 study found that clones differ from their donor, stated: "The bottom line is this. While clones are genetically identical, physical characteristics such as size, weight and hair type may not be the same because the DNA has been modified during the cloning process in such a way that it affects the activity of certain genes."[7]

Even after years of research and the development of new methods for extracting and transferring genetic material, failure rates in most mammal cloning are as high as 99 percent.[8] Even when nuclear transfers produce embryos that are successfully implanted in surrogates, only 3 to 5 percent of these pregnancies produce offspring that live to adulthood.[9] Wilmut implanted 277 cloned sheep embryos in surrogate ewes, from which only 13 pregnancies resulted—Dolly being the only successful birth.[10] Many of the failed clones had devastating defects and deformities.

The FDA justified its rush to approve cloned animals in food, claiming that advances in animal cloning can resolve issues related to poor animal health, animal suffering, and food safety. This is simply untrue. One of the world's leading cloning scientists, Rudolf Jaenisch of the Massachusetts Institute of Technology (MIT), told the *Christian Science Monitor* in 2005: "You cannot make normal clones. The ones that survive will just be less abnormal than the ones that die early. There has been no progress—none—in the last six years in making cloning more safe."[11]

ANIMALS AS AUTOMATONS

At a time when more and more people are increasingly concerned about the treatment of animals raised for food, animal cloning not only raises new and troubling ethical dilemmas as science enters the realm of "playing God," it also presents a stark and unacceptable cruelty. The tremendous suffering of animal clones is not limited to the cloned animals themselves; their surrogate mothers also face great suffering. Animal cloning can frequently result in a condition known as "large-offspring syndrome," in which cloned offspring are larger than normal, resulting in overly stressful Caesarian deliveries for the surrogate mothers long before the normal birth time.[12] In one cattle cloning project, three out of twelve surrogate mothers died during pregnancy.[13] The FDA admits that cow cloning is unique among assisted reproduction, in that "pregnancy losses occur at all stages of gestation." Furthermore, the incidence of certain defects in clones is so much higher than in other techniques that the FDA's argument seems callous and unconvincing. For example, studies have found that large-offspring syndrome occurs in up to 50 percent of clones but is rare in other reproductive techniques.[14] The rate of hydrops, an abnormality that can lead to stillborn animals, early death, and/or death of the surrogate cow, is as high as 42 percent in cloning.[15] In natural breeding or other assisted technologies, the condition is extremely rare, with estimates as low as 1 in 7,500.[16] Following the FDA's logic, a condition that causes cancer in 1 out of 2.5 patients is different "only in degree" from one with a cancer rate of 1 out of 7,500.

Even the cloned animals that survive are likely to suffer a wide range of health problems. Cloned livestock that manage to survive birth tend to require more care than those sexually reproduced. Jonathan Hill, who has worked on cattle cloning at Cornell University, suspects that 25 to 50 percent of clones are born having been deprived of normal levels of oxygen.[17] The neonatal condition of most clones is poor. Rebecca Krisher, an animal reproduction specialist at the University of Illinois at Urbana-Champaign, says, "Almost all of these animals, if born on a farm without a vet hospital . . . probably wouldn't survive."[18]

Abnormalities in cloned animals are common. Late in 2002, scientists at the New Zealand government's AgResearch reported that 24 percent of the cloned calves born at the facility died between birth and weaning. This figure contrasts with a 5 percent mortality rate for noncloned calves. Another 5 percent of cloned calves died after weaning, compared with 3 percent of sexually reproduced calves.[19]

One review of scientific literature, authored by executives at the commercial cloning lab Advanced Cell Technology (ACT), found that nearly 25 percent of cow, sheep, swine, and mouse clones showed severe developmental problems soon after birth. Even this high number likely underestimates the problem: the vast majority of the studies considered for this review had follow-up periods of only a few weeks or months,[20] so many later-developing health problems would not be reflected.

More recent research shows that even clones seeming healthy at birth may not be as normal as they appear, as they suffer from a variety of maladies, including liver failure, pneumonia due to weak immune systems, and cancer.[21] The most likely causes of clones' defects appear to be genetic abnormalities that arise during fetal development. Rudolf Jaenisch and his colleagues at MIT's Whitehead Institute determined that cloned mice in their study had hundreds of improperly expressed genes. These genes resulted in a wide variety of abnormalities, ranging from the very subtle to the catastrophic.[22] In fact, documented accounts of apparently "healthy" clones dying suddenly and unexpectedly are numerous, and cloning scientists have seen the problem so often that one has termed it "adult clone sudden death syndrome."[23]

DESTROYING DIVERSITY, ONE CARBON COPY AT A TIME

While cloning companies promise the production of identical, high-quality animals, scientists warn that cloning is a recipe for disaster. In 2005, a university researcher cautioned that "if there is no genetic variability, disease can affect all the animals simultaneously," potentially wiping out entire herds.[24] Modern livestock breeding techniques have already reduced the genetic diversity of many populations of farm animals. Over 90 percent of U.S. dairy cows are the Holstein variety. Eight of the fifteen breeds of swine raised in the United States in the middle of the twentieth century no longer exist. Similarly, only five breeds make up nearly the entire U.S. poultry flock, and almost all white eggs come from one chicken variety, White Leghorns.[25]

Large-scale commercial cloning of animals would further erode livestock diversity. Entire herds and flocks could share a single genome. A herd with naturally occurring genetic differences will typically include some animals that possess natural resistance to certain diseases, but with genetically identical clones, the protections that diversity provides are lost. The commercialization of cloning would make it difficult, if not impossible, to reverse weaknesses or adverse effects bred into an animal population or species.

CLONED FOOD: COMING TO A SUPERMARKET NEAR YOU

Setbacks in cloning science, including frequent births of deformed animals, have not discouraged biotech companies that want to sell cloning technologies to the beef, pork, chicken, egg, and dairy industries, and thus the safety of food products from cloned livestock is also a major concern. Faced with his continuous failures in cloning, Ian Wilmut has said that commercial production of meat and dairy products from cloned animals should not begin until large-scale, controlled trials have been conducted. Wilmut told the magazine *New Scientist* that study of cloned animals should look not only at one-time samples of food products from clones, but also at the animals' health profiles and life spans. Wilmut warned that even small imbalances in an animal's hormone, protein, and fat levels could compromise the quality and safety of meat and milk.[26]

While the biotechnology industry has already proclaimed the safety of cloned food products, scientists have yet to conduct large, comprehensive studies. An analysis by the National Research Council (NRC) released in August 2002 noted that scant research on the safety of meat and milk from embryo-derived clones existed.[27] As for somatic cell nuclear transfer (SCNT) cloning, food safety issues are even less clear, as the NRC notes:

> The cloning of animals from somatic cells is more recent. Limited sample size, health and production data, and rapidly changing cloning protocols make it difficult to draw conclusions regarding the safety of milk, meat, or other products from somatic cell clones and their offspring.[28]

Additionally, while the FDA argues that clones that survive six months are healthy, MIT's Jaenisch disagrees. He notes that "problems appeared when cloned mice were 15 months old. You would have to wait 15 years to [assess such problems] in bulls."[29] As this suggests, health problems can occur in older clones, and many years of study are needed to assess cloning safety. And, perhaps most egregiously, the FDA's 2008 risk assessment is seriously flawed. For example, the agency found no peer-reviewed studies on meat from cloned cattle, cloned pigs, or their offspring. It found just three peer-reviewed studies on milk from cloned cows—and all three studies showed differences in milk from clones that should have prompted further research. Yet despite the lack of studies, the FDA's assessment found that meat and milk from all these cloned animals and their progeny are "as safe to eat" as food from natural animals. Additionally, even though many studies show troubling health data in clones that appear healthy, the FDA found no studies that investigated the potential for food safety threats from unexpected new proteins or other metabolites in food from clones or their progeny. [30]

In 2005, a study described as a "pilot" study by researchers was hailed by a BIO spokesperson as proof that "the science is clear" on the safety of food from these animals.[31] In fact, the pilot project looked at just two cloned beef cattle and milk from four dairy cows.

Some scientists warn that abnormal gene expression, which likely causes the health problems of clones, is likely to also affect the meat and milk of cloned livestock. In 2002, the NRC noted that studies to confirm or refute this concern had not been done: "There are to date no published . . . comparative analytical data assessing the composition of meat and milk products of somatic cell clones, their offspring, and conventionally bred animals."[32]

High doses of hormones and antibiotics used in cloning present another significant safety concern. Because of the high failure rates of cloning pregnancies and the typical sickly nature of newborn clones, increased levels of veterinary hormones and antibiotics are used in the cloning process. Scientists often infuse the surrogate mothers of cloned livestock with massive doses of hormones to improve the odds that the cloned embryo will implant in the surrogate's uterus. While the clones are typically the genetic offspring of highly prized parents, the surrogate mothers hold no such intrinsic value, and many are destined for slaughterhouses soon after giving birth. The clones themselves, often born with severely compromised immune systems, frequently receive massive doses of antibiotics and other medications.[33] The increased need for antibiotics among cloned animals is not only indicative of the poorer health status of these animals, it also raises the specter of increased antibiotic resistance. Increased application of antibiotics in animal production greatly increases the likelihood that antibiotics commonly used to treat infection in humans will lose their efficacy.[34] Although the commercialization of cloning will likely increase the prevalence of sickly and immunocompromised animals in our food system while simultaneously inhibiting our ability to fight infection in humans, the FDA has failed to address these important food safety issues.

Commercialization of cloned livestock for food production could also increase the incidence of food-borne illnesses, such as *E. coli* infections. Stressed animals are known to produce pathogens, and cloning is likely to increase animals' stress levels.[35] According to the NRC study, "Because stress from [the] developmental problems [of cloned livestock] might result in shedding of pathogens in fecal material, resulting in a higher load of undesirable microbes on the carcass, the food safety of products, especially such as veal, from young somatic cell cloned animals might indirectly present a . . . concern."[36]

REGULATORY FAST TRACK

The FDA admits in its own risk assessment that a vast quantity of animal clones are unhealthy and would not be suitable for the food supply. But the agency has made assurances that it and the U.S. Department of Agriculture (USDA) would be able to pull these animals out of the food supply, and that milk and meat would only come from the so-called healthy clones. Here are two agencies that have failed to protect consumers from *Salmonella* and *E. coli* in countless food products, yet now they are saying they will be able to ensure that only the safe or healthy clones make it into the food supply. Why should the public trust them now?

Another regulatory oversight involves the fate of all the defective cloned animals that die soon after birth or are pulled out of the food supply. These animals—minus a few exceptions—are allowed to be rendered into products such as animal feed, pet food, and even cosmetics such as face creams and lipstick. All without being labeled.

Despite widespread concerns about the introduction of cloned animals, the FDA has pushed ahead with commercial approval. In 2006, the Center for Food Safety and a coalition of consumer, religious, animal welfare, and other groups filed a legal petition to the FDA calling for a mandatory premarket review of food from cloned animals based on the agency's animal drug process under the Federal Food, Drug and Cosmetic Act (FFDCA). Such a review would require rigorous safety testing before food from cloned animals could be marketed, in place of the current unscientific and biased "risk assessment" process. The FDA denied this petition in 2008, and has offered an inadequate explanation as to why animal cloning should be exempted from such rigorous new drug review procedures as are required for other foods derived from animals, such as fast-growing genetically engineered salmon. In addition, the FDA does not require that food products derived from cloned animals or their progeny be tracked or labeled as such. The U.S. Senate has voted twice to delay the FDA's decision on cloned animals until additional safety and economic studies can be completed by the National Academy of Sciences and the USDA, and more than 150,000 Americans wrote to the FDA urging them not to allow clones and their offspring in the U.S. food supply.

In contrast to the U.S. government's lax approach to the risks of animal cloning, in 2008 the Agriculture Committee of the European Parliament called for a ban in the European Union on the cloning of animals for food, and an embargo on imports of cloned animals, their offspring, and products derived from these sources. The European Food Safety Authority also pointed to the health and welfare issues inherent in animal cloning, and the European Group on Ethics in Science and New Technologies remained unconvinced that the animal welfare and ethical implications of cloning could be sufficiently addressed as to make animal cloning acceptable.[37]

Any attempt to adequately assess and regulate animal cloning should require the FDA to conduct multigenerational studies that include investigations of potential food safety threats from unexpected proteins or other metabolites produced by the cloning process. Because of the uncertainty of the long-term environmental impact of cloned animals in the food supply, the FDA should also prepare a full environmental impact statement for each new animal drug application based on the use of cloning. In addition to food safety issues, a federal advisory committee on ethical issues in animal cloning should be created to work with the FDA and provide expertise on the difficult ethical issues raised by animal cloning.

Current food safety and animal welfare regulations cannot adequately address the known animal cruelty and potential food impurity issues associated with cloning. Until that time, the only acceptable course is for a federal ban on commercial production of food products from cloned livestock. Until a ban is enacted, however, labeling is the only way to give consumers a choice in the marketplace. As the lead regulatory agency handling animal cloning in the food supply, the FDA should at the very least require labeling of these novel foods. Anything less than that is a failure of the public trust.

GENETICALLY ENGINEERED FARM ANIMALS

A Brazen Effort to Make Nature Fit the Industrial Mold

JAYDEE HANSON

CORPORATE SCIENTISTS ARE REMOVING *"mothering" genes from hens to enhance egg laying, altering pigs' digestive systems to produce a more "palatable" waste, and even engineering animals to produce profitable pharmaceuticals. Instead of changing factory farming's horrific conditions, agribusiness is redesigning animals to meet industrial specifications—with few government safeguards and porous regulation.*

❖

A genetically engineered hamburger soon may be coming to a restaurant near you. The Biotechnology Industry Organization has said that some twenty animals are in the process of being approved by the Food and Drug Administration (FDA).[1] Instead of changing the factory farm system to fit the physical and psychological needs (and limits) of animals, the livestock industry is developing animals that are permanently altered at the genetic level to better fit the CAFO system—redesigning the very biology of animals so they can become more "efficient" production machines and thereby maximize industry profits.

Genetically engineered animals incorporate genes from other animals, bacteria, and fungi into the genome of the animal through a process called *transgenesis*. Developers of the genetically engineered animals often incorporate whole sections of DNA and multiple genes into an embryo of the new animal in an attempt to get the new genes to work. There are a number of ways to do transgenesis, but the goal of all of the routes is to insert the new genes in a desired genetic sequence into the host animal's DNA while minimizing the harmful effects of the new genes. When the developers finally get the "proper" mix, they often clone that animal to produce others or use traditional breeding techniques.

This radical manipulation of animals includes a wide range of projects: reprogramming animals' maternal behavior; transforming digestive systems to fit corporate feeding practices (the Enviropig would reduce the phosphorus in piles of pig waste generated in feedlots); making inbred Jersey cows with huge udders less likely to develop mastitis; and making transgenic fish that grow faster in crowded pens.

There has been a rush to produce and commercialize these genetically engineered (GE) creatures, and the technology is moving much faster than the regulatory agencies. In fact, the federal agencies responsible for food safety, animal welfare, and environmental protection have not developed transparent policies, or even decided if they will require food safety trials to protect the public from the risks of animal engineering.[2] The FDA, moreover, has decided to regulate all GE animals under their "new animal drug" rubric, not under regulations developed especially to assess the safety of genetically engineered animals.[3] Under this scenario, the FDA assumes that the genetic changes introduced are a "new animal drug" and requires tests to see if the genetically engineered animal tolerates the inserted genes. As with drugs, the FDA keeps the application for a new GE animal secret until the "drug" or, in this case, the genetically engineered animal, is approved. In some cases, the companies or other parties that have developed genetically engineered animals announce that they are applying for approvals. The animals discussed in this essay are mostly those that have been or that are being submitted by their developers to the FDA for approval. The first GE goat was approved in 2009, after an environmental impact statement reviewed only one of the two locations where the goat was being reared and included no food safety trials, despite a history of unapproved animals from other locations getting into the food system.

Perhaps most chilling is the industry's effort to transform animals' basic instincts. Consider the work of researchers at the University of Wisconsin (UW) on egg-laying turkey hens. Imprisoned in factory farm battery cages with no room to move, egg-laying hens are denied their basic maternal instinct to brood over their eggs, which are removed mechanically. These conditions cause considerable distress among the hens, resulting in diminished egg production and loss of profits. One solution to this suffering would be to promote the use of free-range hens that can lay eggs and brood naturally, but this would not suit the profit needs of industrial egg producers. Instead, UW researchers say they have identified the "mothering gene" in these hens and by "silencing" it, removed their brooding instinct.[4] Michigan State University agriculture ethicist Paul Thompson has proposed genetically engineering chickens to be blind as a way of "ethically" helping the chickens cope with crowding.[5]

Another disturbing project aimed at altering farm animals is the so-called Enviropig, the hog industry's strange genetic engineering solution to its environmentally devastating waste crisis. Scientists at the University of Guelph in Ontario, Canada, have created a transgenic pig with altered saliva and digestive tract. Pig manure contains high levels of phosphorus, which is one component of manure that can make it toxic when it leaches into groundwater, lakes, rivers, and oceans. This brave new pig is redesigned to better digest the phosphorus contained in feed grains, purportedly to reduce environmental problems related to the release and use of pig manure. However, the developers of the Enviropig have admitted that their aim is to help pork producers stay within environmental limits on phosphorus pollution and to enable them to cram even more hogs into their already massive industrial farms. One of the Guelph scientists stated, "The environmental limitations on the number of animals they can raise per hectare of land is just squeezing [the hog farming] industry."[6] The University of Guelph scientists have applied for approval from the FDA, but they do not expect approval of these animals as food from the Canadian government.[7]

The industry's push for profit-maximizing also emphasizes larger-size and faster-growing GE animals without much concern for the animals' health or the environmental effects. For years, U.S. taxpayer dollars supported a project of the U.S. Department of Agriculture's

(USDA) Beltsville, Maryland, research center that involved engineering human growth genes into the permanent genetic code of pigs.[8] The head researcher, Vern Pursel, hoped to create huge pigs whose growth would be spurred by the novel human gene. The experiments were a notorious failure, resulting in pigs whose musculature overwhelmed their skeletal structure, making them bowlegged, unable to stand, and hideously deformed. Despite these failures, similar USDA transgenic livestock projects, including the one that produced the transgenic Jersey cow, continue to this day.[9]

Another transgenic pig research program at the University of Illinois' Champaign-Urbana branch put two genes—one cow gene and one synthetic gene—into sows in the hope of increasing their milk production and the piglets' ability to digest milk. The FDA required that the experiment team destroy all the transgenic pigs after the research was completed, but in April 2001, 386 of the pigs born of transgenic parents were sold to a livestock dealer.[10]

Even animals genetically engineered for nonfood purposes may get into the food chain. In 2001, meat from transgenic pigs at the University of Florida was made into sausages after an employee sold three pigs. This 2001 incident may be the first time U.S. consumers unknowingly ate GE meat. The pigs were modified to carry a copy of the rhodopsin gene, which affects eye function.[11] Other companies' employees have refused to say whether they have eaten the meat of animals they have genetically engineered, including those from Hematech, the South Dakota–based company that has produced a cow that does not develop the prions that cause mad cow disease.[12]

Gene researchers have met greater success getting fish to grow larger and more quickly than nature intended. After initial attempts to engineer human growth genes into salmon, they discovered that various fish growth genes were more effective. AquaBounty, a Massachusetts-based company, applied to the FDA in 2000 to market these GE supersalmon, which grow twice as fast as conventional farmed salmon. The fish contain genes from two other fish species, one from another salmon and one from the eel-like Arctic pout. Researchers warn that these mutant fish could carry "Trojan" genes: if these fish are released, or if they accidentally escape into the wild, they could cause the extinction of entire species. As with genetically engineered plants, approval of these fish would provide benefits to the entity that "owns" the organism, but not to the consumer or the environment.

USING ANIMALS AS BIOREACTORS

Beyond transforming livestock to fit CAFOs, agribusiness researchers are now using animals' bodies in place of mechanical bioreactors, thereby turning animals into veritable factories for the production of valuable pharmaceuticals and industrial chemicals. Scientists are working on a variety of so-called biopharm animals, some of which are genetically engineered to synthesize vaccines and other medicines. Cattle and goats have been genetically engineered to secrete human antibodies and growth hormones in their milk. Others are being altered, often with human genes, to produce blood proteins and blood-clotting factors. On February 6, 2009, the FDA approved the first GE animal, a goat genetically engineered to excrete a drug in its milk.[13] While this first goat was not approved as a human food, it was approved without advisory committee meetings focused on the animal's approval or a public comment period as stipulated by FDA's guidelines for approving transgenic animals.[14] GTC Biotherapeutics refers to its GE goats as its "transgenic production platform" on its website. In perhaps the most bizarre example, goats have been genetically engineered to produce spiders' silk for use in bulletproof vests. That project, funded by the U.S. and Canadian military, was abandoned when it proved not to work as expected.[15]

Currently no U.S. laws prevent genetic engineers from marketing meat or milk from these animals, or prevent offspring of GE animals or animals that fed on the milk of "biopharm" mothers from entering the human food supply. The FDA has not indicated whether the meat and milk from these animals will be regulated, and some producers say they hope to market them as food for people.

Consumers have so far resisted efforts to integrate transgenic foods into human diets. After creating transgenic cows to produce a human protein for treating hemophilia, the Dutch biotech firm Pharming Healthcare, Inc. (PHI)[16] suggested donating the animals' meat to a local food bank, but area residents questioned its safety and the company was forced to rescind its offer.[17] The manufacture of milk from transgenic animals is also a concern. PHI originally planned to build a dairy processing plant near its transgenic cattle farm in Craig County, Virginia, but subsequently decided against it.[18] It is not known whether this GE milk will be handled in facilities that process milk for human consumption, and, if so, how the processor will guard against contamination.

HUMAN HEALTH AND FOOD SAFETY CONCERNS

Even as agribusiness prepares to market genetically manipulated animals, there has been minimal public discussion of the many human health dangers that could be introduced by these novel creations. Perhaps most troubling is the engineering of animals containing antibiotic-resistant "markers," designed to help producers confirm that the new genetic material has been transferred into the host. Introducing these marker genes into the food supply via GE animal meat and milk products could render many important antibiotics useless in fighting human diseases.

Genetically engineering animals to be "healthier" for humans to consume is a reported goal of some of the transgenic animal research. Geneticists and cloning scientists at the University of Missouri have mixed DNA from the roundworm *Caenorhabditis elegans* and pigs to produce swine with significant amounts of omega-3 fatty acids, the kind believed to stave off heart disease.[19] The researchers cloned a dead pig that had the gene in the right location, and that clone later produced five "successful" transgenic piglets that the researchers intended to breed. So far, no companies have announced that they plan to use this technology for pork products. In 2002, Smithfield Foods funded cloning research for ProLinia (since purchased by Viagen),[20] but in 2008 Smithfield and Hormel, two of the top U.S. producers of pork products, announced that they would not use cloned animals in their products. Still, any company that wanted to use the University of Missouri pigs would have to get approval for their marketing from the FDA, where these pigs would be evaluated as animals containing a new drug, in this case the modified worm gene.

There is also a serious concern that producing pharmaceuticals in transgenic animals (as well as the practice of genetically altering animals to obtain organs for transplants) could increase the risk of spreading animal viruses to humans. From human immunodeficiency virus (HIV), to chicken and swine flu viruses, to the microscopic prions that transmit mad cow disease to humans, numerous animal pathogens—often barely detectable—can create human diseases and even pandemics. Yet biotech companies seeking to commercialize pharmaceuticals and organs from transgenic animals currently have no means for identifying or eliminating pathogens that might be spread to humans. This hazard would seem to be a significant barrier to large-scale commercialization of medical products from GE farm animals.

The experiments conducted to create GE animals also pose potential new virus threats. Researchers deploy viral vectors that invade the cells of animals and deposit new genetic materials; but these vectors can then recombine with viruses in animals to create new diseases in livestock and humans.[21] Another worry is that if transgenic animals are consumed, these viruses could enter the human food chain.

The very process of genetically engineering animals can make their meat potentially unsafe. Inserting genes and other material into their cells can create new allergens, hormones, or toxins in our food. The technology used to create transgenic beasts, called microinjection—in which the new gene is integrated at random spots in the genome—could activate a host gene that produces a novel toxin or allergen. In a worst-case scenario, microinjection could activate or create a prionlike element, similar to that responsible for mad cow disease, which could then be spread through consumption of transgenic meat.

ANIMAL WELFARE

While humans can lobby to protect their food safety, livestock animals—already subject to great stress, discomfort, and frequent abuse—have no such voice and currently no federal government regulations protecting their welfare. Moreover, the genetic altering of animals threatens to exacerbate factory farm problems and introduces new potential hazards to animal well-being.

One primary risk, according to Joy Mench of the University of California at Davis, is the lack of precision in DNA microinjection.[22]

When injecting DNA into an animal, scientists have no control over where the genes go, and errors can cause deformities and other genetic defects in the animals. The techniques used can be extremely inefficient, with fewer than 4 percent of the animals surviving the process. Of the animals that do survive, many do not express the gene(s) properly and have physical or behavioral abnormalities. These differences in gene expression cause difficulty both for the animals and for assessing the technology.[23] Some of the techniques in use are extremely inefficient in the production of transgenic animals. Efficiencies of production range from 0 to 4 percent in pigs, cattle, sheep, and goats, with about 80 to 90 percent of the mortality occurring during early development. The variability and subtlety of response makes assessment difficult. These "no take" animals could be put into the food supply unless better regulations are put in place.

Reproductive technologies commonly used in genetic engineering, such as in vitro culture, semen collection, egg collection, and cloning can cause stress in animals. In vitro culture methods and cloning, for instance, have been associated with "large-offspring syndrome" in cows, which can cause complications in birthing and developmental problems in offspring. Nearly half of cloned animals have a large-offspring syndrome problem. Given that many GE animals are cloned or offspring of clones, they may have an even greater likelihood of this condition, putting survival of both the surrogate mother and the GE animal at considerable risk.

ANIMAL BIOTECHNOLOGY AND ETHICAL CONCERNS

As companies press ahead with their experiments and marketing efforts, a rich public debate must tackle important questions: Is it ethically acceptable to use human genes in animals to produce biopharmaceuticals? Are these biopharmaceuticals safe?[24] What will be the fate of nonproductive transgenic male offspring, and of transgenic female animals, when they come to the end of their useful lives? How will animal engineering affect certain mammal breeds and their protection under the federal Endangered Species Act?

These ethical questions become yet more concrete when considering the ecological impacts of animal engineering. Here, the risks to future biodiversity and species survival are significant. Professor William Muir, director of the Purdue University High Definition Genomics Center, likens transgenic organisms to exotic species that can invade new areas, disrupting ecosystems and displacing other species.[25] When the gypsy moth was introduced to the East Coast to increase silk production, it did not produce silk but rather quickly proliferated and destroyed plant life across the country. An escaped transgenic organism, Muir says, could pose a similar risk if the new gene was able to adapt and extend its range into different environments. For instance, a freshwater catfish engineered to tolerate saltwater could escape, enter the ocean, and displace established species, posits Muir.[26]

This threat of accidental proliferation gives rise to a Trojan gene scenario. According to Muir, escaped transgenic animals, through interbreeding, can introduce a maladapted new gene into wild populations that lowers the net fitness of the animal. Ultimately, inserting this gene could lead to the extinction of both the escaped transgenic population and its wild relatives. In a process that Muir calls "Darwin on his head," Trojan genes give transgenic animals an initial advantage over their wild counterparts, but, through an ironic twist on natural selection, these genes lower their long-term fitness and threaten to bring the whole species down with them. An escaped male transgenic fish designed to grow larger than normal would enjoy outstanding mating success because female fish see large males as more "fit" than small males. Through this mating prowess, the transgenic male would rapidly spread the transgene through the wild population. Muir (who has conducted research on gene-altered medaka) found that the growth gene engineered into the fish caused a serious maladaption in its offspring, leading to a one-third higher death rate in the offspring.[27] Natural selection, in this case, led to the destruction of the species. In the bleak arithmetic of this Trojan gene, according to Muir, if just 60 genetically altered fish were released into a population of 60,000 native fish, there would be complete extinction in forty generations. This chilling scenario is of urgent concern, not just with fish but with virtually any mobile species.

REGULATORY FAILURES

Despite the many serious warning signs, federal agencies have not addressed how—or even if—they intend to regulate transgenic livestock and fish. While a number of federal statutes apply indirectly to GE animals, none specifically addresses this new technology, and government agencies have failed to develop regulations (as opposed to a nonbinding guidance like the one the FDA issued in January 2009)[28] for how they might be regulated. Neither the USDA nor the FDA has developed standards for transgenic animals that might be imported into the United States.[29]

Among the most worrying threats that remain unresolved by regulation:

- The potentially destructive environmental impacts of escaped transgenic animals have yet to be closely examined or controlled for by regulators.
- The distinct lack of animal welfare standards related to transgenics in agriculture puts animals at risk from a technology that is often imprecise and known to cause health problems and cruel and inhumane suffering in livestock.
- The human health effects of using pharmaceuticals produced in transgenic animals are disturbing, yet not adequately assessed.
- Despite widespread concern about the risks of GE meat and milk entering the human food supply, regulations fail to ensure the separation of transgenic animal products; likewise, there are no laws regarding the fate of unused products, and few means for public input on this key issue. Dead animals from these genetic engineering operations could end up being rendered for cosmetics or animal food.

The chief regulatory authority for transgenic animals invoked by the FDA Center for Veterinary Medicine (CVM) is the New Animal Drug Application (NADA) statute. Under NADA, the genetic materials inserted into some GE animals have been considered new animal "drugs" because they "affect the structure or function" of animals. The statute provides an opportunity for comprehensive regulation, but so far agencies have neglected its use. Developed with conventional drugs in mind, the law is riddled with shortcomings when applied to transgenic animals, including risk assessment problems, lack of criteria for assuring human food safety, and difficulty regulating the offspring of transgenic animals. Additionally, the FDA lacks clear authority to address the broader environmental and ecological concerns related to transgenic animals, making this statute woefully insufficient.

The USDA has some regulatory authority regarding GE animals, but it remains unclear whether the agency will develop an approval process for GE animals. The Animal Health Protection Act gives the USDA's Animal and Plant Health Inspection Service (APHIS) power to regulate the movement and environmental release of some transgenic animals, but the law only covers "livestock" and may exclude other animals. The statute applies narrowly to genetic modifications that may cause livestock diseases or pest problems, and only covers the importation and interstate movement of GE livestock.[30] The Animal Welfare Act was developed to promote humane treatment of research animals, but farm animals are exempt, so it is unclear whether livestock would be covered when they are used to produce chemicals or pharmaceuticals. The Animal Damage Control Act could apply to transgenic animals considered "injurious" to agriculture, but the law may not give APHIS much authority beyond covering responses to escaped GE animals.[31] The overall regulatory landscape is frighteningly barren: without specific guidance relating to transgenic animals, it is unclear how these laws can be applied, and in their current state, they are clearly insufficient to address the many risks inherent in engineering livestock.

Equally troubling is the regulatory system's lack of transparency. The licensing process under the Investigational New Animal Drug (INAD) applications at FDA, for instance, is privileged information. The public has no way of knowing when, or for which product, an INAD application has been filed. This confidentiality enables applicants to skirt the scientific questions and novel issues raised by the technology of genetic engineering. Furthermore, the United States has no labeling requirements for GE foods or animals. While laws require labeling when orange juice is made from concentrate, consumers are left in the dark as to whether the products they buy include genes inserted artificially from another species.

Even more problematic is that the FDA import tolerances for GE animals may not be even as stringent as approvals for animals residing in the United States.[32] A company like AquaBounty may raise its salmon in a country that does not regulate the transgenic salmon as much as the United States might. China is a major developer of cloned and GE animals. The FDA could certify Chinese oversight as adequate with only a cursory review of the Chinese processes.

WHERE DO WE GO FROM HERE?

The FDA has failed to assure the safety of genetically engineered animals; new regulation that requires open, not secret, review of the safety and environmental integrity of GE animals is now needed.

The existing regulatory uncertainties only mask the serious concerns raised by the genetic manipulation of livestock and fish. The failure of the FDA to develop a transparent process for the approval of GE animals, instead using the secretive process of the New Animal Drug rubric, means that consumers will be deprived of basic safety information. The redesigning of animals to fit CAFOs and to produce pharmaceuticals presents many potential risks never before seen in the scientific or agricultural community—and measures must be taken to mitigate these risks before transgenic animals are commercialized. The FDA's inadequate risk assessment of cloned animals, wherein the largest study involved only fifteen animals, makes a secret process for GE animal approval all the more problematic.[33] Moreover, many GE animals are likely to be both cloned and genetically engineered.

As public officials have done little to address these problems, a number of steps must be taken—prior to any product marketing—to protect the environment, animal well-being, and human health.

First, more independent research is required to document fully the environmental and human health effects of GE animals.[34] There is also an urgent need for comprehensive regulations (and not just the general guidance that FDA issued for GE animal approvals, which is not legally binding on either the FDA or the applicants) that specifically address issues related to transgenic animals rather than relying on current measures that may create loopholes or leave areas unregulated.

Second, as there have been no long-term studies to show that GE animals can be safely and humanely produced for food, the Obama Administration, USDA, or FDA should put in place an immediate mandatory moratorium on the marketing of any food products from cloned or GE animals. In regard to GE animals used for production of nonfood products (e.g., pharmaceuticals), because these animals and their by-products have not been approved for human consumption and could pose serious health risks, there must be strict rules and procedures to keep them isolated from other animals and separate from the human food supply. To prevent contamination, these rules must also prohibit the introduction of these GE animals and their offspring to conventional farms. Given the high likelihood that a company rearing transgenic animals could go out of business, approvals of any transgenic animal must assume that the animals could outlive the company.

Finally, a system of labeling and traceability requirements should be developed for all products from GE livestock. Labeling requirements are essential for consumers to make informed choices about the use of nonfood transgenic animal products. The FDA has said that it will only require labeling when the company producing a new animal makes a health claim for the animal—that is, that the animal is healthier than its traditional counterpart. The USDA, however, already requires milk from different species of animals to be labeled with the species' name. Should not transgenic cows' milk that contains the genes of other species be labeled as well?

Perhaps most important, the veils of secrecy and regulatory inadequacy must be lifted, and this dubious new form of industrial agriculture must be exposed and publicly debated. New regulations must be transparent and must include avenues for public input in the product approval process. With so much at stake, public education and debate on the use of transgenic animals is critical. The serious problems of the industrial animal production system cannot be solved—and could be gravely exacerbated—by genetically altering animals to fit into a deeply flawed CAFO model. Public awareness, scrutiny, and outcry are vitally needed to prevent this latest, highly disturbing manipulation of nature in the name of corporate efficiencies and profits. The Obama administration has said that it will use science to make decisions in a transparent way. Drafting legislation that makes food safety, animal welfare, and environmental integrity the ground for any GE animals and putting all new approvals on hold until that legislation and relevant regulations are drafted would be a good start on science-based policymaking.

NUCLEAR MEAT

Using Radiation and Chemicals to Make Food "Safe"

WENONAH HAUTER

RATHER THAN APPROPRIATELY SCALING *animal operations or slowing down disassembly lines, the meat industry is reaching for "technofixes" to ensure the public of food safety. Unfortunately, it's just not that simple. Zapping meat with high-powered radiation—150 million times stronger than human X-rays—has been linked to genetic and cellular damage caused by by-products in irradiated food. Then there's the chemical solution: just sterilize tainted meat with carcinogens.*

❖

If nothing else, you have to give the irradiation industry credit for persistence. After decades of controversy, and numerous attempts to convince consumers to get over their gut-level reluctance to eat something that has been zapped with the equivalent of 150 million chest X-rays, the proponents of irradiation still won't give up. Each year, hundreds of thousands of pounds of ground beef are irradiated prior to being shipped to market. But if the meat industry got its way, this would just be a drop in the bucket; the industry is pressuring the government to allow ever-wider uses of irradiation: from deli meats and hot dogs to baby food and seafood. In 2002, this push for expansion of irradiation included Congress giving the U.S. Department of Agriculture (USDA) free reign to purchase irradiated meat for the government's nutrition programs—including the National School Lunch Program.[1] Fortunately, public outcry has halted schools from accepting or purchasing nuclear meat. Nevertheless, despite public opposition, the meat industry is relentless in its lobbying for massive promotion and expansion of irradiation. And the rationale behind the all-out embrace of irradiation is evident.

THE SILVER BULLET FOR FACTORY FARMS

Industry and regulators see the use of nuclear materials as a silver bullet technology that can save the factory farming system from itself. The horrific conditions in U.S. industrial feedlots and slaughterhouses not only result in unspeakable cruelty to billions of animals, but they also lead to the creation and spread of pernicious pathogens that have caused illness and death.[2]

Under increasing pressure to address the public health threats, CAFO operators and agribusiness corporations are turning their sights on irradiation to kill the dangerous bacteria and other pathogens spawned and spread by the factory farming system. Rather than institute sanitary rules for CAFOs and meatpacking plants that would remove the sources of these pathogens, they propose to use irradiation. Rather than slowing down line speeds in plants—which cause contamination of meat, and of course a plethora of workplace accidents and animal cruelty—they again propose the use of irradiation. Because cleaning up CAFOs and reducing line speeds cost money, the industry and its allies in government see irradiation as the technology that lets them continue to run massive factory farms and the massive slaughterhouses they supply.

Instead of requiring CAFOs and meat plants to abide by strong sanitation and safety standards, backed up by adequate government meat inspection and adequate microbial testing, the USDA has promoted the implementation of technological interventions, such as irradiation and chemical rinses, to "clean up" the pathogenic mess.

Some of these technologies, like chemical rinses, are so harsh they actually change the color and consistency of fecal matter so that it's no longer considered "feces." Since this altered fecal matter doesn't meet the official definition of "feces," the carcass is not condemned. The result is that meat with visible feces on the carcass can be kept on the production line, treated with a chemical rinse, and later sold to the consumer.[3]

FROM FOOD TO MUTAGEN:
THE HEALTH HAZARDS OF IRRADIATION

Irradiation, this purported panacea for food safety, is itself a source of toxic meat. Food irradiation uses high-energy gamma rays, electron beams, or X-rays (all millions of times more powerful than standard medical X-rays) to break apart the bacteria and insects that can hide in meat, grains, and other foods.[4] Radiation is one of the more destructive forces in nature, and simple logic dictates that doses powerful enough to kill living organisms are also powerful enough to fundamentally alter the food itself. Voluminous scientific research has borne this out, finding that while a radioactive assault may kill bacteria or insects, it also destroys a food's vitamins and can significantly alter its chemical composition. As ionizing radiation passes through cells, it can throw electrons out of orbit, breaking chemical bonds and leaving highly reactive free radicals in their wake. These free radicals re-form into radiolytic products (chemicals created in food by the irradiation process), which include both known carcinogens like benzene and formaldehyde, as well as new chemical compounds.[5]

Since the U.S. Food and Drug Administration (FDA) has approved the use of irradiation on major portions of our food supply, we might naturally assume that the overwhelming majority of these studies revealed no mutagenic effects. Not so. At least 12 published journal articles report mutagenic effects from in vivo studies on animals or cells grown on, or exposed to, irradiated substances. Other published studies have explored possible links to colon tumor promotion, impacts on hemoglobin, and other health effects.[6]

Many of these published studies state in frighteningly clear terms the potential hazards posed by these foods:

- "Freshly irradiated . . . diet fed to male mice of both strains caused an increase in early deaths of offspring of females mated to the males in week 7 and to a lesser extent in week 4."[7]
- "Cytogenetic [related to cell DNA] examinations of the developing spermatogonia in 30 mice of each group revealed that cytogenetic abnormalities were significantly more frequent in the group fed irradiated flour than in the control group."[8]

- "Feeding of mice (males and females) for two months before mating with 50% of the standard complete diet (solid cakes) irradiated with 5 Mrads of radiation provokes a significant increase of pre-implantation embryonal deaths."[9]
- "The children receiving freshly-irradiated wheat developed polyploid cells and certain abnormal cells in increasing numbers as the duration of feeding increased and showed a gradual reversal to basal level of nil after withdrawal of the irradiated wheat. In marked contrast, none of the children fed unirradiated diet developed any abnormal cells."[10]

Scientific evidence raising doubts about the safety of irradiated foods continues to accumulate. The most recent studies have focused on a particular group of by-products of the irradiation of meat that fall into a class of chemicals known as cyclobutanones, which are generated when fatty acids in foods are irradiated. This research is particularly important because these by-products are inevitably formed during the irradiation of meat foods and because the results suggest that these chemicals may pose serious health hazards.

CASE STUDY: CYCLOBUTANONES

Thirty years ago, a research team from the University of Massachusetts discovered that the irradiation of certain fats found in common foods such as eggs, beef, pork, lamb, chicken, and turkey produces unique chemical by-products classified as cyclobutanones.[11] These by-products are ubiquitous in irradiated meat products, nonexistent in unirradiated products, and can persist in food samples for a decade or longer.[12] In fact, researchers can so easily detect these cyclobutanones in irradiated foods that they can conclusively test for irradiation based on the presence of the chemicals.

In 1998, scientists at Germany's prestigious irradiation research facility, the Federal Research Centre for Nutrition and Food, found that 2-dodecylcyclobutanone (2-DCB), a common cyclobutanone and a by-product of irradiated palmitic acid, caused genetic and cellular damage in human and rat cells and also produced genetic damage in live rats fed the chemical. Palmitic acid is the most concentrated or second most concentrated type of fat in beef, pork, lamb, chicken, and turkey. It is also common to numerous processed foods, including ready-to-eat sauces, pizzas, and snacks.[13] Perhaps even more frightening than these findings is that so little other research has been done on the human health implications of cyclobutanones. Scientists have identified a number of these substances (aside from 2-DCB) created during the irradiation of other types of common fats. While these cyclobutanones are present in irradiated foods, they have never been tested for their potential to cause cellular or genetic damage in people who consume them.[14]

Tests performed over the past decade demonstrate that the amount of irradiation required to produce cyclobutanones falls well below levels used by the food irradiation industry.[15] FDA officials are fully aware of these studies. They also know that cyclobutanones persist in irradiated foods for years and that cooking does little or nothing to diminish their concentrations. Undoubtedly, these dangerous chemicals exist within portions of our food supply. Why are we eating foods that some studies have shown to damage our cells and our genes? It challenges the imagination to believe that the FDA would approve this technology, while barely mentioning, or even ignoring, studies that show it is unsafe. Yet this is exactly what has happened.

NUCLEAR BAILOUT

On December 8, 1953, President Dwight D. Eisenhower stood before the United Nations and unveiled his plan for a new era marked by constructive, not destructive, uses for atomic energy. Shortly after, his Atoms for Peace program generated a long list of ideas for harnessing atomic energy, including nuclear airplanes, wristwatches, and long johns—even coffeepots that could boil water for a hundred years without a refueling. While most of these ideas thankfully ended up in the dustbin of history, the idea of using radioactive materials to "treat" food survived.

Irradiation has had different homes in the federal government over the decades. During the 1960s, the army did the early research that resulted in FDA approval of irradiation for bacon. But after more research revealed that animals fed irradiated bacon suffered serious health problems, the approval was withdrawn.[16] Two decades later, the army had abandoned its irradiation research program.

In the 1970s, interest in food irradiation was smoldering in other parts of the federal bureaucracy, not because of its potential to deal with food safety or shelf life, but because establishing a domestic use for nuclear waste material such as cesium-137 could solve a persistent problem for the nuclear industry. The Department of Energy (DOE) launched the Byproducts Utilization Program to dispose of the highly radioactive waste from nuclear bomb production by using it for food irradiation and by selling some of the waste to private companies. But the DOE's scheme came to an end in 1988, when a serious accident occurred at a facility near Atlanta where cesium-137 was being used. Radioactive material leaked into a water storage pool, and contaminated water splashed onto food and medical packages being irradiated. Some of the workers carried radioactivity into their homes and cars. The mess cost more than $40 million to clean up, and taxpayers footed the bill.[17]

The cast of characters promoting food irradiation in the early days included Martin Welt, president of Radiation Technology, Inc., which built irradiation plants in New Jersey and several other states. During the 1970s and 1980s, Radiation Technology was cited more than thirty times for various violations at its facility in Rockaway, New Jersey, including throwing out radioactive garbage with the regular trash and bypassing safety devices that protected workers. Welt, a much-quoted advocate of irradiation, was eventually convicted on six federal charges, including conspiracy to defraud the government and lying to federal investigators.[18]

After this rocky start to the commercial food irradiation industry, things didn't really improve. Since the 1960s, dozens of mishaps have been reported at food irradiation facilities throughout the United States and the world. Radioactive water has been flushed into the public sewer system. Radioactive waste has been thrown into the garbage. Facilities have caught fire. Equipment has malfunctioned. Workers have lost fingers, hands, legs, and in several cases their lives. And the new generation of irradiation facilities, which use speed-of-light electron beams from machines called linear accelerators instead of radioactive cobalt-60 or cesium-137, are not without risk just because they don't use nuclear material. These "e-beam" facilities emit ground-level ozone, a toxic pollutant that contributes to smog. And at least two workers have been seriously injured in e-beam plants.[19]

As the irradiation industry and their friends in government continue to push for the use of irradiation on a mass scale, the impact of facilities where irradiation takes place must not be forgotten. The infrastructure required to irradiate a large part of the food supply would require hundreds of these facilities, which would put far too many communities and workers at risk.

IRRADIATION COMING TO A STORE NEAR YOU?

Fortunately, irradiated foods are not yet a significant portion of Americans' diets. Irradiated products still have to be labeled as such, and food manufacturers and processors have been reluctant to market irradiated products because those introduced to date have not sold well. In fact, irradiated products currently for sale claim only a tiny percentage of beef patties, sold mostly in the Southeast and Northeast; some papayas from Hawaii; some mangoes from India; and a few other foods. But despite the limited markets for these products, a new onslaught of regulatory and public relations initiatives seeks to revive the desperate industry. The FDA approved the use of irradiation for spinach and lettuce in 2008, although no companies have yet found a way to bring irradiated greens to the market. And the agency is sitting on petitions to allow the use of irradiation on other "ready to eat" foods such as lunch meats and hot dogs. The USDA is considering a petition from the meat industry that would allow meat packers to irradiate whole carcasses inside the slaughterhouse before they are processed into cuts of meat.

And it's not just approval for more uses of irradiation that the industry wants. Hiding behind their standard claims about the benefits of irradiation, the meat, food processing, and grocery industries continue to try to change Americans' minds about irradiated food. With such a large majority of the public against the technology, the industry is reduced to simply trying to make sure consumers won't know what food has been irradiated by weakening labeling requirements. At present, food must be labeled "Treated by Irradiation" and display a "radura" symbol—usually a small green flower within a circle. After years of pressure from the industry and instructions from Congress, the FDA is also trying to change the rules to allow a less alarming, more familiar term, like *pasteurization*, to be used to label irradiated food.

Not content to stick to covering up contamination in meat, the federal government and agribusiness are pushing irradiation in response to recent bacterial outbreaks in fresh vegetables, including *E. coli*–contaminated California spinach that killed 3 people and sickened more than 200 others in twenty-six states in fall 2006. As it stands now, however, irradiation cannot legally be used to kill bacteria on most vegetables. And the FDA may not have the justification to approve it. Very little testing has been conducted on the safety and wholesomeness of irradiated vegetables—and no published research exists on whether irradiated lettuce and spinach are safe for human consumption.[20] Rather than irradiating fresh vegetables, more care should be taken to prevent the flow of manure from industrialized livestock operations onto cropland, which many believe to be the cause of the California spinach outbreak.

Food irradiation and other technological quick fixes only serve to sustain the inhumane and unacceptable practices of the meat industry. Preventing a future that includes a largely irradiated diet will take a grassroots response that lets food corporations and regulators know that consumers want clean, wholesome food, not irradiation.

Part Seven

PUTTING THE CAFO OUT TO PASTURE

INTRODUCTION

Toward a Humane, Equitable, and Sustainable Food System

Calls for reform of industrial animal food production are becoming increasingly common among scientific commissions, international agencies, activist organizations, chefs, and concerned citizens. Some favor moratoriums on further expansion of certain types of livestock CAFOs. Others are working for bans against the most brutal confinement methods. Legislation to regulate antibiotic use in animal food production, already adopted in some European countries, is now being seriously considered in the United States. Critics argue that full enforcement of existing regulations governing monopoly control of markets and environmental protection, along with elimination of perverse subsidies, is long overdue. Voices are rising for the restoration of tens of millions of acres in the United States now under feed cultivation to permanent pastures for grass-fed livestock production. Animal welfare advocates such as philosopher Peter Singer and activist Erik Marcus go a step further, calling for a citizen movement to dismantle industrial animal production altogether.

The European Union currently leads the world in CAFO reforms. These changes are rooted in a seminal report produced in 1997 by the Farm Animal Welfare Council (FAWC), an independent advisory body established by the British government, that adopted a previously conceived set of principles known as "the five freedoms":

1. Freedom from hunger and thirst—by ready access to fresh water and a diet to maintain full health and vigor.

2. Freedom from discomfort—by providing an appropriate environment, including shelter and a comfortable resting area.

3. Freedom from pain, injury, or disease—by prevention or rapid diagnosis and treatment.

4. Freedom to express normal behavior—by providing sufficient space, proper facilities, and company of the animals' own kind.

5. Freedom from fear and distress—by ensuring conditions and treatment that avoid mental suffering.[1]

The European Union has agreed to phase out the most egregious confinement techniques: battery cages (for laying hens) by 2012, and gestation crates (for pregnant sows) by 2013. Some countries within the European Union are adopting measures to make slaughtering more humane. In 1998, Denmark, a leading hog-producing nation, placed strict regulations on antibiotic medicines in the swine industry.[2] Requiring a CAFO to become less pharmaceutically dependent imposes limits on the size of confinement operations and requires more careful oversight of animals.[3] Denmark's antibiotic restrictions have dramatically reduced the presence of antimicrobial-resistant bacteria, thereby prolonging the effectiveness of these medicines as human safeguards.

Demands are rising for animal food production to become more transparent. Slaughterhouses and feeding operations, for example, could be required to install video monitoring systems or agree to unannounced third-party inspections. CAFO operators could be required to accurately report their use of antibiotics rather than being able to purchase them by the sackload and distribute them without veterinary consult. Actual feed ingredients and detailed manure distribution records could be required and made more publicly available. Freedom of information within government agencies could allow the public to know exactly where taxpayer dollars are being spent to support the industry. None of these disclosures would be radical, but the industry is currently trending away from such transparency.

Still, it is not impossible to imagine a far different and far healthier food and farming system, beginning with a long-term commitment to pasture-based farming. Many have been advocating for some time for an ambitious transformation in U.S. agriculture away from soil-eroding feed grains toward deep-rooted perennial pastures, once again diversifying food production in the corn- and soybean-dominated Midwest. In fact, thousands of family farmers are managing appropriately scaled, grass-fed meat, dairy, and egg farms without raising animals in vile and sordid conditions. These pasture-based rotational grazing systems can be resource-efficient and often have the advantage of not needing energy- and capital-intensive inputs such as heating, ventilation, and cooling systems; expensive housing construction; imported industrial feeds; and mechanized manure management systems. They rely on sound animal husbandry techniques and integrating farm animals into a healthy landscape, using manure as a source of soil fertility. But scaling up will not be easy and will require a new generation of farmers willing to join the ranks of this noble profession; legions of consumers; and the financial, production, and processing infrastructure to support them.

To that end, citizens are calling for a much larger and more responsive role for government subsidies to guide sustainable food production. Reform of USDA farm bill programs—which pump billions of dollars into the economy and largely establish the rules of modern agriculture—is seen as an essential way to fund the transformation to a pasture-based livestock economy through green payments and other incentives. In 2008, Wes Jackson, founder of the Land Institute in Salina, Kansas; author Wendell Berry; and a coalition of sustainable farming advocates called for the launch of a "50-year farm bill" campaign: a succession of five-year plans (the average length of a farm bill) to move the country away from highly erosion-prone feed grain agriculture toward perennial, pasture-based animal systems. Others see farm bill programs as an economic engine to help rebuild regional food systems with funds for organic production research; preservation of traditional and endangered livestock breeds; start-up capital for programs linking local livestock producers with communities of eaters; and mobile slaughtering units to serve smaller regional producers.

If the industry is made to pay its true costs and make its practices transparent, changes in food production and personal consumption habits will evolve naturally. As more people and policy makers understand the enormous price we pay for "cheap" animal food products, we will see a shift in corn and feed subsidies and less tolerance of impacts such as soil erosion or excessive nutrient contamination. Livestock will remain essential for farming systems as well as for the human diet for some time, but ultimately we will realize that no person or country has the right to eat high on the protein ladder if it comes at a cost to the local ecosystem or the planet at large. We need action on all levels immediately, from governmental to individual. The time is now to push for more local, sustainable, humane, transparent, and just systems of food production and eating—in short, to put the CAFO out to pasture.

TOWARD SUSTAINABILITY

Moving from Energy Dependence to Energy Exchange

FRED KIRSCHENMANN

OUR ENTIRE FOOD SYSTEM TODAY *operates within the general frame-work of our industrial economy. But our world has changed. Fuel prices are unstable. Water resources are dwindling. And there are no more "sinks" where we can thoughtlessly bury industrial wastes. We must quickly adapt toward systems of energy exchange rather than energy consumption. Grass-pastured farming allows us to do just that.*

❖

Many citizens today are questioning whether animals can be sustainably included in our food and farming production. Sustainability is, of course, by definition a futuristic concept. The root word *sustain* is simply defined in *Webster's* dictionary as "to maintain," "to keep in existence," to "keep going." Sustainability is therefore a journey, an ongoing process, not a prescription or a set of instructions. So when we ask the question, How do we sustain animal agriculture? we are asking how we can manage animal agriculture so that it can be maintained indefinitely, and we are asking what changes need to be made along the way to accomplish that goal.

Sustaining animal agriculture then requires that we begin imagining the challenges and changes that our future will bring. In his extensive study of history, Jared Diamond pointed out that those civilizations that correctly assessed their current situations, anticipated the changes coming at them, and got a head start in preparing for those changes were the ones that thrived—they were sustainable.

Civilizations that failed in that quest were the ones that collapsed. They were not sustainable.[1] What is true for civilizations is likely also true for business enterprises.

Today, thoughtful citizens increasingly question whether animals belong in our food system at all. They see studies reporting that animals are responsible for a major part of the methane in our environment, one of the most pungent greenhouse gases contributing to climate change. They see reports that point out that a single pound of boneless beef has approximately 2,000 gallons of water embedded in it when the total water use required to raise the corn to feed the animal and process the meat is calculated. They read nutritional guidelines that consistently point out that we eat too much meat. So they wonder whether it might not be more sustainable to eliminate animals from our agriculture and food system altogether.

But from an ecological perspective, such reductionist thinking could produce serious unintended consequences that might create opposite results from those we intended. The problems we need to address may not be the result of animals as such, but of the food and farming system into which we have integrated those animals.

It is important to recognize that our entire food system today operates within the general framework of our industrial economy, which is based on two basic assumptions: (1) that natural resources and other inputs to fuel economic activities are unlimited, and (2) that nature provides unlimited "sinks" to absorb the wastes emanating from those economic activities. Our modern industrial food system, including our industrial animal agriculture, is simply part of that unrealistic economy.

Aldo Leopold recognized both the attractiveness and the vulnerability of industrial agriculture as early as 1945:

It was inevitable and no doubt desirable that the tremendous momentum of industrialization should have spread to farm life. It is clear to me, however, that it has overshot the mark, in the sense that it is generating new insecurities, economic and ecological, in place of those it was meant to abolish. In its extreme form, it is humanly desolate and economically unstable. These extremes will some day die of their own too-much, not because they are bad for wildlife, but because they are bad for the farmers.[2]

As we enter the twenty-first century, the insecurities Leopold perceived are beginning to manifest themselves, and there are urgent reasons to reevaluate the way we produce crops and animals in our food system. Among the many changes we are likely to see in the next fifty years, three will be especially challenging to our current industrial agriculture system—the depletion of our stored *energy* and *water* resources, and our changing *climate*.

The reason these changes will be especially challenging to our current food and agriculture system, including our industrial animal agriculture enterprises, is that our industrial economy of the past century was based on the availability of *cheap* energy, *abundant* fresh water, and a relatively *stable* climate.

The end of cheap energy may well be the first limited resource to force change in our industrial animal enterprises. Our modern industrial agriculture production system is almost entirely dependent on fossil fuels. The nitrogen used for fertilizer to produce the animal feed is derived from natural gas. Phosphorus and potash are mined, processed, and transported to farms with petroleum energy. Pesticides are manufactured from petroleum resources. Farm equipment is manufactured and operated with petroleum energy. Feed is produced and trucked to concentrated animal operations with fossil fuels. The manure is collected and hauled to distant locations with fossil fuels.

As long as fossil fuels were cheap, they made all these inputs available at very low cost. But independent scholars agree that we have now either reached peak oil production or will shortly do so.[3]

Of course, alternatives to fossil fuel energy are available—biofuels and wind, solar, and geothermal energy—so one could theoretically contemplate replacing oil and natural gas with alternative sources of energy to keep industrial animal agriculture viable. But the reality that we must face is that our industrial economy was created on a platform of *stored, concentrated energy* that produced a very favorable energy profit ratio—the amount of energy yield divided by the amount of energy expended to make it available. All alternative energy, on the other hand, is based on current, dispersed energy, which has a much lower energy profit ratio. Consequently, economies that are dependent on cheap energy are not likely to fare well in the future. And that is why the depletion of our fossil fuel resources will require not only that we transition to alternative fuels to produce our food, but also that we transition to a new energy system. Creative new designs for animal production are likely to be part of such new energy systems.

The real energy transition that we must contemplate is converting from an energy input system to an energy exchange system. It is this energy transition that is likely to lead us to consider significant systems changes in the way we produce our crops and livestock. Future systems are less likely to be specialized monocultures and more likely to be based on biological diversity, organized so that each organism exchanges energy with other organisms, forming a web of synchronous relationships, instead of relying on energy-intensive inputs.

A second natural resource that has been essential to industrial agriculture is a relatively stable climate. We often mistakenly attribute the yield-producing success of the past century entirely to the development of new production technologies. In point of fact, those robust yields were at least as much due to unusually favorable climate conditions as they were to technology.

The National Academy of Sciences (NAS) Panel on Climate Variations reported in 1975 that "our present [stable] climate is in fact highly abnormal," and that "the earth's climates have always been changing, and the magnitude of . . . the changes can be catastrophic." The report concluded that "the global patterns of food production and population that have evolved are implicitly dependent on the climate of the present century." It then went on to suggest that climate change might be further exacerbated by "our own activities."[4] In other words, according to NAS, it is this combination of "normal" climate variation plus the changes that will occur from our own industrial economies (greenhouse gas emissions) that could have a significant impact on our future agricultural productivity.[5]

A third natural resource that may challenge our current soil management system is water. Lester Brown points out that while we each need only 4 liters of water to meet our daily liquid requirement, our current industrial agriculture system consumes 2,000 liters per day to produce each of our daily food requirements. A significant amount of that water is consumed by production agriculture. Agriculture consumes over 70 percent of our global freshwater resources for irrigation.[6]

Water tables in the Ogallala Aquifer supply water for one of every five irrigated acres in the United States, but this fossil water bank is now half depleted and is being overdrawn at the rate of 3.1 trillion gallons per year according to some reports.[7] And it now appears that as we attempt to meet our energy needs with alternative fuels, we are putting additional stress on our water resources. According to a 2007 *Des Moines Register* article, the production of biofuels is putting significant additional pressure on our water resources, and climate change is likely to further stress that resource.[8] In 2007, Kansas filed a lawsuit against Nebraska over its use of water from the Republican River, which is used for irrigation and other purposes in both states. Kansas complained that from 2005 to 2006, Nebraska had diverted more than its share of water for irrigation and cost the state of Kansas millions of dollars in losses. In 2009, the arbitrator for the dispute found that Nebraska had indeed surpassed its water allocation and that the state's plans for future compliance with water use remained insufficient. As drought and overuse of water increase, so are the disputes over remaining water resources.[9] Previously, Kansas had sued Colorado over Arkansas River water diverted in Colorado, in part, for agriculture irrigation and use by the city of Denver. Reduced snowpacks in mountainous regions due to climate change will decrease spring runoff, a primary source of irrigation water in many parts of the world, adding stress to our water shortages.

These early indications of stress demonstrate that our new energy, water, and climate changes will intersect and impact each other in many unanticipated ways, making industrial production systems increasingly vulnerable.

It is this new reality that should lead us to reassess the place of animals in our food system. In nature, a healthy, self-renewing ecosystem always has animals integrated into a biological synergy that enables the biotic community to thrive. Despite the fact that we could reduce our energy consumption by eating crop proteins directly in the form of vegetables and cereal grains instead of feeding the grains to animals, there are also significant landscapes that are not suitable for crop production but that are ideal for grazing animals. On our farm in North Dakota, for example, 1,000 of the 3,500 acres we farm are still in native prairie because they are land that is simply not suitable for crop production. That native prairie supports over 150 beef animals that produce protein on grass, and the grass produces considerable ecological capital in the form of habitat for wildlife, sequestering carbon, and numerous other ecological services.

Furthermore, animals are essential to building healthy soils, and, as it turns out, how we manage our soils under the new energy, water, and climate regimes in which we find ourselves can make major contributions to the sustainability of our future farming systems. We know, from both research and on-farm experience, that when soils are managed in accordance with closed regenerative loops that build soil organic matter, the soil's capacity to absorb and retain moisture is significantly enhanced, reducing the need for irrigation. We also know from on-farm experience (as well as from nature's own elasticity) that diverse systems are more resilient than monocultures in the face of adverse climate conditions. And we know from on-farm experience that energy inputs can be dramatically reduced when input/output systems are replaced by recycling systems. Managing soil health based on recycling systems will require more mixed crop/ livestock systems.

Joe Lewis and his colleagues, who worked for many years with the USDA Agricultural Research Services in Tifton, Georgia, for example, clearly articulated the failure of the industrial "single tactic" "therapeutic intervention" strategy when applied to pest management. They point out that while it may "seem that an optimal corrective action for an undesired entity is to apply a direct external counter force against it," in fact, "such interventionist actions never produce sustainable desired effects. Rather, the attempted solution becomes the problem." The alternative, they propose, is "an understanding and shoring up of the full composite of inherent plant defenses, plant mixtures, soil, natural enemies, and other components of the system. These natural 'built in' regulators are linked in a web of feedback loops and are renewable and sustainable."[10]

Approaching pest management, weed control, or animal diseases from such an ecological perspective always involves a web of relationships that require more biologically diverse systems. "For example, problems with soil erosion have resulted in major thrusts in use of winter cover crops and conservation tillage. Preliminary studies indicate that cover crops also serve as bridge/refugia to stabilize natural enemy/pest balances and relay these balances into the crop season."[11] In short, such natural systems management can revitalize soil health, reduce weed and other pest pressures, get farmers off the pesticide treadmill and begin the transition from an energy-intensive industrial farming operation to a self-regulating, self-renewing one. Having animals in a diversified crop/animal system always enhances the possibilities for establishing such self-regulating systems.

Other benefits, such as greater water conservation, follow from the improved soil health, which results from closed recycling systems. As research conducted by John Reganold and his colleagues at Washington State University has demonstrated, soil managed by such recycling methods develops richer topsoil, more than twice the organic matter, more biological activity, and far greater moisture absorption and holding capacity.[12]

Such soil management serves as an example of how we can begin to move to an energy system that operates on the basis of energy *exchange* instead of energy *input*. But more innovation is needed. Nature is a very efficient energy manager. All of nature's energy comes from sunlight that is processed into carbon through photosynthesis and becomes available to various organisms that exchange energy through a web of relationships. Bison on the prairie obtain their energy from the grass, which gets its energy from the soil and from the sun. Bison deposit their excrement back onto the grass, which provides energy for insects and other organisms that, in turn, convert it to energy that enriches the soil to produce more grass. It is these energy exchange systems that we must explore and adapt to our postindustrial farming systems. But very little research is currently devoted to exploring such energy exchanges on a farm scale.

Fortunately, a few farmers have already developed such energy exchange systems and appear to be quite successful in managing their operations with very little fossil fuel input.[13] Converting our farms to this new energy model will require a major transformation.

Our highly specialized monocultures, which are energy-intensive, will need to be converted to complex, highly diversified operations that function on energy exchange. The practicality and multiple benefits of such integrated crop/livestock systems have been established through research,[14] but further research will be needed to explore how to adapt this new model of farming to various thermo climes and ecosystems.

Of course it is always difficult to change systems that have developed infrastructures to support them. But we can begin the transition by moving in the right direction. Intensive confined animal feeding operations can take steps to begin transitioning to a more sustainable future with waste-composting systems and other innovations.

Farmers in many parts of the world are adopting deep-bedded hoop barn technologies for raising their animals in confinement. Hoop barns are much less expensive to construct and have demonstrated production efficiencies that are comparable to nonbedded confinement systems and have proved to be a more welfare-friendly environment for animals.[15] The deep-bedded system allows animals to exercise more of their natural functions; absorbs the urine and manure of the animals, which is then composted and used to build soil quality on nearby land; and also provides warmth for the animals during the winter months. Such hoop structures are now being used in hog, beef, dairy, and some poultry operations and have demonstrated reduced environmental impact and risk.[16]

Tweaking our monoculture confinement operations with such methods may be possible and arguably may be necessary in the short term, but as our energy, water, and climate resources undergo dramatic changes, we will need to transition to much more biologically diverse systems, organized into biological synergies that exchange energy, improve soil quality, and conserve water and other resources. Long-term sustainability will require a transformation from an industrial economy to an ecological economy.

THE GOOD FARMER

An Agrarian Approach to Animal Agriculture

PETER KAMINSKY

DESPITE THE TREND toward confinement and consolidation in the hog industry, there is a growing group of pig farmers turning back to small-scale animal husbandry. Paul Willis, founding farmer and manager of Niman Ranch Pork, is leading a movement to let pigs be pigs—giving them space to roam and root, fresh bedding to nest in, and healthy pasture to graze in. A visit to Willis's farm reveals an agricultural model for the future.

❖

There is not much prairie left in the Corn Belt, where the bison once roamed in the tens of millions and the sky darkened when passenger pigeons in the hundreds of millions passed overhead. Paul Willis, manager and founding farmer of Niman Ranch Pork, has joined a growing movement to restore at least a part of the prairie ecosystem. The wildflowers and grasses he has planted or that have returned on their own have names that must surely have sprung from the tongues of poets: bluestem and Indian grass, pale purple corn-flower, death camus, butterfly milkweed, and rattlesnake master.

Willis is an old-fashioned pig farmer. In our agribusiness age, that makes him as remarkable as such other passing American phe-nomena as a pitcher who can go nine innings and an actor who can sing without lip-synching.

When I first visited him, Paul served me coffee and pie in the farmhouse kitchen, and then took me to see his spread. We crossed the road to a field where young pigs gamboled in the grass, noses twitching in a wind heavy with the scent of flowers and new grass. A few sows lay in the shade of their farrowing huts, where their litters suckled, slept, and moved about.

"Don't approach them too quickly; they are protective mothers," Paul said.

The sows lay there placidly, each one like a nanny sitting on a park bench, taking in the world while her young charges played and tumbled nearby. When one of the sows walked over to the feeder, I slowly approached the back of her hut, a piece of corrugated aluminum bent into an arch, with the floor being nothing more than deeply bedded hay. The tiny piglets, climbing over each other and playfully nipping, were awfully cute. The fact that the natural position of a pig's mouth looks very much like a human smile serves to amplify the affection that such babies elicit.

Willis, and most of Niman's farmers, raise a hog known as a Farmer's Hybrid, not because of extensive research but because it is the hog that Willis has always raised. Its genetics are a multigenic stew that typically contains Chester White, Hampshire, Duroc, and Large White genes. It is bred for flavor, hardiness, and mothering ability. The first is what is most important to the consumer, but to achieve that flavor the animals must be able to thrive well outdoors and raise healthy litters (it costs just as much to maintain a sow that keeps nine piglets to weaning as it does to maintain a sow who loses two of her litter).

"Basically, I am just trying to raise pigs the way we did fifty years ago when being a farmer meant being a family farmer," Willis says. "You raised some corn, some soy, some chickens, a cow or two. You planted fruit trees around the house. And you let your pigs be pigs. Which means you gave them plenty of room, the opportunity to be outdoors where they could root and graze, and lots of straw so that they could have deep, fresh bedding. In the winter, the deep bedding can absorb waste material [although given the choice most pigs will deposit most of their waste outside]. When the hay decomposes, the bed produces its own natural warmth."

Speaking about the comfort of his animals brings Willis to one of the things about which he is most proud. Niman Ranch Pork was the first national livestock company whose practices were approved by the Animal Welfare Institute. The AWI standards include: (1) Pigs must be owned and raised by family farmers personally involved in the business, and they must apply AWI standards to every animal they own. (2) Pigs may never be fed bonemeal or other animal products. (3) They may never be raised in close-quarter confinement and must be given sufficient room to roam, forage, and interact with other pigs. (4) No growth hormones are allowed, and antibiotics are permitted only to treat disease. (5) No tail docking is allowed, and animals may not be weaned before they are six weeks old.

Summing it up, Willis says, in his low-key manner, "It's not rocket science; it's really allowing the animal to be a pig. In other words, what are the natural inclinations of a pig?"

Willis grew up at the old farmhouse that now serves as the head-quarters of Niman Ranch Pork. His life detoured away from the farm for twelve years, but he eventually returned and began raising pigs again. "I was aware of things like free-range chickens on the one hand and the poultry factories and hog factories on the other," Willis said. "I realized that simply raising pigs outside, the way we used to, was becoming pretty rare. I knew there had to be a wider market for it. I had been looking for a way to sell the type of pork that we were rais-ing probably ten years before I met Bill Niman."

Niman Ranch Pork is named after its association with Bill Niman, who founded a cattle ranch in Bolinas, California. His grass-fed beef and lamb had attracted the attention of Alice Waters, the great chef and prophetess of the nationwide interest in fresh, wholesome ingredi-ents. A mutual friend introduced Willis to Niman during a California visit.

"We had lunch at a burger joint in San Francisco," Willis explains. "I told him what I was doing, and he gave me some of the locally raised pork he was selling. I took it back to my sister's, in Brisbane, California, where we prepared it and it was . . . all right."

That's Paul's nice way of saying it wasn't special, so I prodded him on it.

"Actually, it was mediocre. When I returned to Iowa, we packed up a box of frozen chops and roasts and sent them to Bill. He then sent the pork around to various customers, one of them being Chez Panisse [Alice Waters's restaurant]. I'd never even heard of Chez Panisse at the time. Anyway, they all loved the pork. So Bill said, 'Send me thirty hogs.'

"This was really a far cry from what we had been used to doing, which was to call up hog buyers and whoever had the best price locally, you would take your hogs in and they would write you a check and that was it. This was a different deal. The pork went to the West Coast over the weekend. So the pigs had to be at the slaughterhouse on Wednesday, killed on Thursday, chilled on Friday, and shipped out. The meat got there at five-thirty Monday morning. That was a pretty exciting moment.

"Bill said, 'Well, what do you want, what's your price?' That was the first time as a farmer that I wasn't really dealing in a commodity. I had something that *I could put value on!*

"So we came to an agreement. I started out sending hogs, every other week, about thirty-five head, then we'd go to thirty-seven head, forty head, and when I couldn't keep up with the numbers, I started looking for some neighbors and some other farmers I knew. First was Glen Alden, a local, and Bob Gristoff, right from Thornton. We started getting calls from other farmers. That fall . . . I had about thirty, thirty-five farmers involved."

Departing from what was then the norm for farmers—selling to a packinghouse and collecting the money on the spot—Willis had to figure out a new way to get the farmer paid. "Through the Packers and Stockyard Act, farmers must be paid within a couple of days. With Niman, the cash flow situation was different. A pig comes from the farm, goes to a packing plant, then to California, then to a customer, and you, the farmer, have to wait weeks before the money comes back to you.

"So the pork company was created to enable us to pay the farmers right away, out of cash flow. We made it a requirement that each of our farmers would pay a capital contribution each time a pig was sold. It started out at one penny a pound. That was matched by Niman Ranch in California. So we as farmers put money into the company to build up a reserve, to be able to buy pigs from ourselves, and the parent company would reimburse the pork company. That penny a pound also built the farmer's equity in the company.

"The commodity business is all about doing more and doing it cheaper, but our thinking is, if you're raising the best pork, you should be paid the best price. We decided to pay around fifteen dollars a hog over the market price. We also established a floor for those times when the local market falls below a certain point. In 1998, hog prices went to eight cents a pound. Niman Ranch paid forty-three and a half cents at that time. The good part was that we saved people's farms; we made a big difference. The bad part was that we weren't able to buy all of everybody's pigs at the time."

Willis related to me his company autobiography in bits and snatches over the course of a day, much punctuated by incoming calls on his cell phone. We drove through the rolling green Iowa country-side, with its old-fashioned red barns, easy on the eyes, even soothing. Everything was, to outward appearances, as it had always been since the late nineteenth century, with the exception that here and there, standing out from the landscape into which they would never blend, were low white buildings with peaked roofs.

"See over there?" Paul said. "That's a fifteen-hundred-sow opera-tion." He was referring to a confinement operation. "Everybody says they don't want to see more of them, but some farmers are up against it and see it as a way out." When small farmers find themselves pit-ted against factory farms, the economics often force them to give in despite the long-term benefits of small-scale farming.

The family farm—a symbol that is much praised by politicians but that is being driven to extinction by public policy—represents one way of dealing with the land, the plants that grow on it, the live-stock that is raised there, the wildlife that somehow manages to find a way to freeload on the edges of fields, woodlots, and uncultivated set-asides. I think of this outlook as the Agricultural Way, or, as the historians of rural life say, the Agrarian Way: agrarian, with its con-notations of populism and land stewardship—not merely planting, raising, and harvesting in the shortest period of time. What goes on in the sugar plantations of Florida, the chicken factories of Arkansas, the hog factories of North Carolina (and Iowa, and Illinois, and Colorado, and more) is decidedly not agrarian nor is it truly agricul-ture: it is industry.

Industry is about qualification, standardization, risk manage-ment. It consumes resources and therefore depletes them. The agrar-ian approach, on the other hand, is about managing resources sus-tainably, creating while consuming, renewing while reaping. There are no factories, that I know of, that have been around for five hundred years, yet there is land the world over that has been managed agriculturally for hundreds if not thousands of years: the vineyards of France, the cattle-supporting pampas of Argentina, the oak savannas of western Spain, the rice paddies of Indochina. The industrial model seeks to control nature; the agrarian seeks to manage it. The former consumes more and more resources to maintain output; the latter can go on producing forever.

With his small, multigenerational family farm, with his acres of reclaimed prairie, his woodlots with soil-conserving trees, his use of manure from his animals to fertilize the fields that produce the feed that sustains the animals that, completing the circle, produce the manure that starts the cycle all over again, Willis represents one thread of American agricultural history. The other thread—the one of the endless frontier and the genetically engineered and petrochemical-based "Green Revolution"—has been wildly profitable (for the shareholders of agribusiness corporations), but it is inevitably ruinous for the ecology.

The alternative to this approach is diversified farming of the kind that typified family farms and that, in some measure, is practiced by supporters of sustainable agriculture such as Willis. He is among the most influential of a very few who are employing modern business practices in the service of traditional agriculture.

"The Polish peasants' farmers union had a conference," Willis says as he recalls an event he was invited to. "They had farm leaders, veterinarians, animal welfare people, environmentalists, and—this really impressed me—they had philosophers and they gave them equal billing! It made sense. I mean, the whole idea was about basic questions of how we and the animals live. And the thought struck me, 'Gee, I wonder if at our next conference at Iowa State we could get some philosophers.' You know, in the farm business they never want to make decisions unless they are based on sound science. But you can manipulate science to whatever your objective is. Philosophers could help."

"You mean like Wendell Berry at your next farrowing conference?"

"Sure, why not?" he said.

CHANGING THE LAW

The Road to Reform

PAIGE TOMASELLI AND MEREDITH NILES

FROM A LEGAL PERSPECTIVE, *there is a lot of blame to go around when assessing the far-reaching devastation caused by animal factory food production. First is our failure to put laws in place, or the passage of laws that grant factory farms free passes on animal rights and environmental violations. Then there is a lack of enforcement of laws that do exist. The European Union has shown global leadership with legal reform. It's our job to follow their lead and then go even further.*

❖

In the state of California, the historic nature of the 2008 election went far beyond the White House. For the first time, residents of the most populous state in the union went to the polls to cast their opinion on the welfare of farm animals. The ballot included Proposition 2, a statewide referendum poised to ban veal crates, battery cages for egg-laying hens, and gestation crates for pigs by mandating that animals have sufficient space to lie down, stand up, fully extend their limbs, and turn around freely. Animal welfare, environmental, and public health organizations throughout the country championed the measure as an effective way to end animal abuses and blatant food safety violations, and to set the stage for additional state and federal initiatives. While supporters of Proposition 2 organized grassroots efforts throughout the state, the industry launched its own smear campaign in a desperate attempt to continue their severe factory farming confinement practices.

Hidden behind the misnomer "Californians for Safe Food," the factory farming industry launched a public campaign rife with scare tactics. Misleadingly promoting the use of confinement crates and cages as a means to protect the public from bird flu, salmonella, and a host of other diseases, it called Proposition 2 "unnecessary, risky and extreme."[1] The campaign appealed to people's wallets by asserting that Proposition 2 would cost $600 million and bankrupt the California egg industry.[2] Donations poured in from agribusiness corporations and industrial farms, mounting to more than $8 million. Nearly 60 percent came from outside the state of California,[3] an example of corporate factory farming creating a loss of local democratic control.

Fortunately, California residents saw through industry-funded fearmongering. Proposition 2 passed by an overwhelming vote of 63.5 percent, with nearly twice as many people voting for the statute as against it.[4] It was a historic first step to end some of the worst abuses of factory farming in the United States. With nearly 12 percent of the total U.S. population, California by its vote on Proposition 2 sent a message to the rest of the country and our lawmakers that people care about animal welfare and want action. While Proposition 2 should be celebrated as a victory for animals and democratic local control, its necessity highlights the nation's huge factory farming problem. If federal legislation and regulations were enforced, if government required the industry to pay for its true environmental costs, and if our agencies were fully funded to regulate factory farms, initiatives like Proposition 2 would likely be unnecessary.

BARELY THERE: CURRENT U.S. REGULATIONS

Numerous U.S. laws and regulations claim to oversee factory farms. Unfortunately, inconsistent adoption and enforcement along with blatant industry exemptions from a variety of rules have created regulatory loopholes and incessant violations, leading many to believe that laws regulating factory farms don't even exist. In fact, dozens of environmental and animal welfare statutes on both a state and federal level at least purport to address some portion of the overwhelming problems caused by factory farms.

ENVIRONMENTAL STATUTES   The Clean Water Act (CWA)[5] is the main law charged with regulating water pollution, including toxic animal manures at factory farms; however, application has thus far been undercut by loose enforcement and widespread industry exemptions. The Clinton administration Environmental Protection Agency (EPA) attempted to fix this problem and create a regulation holding concentrated animal feeding operations (CAFOs) accountable for cleaning up their waste.[6] The Bush administration immediately vacated this regulation and in 2003 issued its own rule, creating major CWA loopholes, such as exempting "land applied waste" (manure spreading) as a point source of pollution.[7] When faced with a legal challenge, the United States Court of Appeals for the Second Circuit sided with environmentalists on several counts, holding that the rule failed to hold CAFOs accountable for their waste. The court, however, sided with industry on the argument that only CAFOs that generate "actual discharges" must apply for permits.[8] In practice, this left a significant number of CAFOs outside of the CWA permit process, creating a self-certifying system in which CAFOs can claim they are not discharging pollution and thus do not need a permit.

In response to the court decision, the EPA published a new rule in November 2008. While the new rule requires permits for discharges from land applications of manure,[9] it remains riddled with loopholes. The rule relies on factory farm operators to self-determine whether their waste dumping activities are considered "discharges" and subject to regulation under the CWA.[10] The new rule effectively allows CAFOs to claim that waste not directly pumped into rivers or streams is not a "discharge" requiring a permit. The rule concurrently established a voluntary permitting system for CAFOs proposing to not discharge; yet voluntary permits are not open for public participation or regulatory review and do not exclusively prohibit CAFOs from being able to obtain "nondischarge" status even after a documented discharge. The result of this regulatory rigging is that the CWA requirements cater to factory farming and allow CAFOs virtual self-regulation at the expense of the environment and human health.

When it comes to regulating CAFO air pollution, the situation is no brighter. Globally, a shocking 18 percent of human-caused greenhouse gas emissions come from the livestock industry, according to the UN Food and Agriculture Organization, although some experts feel the contribution could be as high as 51 percent.[11] Increasingly, scientific studies are demonstrating that factory farms exacerbate greenhouse gas emissions and concentrate toxic air emissions into local areas,[12] which adversely impact rural neighborhoods and farm worker health.[13]

The Clean Air Act (CAA)[14] is the major piece of federal legislation charged with enhancing air quality and promoting public health and welfare.[15] The CAA establishes a cooperative state-federal scheme for overseeing and improving the nation's air quality.[16] While the CAA does *not* exempt agricultural sources from its substantive or procedural mandates, factory farms have historically evaded regulation. They are considered "stationary sources" under the CAA and are thus obligated to comply with the CAA's "New Source Review" permitting requirements. Whether a CAFO facility actually triggers these permit programs, however, is currently being litigated.[17]

While some CAFO air pollutants are regulated under the CAA and are therefore subject to its mandates, the most significant—nitrous oxide, methane, carbon dioxide, and ammonia—are not.[18] Hydrogen sulfide, a deadly toxic gas produced during manure degradation, is subject to only minimal monitoring and sickens or kills farm workers yearly.[19, 20] Until recently, excessive releases of ammonia and hydrogen sulfide were regulated under the toxic air emissions reporting requirements of both the Superfund law—the Comprehensive Environmental Response, Compensation, and Liability Act (CERCLA)[21]—and the Emergency Planning and Community Right-to-Know Act (EPCRA).[22] Unfortunately, a late-term Bush administration regulation exempted the reporting of such toxic air emissions from CAFOs.[23] The Bush-era EPA noted that "[t]he Agency believes that a federal response to such notifications is impractical and unlikely,"[24] thereby setting the precedent that laws not easily enforced can be eliminated at the expense of the environment, farm workers, and communities in dangerous proximity to sickening and potentially deadly levels of toxic air emissions.[25] In early 2009, the Center for Food Safety, with other environmental and public interest organizations, filed suit challenging the legality of this exemption.[26]

ANIMAL WELFARE STATUTES Regulation of farm animal welfare at a federal level is almost nonexistent in the United States. The Animal Welfare Act, the most notable federal legislation, protects animals only as instruments of interstate commerce and entirely excludes factory farm animals and fish.[27] As a result, horrific animal abuses that could imprison someone if performed on a domestic animal are perfectly legal and acceptable for farm animals.

Ironically, farm animal welfare is most protected at the time of the animal's death. The Humane Slaughter Act aims to prevent needless suffering and slaughtering of conscious animals.[28] Lax enforcement, in part because of the more than 9 billion animals slaughtered yearly,[29] allows factory farms to disregard slaughter laws. Unfortunately, even if the Humane Slaughter Act was enforceable, the law explicitly exempts chickens, which represent over 95 percent of animals slaughtered for food in the United States.[30]

State anticruelty laws often suffer from the same flaws as federal laws.[31] In the past two decades, factory farm interests have convinced states to add "common farming exemptions" (CFEs) to state statutes, legitimizing farm animal abuse. The exemptions use "common," "customary," "established," and generally "accepted" practices within the industry to justify inhumane treatment.[32] For instance, the Nevada anticruelty laws "do not prohibit or interfere with established methods of animal husbandry, including raising, handling, feeding, housing, and transporting livestock or farmed animals."[33] These CFEs empower the farming industry to self-determine farmed animal cruelty for their own benefit, rather than in the best interest of animal welfare.[34]

Public interest organizations, including the Center for Food Safety and the New Jersey Society for Prevention of Cruelty to Animals, paved the way to challenging such regulations with litigation in New Jersey when that state amended its animal cruelty law.[35] The organizations challenged numerous provisions of the regulations, including a CFE for all "routine husbandry practices." The court determined that the protection of routine husbandry practices was arbitrary and capricious, because it failed to comply with the law stating that practices must also be humane. Such challenges to CFEs are highly dependent on language specifically written into the exemptions, and the New Jersey Supreme Court noted that this type of challenge might not prevail in other states because many states chose to not require practices to be humane.[36]

Even when state anticruelty laws do not contain CFEs, enforcement is rare. State anticruelty laws are criminal statutes, which status prevents private citizens from enforcing them.[37] Instead, local district attorneys have exclusive enforcement abilities, but limited resources and priorities for animal welfare prosecutions, resulting in little enforcement and few prosecutions.

Despite the current climate, there is new hope in the battle for state welfare protections. As public awareness of animal welfare issues has grown, an increasing number of states have passed laws to end the worst animal abuses at factory farms. Prior to California's Proposition 2, Florida, Arizona, and Oregon had banned pig gestation crates, and Arizona and Colorado had banned veal crates.[38] These laws are notable steps toward a nationwide commitment to animal welfare.

ANTIMONOPOLY REGULATIONS In addition to blatant violations and exemptions for factory farms under our nation's environmental and animal welfare laws, a significant portion of the CAFO problem lies in the structure of the industry. The vertically integrated nature of the animal agriculture system and a lack of antimonopoly enforcement have enabled livestock processors to exhibit immense control over the entire system. Large-scale CAFOs are often tied directly into processors and distributors, yet small-scale livestock producers face dwindling markets and rely on a handful of large corporations to buy, process, and sell their product, increasing the economic power that processors hold over producers. As of 2004, only four firms controlled 80 percent of beef slaughter, 64 percent of hog slaughter, and 57 percent of sheep slaughter in the United States.[39]

Congress enacted the 1921 Packers and Stockyards Act (PSA)[40] to safeguard the livestock industry against monopolies and collusion. The law provides that it shall be "unlawful for any packer or swine contractor . . . to make or give any undue or unreasonable preference or advantage to any particular person or locality in any respect whatsoever."[41] The U.S. Department of Agriculture's (USDA's) Grain Inspection, Packers and Stockyards Administration (GIPSA) administers the PSA but unfortunately has never defined what "undue and unreasonable preferences" actually mean. As a result, courts have interpreted the law to mean that undue preferences must have anticompetitive impacts to be a violation of the PSA. This interpretation of the PSA forces farmers suing for "competitive harm" to prove how the behavior of one company has negatively impacted the competitiveness of the entire industry.[42] Recently, however, the Fifth Circuit Court of Appeals held that a plaintiff does not need to prove an adverse effect on competition to prevail, a conclusion in tension with sister appellate courts.[43] It appears that the Supreme Court or a congressional action will be needed to decide the issue.

VEGGIE LIBEL LAWS In 1996, Oprah Winfrey devoted an episode of her talk show to mad cow disease and learned that some American cattle were fed ground-up meal from dead livestock, potentially exacerbating mad cow disease.[44] The National Cattlemen's Beef Association has a voluntary ban on ruminant-to-ruminant feeding; however, Oprah's guest, Howard Lyman, insisted he had personally witnessed the practice and that there are USDA statistics to back it up.[45] Oprah then made history after decrying: "It has just stopped me cold from eating another burger!"[46] Oprah did not realize that her words would land her in a lawsuit[47] that utilized "veggie libel laws," also known as "food disparagement laws," which make it easier for food industry interests to sue critics, opponents, and concerned citizens for speaking out against industry practices. Veggie libel laws have been passed in thirteen states: Alabama, Arizona, Colorado, Florida, Georgia, Idaho, Louisiana, Mississippi, North Dakota, Ohio, Oklahoma, South Dakota, and Texas. According to these laws, industry can file a claim against any individual if it suffers damages as a result of this person's disparagement of a perishable food product.[48] Veggie libel laws are controversial free-speech inhibitors, and the constitutionality of these laws remains uncertain. Still, publications about the food industry have been delayed because of the fear these laws generate,[49] and lawsuits have been filed against individuals speaking out against food safety.

THE EUROPEAN APPROACH: A MODEL IN THE MAKING

While U.S. regulators have undertaken significant efforts to protect and defend industrial factory farming at the expense of public health, animal welfare, and the environment, other governments have chosen to regulate animal agriculture in a different way. In particular, many European countries and the European Union as a whole have become a blueprint for animal production, establishing an oversight system that protects industry interests and animal welfare, the environment, and public health at the same time. While not perfect, the European model offers many examples and opportunities that the United States could rely on in overhauling its own system.

THE EUROPEAN UNION REGULATORY SYSTEM AND ANIMAL WELFARE LEGISLATION Historically, the United States has utilized environmental statutes to regulate factory farms; conversely, the European Union (EU) has regulated these farms more often through animal welfare directives and continues to implement new regulations and enforce those already in place. Within the EU system,[50] directives outline a final goal but give member states the ability to implement rules how they see fit, often resulting in more stringent requirements.[51] The European Convention on Farm Animals laid the foundation for farm animal welfare in the EU by regulating pain and suffering and outlining general welfare conditions, freedom of movement, and environmental conditions. Enforcement of the convention has been implemented through daily inspections to monitor both animal welfare and technical equipment.[52] Several farm animal welfare directives have since followed, including the establishment of the Welfare Quality Project, which aims to develop a single, clear regulatory framework for animal health. The recent adoption of the Animal Health Strategy under the motto "Prevention is better than cure"[53] demonstrates the continued interest of the EU in advancing and evolving animal welfare statutes.

SPECIES-SPECIFIC WELFARE PROVISIONS While the EU is developing its broader animal welfare policy, it has also enacted species-specific directives to phase out some of the cruelest practices, including gestation crates, veal crates, and battery cages, all still common in the United States. Such directives are markedly changing the way factory farms are run by reducing the number of animals that can be handled, inspected, and cared for daily. In the case of pigs, the European Commission enacted two welfare directives: one reducing confinement[54] and the other eliminating and reducing painful procedures like tail docking, castration, and early weaning.[55]

The chicken and cattle industries have also been a focal point to stop animal welfare abuses in the EU. Recent directives established stocking density rates for broiler chickens, allowing 30 percent more space per bird than in the United States, and included recommendations on farm worker training and requirements for lighting, feeding, litter, noise, and ventilation.[56] Other regulations stopped the introduction of new battery cages as of 2003 and banned all battery cages as of 2012.[57] Norway has effectively banned beak clipping and burning[58] by requiring a veterinarian to conduct all surgical procedures and medical treatment, and the United Kingdom prohibits the deprivation of food, water, and light.[59] And in 2008, the EU established minimum standards for the protection of calves by effectively banning veal crates.[60]

EUROPEAN UNION SLAUGHTER LEGISLATION The EU also has long-established welfare practices for slaughter, and more recent regulations have continued to evolve the EU standards. In 2008, the EU proposed a regulation, developed with input from a variety of stakeholders, that increases responsibility for animal welfare by directing operators to recognize physical comfort and to prevent injury, disease, pain, aggression, lack of feed or water, and adverse interaction. It also regulates killing methods and worker competency by requiring that personnel handling and/or slaughtering animals must possess a certificate of competence.[61]

ANTIBIOTICS AND GROWTH HORMONES European countries have also made significant progress in reducing or eliminating the use of unnecessary antibiotics in animal production. Antibiotics are given to farm animals to treat illness, prevent disease, or promote growth. The use of antibiotics to promote growth, also known as nontherapeutic use, has created significant controversy because of its link with antibiotic resistance, and the perpetuation of unhealthy and unsafe farm conditions. Some European countries have banned the use of a variety of antibiotics frequently used for people. In the early 1970s, the United Kingdom banned the use of penicillin and tetracycline for growth promotion. Later, Sweden took the initiative one step further by banning the use of all growth-promoting antibiotics in farm animals.[62] The most studied case, however, is the Denmark ban.

In 1998, Denmark banned antibiotic growth promoters in pigs and chickens and began pioneering reductions in agricultural use of antibiotics by assembling the world's most comprehensive data on antibiotic use and antibiotic-resistant bacteria.[63] The Danish ban created significant declines in resistant bacteria in pork and chicken. For example, antibiotic-resistant bacteria in those animals dropped from 60–80 percent to 5–35 percent.[64] Based on such impressive results, the WHO recommended a ban on antibiotics for growth promotion in 2003. That same year, the EU passed a regulation banning the use of growth-promoting antibiotics in animal feed. While critics often point out that the Danish ban led to a rise in antibiotics used therapeutically, Denmark's overall antibiotic use has declined more than 50 percent, while overall productivity has increased by 43 percent.[65]

Since the early 1980s, the EU has also criticized the use of hormones in factory farming and introduced legislation banning the practice. The EU prohibited the use of hormones for nontherapeutic purposes in 1985 and banned the importation of U.S. beef in 1988 to avoid importing hormone-treated meat.[66] The issue is controversial, especially in the United States, where there is no such ban and hormone and antibiotic use in livestock production is widespread. While the EU no longer bans all U.S. beef, the EU continues to ban imports of hormone-treated beef and only allows beef imports that are certified as produced without the use of hormones.[67]

ENVIRONMENTAL LEGISLATION The EU's initiatives on animal production go beyond animal welfare and public health to also include tracking and regulating the environmental effects of agriculture. The Thematic Strategy on Air Pollution is an EU initiative that brings existing air quality legislation under a single umbrella, focusing on five key pollutants, including ammonia. The strategy proposes to broaden clean air laws to include more sectors like agriculture and to reduce ammonia emissions from fertilizers and manure. It is based on an earlier Nitrates Directive, which recognized that "common action is needed to control the problem arising from intensive livestock production."[68] The legislation directed member states to identify vulnerable zones and to establish codes of good agricultural practice and action programs to reduce pollution.

The EU also recognizes agriculture as a major contributor to climate change and has spent two decades trying to reduce agricultural greenhouse gas emissions. Agricultural emissions decreased by 20 percent from 1990 to 2005 as a result of a decline in livestock numbers, more efficient application of fertilizers, and better manure management. The reduction of farming emissions is much higher than the overall EU emissions reductions of about 8 percent.[69] Early identification of sources of greenhouse gas emissions coupled with legislative action achieved dramatic results that are yet to be realized in the United States under any uniting federal greenhouse gas reductions act.

THE ROAD TO REFORM: SOUND POLICIES TO CREATE CHANGE IN THE UNITED STATES

While the EU has had challenges in implementing animal legislation, it has made significant strides in adopting progressive laws to better address the environment, human health, and animal welfare issues involved with factory farms. The United States has a variety of opportunities to initiate policy changes that go above and beyond the EU model.

STRENGTHEN AND ENFORCE EXISTING ENVIRONMENTAL LAWS

Many rules and regulations exist to address the environmental and health concerns of factory farms in the United States, yet these laws are rarely enforced. Factory farms are not monitored or inspected on a routine basis, making it relatively easy to ignore laws and skip enforcement.[70] Government agencies are not allocated sufficient resources to effectively monitor regulatory compliance, and some laws actually allow for industry self-regulation. To effectively regulate animal factories, the existing regulatory framework must be strengthened to eliminate industry self-regulation and animal farming exemptions. As a first step, the government agencies charged with overseeing farms—including the USDA, the FDA, and the EPA—must receive appropriate funding so they can adequately enforce existing environmental laws, with the ultimate goal of protecting the environment and human health.

Additional recommendations to strengthen and enforce existing environmental laws include, but are not limited to, the following:

- Place a moratorium on new factory farms and on expansion of existing facilities by the EPA until adequate environmental and health safety standards are in effect.
- Develop a standardized federal approach for regulating air pollution from factory farms under the Clean Air Act.
- Require all factory farms to treat sewage.
- Allocate appropriate funding and introduce legislation to allow for the tracking and reporting of water and air emissions from factory farms for a national collection database.
- Amend existing regulations that allow for industry self-regulation, such as National Pollution Discharge Elimination System (NPDES) permitting rules under the Clean Water Act.
- Enact legislation and implement regulations, including regulation of greenhouse gas emissions from animal production as a source of emissions and a significant hot spot for mitigation.

EXPAND FEDERAL AND STATE ANIMAL WELFARE LAWS A 2007 poll indicates that 75 percent of the U.S. public would like to see government mandates for basic animal welfare measures.[71] Animals raised for food that are treated well and allowed to exhibit natural behavior are healthier and safer for human consumption.[72] While the cruelest practices are banned or are currently being phased out in the EU, there are no federal anticruelty laws addressing farm animal welfare in the United States. Animal welfare measures must be instituted at both the state and federal level to improve food quality and safety—for example: (1) minimum federal humane farming legislation that acts as a floor, not a ceiling, permitting states to continue to pass stricter anticruelty legislation, and (2) state anticruelty legislation that quickly phases out the cruelest farming practices—gestation crates, farrowing crates, veal crates, and battery cages. Adding citizen suit provisions to these laws will enable individuals, not just state attorneys general, to have enforcement power.

PROMULGATE ANTIBIOTICS LEGISLATION According to the Union of Concerned Scientists, animal producers in the United States use as much as 84 percent of all antimicrobials in the United States.[73] The World Health Organization has noted that "this ongoing and often low-level dosing for growth and prophylaxis inevitably results in the development of resistance in or near livestock, and also heightens fears of new resistant strains 'jumping' between species."[74] Furthermore, scientific evidence suggests that ending the routine feeding of antibiotics to farm animals has important public health benefits[75] and does not adversely affect food safety, environmental quality, or consumer food prices.[76] While the FDA admits that "antimicrobial drug residues present in food from food-producing animals may cause adverse effects on the ecology of the intestinal microflora of consumers,"[77] very little is being done to reduce antimicrobials in U.S. animal agriculture. It is therefore critical that the U.S. government (1) phase out and ban current use of antimicrobials for nontherapeutic purposes, especially those that are important for human medicine, such as penicillins, tetracyclines, and stretogramins, and (2) ban new approvals of antimicrobials for nontherapeutic uses.

REFORM CROP AND ANIMAL SUBSIDIES A variety of crop and environmental subsidies exist that either directly or indirectly benefit factory farms. In the United States, most animals in CAFOs eat a diet based on corn and soy, heavily subsidized and cheap for factory farms. While chicken and hog farms benefit from crop subsidies,[78] large cattle operations are most subsidized by cheap grain production. The 168 largest beef feedlots, averaging over 32,000 animals each, sell more than 64 percent of feedlot cattle and represent about 74 percent of beef CAFOs. On average, each feedlot receives about $2.2 million in grain subsidies annually, and nearly $35 billion was given to factory farms between 1997 and 2005.[79] Unfortunately, a lack of national data keeping makes it nearly impossible to document the total payments disbursed, often creating loopholes in which wealthy farmers receive subsidy payments they are not qualified to receive. Furthermore, the recent boom in corn ethanol production and subsidies, unwarranted because of the demonstrated inability of corn ethanol to reduce greenhouse gas emissions,[80] also provides indirect

subsidies for factory farms. Distiller grains, a by-product of the ethanol industry, sold to factory farms as a feed supplement, increased 37
percent between 2007 and 2008 and by 63 percent between 2007 and
the expected 2009 usage.[81]

Recommendations to reform animal and crop subsidies include,
but are not limited to, the following:

- Reduce crop subsidies for large commodity crops, including corn
  and soy, and redirect money toward pasture-based and organic
  animal production.
- Continue to require a pasture standard in organic certified animal products.
- Work to reduce or phase out corn ethanol subsidies, which contribute distiller grains to animal diets at a cheap cost to factory
  farms.
- Establish a national data-keeping system to track crop subsidy
  payments and put a check on subsidies to the largest farms outside the income limit.

The Environmental Quality Incentives Program (EQIP) began in
1996 as a means to provide a cost share and incentives program for
farmers who were engaged in conservation practices such as wetlands
preservation, grassland management, and tree planting on highly
erodible croplands.[82] Initially, the funding for EQIP was given on a
cost-effective basis, and payments were capped at $10,000 per year
or $50,000 over five years. Notably, payments could not be used for
the construction of animal waste storage facilities. In the 2002 farm
bill, EQIP funding changed dramatically as the annual cap was
completely eliminated, making it feasibly possible for one facility to
receive $450,000 in EQIP payments in one year. Funding changes
also made it increasingly easy for factory farms to receive funding
under the EQIP program, since Congress designated that at least
60 percent of the EQIP payments must be used for livestock-related
practices. At the same time, Congress reversed the former restriction
on payments for manure storage facilities and prohibited considering cost effectiveness when reviewing EQIP applications. As a result,
CAFOs were no longer excluded from EQIP funding and have been
heavily subsidized by the EQIP program since 2002.

To reverse the practice of allowing factory farms to receive payments for merely cleaning up their pollution, we recommend the following:

- Establish new EQIP caps and focus payments on cost efficiency, not just the presence of pollution. Caps will force factory farms to clean up their own pollution and not rely on government funding to do so.
- Reduce EQIP payments for construction and expansion projects at factory farms that allow farms to get bigger on taxpayer dollars, and focus more funding on management-based conservation practices.
- Appropriate money to track EQIP contracts by livestock size, type, manure amount, and funding size to better regulate programs and eliminate subsidies to CAFOs.

INCREASE TRANSPARENCY Factory farms remain mysterious and guarded entities, and congressional mandates have allowed this secrecy to continue by explicitly prohibiting opportunities for public participation, right-to-know, and Freedom of Information Act (FOIA) requests. In the 2002 farm bill, a section titled "Privacy of Personal Information Relating to Natural Resource Conservation Programs" prohibited the USDA from releasing information about contracts received through programs like EQIP.[83] In practice, this makes it next to impossible to understand the ways in which funding has been used. There is also an increase in denying public participation in the regulatory process, most recently in the 2008 CAFO discharge rule that prevented public participation in the voluntary permitting system.

Recommendations to increase transparency and the public right to know include the following:

- Increase the public's right and ability to access information regarding Natural Resources Conservation Service (NRCS) and EQIP programs, through FOIA or otherwise.
- Promote the importance of including mandatory third-party inspection provisions in new state and federal legislation.
- Challenge the constitutionality of veggie libel laws in states, as well as laws that make photographing factory farms illegal.

A BLUEPRINT FOR ACTION

The passage of Proposition 2 in the 2008 election demonstrates that there is reason to be hopeful about the future of factory farm regulations in the United States. The residents of California exercised their democratic right to reform our political system and stood strong against industry interests that have received a free pass for far too long. Yet it is clear that we cannot and should not have to rely on individuals and states to address endemic national problems associated with industrial factory farms. The status quo of factory farming can no longer be propped up by ineffective and unenforced policies at the expense of our animals, the environment, and public health.

In Europe, regulating factory farms through animal welfare, environmental, and health and safety provisions is a priority and offers a basic blueprint for the ways that the United States can alter its most egregious practices. For too long the U.S. regulatory system has allowed factory farms to stay hidden from public view and out of our political discussions. The American people continue to voice their opposition to factory farms by shopping at farmers' markets, purchasing organic products in unprecedented numbers, and exercising local control by passing local and statewide ordinances. But public action must be coupled with mandating national policies to end subsidies to animal farm factories that are desecrating rural areas, damaging public health, and harming our environment. Simultaneously, regulations already in place in the United States must be expanded and reinforced with appropriate funding. Recent victories such as Proposition 2 have provided an ideal climate for change. Failure to act will allow industrial factory farming to persist despite well-intentioned individuals and local regulations.

A CHEF SPEAKS OUT

Making the Case for Taste

DAN BARBER

BENEATH OUR APPETITE *for sizzlin' sirloins and juicy lamb chops lies a not so palatable truth: the grain-fattening mania of industrial animal farming has been unkind to animals and destructive to the environment, and has left us too dependent on oil. More than that, most American meat doesn't taste very good. Truly great cooking, the food that evolved out of the world's thriving peasant cuisines, has always been regional and distinctive. It can't be any other way.*

❖

On an early July morning a few years ago, I walked out to where the lambs were grazing and watched Padraic, the livestock assistant at Stone Barns, getting ready to move the one hundred or so lambs to a new paddock of grass. I had thoughts, if not visions, of the Marlborough Man. Padraic is six feet four inches, with chiseled features and piercing eyes, and as he tipped his cowboy hat up to the sun I waited for him to open a can of Skoal or crack a leather whip to keep the lambs moving. Instead Padraic called out in a gentle coo, opened the fiberglass fence, and gently waved the first lamb onto the new grass. "That a girl," he said, tapping her on the rump.

Until that moment I thought I knew good lamb. I had certainly sourced enough from local farmers over the years, and I had roasted enough chops and braised enough shanks to recognize a well-raised lamb when I ate it.

What I didn't know, and what I hadn't stopped to consider was, *What does a lamb want to eat?* It's a strange question, but out in the field watching the lambs excitedly trot to new grass, without being pushed or cajoled, it wasn't hard to recognize that they actually cared quite a lot about what they ate. You could even call them picky. They moved quickly over certain grasses to get to others—to nosh on clover and mustard grass, avoiding horse nettle and fescue along the way. They resembled hungry, aggressive diners at a New York City buffet table.

That's just it, lambs on a grass diet don't so much get fed as work to feed themselves, and the distinction is not small. Their diets, and most likely their pharmacological needs, are integrated into the rhythms of the seasons, just like fruits and vegetables.

Grass-based farming, a philosophy as much as a methodology, has been called inefficient. It's been called many other things too: expensive and elitist, and highly impractical. "You can't feed the world that way" is the frequent rebuke, as if shepherding animals onto fresh forage was as outdated as the horse and buggy. It's time consuming and labor-intensive, and it requires you to be attuned to the soil and grasses, among many other supposedly needless worries.

Yet what I saw as I stood there watching Padraic was not a nostalgic image of America's agrarian past, but a vision for the future of the whole of animal husbandry. And (so long as I'm generalizing) it might also be a look at the future of food. Why? Because there's been a dirty little secret about our sirloins (and our chicken breasts and our pork chops). It's not just that the industries responsible for raising our meat are mired in a system that's cruel to animals, or that their practices are destructive to the environment, or even that they have grave effects on our health: we've known about all of that for many years. No, what's becoming more and more clear is that most American meat—insert your favorite cut here—doesn't taste very good.

Take America's Colorado lamb, famous for those perfectly uniform and fatty chops. Since fat carries flavor and retains moisture, it's pretty easy to have a moist and juicy bite of industrially produced lamb. But as Garrison Keillor said, "You can taste the misery in every bite." A chef might say that the misery you're tasting is greasy fat. Greasy fat is not natural fat. Greasy fat coats your mouth. It's sweet, soft, and nutty, and it tastes nothing like the animal you're eating. It also surrounds a kind of watered-down version of what lamb could be, which is deceptive after unwrapping that Cadillac-size chop from the butcher. What you've really got is lamb-lite.

An added insult: most lamb recipes instruct you to "remove fat cap and discard." We do this without thought, as if we're unpacking groceries. It's how professionals do it too. When I was training to butcher meat, part of my job included cleaning twenty racks of lamb for dinner service every afternoon, and with each rack the head butcher showed me how to pull off the two solid inches of fat covering the loin and discard it in the trash. Taking it to the dumpster, I thought about the irony. The restaurant paid the highest price for the most coveted part of the animal, only to toss 10 percent of it in the trash? When I asked the old French butcher why the chef wanted the fat removed, he looked at his young apprentice with a raised eyebrow: "It's disgusting, so much fat."

That excess fat comes from lamb fed a truckload of corn, which in turn came from an ocean of cornfields—cornfields made possible by fertilizers and pesticides, and $300,000 combines. Add to that the trucking and processing of corn and you can sum up the process, and define the thick coat of fat, in one word—oil.

For the last thirty years, environmentalists and small farmers (and, if I may add, chefs) have weighed in to suggest that this is several kinds of madness. In light of the dire health and environmental warnings, they made inspiring, superhuman attempts to wean our big food chain off its addiction to oil. But all along, the industrial agriculture juggernaut simply responded: If we're feeding more people more cheaply, and using less land, how terrible could our food system be?

Therein lay the justification, the motivation—the business plan, really—of American animal agriculture.

That is, until now. Thanks to dwindling world supplies, we're spending more for our oil today (a whopping $80 a barrel at the time of this writing versus an average price of just $20 a barrel for the last fifty years), and we're expending more of it. In 2008, American retail food prices went up 4.5 percent; wholesale prices, 30 percent. Corn alone was over $5 a bushel, up from $3.

There are many reasons for these price jumps, including America's wasteful ethanol subsidies and the world's increased demand for meat. But a closer look only leads you back to oil—the demand for that corn-fattened meat is being satiated by more grain; grain is more expensive because of demands for ethanol; ethanol is expensive because of the oil it takes to extract and transport; and oil is getting more expensive because there's less oil.

So what is there to celebrate? Quite a lot, actually. For the first time in the last half century, small and midsize farms that focus on rotational grazing—the best stewards of the land—are beginning to gain a competitive advantage. These farms aren't as reliant on fossil fuels. They use less large machinery and fewer chemical amendments, and they have significantly lower transaction costs. Farmers like Padraic, standing in the field shepherding their herd, might look like portraits of America's agrarian past, but in fact they're more like savvy businessmen, removing their most expensive input (grain) and replacing it with a free energy source (grass). And these farmers, almost without exception, are producing the kind of meat we want to eat—delicious and richly textured, without flab or a greasy aftertaste, and with a flavor that changes throughout the year.

John Jamison is another of them. Jamison supplies lamb to some of the best restaurants in the country, but he still gets excited explaining the "inconsistency" of his product to chefs like me. "Oh yeah, you can taste the difference—by age, by diet. You'll get stronger-flavored lamb in May and June based on the young wild garlic and onions, and then a leaner taste in late summer from the wildflowers. In fall you start to see the cold-season grasses, giving you the most mature and delicious fat of the year."

When I first met John, I asked him how he got started. "My wife, Sukey, and I were a couple of hippies who didn't want Woodstock to end," he said. It was in the aftermath of the oil crisis. The price of gasoline had quadrupled in just a few months, from twenty-five cents a gallon to over a dollar. And the combination of falling supplies and international unrest caused grain prices to double or triple.

Along came the development of tensile wire fencing that could be set up and moved by one person (the brainchild of John Waller, not surprisingly a native of New Zealand, where grass-fed livestock is the only game going). "That was really the beginning of intensive rotation, because it could be done by one person, and you saved money on grain. For us, it just seemed economical."

The Jamisons set up a successful grass operation on 200 acres in western Pennsylvania, but Waller's philosophy never went mainstream. The oil crisis ended and the era of cheap fuel returned, and so did status quo methods of confined animal feedlots. For many years it was difficult for the Jamisons to compete with grain-fed operations—and lamb in this country was already a tough sell—but in 1987 their luck changed. That's when French chef Jean-Louis Palladin, then the most respected chef in the country, called out of the blue, asking the Jamisons to deliver a few lambs for a congressional dinner at the Watergate Hotel.

"I remember we got lost on our way there, so we didn't arrive until the night before the event. Sukey and I walked up to the kitchen, both carrying the lambs on our backs. And we just knocked on the door."

Palladin soon came out to inspect the Jamisons' product. He ran his hands along the carcass, and stuck his nose deep into the lamb's cavity. "He had an enormous mane of wild hair and thick, oversized glasses, but he stuck his entire head into the carcass, breathing in, as if he was about to taste a vintage Bordeaux."

With Palladin's blessing, John and Sukey were soon receiving orders from chefs around the country. "It's a funny thing," John said. "Here we were adhering to our ideals from the sixties—living simply, improving the land, making the world a better place—and trying to farm in the great French peasant tradition. Along comes a Frenchman, feeding some of the wealthiest and most influential Americans, who helps make our product famous in America."

Jean-Louis Palladin's contribution to gastronomy was enormous, and well documented. But his most lasting contribution might be helping to ensure the success of the Jamisons, who have gone on to inspire livestock farmers all over the country. These farmers allow us to envision a future for raising livestock where the farming model isn't rooted in the General Motors mindset—take more, sell more, waste more. Instead, the motivation is to keep our eyes firmly planted on the sun, our planet's greatest source of free energy, and figure out how to better profit from what's pouring down every day.

"The best part of meeting Jean-Louis was just after he tasted our lamb. I'll never forget when he took the first few, frantic bites," John said. "He suddenly got all quiet. His eyes welled with tears. Tearing off a piece of butcher paper, he quickly drew an outline of France, describing the different flavors of the lamb from each region."

Variation, the enemy of conventional animal husbandry, is avoided through a constant diet of grain. Palladin saw it differently, and appreciated what every chef, and every serious eater, knows instinctively. Truly great cooking, the food that evolved out of the world's thriving peasant cuisines, is regional and distinctive. Until recently, it had never been any other way.

Palladin never bought into the grain-fattening mania of animal farming, not because it was destructive to the environment, or because it left us too dependent on oil, but because it never produced anything really good to eat.

"Jean-Louis used to call me after a delivery," Jamison told me, "and he'd tell me the exact age of the lamb that was delivered, and then he'd list for me the different grasses they were eating. It was incredible—he was telling *me* what they were eating." John paused, and then added, "At those moments I felt strangely, even pleasantly, confused—it was like, who's the chef and who's the farmer? There just didn't seem to be much difference."

DISMANTLEMENT

A Movement to Topple Industrial Animal Agriculture

ERIK MARCUS

DESPITE THE EMERGENCE of three movements to reform industrial animal production—vegetarianism, animal rights, and animal welfare—change has been slow to take root. Consumption of animal products is rising while the industry grows ever more powerful and secretive. Perhaps it's time for a fourth long-range movement against industrial animal suffering: dismantlement.

❖

A Gallup Poll released in May 2003 found that 96 percent of Americans believe that animals deserve some protection from harm and exploitation.[1] A nationwide survey conducted in 2008 by University of Michigan economists showed that 69 percent of people polled would actually vote to prohibit the use of sow gestation crates in pork production.[2] And 62 percent of Americans favor the passage of strict laws protecting the welfare of animals raised on farms.[3]

Improved attitudes toward animals have led to progress on many fronts. The fur industry has been severely weakened by the work of animal activists. Sixteen cities, out of concerns over cruelty, have banned circuses that feature animals.[4] And between 1990 and 2008, voters passed twenty-two animal welfare initiatives that were put on state ballots.[5] Meanwhile, penalties for animal cruelty are becoming more widely enforced. The year 1999 marked the first time that factory farm workers received felony-level indictments for animal cruelty.[6] In 2002, three men pleaded guilty to felony animal abuse charges for torturing a calf to death. In addition to the felonies, the men were also convicted of misdemeanor offenses for tormenting the calf in front of his mother, thereby inflicting psychological distress on the cow.[7]

Undercover videotapes released by the Humane Society in early 2008 exposed employees of the Westland/Hallmark Meat Company in Chino, California, brutally forcing animals to their feet so they could be ruled as fit for slaughter. The ensuing investigation resulted in the largest meat recall in history, the incarceration of two employees, and, ultimately, the closure of the slaughter plant. Incidentally, Westland/Hallmark's largest distribution client was a distributor to the National School Lunch Program.

Perhaps the most important task of the animal protection movement is to ensure that vegan advocacy materials are disseminated far and wide. Small and relatively new organizations like Vegan Outreach, Compassion Over Killing, and Mercy for Animals have been doing a remarkable job of exposing millions of young people to this information.

While animal protection groups are growing in size and influence, the natural foods industry is knocking down the barriers that keep people from becoming vegan. It's constantly getting easier to eat a cruelty-free diet. Today, there are well over a hundred exclusively vegan cookbooks, and the market for vegan convenience foods has become crowded with fantastic products. Sales of organic foods in the United States have jumped from $1 billion in 1990 to $20 billion in 2007.[8] The largest U.S. retailer of natural foods, Whole Foods Market, started with one store in 1980 and had grown to 280 stores by 2009.

The burgeoning market for vegetarian foods has prompted the food industry's largest companies to invest heavily. In 1999, Kraft Foods purchased Boca Burger, and Kellogg's bought analog meat producer Worthington Foods. Soymilk has become so popular that it is now carried in just about every supermarket in America, and it's also available at Starbucks coffeehouses.

TRENDS IN U.S. MEAT CONSUMPTION

Considering the developments that have occurred in recent years, it might seem as though farmed animal protection efforts are on an unstoppable roll. But the only way to maintain such optimism is to ignore the one statistic that matters most: the amount of meat eaten per person in the United States. That quantity has been steadily on the rise, despite the best efforts of the animal protection movement. In 2007, America's meat and poultry consumption hit an all-time high of 222 pounds per person. American slaughterhouses killed 9.5 billion animals in 2008, up from 3.36 billion animals in 1975.

But aren't there at least a higher percentage of vegetarians and vegans in America today than ever before? This would seem a reasonable expectation, given the increasing visibility of vegetarian options. Unfortunately, surveys don't indicate that any substantial progress has been made in convincing Americans to stop eating animal products. As of 2009, only about 3 percent of Americans follow a vegetarian or vegan diet.[9]

It's an incredibly discouraging situation. Every year, the animal protection movement grows larger and richer. Meanwhile, increasing numbers of delicious vegan foods come to market, obliterating any excuses that a vegan diet is hard to follow. Yet each year the number of animals slaughtered sets a new record. Even in regard to welfare issues, the situation has deteriorated in several respects. Since the start of the modern animal protection movement in the mid-1970s, factory farming's grip on animal agriculture has tightened with each passing year.

None of this analysis is intended to belittle the efforts of people who work to keep animals from harm. If the modern animal protection movement had not come into existence, conditions for farmed animals would doubtless be even worse than they are today. But we owe it to the animals to continually assess the work done on their behalf, and to come up with ever-improving ways to make a difference. The sad but painfully obvious truth is that the modern animal protection movement has, so far, largely failed in its three most important tasks:

- Increasing the percentage of Americans who are vegetarian or vegan
- Encouraging nonvegetarians to reduce their consumption of meat, dairy products, and eggs
- Diminishing the suffering of farmed animals

I am convinced that these failures can be halted. By looking at how the animal protection movement has evolved since the 1970s, it's possible to determine where the movement has gone off course. We need to understand where mistakes were made and to take corrective action where appropriate. The remainder of this essay will analyze what has gone wrong with the animal protection movement, and how we can remedy the situation.

THE THREE EXISTING MOVEMENTS FOR ANIMAL PROTECTION

Animal agriculture can be likened to a giant. It is simply too big and too strong for any one approach to defeat. Fortunately, there are three different movements—vegetarian, animal rights, and animal welfare—that work to protect farmed animals. Each of these movements undermines animal agriculture in a unique way and specializes in attacking a different vulnerability. We have a vegetarian movement that awakens the public to the benefits of meat-free eating and helps people to make the switch. We've got an animal rights movement that inspires people to question the ethics of eating animals. And last, we have a welfare movement that anyone can become involved with, to remove some of the cruelty from animal agriculture.

LIMITATIONS OF THE VEGETARIAN MOVEMENT

The vegetarian movement, as it currently exists, is weak in two areas. The first weakness—the one that could readily be addressed—pertains to the arguments the movement makes to support vegetarian and vegan eating. The vegetarian argument often seems to claim that vegan eating is a panacea for all health and environmental ills. Several of the best-selling vegetarian advocacy books published since the 1970s have devoted about equal space to the issues of health, the environment, and the animals. In consequence, when creating outreach materials, vegetarian societies usually give these three areas equal amounts of attention, sometimes using arguments of questionable accuracy.

For the vegetarian movement to gain credibility and persuasiveness, its leaders would do well to reduce the attention they give to health and environmental concerns. There's no need for vegetarian advocates to renounce all claims regarding health and the environment, but these arguments need to be made with great care, and they should be tailored to specific food choices and diets. With this approach, vegetarian activists can reshape their outreach arguments to achieve greater credibility.

The second weakness in the vegetarian movement is unlikely to be adequately addressed: the fact that most vegetarian groups emphasize celebration over action. One of the great strengths of the vegetarian movement is that it puts a friendly face on the idea of eliminating animal products from the diet. Around the country, most vegetarian groups are geared toward organizing social activities—potlucks, outings, turkey-free Thanksgiving celebrations, and so forth.

Every town needs a strong, vibrant vegetarian society. The situation confronting farmed animals no doubt improves whenever people gather to extol nonviolent eating. But there is only so much that can be accomplished through celebration. While vegetarian groups are terrific at organizing social events, they tend to be fundamentally unsuited to carrying out work that is more action oriented. It's not that vegetarian groups should be done away with—far from it!—but rather that they should be joined by groups that take a more activist role in undercutting the strengths of animal agriculture.

LIMITATIONS OF THE ANIMAL RIGHTS MOVEMENT

To the extent that the public understands animal rights philosophy, that understanding is probably embodied by the PETA (People for the Ethical Treatment of Animals) slogan: "Animals are not ours to eat, wear, experiment on, or use for entertainment."

There are certainly activists who agree wholeheartedly with this absolutist position. But the movement's literature actually includes a number of books that take a more nuanced view of matters. Chief among these is Peter Singer's *Animal Liberation*, as well as his other writings. Grounded in utilitarianism, Singer's philosophy seeks to shape a world with the least amount of suffering. Doing so means paying attention to the times when the interests of people come into conflict with the well-being of nonhuman animals. Under Singer's philosophy, for example, it would be morally desirable to painlessly kill a thousand mice if the knowledge gained would spare tens of thousands of humans from an agonizing death.

Unfortunately, as far as the general public is concerned, all animal rights activists are dead set against any form of animal use, regardless of how little or how much humans stand to benefit. This makes animal rights philosophy poison when it comes to publicly debating animal agriculture. When animal defenders and livestock producers trade jabs on television and radio, or are quoted in articles, neither side has the opportunity to develop a sustained and coherent argument. All the public hears are sound bites. And it is here that the comprehensive nature of animal rights philosophy becomes a terrible liability for the defenders of farmed animals.

Time and again, factory farm interests have been able to wrest the discussion away from brutal practices of animal agriculture and into the thorniest thickets of animal rights philosophy. Activists are then left with the unenviable task of explaining why they are against animal testing that could produce treatments for diseases that are currently incurable.

Animal rights philosophy has much to say about the ethical questions that arise when the interests of humans and animals come into conflict. Unfortunately, it's impossible to hold the spotlight on factory farm cruelty when animal rights philosophy is involved in the argument. People working against animal agriculture must be aware that animal rights arguments are often too complex to be put before the public productively. The argument against factory farming needs to be simple, easily understood, and primarily focused on the miseries suffered by farmed animals. Farmed animal protectionists would therefore do well to avoid debating philosophy in public. Instead, the public should be given a far simpler argument—that animal agriculture is inherently cruel, is uniquely resistant to reform, and therefore ought to be eliminated.

LIMITATIONS OF THE ANIMAL WELFARE MOVEMENT

Welfare reforms have arguably produced greater gains for farmed animals than anything initiated by the vegetarian or animal rights movements. Yet, for all its potential, there are still severe limitations to what can be accomplished by the welfare movement. Welfare reformers have limited resources and must focus attention on animal agriculture's most indefensible cruelties. Such a triage system leaves lesser cruelties unaddressed.

It's true that, over time, the welfare movement will work its way down to eradicating lesser cruelties. The trouble is that animal agriculture is a moving target and is continually developing new methods for raising animals. If there's one thing we can be sure of, it's that the people who brought the world beak searing, gestation crates, and battery cages are certain to dream up comparably cruel innovations in the future. So, while welfare reformists busy themselves getting rid of the worst of today's cruelties, the industry is rapidly devising new practices for tomorrow. What's worse, the rollout of new practices is usually gradual, and it may be some time before new cruelties become widespread enough to gain the attention of welfare reformers.

The trouble with welfare reform is that it is always behind the curve. However effective at gradually getting rid of existing cruelties the welfare reform movement may be, it will always be powerless to prevent new cruelties from emerging.

BUILDING A FOURTH MOVEMENT

These three existing movements—vegetarian, animal rights, and animal welfare—each play an indispensable role in farmed animal protection. The vegetarian movement seeks to wean people away from a lifetime of animal-centered eating. The animal rights movement works to modify society's exploitive beliefs about animals. And the animal welfare movement, piece by piece, puts an end to some of the worst cruelties carried out by animal agriculture.

While these three movements provide an excellent and much needed defense of farmed animals, not one of these movements delivers much in the way of an offense. I believe we urgently need an all-new movement expressly designed to identify and strip away the primary assets of animal agriculture. The surest way to eliminate animal agriculture's cruelties is to seek to eliminate animal agriculture itself. To accomplish this, we need a new movement expressly designed to go on the offensive, with the purpose of ushering animal agriculture out of existence. It's within our power to build such a movement. While animal agriculture surely can't be abolished over-night, we need to begin taking the first steps down that road.

A movement that strives to weaken and one day topple animal agriculture will perfectly complement the work already being done by the vegetarian, animal rights, and animal welfare movements. For the first time, the animal protection movement will have an offense as powerful as its defense.

CREATING A DISMANTLEMENT MOVEMENT

I call this movement the dismantlement movement, and it is built upon an audacious premise—that activists are capable of banding together to undercut and ultimately eliminate the industry of animal agriculture. Even the most radical elements of the animal protection movement have never set an explicit goal to eliminate animal agri-culture. I think activists have kept quiet about this matter because nobody wants to appear out of touch with reality. But until we begin working toward the goal of ending animal agriculture, the fate of America's farmed animals will remain sealed. The 10 billion farmed animals that die in America each year need us to be brave enough to begin a grand task—one that will likely take several generations to complete.

The name *dismantlement* carries with it the underlying mental-ity of how animal agriculture can be overcome. *Dismantlement* is a word lacking any implication of hysteria or violence. Rather, the word suggests that animal agriculture can be taken apart in the systematic manner of a mechanic taking apart an engine—thoughtfully, calmly, and one piece at a time. Believe it or not, despite animal agriculture's size and strength, there is good reason to expect that a concerted effort could one day topple the industry.

One sign of the vulnerability of the factory farm industry can be seen in recent efforts to pass laws that would criminalize public entry or photography in animal agriculture facilities. Missouri state legisla-tors, for example, introduced a law to make it a felony to photograph or videotape "any aspect of an animal facility." A similar Texas bill would have served violators a $10,000 fine and jail time. Although these proposed laws were unsuccessful, antitrespassing laws have been passed to shield factory farms in Oklahoma and California.

By pushing for the creation of these laws, animal agriculture has tipped its hand about its greatest fear. The industry has decided that, at all costs, the public must remain ignorant about how farmed animals are treated. The industry can exist in its present form only as long as the public is kept in the dark about animal treatment.

CHOOSING DISMANTLEMENT'S FIRST CAMPAIGNS

Most of the dismantlement movement's initial efforts should be directed toward outreach. The work to dismantle animal agriculture is in its infancy, and it will be many years before we have the numbers needed to create substantial change. So our first task is to promote movement growth as quickly as possible.

But even with our current minimal resources, we can begin stripping away three of animal agriculture's most important assets. Right now, animal agriculture benefits tremendously from school lunch programs, grazing subsidies, and U.S. Department of Agriculture (USDA) nutrition guidelines. The dismantlement movement should seek reform in these areas, and the public will side with us if we adequately publicize what is at stake.

REFORMING SCHOOL LUNCH PROGRAMS

Animal agriculture benefits enormously from the National School Lunch Program (funded primarily through the Child Nutrition Act). In 2005, the program spent more than 60 percent of its food budget for meat and dairy products, and less than 5 percent for fresh fruits and vegetables.[10]

Back in 1946, when Congress initiated the National School Lunch Program, it made sense to offer America's children subsidized meals that were loaded with fatty meats and dairy products. Malnutrition was a pressing problem, and what little was known about nutrition made it appear wise to feed children substantial amounts of animal products. But given what nutrition science has learned since the 1940s, there's no longer any justification for basing school lunches on animal products. In America today, childhood malnutrition has been largely replaced by childhood obesity.

Today's National School Lunch Program starts millions of children each year down the road to a lifetime of unhealthy food choices. I'm not at all suggesting that the program should be eliminated, and it's naïve to think that it can be reformed overnight. But as it currently exists, the National School Lunch Program is nothing more than a dumping ground for animal agriculture's excess capacity.

Today our schools need an entirely different meal-planning approach. It has been demonstrated that children love to try interesting plant-centered meals, as long as schools make an effort to engagingly teach the importance of a healthy diet. Lunch programs that emphasize quality food preparation can start children on a lifetime of more healthful eating. What's more, since these revamped lunch programs would emphasize whole grains and vegetables instead of meat and cheese, significant savings in tax dollars would result. A report by the Institute of Medicine in October 2009 made recommendations to the USDA on calorie limits for school lunches as well as suggesting an increase in legumes, fruits, and vegetables, including dark greens and orange vegetables.[11]

Activists are now working to get the National School Lunch Program out of the hands of the USDA, and to assign the program to either the Department of Health and Human Services or the Department of Education. Jonathan Safran Foer's 2009 book *Eating Animals* calls for the National Institutes of Health to take over the task of formulating purchasing allocations for the National School Lunch Program. Dismantlement activists ought to contribute time and money to these efforts.

ENDING GRAZING SUBSIDIES

Grazing subsidies constitute a second abuse of tax dollars that an informed public would never allow. A 2005 report estimated that federal grazing programs cost U.S. taxpayers at least $123 million per year.[12] The reason the U.S. government loses money on its grazing program is that it rents land in arid landscapes to ranchers at far below market rates. Given the health and environmental consequences of beef production, as well as the surprisingly small amount of food that public lands grazing generates, there's no reason to think that an informed public would tolerate the long-term continuation of grazing subsidies that currently exist.

PUTTING THE NATIONAL INSTITUTES OF HEALTH IN CHARGE OF NUTRITION ADVICE

The third, and perhaps most vulnerable, of government programs benefiting animal agriculture relates to the nutrition guidance issued by the U.S. Department of Agriculture. There is simply no justification for the agency charged with overseeing food production to offer nutrition advice to the public.

The USDA was formed in 1862 with the mandate to provide farmers with support, information, and productive seed varieties. During the Great Depression, the USDA initiated subsidies and other programs to benefit farmers. As farmers became increasingly dependent on the USDA, the agency was also given the task of formulating nutrition advice for the public.

From the beginning, the USDA's nutrition advice has been written with an eye to furthering the business interests of animal agriculture. Every five years, the USDA issues a new set of nutrition guidelines. And every time these guidelines are revised, the new edition is drafted by a committee made up largely of representatives from the meat, dairy, and egg industries. These people have no business sitting on government committees that make public health recommendations.

It was a betrayal of public trust when the government first handed the job of setting nutritional guidelines to the USDA. This task should be reassigned to the National Institutes of Health (NIH)—the agency that should have been given the job in the first place. The NIH ought to base its nutrition recommendations on the best science available. It's absurd that agriculture interests, whether dairy farmers or blueberry growers, are allowed to sit on boards that formulate the government's nutritional advice.

LOOKING AHEAD

The struggle to win each of these reforms will doubtless be long and difficult, but victory is obtainable. That's because, with each of these issues, the public good is currently being sacrificed to the interests of animal agriculture. As these injustices are brought to light, Americans will surely side with the dismantlement movement's calls for reform. By the time these reforms are won, the dismantlement movement will be large and powerful enough that a new range of opportunities will be plainly visible. Of course, the speed at which we make progress depends on how many people become active in dismantlement, which is why outreach must remain our primary task.

Already, there are hundreds of activists across America who can serve as the core of this new movement. Our success will be determined by our commitment and by our willingness to collaborate in innovative ways. In my own activism, I devote the bulk of my energies to inspiring people to work for dismantlement. Together, we can direct our collective abilities to ensure that animal agriculture's remaining years are as few as possible.

THE FARMER'S BIND

Scaling Up for a Different Kind of Agriculture

BECKY WEED

OUR FOOD AND AGRICULTURE SYSTEM *is caught in a whirl of contradiction. Farmers feed the world but are dependent upon subsidies that can harm communities and ecosystems. Ranchers strive to give young calves a healthy life on the range, only to sell them to confinement feedlots where they fatten on corn, degrading their digestion and our diets, trapped in their own waste. The eaters that support this system are also complicit. But sooner rather than later, we need to move beyond a world of blame toward a world of solutions.*

❖

An Ethiopian agricultural official landed at my lunch table a few years ago in the midst of an organic livestock conference in Minnesota sponsored by IFOAM, the International Federation of Organic Agriculture Movements. He puzzled aloud, "I'm really confused. For decades we've been hearing from developed nations, 'You have to learn to intensify your agriculture,' but here, at this conference, these people are telling us that our extensive systems, our 'natural' animals, might be valuable. I don't know where to turn."

Join the club, I thought to myself, for I too was reeling from the ironies of the livestock agenda.

Big surprise, I jeered inside, for the guideposts set for this Ethiopian man by a collage of aid agencies, agricultural academics, domestic political realities, and the simple force of hunger are not fundamentally different from our own American history of contradictory guideposts over the last century. In revealing his own exasperation at mixed messages and missions, this Ethiopian man had touched a nerve in me I hadn't realized was so raw.

Only in retrospect do I articulate the sense of schizophrenia in farming that has been brewing. The irony is so commonplace that we are almost inured to its jolts: we feed the world, but our subsidies damage everyone's ability to feed themselves; we protect open space, but we destroy biodiversity; we represent lauded agrarian roots, though we epitomize the pathologies of industrialization; we call ourselves "the first environmentalists," while our job is to exploit nature's bounty; our intimacy with animals is legendary, but our mechanistic exploitation of animals seems boundless; we literally cultivate beauty as we obliterate wildness.

We invoke these dichotomies so regularly, and with such expedience, that our natural compulsions toward coherence seem worn out and cast aside: the U.S. Congress sings praises to the family farmer, while repeatedly voting in farm bills that destroy the same; humane and human-scale small farms fill our children's books and school field trips while the residue of corporate-scale production fills their school lunch programs; we hammer out hardball trade agreements "to promote agriculture," but we cast a blind eye to the overseas farmer and consumers forever altered by such "free trade"; we strive to raise children who are proud to "feed the world," but our own struggles with bankruptcy, diminishing prestige, and/or dependence on nonfarm income cast a different shadow and drive many of our youth off the land.

The dilemmas implicit in these polar perceptions and habits are so troubling, and so intractable, that we seem stuck like iron filings over a magnet, both repelled by, and caught up in, one another's fields. For observers of agriculture, that's manageable. Landing somewhere in the range between critic and cheerleader, observers can reconcile the polar pulls by taking solace and enlightenment in their own conscious and intentional eating habits and professional endeavors. But those of us who are farmers are caught up in a different force field, compelled to land somewhere along the spectrum between complicity and victim status, often uncertain of just what position we hold. Farmers, ranchers, and factory workers involved in livestock agriculture illustrate the quandaries most starkly, for our relationships to live creatures leave little room for ambiguity about consequences.

A midwestern hog farmer, leveraged in debt to hog confinement facilities once built in an attempt to add value to his corn and soybeans when prices were low, is now confined himself by high grain prices and an animal factory that bears no resemblance to his childhood memory of pigs. A laborer in a southeastern chicken "farm," likely an immigrant accepting wages that most Americans would spurn for such work, performs unspeakable acts on caged birds—as he struggles to make a decent home for his own children. Even the western rancher, at least one remove from the dreariness of ultraintensive livestock agriculture and keeper of the independent cowboy archetype, is intimately tied to a cattle feedlot system that treats his calves in ways that would be anathema on his own ranch. Is he complicit because he "uses" an industrial ag infrastructure to maintain his glorious lifestyle while others do the dirty work? Or is he victim because he busts his ass and takes real risks to make it in a commodity universe that has prices so far from parity with nineteenth-century goods that we barely even joke about the discrepancies anymore?

Even those of us who are working in different versions of agriculture in small pockets all over the world, tied more closely to our animals' full life cycle and to our human customers, harbor little illusion that we are free from the factory fray. Although we may take pride and solace in our local land and animal stewardship, we daily face the harsh reality of our larger enclosure. Whether it's the glass ceiling of prices over a commodity atmosphere, the seemingly irreconcilable walls between niche-market values and the desirable goal of good food for everyone, or the floor of landscape degradation that extends way beneath even the most precious farm gate—we are all boxed in.

When I first learned of the idea for this book, I rolled my eyes and wondered, Who needs another devastating exposé? Will the condemnations alone move us out of our binds in modern food consumption? Our animal factories may not find their biggest threat from distressed citizens who worry about the size of chickens' cages and the stench of corn manure deep in cattle feedlots. Sincere and legitimate as those animal welfare concerns may be, they have not shown the power necessary to bring our industrialized animal houses down, at least not yet. Upton Sinclair started this campaign generations ago, but the Farm Bureau triumphantly published a survey of Americans as recently as 1999 showing that three-fourths of consumers think farmers do a good job taking care of farm animals, and the statistics on mainstream meat and dairy consumption appear to corroborate their case. Is it satisfaction, or resignation? Like Jefferson's characterization of what slavery does to the master, it may be time to consider the haunting possibility that the animal factory itself degrades the administrators as much as the inmates, mixed metaphors and all.

Are there signs that our own massive machine could collapse under its own weight? Forget for a moment the possibilities of uncompetitive markets, the revolving doors between industry and regulators, real and corrupt though they may be in some instances. It's enough to consider the more profound degradation we are instituting via the earth itself: both the confinement apparatus and the well-intentioned cropping systems that sustain it are degrading the earth's natural infrastructure as surely as slavery degrades the psyche. Consider pollinators, or hydrologic cycling, or predator-prey relationships among everything from bugs to megafauna, or carbon cycling in soils and the atmosphere, or fisheries' reliance on oxygenated runoff. We have been messing with all of it.

Back at the Minnesota conference, covering everything from ultraintensive Danish chickens to midsize hog and cattle models of the midwestern United States to wandering, semiwild beasts in the poorest provinces of India, these organic farmers and researchers from around the world were like minded in their dedication to chemical-free farming, but all over the map in terms of scale and intensity. Both the Ethiopian man and I, a Montana sheep rancher, could accept that there is no recipe for the "correct" size for success, for we are accustomed to the notion that nature also runs a spectrum in size and intensity, from anthills to snow leopard habitat. But is it out of line to yearn for some criteria for identifying, designing, and managing an *appropriate* scale for agricultural production, and the necessarily coupled systems of processing and distribution? Who is setting the guideposts? We could simply accept our fate as one of gaming a long string of trade-offs, or we could seek a more strategic plan.

Economies of scale have busied the calculators of industrial food strategy for at least a century, primarily in the name of growing more food, a mission that seems so basic and admirable that we do not question it. The arithmetic of scaling up to achieve commodity efficiency is indeed compelling, and in recent decades, my midcareer peers have joined this calculating vortex while kneeling at the altar of the "free market." I look back now and see that three-quarters of the Harvard class of 2007 went to work in the "financial services" industry. That fraction has ramped up steadily from about 20 percent in 1970.[1]

Large percentages of graduates from other Ivy League institutions similarly gravitated to the financial sector, and land grant university graduates who populated the midlevel leadership of agribusiness did their bidding. To be sure, only a small portion of the financial sector leadership had anything to do with food systems, but that is part of the point: we have allowed agriculture to be governed by a financial sector that has either selected the scale and mode of biological systems with the tools of an Economics 101 lecture or has been clueless altogether. Is it any wonder we face disruptions?

The midlevel land grant support force, though far less inept in the world of domestic livestock and crops, and admirably sensitive to the merciless statistics of population growth versus food supply projections, seems to boast a similar dose of denial about how the Earth works. These days, automobile industry analysts are cackling with incredulity at American manufacturers who in the 1980s projected millions of car sales to China, while at the same time ramping up production of Hummers at home. Did they assume that petroleum could remain cheap after a few decades of that? It's hard not to ask if today's agricultural theorists are not making the same mistake in their own fields of corn, hogs, cows, and ethanol, even *with* the benefit of automotive hindsight.

Perhaps it is time to apply the same zeal to our selection of scale that we once applied to our worship of its expansion. Examples of such efforts, all requiring adjustments of scale, are abundant, diverse, and underway:

- The grass-fed meat movement
- Distribution systems that use renewable fuels, modern information tools, and creative partnerships among producers to empower rather than degrade local production systems

- Cropping systems that enhance beneficial predators and pollinators rather than degrading them
- Grower networks that empower decentralized production and overcome limitations of small size
- Husbandry techniques that acknowledge and make use of natural animal behaviors rather than suppressing them

No doubt readers could add more, and with increasing frequency I encounter twenty- and thirty-something visitors who show up without degrees in financial services, but rather with a roll-up-the-sleeve passion to seek new models, new scales. The imperative now is to stop viewing these experiments and these young people as fringe romanticizations of bygone eras or yuppie pretenders, and to subject them instead to both the support and rigorous evaluation that reform movements and reformers merit.

The myriad consequences of such "experiments" are inspiring. They include more humane working conditions for people and animals; more beneficial distributions of fertilizers and wastes; carbon sequestration via grassland restoration; reduced dependence on petroleum-based tillage and transport; efficiencies yielded by integrated cropping and livestock systems; reduced vulnerability to industrial-size food safety fiascoes; increased animal health resilience in response to diversity and decentralization; and restoration of human and wildlife communities.

However, the full potential of such consequences is constrained by competition with a commodity system, and by a belief system in the seats of power that still perceives the centralized commodity system to be robust. Having run the experiment on scaling up for many decades now, we have discovered limits to its design. We need not throw the baby out with the bathwater, and we need not spend all our time decrying the ugliness of our errors (many were well intentioned), but we can use those discoveries to qualitatively redesign our schemes for agriculture. Doubters need only examine the list of scaling-up "errors" that generated the innovations listed above: inhumane working conditions for people and animals; inane distribution of resources that turns fertilizer into hazardous waste; carbon emission via excess tillage and grassland destruction; extreme and consequential dependence on petroleum-based tillage and transport; inefficiencies yielded by decoupled livestock and monocropping systems; proven vulner-ability to industrial-size food safety fiascoes and animal health crises; and fraying of human and wildlife communities.

If we ran our economic models through a filter that understands how the earth works, rather than merely the prestigious but provincial arithmetic of economies of scale, we might find the means to invest more wisely in the innovations already underway: pollination, predation, nitrogen fixation, wetland filtration, carbon cycling, and so on. These are the criteria missing from the lectures delivered to, and delivered by, the founders and funders of the factories.

Only by reconciling these and other natural processes with new adaptive systems for feeding ourselves will we update our designs, and only then will we reconcile the schizophrenic self-image that haunts farmers today. It is natural and legitimate for concerned citizens outside agriculture to point their ethical queries at the animal factories, but as farmers, we must take the lead in pointing the ethical query back at citizens, and at ourselves. As long as we collectively defend a regime that dominates itself with subsidized corn and soybeans to feed the factory (and now the gas tank), we *are* complicit. If the binds of finance and personal aging are too tight to liberate us from this circle of wagons (and for many people they truly are), then, at a minimum, let's at least encourage our children to throw off the traces.

HEALING

Restoring Health, Wealth, and Respect to Food and Farming

JOEL SALATIN

WHAT WOULD BE THE OPPOSITE *of centralized production? It sounds like lots of small farms, maybe even family farms: smaller, diversified, symbiotic, synergistic, and multispeciated. And lots of farmers. In fact, across the country, farmers are demonstrating that small- and medium-scale animal production is both economically viable and environmentally sustainable.*

❖

Every eater has a role in creating a new food and farming paradigm that honors the pigness of the pig, offers transparency from field to fork, and ultimately provides cultural healing. Here at Polyface Farm, nestled in Virginia's Shenandoah Valley, we apply the healing test to every decision. If it doesn't heal, it's not acceptable. Healing comes in many dimensions.

SOIL Organic matter should build, not only to add tilth and water retention capacity, but also to sequester more carbon and provide a smorgasbord for the billions of critters that make up the microbial community. Perhaps an appropriate blessing would be: "May your earthworms copulate freely, and their tribe increase."

WATER Muddy rivers should be a thing of the past. Clear-running streams and ponds brimming with aquatic life should be normal. Here's a thought: Imagine if all the petroleum, labor, and machinery devoted in the last century to plowing, planting, and harvesting grains to feed multistomached herbivores (which shouldn't eat grain in the first place) had been devoted to building ponds and installing gravity-based water lines across America's landscape. Had such a resource allocation occurred, by this time the United States would no longer have floods or droughts because we would have nearly re-created Eden.

LANDSCAPE The field, forest, and riparian edge zones that indicate vibrant, diversified flora and fauna would crisscross the land. Gone would be miles of monocropping. Gone would be stream bank cave-ins. Dust storms and gullies would be a thing of the past. A haven for multitudinous species that require two environments for healthy living, the landscape would team with multispecies, some wild and some domestic.

EROSION Despite the billions of dollars spent on soil conservation efforts, the United States is still losing soil faster than it is being built. This is a disgrace. Unless and until we as a culture actually build soil faster than we are depleting it, healing cannot come to America's food system.

ANIMALS Commercial domestic livestock in America suffers abuse that should become a thing of the past. Healing will require eaters to individually and collectively quit patronizing these abusive prac-tices, opting instead for pasture-based, compost-driven, locally grown and processed meat, poultry, and eggs. A culture that views pigs as inanimate piles of protoplasmic structure to be manipulated however cleverly the human mind can conceive will view its citizens the same way—and other cultures. It is how we respect the least of these that creates an ethical, moral framework on which we respect the greatest of these. Providing a habitat that allows the pig to fully express its physiological distinctiveness is the starting point.

PLANTS Ever since chemist Justus von Liebig told the world in 1837 that plants were composed only of nitrogen, phosphorus, and potas-sium, incomplete soil management has gradually sickened plants. It's time to heal them with complete soil nutrition, proper plant commu-nities, and respectful husbandry.

FARMS Rather than being environmental and social liabilities, heal-ing farms exude aesthetic and aromatic attraction. Relegated to the edges of humanity because of their noxious dust, odors, pollution, chemicals, and abusive animal practices, farms must be re-embedded in communities and villages. Farms should be places where people like to congregate. Healing requires that a kindergarten class can enjoyably sit down among the chickens. If youngsters don't think the farm is "awesome and cool," their disdain will inherently carry over to a disdain of the food they eat. Loving the plate starts with loving the farm, and loving to be on the farm, and loving all that happens at the farm.

FARMERS No culture has so quickly and completely decimated its agrarian base as the United States. We now have nearly twice as many Americans in prison as we have farmers, and our nation's leaders are proud of this statistic. So proud that they think we should export this kind of farming around the world and that other cultures should emulate our success. The stereotypical redneck, trip-over-the-transmission-in-the-front-yard, tobacco-spittin' flunky farmer causes rural brain drain as the best and brightest leave for city lights, 401(k) plans, paid medical, and paid vacations. Rather than priding ourselves on how few people need to be farmers, we should respect and honor the nation's resource stewards. This must start in the collective consciousness before it can permeate to economic and physical returns.

REAL FOOD In a nation where parents are blessed for feeding their children Twinkies and Cocoa Puffs but cannot choose heritage-based raw milk, we have a long way to go before claiming we've healed our food system. The nutritionists, in true Greco-Roman Western reductionist linear systematized fragmented disconnected compartmentalized thinking, have dissected food components into parts and pieces. Generally, healing food is anything that was available before 1900; whatever the amalgamated, extruded, irradiated, reconstituted, genetically adulterated, industrial-prostituted manipulators offer is foreign to our 3 trillion intestinal micro flora and fauna. Food must replace pharmaceuticals as the best healer.

DIGESTIVE COMMUNITY Each of us has 3 trillion critters in our digestive system that metabolize our food. That's a lot of committee meetings, school diplomas, marriages, and retirement programs. In the continuum of human history, the industrial food blip, which is really a petroleum blip, is definitely a blip. These critters have never heard of Democrats or Republicans, or Robert's Rules of Order or the Geneva Convention, for that matter. They have been assaulted with corn syrup, tomato-pepper–human DNA–adulterated combinations, nutrient-depleted carrots, and toxin-laced feedlot beef. We must heal them with a historically consistent diet.

ENERGY The average food calorie requires some 14 calories in energy; this is a backward reality. Food should be produced using solar energy and be a net energy gain, not a drain. Efficient local distribution systems and grass-based livestock production can and must replace the energy-dependent industrial animal confinement system. The only reason that industrial food production has appeared efficient has been the abundance of cheap fuel; properly priced fuel will expose this charade for what it always has been.

THOUGHTFUL EATING, CONSCIOUS DINING We struggle to articulate the social, familial congeniality surrounding the dining experience. I like to call it reconnecting with our dinner dance partner. When the only association we have with our dinner dance partner is a plastic wrapper and the microwave, the historically intimate dining experience has been relegated to a one-night stand. Where's the romance, the courtship, the consciousness of decision leading up to the intimate act of ingestion? We must heal this dinner relationship, affectionately, respectfully, and knowledgeably.

LIVING For the first time in human history, people can move into a community, hook a water pipe into one coming in, the sewage pipe into one going out, buy food at the Wal-Mart from unknown sources, flick on a light switch for energy from who knows where, and build a house out of materials covered in bar codes from Home Depot. We don't have to know the local ecology, economy, society, climate, agriculture, or anything. Just hook up. Such a noninvolved existence inherently breeds contempt for the community that sustains our existence: physical, spiritual, mental. Respecting our humanness requires that we respect—by appreciating our codependence on—that community of air, water, plants, animals, soil, and microbes.

That's a lot of healing to do. Ours is not the first culture to face a large healing agenda. We did not get where we are overnight, and we will not get out of it overnight. As a Christian libertarian environmentalist capitalist, I am not waiting around for government agencies, grants, or legislation to effect the healing. Even though you may be fully aware of our collective cultural food sickness, be assured that the overriding consensus of our culture is still running pell-mell toward the industrial food system.

The industrial food system's plans to clone, genetically modify, irradiate, and microchip every morsel of food is apparent and moving forward at warp speed. That you and I react to this agenda with horror does not deter it in the least. Whatever can be grown faster, fatter, bigger, and cheaper is Wall Street's mantra, the cry of the pinstripe-suited conquistadors commanding their field minions from high-rise offices in Metropolis, USA.

In fact, these experts, both USDA and corporate, view farm ponds as a landscape menace because they attract waterfowl, the alleged culprit in avian flu transmission. I've been called a bioterrorist for letting my pastured poultry commiserate with red-winged blackbirds, who in turn transport deadly viruses to the scientific, environmentally controlled concentration camp factory industrial houses. Perhaps one of the biggest shocks to the countless visitors who tour our farm to enjoy the aesthetic and aromatic romance of pasture-based livestock production is when I explain to them that within our conventional agrarian community, Polyface Farm is viewed as a threat. We don't vaccinate, medicate, eradicate, complicate—we just don't do what farmers are supposed to do. And that's threatening.

What would be the opposite of centralized production? Sounds like lots of small farms, maybe even family farms. But for sure, smaller, diversified, symbiotic, synergistic, multispeciated farms. And lots of farmers.

I'm convinced that if the industrial dairy cartel had their way, they would prefer one massive genetically modified cow somewhere around Lincoln, Nebraska, with huge pipes hooked up to her four teats. Each 30-inch-diameter pipe would go to a fourth of the United States—one up toward New England; one down toward Alabama and Florida; one toward the Southwest, terminating in Los Angeles; and the other toward San Francisco Bay. The massive cow would eat a train-car load of grain and silage per bite and poop a train-car load every fifteen seconds. Thus the railroad would simply make a loop from front to back, with cars unloaded and reloaded every few minutes. This twenty-four-hour-per-day behemoth would be the ultimate economies-of-scale producer, and no farmer would be required to hook up, unhook, care for, or look after anything.

Global positioning satellite–guided John Deeres would plant and harvest corn with mechanical precision and dump it into the train cars. A robotic soil injector would dispose of the manure from the incoming train before it looped around to be loaded for the return trip. This would all be efficient and free up farmers to punch computer buttons in Dilbert cubicles for multinational corporate officers at the end of the expressway. Oh, and they could pick up their milk on the way home. Sounds fun, don't you think?

Back to a less obscene vision, I see thousands and thousands of diversified farms serving their bioregional locavores. Imagine walking down the grocery aisle of any supermarket in the United States. Think how many products on those shelves could be produced within 100 miles of the establishment. Not coffee or spices maybe, or bananas or tea, but the list of possibilities is enormous: dairy, fruits, vegetables, meats, poultry, eggs, grains. If all that could be grown and marketed within 100 miles actually were, it would fundamentally change our food system beyond recognition.

And lest anyone think the local idea is quaint and cute but not really practical, consider that virtually all metropolitan areas could feed themselves within 30 miles. Since losing free petroleum from the old Soviet Union, the approximately 2.1-million-person city of Havana, Cuba, now grows 75 percent of its food within the city limits.

The reason the butcher, baker, and candlestick maker were chased out of town during the last century was because cities became antihuman in their smells, pollution, unsightliness, and treatment of people. And whenever economic sectors move to the edges of humanity, they always take environmental, social, and economic shortcuts because neighbors are not around to see what goes in the front door and what comes out the back door. A transparent food system must always be embedded in the community with a fairly open-door policy.

The U.S. Department of Agriculture considers it a food production health risk to let visitors come to farms. After all, people might carry disease to the animals or plants. What does it say about our food when it suffers such immunodeficiency that eaters cannot touch, smell, or look at it until it falls onto our plates from a plastic bag? Any food production model divorced from humans will produce an anti-human dinner. Appropriately scaled, aesthetically and aromatically romantic farms require diversity, synergism, lots of healthy relationships, and a nurturing rather than manipulative attitude. Indeed, the model must follow nature's patterns.

That means that cows don't eat dead cows even if doing so will grow them faster, fatter, bigger, cheaper. It means planting square miles of narrow-genetic-based potatoes is not efficient; it is vulnerable to disease. It means pouring concrete and planting rebar is not the secret to health. It means omega-3 and omega-6 fatty acid ratios are as important as egg production percentages. It means the why is as important as the how. And it means a moral and ethical boundary exists to keep human cleverness from exceeding its ability to metabolize its own inventions.

Perhaps the single most telling measure of our culture's ailing food system is the declining number of farmers, the notion that fewer people on the rural landscape is a good thing. I would suggest that a healthy farming sector would house many, many more loving stewards rather than fewer. And that having more eyes and hands on the landscape, to care for it, would be a great thing. When will people who think it's progress when more teens show up for river clean-up day realize that more farmers will steward the landscape better than a few megafarms?

Second, the opposite of centralized processing would indicate local abattoirs (slaughterhouses), canneries, cottage industry, and church kitchens. During the industrial era, a host of food safety regulations developed to protect citizens from shortsighted processors. But these regulations, unfortunately, have criminalized these embedded community-scaled processing facilities to the point that they literally do not exist.

The pendulum has swung far too much to one side and, in over-correcting for the abuses detailed in Upton Sinclair's 1906 iconic *The Jungle*, has virtually annihilated the neighborhood processing infrastructure. Where are the canneries? Where are the local butchers? The infrastructure overhead required to make one quiche and sell it to the neighbor is of such magnitude that embryonic businesses cannot be born.

Our culture encourages people to go out on a 70-degree November day and gut-shoot a deer with Creutzfeldt-Jakob disease; drag it a mile through the squirrel dung, sticks, and rocks; display it prominently on the hood of the Blazer in the afternoon sizzling sun; then take it home and pull it up in a backyard tree for a week under roosting starlings and sparrows. Then it can be skinned, cut up on a board in the backyard, and fed to the children. And this is all considered a wonderful thing.

But try selling one T-bone from a beef butchered on an appropriately temperate day and kept in a stainless steel walk-in cooler before being cut up, and the government will arrest you for selling uninspected meat. Make no mistake, these regulations are not about food safety; they are about denying market access to innovative competitors and keeping the current oligopolistic players in the game.

A truly transparent, decentralized food processing system needs a constitutional amendment to guarantee all Americans the freedom to choose the food they want to feed their 3-trillion-member internal community. We have the freedom to own and use guns, assemble, and practice our religion. But what are those freedoms if we cannot choose what to feed our bodies to give us the energy to shoot, pray, or preach? The only reason the framers of our Bill of Rights did not guarantee us the freedom of food choice is because they could not have envisioned a day when an American could not purchase a glass of raw milk or a pound of sausage from a neighbor.

Interestingly, any food item can be given away; it just cannot be sold. What is it about the selling that suddenly makes it a hazardous substance? And notice that the prohibition is only on the selling, not the consuming or buying. Most hazardous substances like pharmaceuticals and illegal drugs contain prohibitions on both buyer and seller. But on food, the prohibition is only on the seller. If you can procure illegal food, you can consume it freely and feed it to your children. Obviously, the food police do not really think this is dangerous food.

The kind of food system I envision does not exist because it has been summarily chased from our communities. Why can't I get donuts from Aunt Matilda next door, pot pies from the homeschooling family down the street, milk and cheese from the dairy farmer deacon at church, and sausage from the acorn-fattened pigs up the road? If we really want an educated eater, the quickest way to accomplish that is to let people opt out of government-sanctioned food. The choices would stimulate study and discussion, research and discovery as people took responsibility for their own food choices.

For those too timid to take responsibility, the supermarket is ready and waiting with government food. But as soon as people began eating food free of corn syrup, feeling better and exiting hospitals, word would get around, and entrepreneurial community processors would proliferate beyond what we can imagine today. Innovation requires embryonic prototypes, but when these embryos, because of arbitrary and capricious, inappropriate food police, must be too big to be birthed, what could be never exists.

The industrial system that gave us economies of scale eventually exceeded its own efficiency. We can hear that excess every day, screaming from the bowels of the food industry: *Campylobacter, E. coli, Salmonella, Listeria, bovine spongiform encephalopathy, avian influenza*. These words are nature's language, begging us: "Enough!" When will we listen? When will we trade our conquistador hats for caretaker hands? And when will we realize that four-legged salamanders for our grandchildren's world are certainly as important as today's Dow Jones Industrial Average?

One doesn't have to be compromised for the other. Community-friendly processing—thousands of medium and small businesses—can efficiently and effectively meet all the demands of a growing population. But these entrepreneurs must be emancipated from the slavery of the food police by giving them access to neighbor customers. Most of the government food in the supermarket is tainted with substances that did not exist a mere 100 years ago. I wonder how in the world our species survived until that blue USDA logo appeared? Our current epidemics of type 2 diabetes, heart disease, and obesity are perhaps traceable directly to eaters' abandoning the foods of our forebears and eating government food instead.

Indigenous, heritage-based food is what our 3-trillion-member internal communities are used to. Being a good neighbor to those communities is what all of us should aspire to be. That food will be found in our kitchens and neighborhood processors.

Finally, the opposite of long-distance transportation sounds like . . .

well, it sounds like local, don't you think? From farmers' markets to community-supported agriculture to metropolitan buying clubs to farm gate sales, I envision a local food network that services a bioregion.

A truly functional, competitive local food system must have a smaller distribution energy footprint than the industrial system. And that will take some doing, because right now farmers' markets have a larger footprint than Wal-Mart. Even though the average farmers' market vendor is traveling only 40 miles one way, he is transporting only a couple of hundred pounds of product. When compared with the 1,500-mile Jolly Green Giant truck run, the shorter distance does not compensate for the much tinier volume carried.

Farmers must network to achieve similar economies of scale in hauling their products to population centers. To attain a credible competitive edge, a local system will necessarily involve what I call food clusters consisting of six basic components: production, processing, accounting, marketing, distribution, and customers.

PRODUCTION Somebody has to produce something to eat.

PROCESSING The raw material normally must be put in marketable form. Most people don't want to go out on the back stoop and butcher their chicken for dinner. In fact, today many people don't realize that a chicken actually has bones. "You mean there's more than skinless, boneless breast?"

ACCOUNTING Someone must watch the money, balance the check-book, pay the invoices, bill out sales. This is more than putting all the income in one box and the outgo in another box and hoping the income is higher than the outgo.

MARKETING In any successful business, at least one person must be a gregarious storyteller schmoozer. If you don't have one, you don't have a whole. And this is where too many farmers drop the ball. Many people farm because they really don't like to interact with people. But you can't have a viable food system without linking producers with consumers.

DISTRIBUTION You have to get the food to where people are. Whether that's a scheduled drop point, retail store, farmers' market, or UPS shipping point, a viable food system requires toting the stuff from point A to point B, and it had better be done efficiently. This is where most local food systems break down. Rather than every farmer owning a delivery van, the distribution needs to be operated as a separate, stand-alone business that services many farmers and many customers. Here at Polyface, we put food from a dozen other producers on our delivery vehicle every week. This moves our small operation into an economy of scale that competes even with the big boys.

CUSTOMERS Perhaps this seems too obvious, but if you're located 100 miles from a Coke machine, the essential customer element of a local food system can be a challenge. I admit that I don't have all the answers for those remotest of places. I do know that if everyone who could participate in a local food system just would, it would so fundamentally change America's food system that morphs would occur that we cannot even envision today. At the end of the day, eaters—all of us—must share the responsibility for creating a local food system. It can't all be done by farmers. It can't all be done by farmers' market masters. It can't all be done by distributors.

The shared responsibility for a local food system to work is palpable. Many of us farmers become frustrated by the apparent notion that we have to be the ones to do all the innovation.

Imagine millions of kitchens taking in nonmanipulated food, preparing it for grateful families, and enjoying convivial conversation and communion around the table. That is how we close the loop back to the farmer, back to the land, back to the earthworm.

Notice I have not asked for a single government program, no agency grants, and no legislation except the freedom of food choice. All noble causes find their impetus from charismatic individuals who awaken on the inside, one by one, to the needs of the moment. At this moment, millions of us can be newly awakened to the need for healing, and we can make it happen. Today. Maybe for some it will be just preparing one meal from scratch this week. Maybe for some it will be eating one sit-down meal a month, as a family or a couple.

For others, it will be moving from the supermarket to the farmers' market and then visiting some of the farmers. For many, it will require giving up some TV time and video games to reconnect with the vibrant, pulsing biological community in and around us. Living in that awareness will heal our food system, our bodies, and our land.

VOTE WITH YOUR FORK

It's Time for Citizens to Take Back the Food System

DANIEL IMHOFF

THE GREAT CHALLENGES *of our time—changing climate, diminishing fossil fuel resources, disappearing species, and exploding nutritional epidemics such as obesity—cannot be addressed without fundamental changes in our approach to food and agriculture. Citizens can help to shape a different kind of food and farming system by voting with their forks: with the foods they buy, their lifestyle decisions, the ballots they cast, and the vigilance they pursue with elected officials. Time is of the essence.*

❖

On a cold winter morning, six volunteers gather at a wooded opening on a low-flowing creek, which eventually mingles with North Carolina's heavily polluted Neuse River. To avoid trespassing on land owned by the industrial hog operation upstream, the citizen scientists—members of the Neuse River Foundation Sampling Team—are equipped with long-handled dipping cups . . . and river kayaks, in case they need to paddle lawfully into deeper U.S. waters. It's a duty not without risks: from angry factory farm operators and workers, aggressive dogs, and poisonous snakes like copperheads and water moccasins.

Alerted by flyover teams that local CAFO operators have been spraying liquid swine waste onto fields in advance of impending rains, the volunteers carefully take and label a number of water samples. These will later be tested for fecal bacteria, metals, nutrients, and other contaminants. With their rivers and creeks polluted by wastes from dozens of CAFOs that concentrate between 12,000 and 20,000 hogs, the volunteers have learned to professionally monitor water-ways for Clean Water Act violations. While government enforcement agencies have largely turned a blind eye to the fouling of their public resources, these volunteers are supported by a cadre of attorneys, amateur pilots, scientists, and activists. More broadly, they exemplify just one of dozens, if not hundreds, of local citizen groups fighting to clean up communities reduced to ecological sacrifice zones by industrial animal agriculture.

AN ISSUE FOR OUR TIME

Food—what we eat and how we produce it—is rapidly becoming one of the defining issues of our time. Like the citizen scientists volunteering with the Neuse River Foundation, people around the United States are taking a greater interest and responsibility in making sure the foods they purchase are good, clean, and fair. They are shortening the distances between farm fields and tables by signing up for weekly deliveries from community-supported agriculture (CSA) operations, patronizing farmers' markets and truck stands, choosing to eat in season, and raising chickens and growing food in urban and rural backyards and community gardens. They are looking for meat, eggs, and dairy products that have been produced according to humane standards, raised on grass, distributed by self-governing cooperatives, and administered antibiotics only if necessary or prescribed by a veterinarian. They are establishing regional food councils, setting ambitious targets for amounts and percentages of foods to be produced and consumed locally, and conducting open discussions about what food security means to their communities. They are challenging government officials to limit egregious agricultural farm bill subsidies, to uphold environmental and antitrust laws that are already on the books, to regulate the use of antibiotic medicines in CAFOs, and to turn away from the agribusiness lobbies in Washington, DC, all too eager to dictate the country's—and by extension, the world's—food and agriculture policies.

Contrary to what industry and their affiliated think tanks and land grant universities might lead us to believe, massively concentrated confinement animal agriculture is not inevitable. We do not need CAFOs to feed a hungry world. And we certainly won't have a world worth passing on to our children and grandchildren if we keep pretending that we do. It's not too late to profoundly change the way we farm and distribute food, to rethink our diets, or to create healthy food systems. How we get there will be no easy task. Nor will it come through simplistic or uniform solutions.

Yet of all our modern economic activities, food and farming systems may be the easiest to decipher in terms of energy consumption, input flows, and extractive demands from the earth's limited biological and mineral resources. Redesigning our food systems to be healthy and regionally diverse might actually be our best offensive strategy for addressing the critical challenges of environmental degradation, population, declining health, and resource consumption ahead of us.

"GETTING PERENNIAL BEFORE THE NEXT CENTENNIAL"

Among our first difficulties is the need to restore our compact with other animal species. By relegating animals to live as protein machines, slaughtering them by the billions, and forcing them to live in unspeakable conditions on top of their own waste, we have broken our contract with the animal world. We must find our way forward (not backward, as some might argue) to a world in which the values of care, decency, and informed husbandry guide our production as well as our consumption of all foods. These values may ultimately be backed up by a universal declaration of animal rights that establishes an ongoing standard of care for all domesticated animals.

Rather than forcing crops and animals to fit the cold parameters of manufacturing and monoculture, farms of a healthy food system will be modeled after nature's systems. The food animals we do raise will live in more natural surroundings and eat a diet they are more accustomed to: pastures and diverse mixtures of deep-rooted plants as well as sustainably farmed grain crops. Rather than being dependent on enormous amounts of fossil fuels, future farming systems will take advantage of renewable forms of energy as much as possible. The milk, meats, eggs, and other crops they do provide will be nutritious and feature local flavors and characteristics. The manure they generate will provide essential fertilizer for local farms. Farmers and eaters will not steal from the future to thoughtlessly gorge themselves today. Healthy foods must come from healthy lands and animals managed by knowledgeable and well-appreciated farmers. In turn, they will make for healthy consumers. In fact, thousands of such diverse, family-oriented farms are producing foods across the country in just that way.

For far too long we in the United States have lived under the shadow and illusion of the "Get Big or Get Out" mantra. This idea originated in the Cold War era under Secretary of Agriculture Ezra Taft Benson and was later engrained as the national farm policy goal in the 1970s. Adopted hook, line, and sinker by the agricultural economists, "Get Big or Get Out" policies determined that U.S. farmers should become feeders of the world and that only the biggest industrial growers should survive. These industrial-scale policies have given us the grain monocultures, the overcrowded animal factories, the monopolistic agribusinesses, and the tragic disappearance of family farmers in the second half of the twentieth century. Government policies have also helped to bolster the idea that bigger and more specialized is the only way to feed the population and that small- and medium-scale alternatives will never be able to perform or measure up. But this is a self-fulfilling prophecy. The rules, regulations, and subsidies have been designed to facilitate control of markets by a relatively small number of extremely large and powerful corporations and producers. A revived food system driven by diversified regional farms has not been put to the test in our modern era.

Moving forward, grass-based animal production can and should become a key component of a national healthy food and farming strategy. A continentwide shift to more permanent grasslands would actually help to capture and store carbon rather than releasing it into the atmosphere—slowing agriculture's climate change impacts (which are formidable and perhaps reversible) and potentially creating new markets for conservation-based food production. Restoring tens of millions of highly erodible acres of corn, soy, and hayfields to permanent, deep-rooted, moisture-absorbing, ground-protecting plants will not only provide food high in omega-3 essential fatty acids but will also help to ensure that we pass on the basic building blocks of food production—fertile soils and clean water—to our children and grandchildren. This twenty-first century course correction might be summed up by a new mantra for food and agriculture. Rather than a survival of the biggest based on animal factories and soil-eroding, chemical-intensive monocultures of annual feed crops, we must "Get Perennial Before the Next Centennial."

RESTORING REGIONAL FOOD WEBS

Our food animals of tomorrow are in dire need of genetic restoration. The biological lineages of modern livestock have become so freakishly specialized and genetically homogenized that many species can't even breed without artificial insemination—commonly with frozen DNA harvested from a few select, long-dead animals. Saving strong lines of livestock breeds, subsets of breeds, and landrace breeds that have been adapted to particular regions and climatic zones rather than the confines of the industrial food pipeline must surface as a national priority: among as many breeds, in as many regions, and as quickly as possible. We should protect the world's agricultural diversity even if it only serves as an insurance policy against catastrophic diseases or other problems that could sweep through extremely vulnerable commercial breeds.

And because the CAFO industry has become so vertically concentrated and dominated by huge corporate conglomerates—"from semen to cellophane" or "from piglet to pork chop"—our regional food production capacities will have to be rejuvenated. Perhaps most daunting is the need for a whole new generation of farmers and food producers. With nearly two-thirds of the country's farming population over the age of fifty-five, and the costs and knowledge requirements of entry so steep, recruiting the young people required to restore regional food webs will be a profoundly challenging task.

Yet one can, in fact, envision the revitalization of regional food production as an economic and organizing force for many decades to come. Converting healthy foods into value-added products can create new jobs and business opportunities. Regional hatcheries, local feed mills, and mobile and small-scale slaughtering facilities can become an economic engine driving a transitional economy forward. Shifting health care and regional development goals to emphasize healthy food production can also transform economic priorities. Primary considerations could include incentives for soil and water conservation, grass farming, and feeding children in schools from well-run local farms.

HEALTHY FOOD AS AN ECONOMIC FORCE

The rise of regional food production systems could become a driving force in a new economic system that attempts to wean our economy from excessive dependence on fossil fuels and far-away produced goods. Because the food system is responsible for at least one-third of greenhouse gas emissions (and perhaps much more than that)—a staggering toll no matter how you look at it—lowering the carbon footprint of agriculture seems like a logical and urgent place to start addressing climate change.

In a world pummeled by both an obesity epidemic and chronic hunger, it is entirely possible that nutritious foods could become one of our best forms of preventive health care. According to the American College of Surgeons, at least seventy cents of every new health care dollar created in the United States is spent on treating some malady related to the obesity and overweight crisis sweeping the country and now the globe. Such expenses are preventable if the food system can be less centered around dumping cheap fatty animal products and high-calorie processed foods on an increasingly sedentary public. With concerns about food safety on the rise—chemical contamination, pathogenic diseases, and other threats—regional food webs may become our best safeguard against uncertainty. We have an easier time tracking among smaller producers distributing foods regionally than with huge operations that comingle foods (and animals and other ingredients) from different producers and scatter them through vast distribution networks.

REDEFINING HEALTHY FOOD

Such a broad system overhaul may require a whole new way of defining what healthy food is, what it can mean to society, and what kind of priority levels it must assume among consumers, producers, government agencies, and all other involved parties. At the Slow Food Nation Summit, held in San Francisco in August 2008, the Declaration for Healthy Food and Agriculture was released to the public as part of a multiyear effort to build a citizen movement. The declaration, already signed by tens of thousands of people, defines healthy food with a twelve-point platform, which can help to inform our discussion as we move forward.

A healthy food and agriculture policy:

1. Forms the foundation of prosperous and secure societies, healthy communities, and healthy people.

2. Provides access to affordable, healthy food to all people around the globe.

3. Protects the finite resources of productive soils, fresh water, and biological diversity.

4. Strives to remove fossil fuel from every link in the food chain and replace it with renewable resources and energy.

5. Originates from a biological rather than an industrial mindset.

6. Prevents the exploitation of farmers, workers, and natural resources; the domination of genomes and markets; and the cruel treatment of animals by any nation, corporation, or individual.

7. Upholds the dignity, safety, and quality of life for all workers.

8. Fosters diversity in all its relevant forms: diversity of domesticated and wild species; diversity of foods, flavors, and traditions; diversity of ownership.

9. Commits resources to teach children the skills and knowledge essential to food production, preparation, and nutrition.

10. Requires a thorough national dialog and allows regionally adopted guidelines regarding technologies used for production.

11. Enforces transparency so that citizens know how their food is produced, where it comes from, and what it contains.

12. Promotes economic structures and supports programs to nurture the development of just and sustainable regional farm and food networks.

VOTING WITH OUR FORKS

The reality is that the scale of problems related to population growth, economic development, and food production is enormous. The good news is that food is an issue most of us can do something about. We are all eaters, and the acts of eating and of producing our food bind us to one another and to the earth. We can "vote with our forks" through the meals we cook and purchase. We can do our best to support a healthy food system as defined above, though it might take more sacrifice than we think. In so doing, we contribute to one of the most powerful world-shaping forces.

And while we can vote with our forks in choosing the foods we provide for our homes, places of work, and communities, we also need radical reforms to public policies and laws. Voting with our forks requires becoming more educated about policy issues that affect our food system and casting our ballots accordingly. Knowing what we now know of the billions of U.S. Department of Agriculture farm bill dollars that are spent annually to prop up the CAFO industry at the expense of the small family farmer, there should be "No Subsidization Without Social Obligation." Taxpayer dollars spent on subsidy programs should be targeted to create a healthy and sustainable world— not to give handouts to huge corporations for cheap monoculture feed grains or the construction of toxic manure containment systems.

Every elected official must have a position on the food system and make it well known among constituents. Every elected official should have a policy on the present and future of CAFOs as well as a stance on grass-based pasture farming. But no government representatives will take these issues seriously unless eaters demand a shift toward healthy non-CAFO food for everyone—not just for those who can afford it.

The good news is that the eaters (aka taxpayers) solidly outnumber all other voting blocks. We can only hope that we wake up in time and, like the community activists around the country fighting for a better food system, take up the yoke of vigilance and hold each other accountable. Our pursuit of healthy food and agriculture can be a unifying and positive force if we make the connection that each time we cast a vote with our forks—with our buying decisions and our ballots—we send out a profound signal about the type of world we want to live in.

KNOW WHERE YOUR FOOD COMES FROM

Nowhere in any other human industry does one find the breadth of environmental impacts found in animal food production. Yet this is just one component of what could be called the "Mother of all crises": *the Extinction Crisis*. As you eat each meal, try to understand and visualize how your food is produced and how it contributes to the present state of the world.

- **Land use**—What types of habitats were originally converted to produce the food you are eating?
- **Beauty**—How has natural beauty been compromised as a result of your food choices?
- **Chemically saturated feed**—Have fields been drenched with fertilizers and pesticides to produce feed for your meat, milk, or eggs?
- **Massive monocultures**—Did the feed for your animal products come from corn, soy, and hay monocultures or from managed pastures?
- **Heavy carbon footprint**—How much oil goes into feeding, transporting, and processing the food you are eating? What about the greenhouse gas emissions involved?
- **Social costs**—What happens to our culture as farms become factories and farmers become low-wage contractors or disappear altogether because we want abundant cheap food?
- **Health costs**—What are the medical and economic impacts of a diet heavy in saturated animal fats?
- **Animal welfare**—What does it mean if we support corporations that treat animals like inanimate production units?
- **True costs**—Can you make food choices that are healthier for people, the land, and our future?

Environmentalism begins at the breakfast table. Maybe you can develop an eater's manifesto of your own.

WHAT YOU CAN DO

- Refine, reduce, and replace animal products.
- Consider eating smaller amounts of animal food products. Carefully seek out grass-fed and grass-finished beef and dairy products and pasture-raised pork, poultry, and egg products for those you do buy.
- Learn about vegetarian cooking. Consider "Meatless Mondays," as advocated for by the Johns Hopkins University Center for a Livable Future, or avoid factory-farmed animal products altogether by switching to a plant-based diet.
- Purchase meat, eggs, and dairy products from local farmers on the farm or at farmers' markets, or by buying a share from a local farmer as part of a community-supported agriculture (CSA) program or local buyers' group.
- Read labels. Does the product contain artificial growth hormones or genetically engineered ingredients? Eggs that are merely labeled "cage-free" or "free-range" but not certified by a third party may not necessarily be ensuring the hens' welfare.
- Choose meats from animals that were not given "nontherapeutic" antibiotics—indicated by labels such as "USDA Certified Organic" or "no antibiotic use." Look for the Humane Farm Animal Care label. Foods with this label come from humane sources that are inspected annually. Select certified organic meats, eggs, and dairy and those clearly labeled as using only vegetarian animal feed.
- Honor where your food comes from. Consider spending a little more on better sources and better qualities of meat and animal products, a little less often. Learn as much as you can about bringing the most flavor out of your cooking. Be creative with leftovers.
- Don't support companies that don't care about animal rights.
- Ask your local grocers and restaurants to offer humanely raised foods and fresh, locally grown products from small producers.

WHAT POLICY MAKERS CAN DO

What we all do in our personal lives matters, but more important, the livestock sector must be required to pay the true costs of production and to become financially accountable for any harm it causes.

Decentralization of production through smaller, locally adapted operations is the only way to spread wastes appropriately across the landscape. Subsidies for cheap grain, water, grazing leases, and other means of production must be replaced by mechanisms and incentives to reward producers and landowners for environmental protection and stewardship.

The following policy steps are essential to bringing the CAFO production system into environmental, ethical, and economic compliance, as recommended by leading organizations and scientific panels.

- Phase out the use of antimicrobials for nontherapeutic (i.e., growth-promoting) purposes in food animals to reduce the risk of antimicrobial resistance to important human medicines.
- Regulate or phase out the most egregious, intensive, and inhumane forms of animal factory confinement, such as battery cages (for laying hens); gestation crates (for sows); restrictive farrowing crates (for sows); veal crates (for male dairy calves); tethering; force feeding of geese and ducks; tail docking of dairy cattle as well as hogs; and forced molting of laying hens by feed removal.
- Phase out the construction of new CAFOs and the expansion of existing facilities.
- Establish and enforce strong pollution laws and water use permits, as well as pollution reporting requirements for CAFO producers to protect all citizens from the adverse environmental and health hazards of improperly handled waste.
- Reduce the number and scope of exemptions for agriculture operations from existing or proposed environmental and animal cruelty laws.
- Impose strict regulations on the hazardous substances contained in manure.
- End air emission monitoring study programs that essentially allow factory farms to violate air quality standards. Develop new regulations that would reduce emissions of ammonia and other air pollutants from CAFOs, and ensure that CAFO operators cannot avoid such regulations by encouraging ammonia volatilization.
- Address the concentration of corporate power in livestock markets by strict enforcement of antitrust and anticompetitive practice and

by enacting other measures to increase competition in the livestock industry.

- Create and fund programs that revive animal husbandry practices and training.
- Protect all domestic livestock—including poultry—under state, national, and universal codes of conduct for animal welfare.
- Reform policies that encourage the overproduction of corn, soybeans, and other commodities that has resulted in cheap feed for animals in CAFOs. Replace feed crop subsidies with programs that strengthen conservation and support prices when supplies are high (rather than allowing prices to fall below the costs of production).
- Allow local governments to regulate CAFOs through their health or zoning laws.
- Reduce the use of U.S. farm bill conservation dollars that fund CAFO waste management under the Environmental Quality Incentives Program (EQIP), and shift support toward sound animal farming practices.
- Revise slaughterhouse regulations to facilitate larger numbers of smaller processors, including eliminating requirements not appropriate for smaller facilities.
- Take public health measures such as providing adequate numbers of federal inspectors or empowering and training state inspectors.
- Substantially increase funding for research to improve alternative livestock production methods—especially those that are pasture-based—that are beneficial to the environment, public health, and rural communities.
- Phase out the use of blood, manure, slaughterhouse waste, and other animal products in feed for any farm animal.
- Train animal industry workers on how to prevent animals from becoming downers and how to deal humanely with those that are suffering.
- Require country-of-origin and accurate processing labels for all animal products and products containing animal by-products, to provide consumers with information about where their food is coming from and a way to check for adequate animal welfare and food safety policies.
- Strongly enforce regulations pertaining to CAFOs, including more inspectors and inspections, better monitoring and enforcement of manure-handling practices, and measurement of the effectiveness of pollution prevention practices.

Special thanks to the Pew Commission on Industrial Farm Animal Production, the Union of Concerned Scientists, and Food and Water Watch for contributing to these recommendations.

CONTRIBUTORS

DAN BARBER is one of the United States' most highly celebrated chefs. He began farming and cooking at his family farm, Blue Hill Farm, in the Berkshires, where he gained appreciation for locally grown and seasonal foods. He is the co-owner of two acclaimed restaurants, Blue Hill in New York City, and Blue Hill at Stone Barns, located on an 80-acre working farm 30 miles north of midtown Manhattan. In 2009, *Time* magazine featured him in its "*Time* 100," an annual list of the world's most influential people.

WENDELL BERRY is a working farmer in north-central Kentucky and the author of more than thirty books of poetry, essays, and novels. He has received fellowships from the Guggenheim and Rockefeller foundations, a Lannan Foundation Award, and a grant from the National Endowment for the Arts. His many books include *The Unsettling of America, What Are People For?* and *Citizenship Papers.*

DONALD E. BIXBY is the retired executive director and technical program manager of the American Livestock Breeds Conservancy (ALBC), the pioneer agency in breed conservation in the United States and an internationally recognized leader in genetic conservation in livestock and poultry. He helped to establish the USDA Agricultural Research Service's National Animal Germplasm Program and continues as liaison to the gene bank. In 2000 he was honored by Slow Food International for the work of ALBC in conserving genetic diversity in the farm animal species. The Seed Savers Exchange further recognized his efforts with its Award of Merit in 2007.

STEVE BJERKLIE has covered the meat and poultry industry for a variety of publications since 1980. At present he is a contributing editor for *Meat & Poultry*, the industry's leading trade journal, and has been a correspondent for *The Economist* magazine since 1996.

CHRISTOPHER D. COOK is an award-winning investigative journalist and writer whose work has appeared in *Harper's, Mother Jones*, the *Christian Science Monitor*, the *Los Angeles Times, The Nation*, and *The Economist*. He is the author of *Diet for a Dead Planet: Big Business and the Coming Food Crisis.*

JAY GRAHAM is a former researcher for the Johns Hopkins University Center for a Livable Future. The center promotes research and education about the complex relationships among diet, food production, environment, and human health. The center was also a leading participant in the Pew Commission on Industrial Farm Animal Production's 2008 report *Putting Meat on the Table: Industrial Farm Animal Production in America.*

JAYDEE HANSON is a policy analyst for the Center for Food Safety on issues related to animal cloning and animal genetic engineering. He also works for the center's sister agency, the International Center for Technology Assessment (ICTA), where he directs work on human genetics, including stem cell research, cloning, and gene/embryo patenting.

WENONAH HAUTER is the executive director of Food & Water Watch and has worked extensively on energy, food, water, and environmental issues at the national, state, and local levels. She has an MS degree in applied anthropology from the University of Maryland and coauthored *Zapped: Irradiation and the Death of Food.*

EMMETT HOPKINS is a researcher and writer for Watershed Media. He previously studied and worked on sustainable food systems at Stanford University.

LEO HORRIGAN is a senior staff member at the Johns Hopkins University Center for a Livable Future. The center promotes research, education, and advocacy about the complex relationships among diet, food production, environment, and human health. The center was also a leading participant in the Pew Commission on Industrial Farm Animal Production's 2008 report *Putting Meat on the Table: Industrial Farm Animal Production in America.*

DANIEL IMHOFF is the author of numerous essays and books, including *Food Fight: The Citizen's Guide to a Food and Farm Bill; Farming with the Wild: Enhancing Biodiversity on Farms and Ranches;* and *Paper or Plastic: Searching for Solutions to an Overpackaged World.* He is the cofounder of Watershed Media, a nonprofit research institution and publishing house, and cofounder of the Wild Farm Alliance, a national organization that promotes farming systems that accommodate wild nature.

PETER KAMINSKY is the author of numerous books including *The Elements of Taste.* His forthcoming book is *Culinary Intelligence: A Hedonist's Guide to Eating Healthy.* He is the former Underground Gourmet for *New York* magazine and his Outdoors column has run in the *New York Times* for two decades. The excerpt in this book is from *Pig Perfect: Encounters with Remarkable Swine,* which his agent describes as "a study in hamthropology."

ROBERT F. KENNEDY JR. founded, and is the current president of, the Waterkeeper Alliance, a network of 157 groups worldwide working to preserve and protect aquatic ecosystems. Kennedy serves as codirector of the Environmental Litigation Clinic at Pace University School of Law and is a senior attorney for the Natural Resources Defense Council. He is the author of many books, including *Crimes Against Nature: How George W. Bush and His Corporate Pals Are Plundering the Country and Hijacking Our Democracy.*

ANDREW KIMBRELL is a public interest attorney, activist, and author. He has been involved in public interest legal activity in numerous areas of technology, human health, and the environment, and has written and edited several books on a variety of issues, including *Fatal Harvest: The Tragedy of Industrial Agriculture* and *Your Right to Know: Genetic Engineering and the Secret Changes in Your Food.*

FRED KIRSCHENMANN is a Distinguished Fellow at the Aldo Leopold Center for Sustainable Agriculture at Iowa State University and the president of the Stone Barns Center for Food and Agriculture. He farms over ten grains and oilseeds on 3,500 acres in North Dakota that include integrated livestock.

ANNA LAPPÉ is a national best-selling author and a sustainable food advocate whose writing has appeared in the *Washington Post*, the *San Francisco Chronicle*, the *Los Angeles Times*, and the *International Herald Tribune*. She is the author of *Diet for a Hot Planet: The Climate Crisis at the End of Your Fork and What You Can Do About It*, and coauthored *Hope's Edge: The Next Diet for a Small Planet* with her mother, Frances Moore Lappé, and *Grub: Ideas for an Urban Organic Kitchen* with eco-chef Bryant Terry.

CHRISTOPHER MANES has written on topics as far ranging as anthropology, philosophy, religion, postmodern environmentalism, medievalism, linguistics, and law. He is best known for his book *Green Rage: Radical Environmentalism and the Unmaking of Civilization*, which was nominated for a *Los Angeles Times* Book Prize in science.

ERIK MARCUS is the author of *Meat Market: Animals, Ethics, and Money*, and *The Ultimate Vegan Guide*. He publishes a daily blog at Vegan.com and has spoken to audiences in more than a hundred cities.

SHAWN MCKENZIE is a senior staff member at the Johns Hopkins University Center for a Livable Future. The center promotes research, education, and advocacy about the complex relationships among diet, food production, environment, and human health. The center was also a leading participant in the Pew Commission on Industrial Farm Animal Production's 2008 report *Putting Meat on the Table: Industrial Farm Animal Production in America.*

ANNE MENDELSON is a freelance writer who specializes in food and culinary history. She is the author of *Stand Facing the Stove* (a history of *The Joy of Cooking* and its authors) and has written three Mexican cookbooks with chef-restaurateur Zarela Martínez. Anne has written for *Gourmet*, *Saveur*, and the *New York Times.*

MEREDITH NILES is the former director of the Cool Foods Campaign at the Center for Food Safety, which educates the public about how food choices affect global warming and promotes sustainable alternatives and policies, such as organic, local, and whole foods and reducing meat consumption.

MARTHA NOBLE is a policy specialist at the National Sustainable Agriculture Coalition and cochairs the Clean Water Network's Feedlot Work Group. She received a law degree from the University of California at Berkeley and served for a decade as a research professor and staff attorney with the National Agricultural Law Center at the University of Arkansas, Fayetteville.

TOM PHILPOTT is a cofounder of Maverick Farms, in Valle Crucis, North Carolina, and food editor at Grist.org, where he writes the Victual Reality column.

MICHAEL POLLAN is the Knight Professor of Journalism at the University of California at Berkeley's Graduate School of Journalism and the author of five books, including *In Defense of Food: An Eater's Manifesto*; *The Omnivore's Dilemma: A Natural History of Four Meals*; and *The Botany of Desire: A Plant's-Eye View of the World*. He has received the Reuters/World Conservation Union Global Award in environmental journalism, the James Beard Foundation Award for best magazine series in 2003, and a Genesis Award from the American Humane Association.

BERNARD E. ROLLIN is University Distinguished Professor of Philosophy, and holds professorships in philosophy, biomedical science, and animal science at Colorado State University in Fort Collins, Colorado. He is the author of numerous books on animal issues, including the award-winning *Animal Rights and Human Morality*, and over five hundred articles. He was recently a member of the Pew Commission on Industrial Farm Animal Production, which produced the landmark report *Putting Meat on the Table: Industrial Farm Animal Production in America*.

JOEL SALATIN is a full-time farmer at Polyface Farm in Virginia's Shenandoah Valley. A third-generation alternative farmer, Salatin is one of the world's leading innovators in the intensive rotational grazing movement. He holds a BA degree in English, is the author of numerous books, and writes extensively in magazines such as *Stockman Grass Farmer*, *Acres U.S.A.*, and *American Agriculturalist*.

ERIC SCHLOSSER'S work has appeared in *The Atlantic*, *Rolling Stone*, *Vanity Fair*, *The Nation*, and *The New Yorker*. He has received a National Magazine Award and a Sidney Hillman Foundation Award for reporting. His groundbreaking book *Fast Food Nation: The Dark Side of the All-American Meal* helped to change the way that Americans think about what they eat. It has been translated into more than twenty languages.

MATTHEW SCULLY has served as literary editor of *National Review*, as a senior speechwriter to President George W. Bush, and as a speechwriter to 2008 Republican presidential nominee John McCain and vice presidential nominee Sarah Palin. He is the author of *Dominion: The Power of Man, the Suffering of Animals, and the Call to Mercy*.

REBECCA SPECTOR is the West Coast director of the Center for Food Safety. She has worked in the environmental and agricultural sector for nearly twenty years, for organizations including Green Seal, and Mothers and Others for a Livable Planet. She was the associate editor of *Fatal Harvest: The Tragedy of Industrial Agriculture* and *Your Right to Know: Genetic Engineering and the Secret Changes in Your Food.* Rebecca holds an MS degree in environmental policy from the University of Michigan's School of Natural Resources and Environment.

KEN STIER is a journalist with more than twenty years' experience covering domestic and international affairs for major newspapers and magazines. His work has appeared in *Fortune, Time,* and *Newsweek.*

STEVE STRIFFLER holds the Doris Zemurray Stone Chair in Latin American Studies at the University of New Orleans, where he teaches classes on Latin America, immigration, and labor. Striffler's books include *Chicken: The Dangerous Transformation of America's Favorite Food; In the Shadows of State and Capital: The United Fruit Company, Popular Struggle, and Agrarian Restructuring in Ecuador, 1900–1995; Banana Wars: Power, Production, and History in the Americas;* and *The People Behind Colombian Coal: Mining, Multinationals, and Human Rights.*

KENDALL THU is an associate professor of anthropology at Northern Illinois University. He is editor of *Culture & Agriculture* and a fellow in the Society for Applied Anthropology. He served a two-year term on the National Agricultural Air Quality Task Force under Secretary of Agriculture Dan Glickman.

JEFF TIETZ has written for *Rolling Stone, The New Yorker, Harper's, Vanity Fair,* and *The Atlantic.* His work has appeared in the anthologies *Best American Magazine Writing* and *Best American Crime Writing.* He lives in Austin, Texas.

PAIGE TOMASELLI is a staff attorney at the Center for Food Safety, where she uses litigation and policy to curtail industrial agriculture production methods such as the proliferation of genetically engineered crops, concentrated animal feeding operations, and the widespread use of sewage sludge.

DOUGLAS R. TOMPKINS is a long-time wilderness advocate, mountaineer, skier, farmer, kayaker, pilot, and environmental/conservation activist. He founded The North Face and cofounded the apparel maker Esprit. In 1990 he left business to work on creating large-scale conservation areas and national parks in Chile and Argentina. He and his wife, Kristine Tompkins, have preserved more than 2 million acres of land for the conservation of biodiversity, including the eight-hundred-thousand-acre Pumalin Park in Chile. In 1990 he founded the Foundation for Deep Ecology, which has been a key supporter of grassroots environmental NGOs and has produced numerous activist campaign-related books, including *Clearcut*, *Welfare Ranching*, *Fatal Harvest*, *Thrillcraft*, and *Plundering Appalachia*.

BECKY WEED is the co-owner of the certified organic Thirteen Mile Lamb and Wool Company, which raises sheep on grass and processes wool and other natural fibers in a small mill in Belgrade, Montana. Thirteen Mile products are predator-friendly—that is, only nonlethal methods are used to protect the flock from native carnivores. Weed is a former member of the Montana Board of Livestock and a cofounder of the Wild Farm Alliance.

GEORGE WUERTHNER is an ecologist, writer, and photographer who has published thirty-four books on geography, national parks, wilderness, conservation history, and environmental issues. In researching those books, he has traveled extensively throughout the western United States and has been to every major mountain range in the West. He has a particular interest in public lands and wildlands.

RESOURCES

Alliance for the Prudent Use of Antibiotics (APUA)
Aims to strengthen society's defenses against infectious disease by promoting appropriate antimicrobial access and use and by controlling antimicrobial resistance on a worldwide basis.
(617) 636-0966
www.tufts.edu/med/apua

ATTRA (National Sustainable Agriculture Information Service)
Formerly Appropriate Technology Transfer for Rural Areas; provides information and other technical assistance to farmers, ranchers, extension agents, educators, and others involved in sustainable agriculture in the United States.
(800) 346-9140
www.attra.org

Center for a Livable Future (CLF)
Engaged in research, educational outreach, and community action in its program areas of farming, eating, and living for our future.
(410) 502-7578
www.jhsph.edu/clf

Center for Food Safety (CFS)
A nonprofit public interest and environmental advocacy membership organization established in 1997 to challenge harmful food production technologies and promote sustainable alternatives.
(202) 547-9359
www.centerforfoodsafety.org

Clean Water Action
A 1.2-million-member political action group working to protect the environment, public health, economic well-being, and community quality of life; several state offices are involved in factory farm issues. See website for regional office contact information.
www.cleanwateraction.org

Clean Water Network

A coalition of more than 1,200 U.S. public interest organizations representing more than 5 million people working together to strengthen and implement federal clean water and wetlands policy.
(202) 547-4208
www.cleanwaternetwork.org

Environmental Integrity Project

A nonpartisan, nonprofit organization established in 2002 by former Environmental Protection Agency enforcement attorneys to advocate for more effective enforcement of environmental laws.
(512) 637-9479
www.environmentalintegrity.org

Food and Water Watch

A nonprofit consumer organization that works to ensure clean water and safe food.
(202) 683-2500
www.foodandwaterwatch.org

Holistic Management International

A nonprofit organization dedicated to restoring the health of degraded private, public, and communal grasslands worldwide.
(505) 842-5252
www.holisticmanagement.org

Institute for Environmental Research and Education (IERE)

Provides a Sustainable Agriculture Program designed to help farmers produce meat, dairy, and other farm products that are safer for people and for the environment and that use that improved quality as a marketing tool.
(206) 463-7430
www.iere.org

Keep Antibiotics Working

A coalition of health, consumer, agricultural, environmental, humane, and other advocacy groups with more than 10 million members dedicated to eliminating a major cause of antibiotic resistance—the inappropriate use of antibiotics in food animals.
(773) 525-4952
www.keepantibioticsworking.com

Kerr Center for Sustainable Agriculture

A nonprofit education foundation whose mission is to assist in developing sustainable food and farming systems.
(918) 647-9123
www.kerrcenter.com

Land Stewardship Project

Works to create a food system that protects soil, water, and wildlife resources; that promotes fairness and economic opportunities for family farms and rural communities; and that provides safe and healthful food for all people.
(612) 722-6377
www.landstewardshipproject.org

National Resources Defense Council (NRDC)

One of the nation's most active environmental action groups, combining the grassroots power of 1.2 million members and online activists with the courtroom clout and expertise of more than 350 lawyers, scientists, and other professionals.
(212) 727-2700
www.nrdc.org

National Sustainable Agriculture Coalition (NSAC)

Works to support small and midsize family farms, protect natural resources, promote healthy rural communities, and provide nutritious and healthy food to consumers.
(202) 547-5754
www.sustainableagriculture.net

Pew Commission on Industrial Farm Animal Production (PCIFAP)

Independent commission formed to conduct a comprehensive, fact-based, and balanced examination of key aspects of the farm animal industry— through the lenses of veterinary medicine, agriculture, public health, business, government, rural advocacy, and animal welfare.
(301) 379-9107
www.ncifap.org

Stockman Grass Farmer

Since 1947, a publication devoted solely to the art and science of making a profit from grassland agriculture.
(601) 853-1861
www.stockmangrassfarmer.net

Stone Barns Center for Food and Agriculture

A nonprofit farm, educational center, and restaurant in the heart of Westchester County that works to celebrate, teach, and advance community-based food production and enjoyment.
(914) 366-6200
www.stonebarnscenter.org

Sustainable Table

Celebrates local sustainable food, educates consumers on food-related issues, and works to build community through food.
(212) 991-1930
www.sustainabletable.org

Union of Concerned Scientists

Combines independent scientific research and citizen action to develop innovative, practical solutions and to secure responsible changes in government policy, corporate practices, and consumer choices.
(617) 547-5552
www.ucsusa.org/food_and_agriculture/science_and_impacts/impacts_industrial_agriculture/cafos-uncovered.html

U.S. Environmental Protection Agency (EPA)

Government agency working to protect human health and the environment.
Animal Feeding Operations: www.epa.gov/oecaagct/anafoidx.html
CAFO Effluent Guidelines: www.epa.gov/guide/cafo

Waterkeeper Alliance

Connects and supports local Waterkeeper programs to provide a voice for waterways and their communities worldwide, championing clean water and strong communities.
(914) 674-0622
www.waterkeeper.org

Wild Farm Alliance

Promotes agriculture that helps to protect and restore wild nature.
(831) 761-8408
www.wildfarmalliance.org

ANIMAL WELFARE / ANIMAL RIGHTS

American Humane Association

Created the first welfare certification program in the United States (American Humane Certified) to ensure the humane treatment of farm animals.
(800) 227-4645; (303) 792-9900
www.americanhumane.org
www.thehumanetouch.org

Animal Welfare Institute

A nonprofit charitable organization working to reduce the sum total of pain and fear inflicted on animals by humans—with an emphasis on cruel

animal factories that raise and slaughter pigs, cows, chickens, and other animals.
(202) 337-2332
www.awionline.org

Compassion in World Farming

Founded in 1967 by a British farmer who became horrified by the development of modern intensive factory farming; campaigns peacefully to end all cruel factory farming practices.
+ 44 (0)1483 521 950 (international)
www.ciwf.org.uk

Farm Sanctuary

Works to end cruelty to farm animals and promotes compassionate living through rescue, education, and advocacy.
(607) 583-2225, ext. 221
www.farmsanctuary.org

Humane Farming Association

Protects farm animals from cruelty; the public from the dangerous misuse of antibiotics, hormones, and other chemicals used on factory farms; and the environment from the impacts of industrialized animal factories.
(415) 771-2253
www.hfa.org

Humane Society of the United States: Factory Farming Campaign

As the largest animal protection organization in the nation, takes a leadership role on farm animal advocacy issues.
(202) 452-1100
www.hsus.org/farm

PETA (People for the Ethical Treatment of Animals)

As the largest animal rights organization in the world, focuses its attention on four areas: factory farms, laboratories, the clothing trade, and the entertainment industry.
Animal cruelty hotline: (757) 622-7382
www.peta.org

ShedYourSkin.com

A campaign promoting alternatives to wool, fur, and leather: "Join kind people everywhere and shed your skins—wear only compassionate, animal-free clothing."
www.shedyourskin.com

World Society for the Protection of Animals (WSPA)

Has promoted animal welfare for more than twenty-five years, concentrating on regions of the world where few, if any, measures exist to protect animals.
(800) 883-9772
www.wspa-usa.org

SOCIAL AND ECONOMIC JUSTICE FOR FARMING COMMUNITIES

Center for Rural Affairs

Works to establish strong rural communities, social and economic justice, environmental stewardship, and genuine opportunity for all while engaging people in decisions that affect the quality of their lives and the future of their communities.
(402) 687-2100
www.cfra.org

Corporate Agribusiness Research Project

A public interest project reinstituted in 1996, sponsored by Voice for a Viable Future; seeks to provide a central, accurate, in-depth source of information about corporate agribusiness's economic, social, and environmental impacts on family farmers, rural communities, ecosystems, labor, and consumers.
(425) 258-5345
www.thecalamityhowler.com

Farm Aid

Raises public awareness about the plight of the American family farmer and provides assistance to families whose livelihood is dependent on agriculture.
(617) 354-2922
www.farmaid.org

Farmer's Legal Action Group, Inc. (FLAG)

A nonprofit law center dedicated to providing legal services to family farmers and their communities to help keep family farmers on the land.
(651) 223-5400
www.flaginc.org

Institute for Agriculture and Trade Policy (IATP)

In 1986 began documenting the underlying causes of America's rural crisis and proposing policies to benefit farmers, consumers, rural communities, and the environment.
(612) 870-0453
www.iatp.org

National Family Farm Coalition

Represents family farm and rural groups whose members face the challenge of the deepening economic recession in rural communities.
(202) 543-5675
www.nffc.net

Socially Responsible Agriculture Project

Educates the public about the problems caused by factory farms, and works to help communities protect themselves against the devastating impacts of these facilities.
(208) 315-4836
www.sraproject.org

DIVERSITY PROTECTION

American Livestock Breeds Conservancy

Founded in 1977, the pioneer U.S. organization working to conserve historic breeds and genetic diversity in livestock.
(919) 542-5704
www.albc-usa.org

Rare Breeds International

The only international nongovernmental organization working to prevent the loss of diversity in global farm animal genetic resources through encouraging and supporting relevant activities and research by NGOs and governments; offers information on events and links to national organizations.
+ 00 (3) 023109-98683 (international)
www.rarebreedsinternational.org

Rare Breeds Journal

A complete guide to the alternative livestock industry covering a variety of rare and minor breeds of livestock.
(308) 665-1431
www.rarebreedsjournal.com

Slow Food: Ark of Taste

Rediscovers, catalogs, describes, and publicizes forgotten flavors.
List of Ark foods: www.slowfoodusa.org/index.php/programs/details/
ark_of_taste
Local producers of Ark foods: www.localharvest.org/ark-of-taste.jsp

Slow Food Foundation for Biodiversity

Supports projects in defense of food biodiversity in more than fifty countries and promotes a sustainable agriculture that respects the environment
and the cultural identity of local people and promotes animal well-being.
+ 39 0172 419 701 (international)
www.slowfoodfoundation.org

FINDING SUSTAINABLE ANIMAL PRODUCTS

American Grassfed Association

Protects and promotes true grass-fed producers and grass-fed products
through national communication, education, research, and marketing
efforts.
(877) 774-7277
www.americangrassfed.org

American Pastured Poultry Producers Association (APPPA)

Website lists members to help consumers find pasture-raised poultry.
(888) 662-7772
www.apppa.org

Chefs Collaborative: Local Food Search

Culinary organization that provides its members with tools for running
economically healthy, sustainable food service businesses, with a special
focus on seafood.
(617) 236-5200
www.chefscollaborative.org

Eat Well Guide

A free online directory of thousands of family farms, restaurants, and other
outlets for fresh, locally grown food.
(212) 991-1858
www.eatwellguide.org

Eat Wild

A source for information about the benefits of raising animals on pasture; links to local farms that sell all-natural, delicious, grass-fed products; and a marketplace for farmers who raise their livestock on pasture.
(866) 453-8489
www.eatwild.com

Food Routes

A national nonprofit dedicated to reintroducing Americans to their food—the seeds it grows from, the farmers who produce it, and the routes that carry it from the fields to our tables.
(570) 673-3398
www.foodroutes.org

Grass-Fed Livestock Producer Contacts

A listing of grass-fed beef, sheep, pig, bison, and goat producers compiled by the University of California Cooperative Extension Service and California State University, Chico, for the purposes of providing scientific information on grass-fed livestock.
www.csuchico.edu/agr/grassfedbeef/producer-contacts/index.html

Humane Farm Animal Care

Offers Certified Humane Raised and Handled certification, the only U.S. farm animal welfare and food labeling program dedicated to improving the welfare of farm animals from birth through slaughter for the 10 billion farm animals raised for food each year.
(703) 435-3883
www.certifiedhumane.org

Local Harvest

An organic and local food website, maintaining a public nationwide directory of small farms, farmers' markets, and other local food sources.
(831) 515-5602
www.localharvest.org

Seafood Watch

A Monterey Bay Aquarium program designed to raise consumer awareness about the importance of buying seafood from sustainable sources; recommends which seafood to buy or avoid and helps consumers to become advocates for environmentally friendly seafood.
(831) 648-4800
www.montereybayaquarium.org/cr/seafoodwatch.aspx

Smart Seafood Guide

A guide created by Food and Water Watch to help consumers find sustainable seafood and make informed choices.
(202) 683-2500
www.foodandwaterwatch.org/fish/seafood/seafood-guide/
national-seafood-guide

VEGETARIAN / VEGAN EATING

FARM (Farm Animal Rights Movement)

A nonprofit, public interest organization promoting vegan, plant-based diets to save animals, protect the environment, and improve health.
(301) 530-1737
www.farmusa.org

GoVeg.com

A website created by PETA to provide information and resources for vegetarian eating.
www.goveg.com

Imitation Meat Resources

www.bocaburger.com
www.lightlife.com
www.seeveggiesdifferently.com
www.slate.com/?id=2059720 (includes taste testing and rankings)
www.yvesveggie.com

Vegetarian Protein Sources

www.happycow.net/vegetarian_protein.html
www.vrg.org/nutrition/protein.htm

A GLOSSARY OF
CAFO TERMS AND EUPHEMISMS

agricultural storm water Runoff that has been polluted by manure and can infiltrate water sources off-site from where the manure was applied.

alternative animal production Animal farming other than CAFOs; includes sustainable practices such as access to pasture and maintaining animals at a low-enough density that the nearby land can safely absorb their manure.

animal unit (AU) Counting method allowing comparison between livestock species; e.g., as defined by the EPA, 1 AU equals 1 beef cow of feedlot size, typically at least 500 pounds, or 2.5 hogs over 55 pounds.

battery cage Industrial cage system that confines multiple egg-laying chickens; typically provides less than 1 square foot of space per animal.

bioaccumulation Accumulation of toxins in the fat of an animal; such toxins can move up the food chain through the rendered fat from slaughtered animals, later used as a protein supplement for other livestock; ultimately this bioaccumulation of toxins can be passed on to humans who consume animal products.

biogas Combustible fuel produced from the methane in CAFO manure.

biological diversity The variety and number of organisms in a given area, with an emphasis on native species.

CAFO (concentrated animal feeding operation) Feeding facility with at least 1,000 animal units; defined by the EPA as containing one of the following: at least 700 dairy cows; 1,000 beef cattle; 2,500 hogs over 55 pounds; 30,000 broiler chickens producing wet manure; 125,000 broiler chickens producing dry manure; or 82,000 laying hens; smaller operations are classified as CAFOs when they discharge manure directly into waterways.

cake Poultry manure combined with absorbent material that has formed a layer of "cake" on the bottom of a poultry shed.

captive supply An economic advantage for a packing company, in which the corporations that slaughter, process, and distribute animal food products also own the animals raised either by their own CAFOs or by contract growers.

cold pasteurization Irradiation or exposure of meat (and other foods) to nuclear radiation to kill potential pathogens.

commodity crops Crops that are eligible to receive subsidies under Title I of the U.S. federal farm bill; includes corn, wheat, rice, soybeans, and cotton.

common farming exemptions (CFEs) U.S. state laws designed to exempt factory farms from animal cruelty laws; use terms such as *common, customary, established,* and *generally accepted* practices within the industry to justify inhumane treatment of farm animals.

contract grower Farmer contracted to grow animals based on an agreement to house, feed, and maintain animals supplied by a processor and return the animals for processing when ready.

conversion efficiency Amount of feed needed to produce a unit of animal product.

CR4 (four-firm market concentration) Amount of market share held by the four largest companies within an industry; a value higher than 40 percent often indicates levels of concentration that interfere with basic supply-and-demand mechanisms.

dead zones Bodies of water with low oxygen content; created when nutrients such as fertilizers from feed production and animal wastes overwhelm an aquatic environment. Pollution from CAFOs contributes to dead zones in the Gulf of Mexico and estuaries along the East Coast that can no longer support fish and shellfish.

direct subsidy Payment to a business that reduces or compensates for production costs—e.g., direct subsidies provided in U.S. farm bills have compensated grain farmers when market prices fell below the cost of production.

distillers grains with solubles Residue that remains after corn has been fermented to produce ethanol; commonly used as a cheap livestock feed; have been shown to result in significantly higher ammonia emissions in manure.

diversified farm A farm that raises both livestock and crops; more generally, a farm that raises multiple crops or crops and livestock.

docking Clipping the tails of piglets or dairy cows to accommodate intensive animal concentrations and conditions of confinement.

downer animal An animal too sick, diseased, or disabled to walk on its own; slaughtering a downer animal for food production has been banned in the United States.

***E. coli* O157:H7** A virulent and potentially lethal strain of a bacteria associated with grain-fed cattle and hamburger; the U.S. Department of Agriculture banned the sale of meat contaminated with the disease after a deadly outbreak was traced to Jack in the Box restaurants.

Emergency Planning and Community Right-to-Know Act (EPCRA) Provisions that help increase the public's knowledge of and access to information on chemicals at individual facilities, their uses, and releases into the environment.

Environmental Quality Incentives Program (EQIP) Government-funded U.S. farm bill "conservation" program that has historically paid CAFO operators up to $450,000 to aid in waste processing.

eutrophication Degradation of a body of water due to the growth and subsequent death of vegetation that lowers oxygen content as it decays; results in the death of fish and other aquatic organisms.

externalized costs Environmental, social, and health costs related to pollution that are borne by society instead of the enterprise responsible—e.g., health problems resulting from air pollution caused by CAFO animal waste.

farm bill Package of federal laws that establish U.S. agricultural policy and economic incentives; typically renewed every five years.

farrowing crates Restrictive stalls where pregnant sows are moved right before giving birth, designed to separate the mother pig from her nursing piglets; the stalls are so small that the sow can only stand up and lie down.

feathermeal Undecomposed feathers from slaughtered poultry broken down by heat and pressure; sometimes used as a feed supplement.

feedlots Confinement areas housing thousands of beef cattle to be fattened on grain prior to slaughter; generally open to the air or partially roofed.

feed-to-meat conversion rate Measure of an animal's efficiency in converting feed mass to increased body mass.

finishing operations Facilities where animals—e.g., beef cattle, hogs, broilers, or chickens—are fattened on grain prior to slaughter; large finishing operations are usually CAFOs.

food disparagement laws (veggie libel laws) Laws adopted by U.S. state legislatures intended to prosecute the disparagement or dissemination of false information that a perishable food product or commodity is not safe for human consumption; it is still untested whether these laws are defensible under the federal constitution.

Food Safety and Inspection Service The public health agency of the United States Department of Agriculture (USDA) responsible for ensuring that the nation's commercial supply of meat, poultry, and egg products is safe, wholesome, and correctly labeled and packaged.

forage Plant material eaten by grazing livestock—e.g., alfalfa, grasses, stems, and leaves.

fugitive manure Manure that leaks out of storage lagoons, becomes volatilized in the atmosphere, or seeps into waterways in other manners.

gestation crate 7-foot by 2-foot metal enclosure used in intensive pig farming, in which a female breeding pig (sow) may be confined during pregnancy—in effect for most of her adult life.

growth promoters Arsenicals, antibiotic medicines, growth hormones, and other additives used to speed weight gain in animal factories.

Humane Slaughter Act Federal law passed in 1958 requiring that food animals be stunned into unconsciousness prior to their slaughter; 90 percent of all animals slaughtered in the United States are chickens, but birds are excluded from the act.

indirect subsidy Support received as a result of direct subsidies paid to another party; e.g., corn subsidies result in indirect subsidies for CAFO producers when they are able to purchase feed at artificially low prices.

industrial agriculture complex Ownership or control of multiple stages of production by a single entity—e.g., in animal production: meat processors, agriculture commodity groups, scientists paid by the industry, and government representatives and policy makers sympathetic to industry.

inputs Supplies used to produce livestock—e.g., feed, water, energy, infrastructure, and antibiotics.

knock box First station on a beef slaughter line, where the cow is rendered brain dead ("insensible") with a bolt pistol.

lagoon Massive open-air holding facility that stores liquid CAFO urine and feces; may be lined or unlined; depending on size, construction, and location may be susceptible to leakage, overflow, or evaporation with the potential to pollute water sources.

litter Mixture of poultry manure, excess feed, and bedding material (such as wood chips) that builds up in broiler facilities; commonly mixed in with feed for other livestock as a cheap source of protein.

livestock Animals raised for meat, milk, and eggs.

mad cow disease Bovine spongiform encephalopathy (BSE); fatal, neurodegenerative disease in cattle, thought to be caused when cows eat the brain or spinal tissues of animals infected with the disease.

manure injection Incorporation of manure into the soil by pumping it into shallow or deep furrows across fields to help control odor, conserve nutrients, and decrease runoff.

methicillin-resistant *Staphylococcus aureus* (MRSA) Multidrug-resistant bacterium created by excessive use of antibiotics in animals and humans; responsible for difficult-to-treat and sometimes fatal infections in humans.

nutrient banking Spraying of liquid manure on snow as a method of disposal; has the potential to become surface runoff as the snow begins to melt.

plumping Injecting salt water, seaweed, chicken broth, or other animal proteins such as beef or pig wastes into chicken to "enhance" its mass and flavor.

point source Single and identifiable localized source of air, water, thermal, noise, or light pollution.

prion Protein suspected of carrying BSE, or mad cow disease.

processing Slaughter of livestock, carcass dressing, packaging, and distribution of finished animal products.

recycling Practice of feeding slaughterhouse scraps and rendered animal wastes back to livestock.

reservoirs of resistance Community of genetic resources—both disease causing and non–disease causing—that carry resistance to antibiotics;

can carry the genetic material (resistance genes) that may eventually be transferred to an organism that can cause disease in humans.

reverse protein factories Feeding operations that consume far more animal or plant protein than they ultimately provide.

rotational grazing Method of raising livestock on pasture in which the animals are moved periodically so that no single area is overgrazed; rate of livestock movement is based on optimum grazing levels for different forage species under different environmental conditions.

ruminant-to-ruminant feeding bans Regulations adopted by many countries designed to prohibit nearly all tissues from ruminants—cows, sheep, and goats—from being fed to ruminants; experts question, however, whether enough is being done to prevent materials from entering the feed supply through loopholes in the system.

specified risk materials (SRMs) Cattle body parts that are disallowed for cattle feed but that can be used for nonruminant protein supplements—e.g., skull, brain, eyes, parts of vertebral column, spinal cord, trigeminal ganglia, and dorsal ganglia of cattle over thirty months of age, as well as the tonsils and distal ileum.

sprayfield Land close to a manure storage facility that is fertilized with liquid manure.

subsidies Payments that artificially support an industry by offsetting its costs of production or by compensating producers for low market prices.

subtherapeutic doses Antibiotics given in a quantity below the level used to treat disease; often used as a method of growth promotion; can lead to antibiotic resistance in bacteria.

transgenic animal Animal whose genome has been modified to carry a gene from another species using a recombinant DNA technology—e.g., a transgenic dairy cow that produces a milk protein that kills the bacteria responsible for causing mastitis.

vat meat Manufactured animal flesh that has never been part of a complete animal (also known as in vitro meat or cultured meat); not to be confused with imitation meat, which is a vegetable food product.

vertical integration Corporate control of multiple stages of production (e.g., feed mills, hatcheries, breeding facilities, processing facilities, distribution outlets) "from squeal to meal" or from "semen to cellophane."

volatilization The transformation of pollutants (such as the ammonia in manure) into their airborne form.

SELECTED BIBLIOGRAPHY

Berry, Wendell. *The Way of Ignorance.* Berkeley: Counterpoint, 2005.

Bixby, Donald E., Carolyn J. Christman, and Cynthia J. Ehrman. *Taking Stock: The North American Livestock Census.* Granville, OH: McDonald and Woodward, 1994.

Center for Food Safety. "Not Ready for Prime Time: FDA's Flawed Approach to Assessing the Safety of Food from Cloned Animals." Center for Food Safety, March 26, 2007.

Clancy, Kate. *Greener Pastures: How Grass-Fed Beef and Milk Contribute to Healthy Eating.* Cambridge, MA: UCS Publications, 2006.

Cook, Christopher D. *Diet for a Dead Planet.* New York: New Press, 2006.

Evans, B. R., and George G. Evans. *The Story of Durocs: The Truly American Breed of Swine.* Peoria, IL: United Duroc Record Association, 1946.

Fearnley-Whittingstall, Hugh. *The River Cottage Meat Book.* Berkeley: Ten Speed Press, 2007.

Foer, Jonathan Safran. *Eating Animals.* New York: Little, Brown, 2009.

Food and Water Watch. *Turning Farms into Factories: How the Concentration of Animal Agriculture Threatens Human Health, the Environment, and Rural Communities.* Washington, DC: Food and Water Watch, 2007.

Goodall, Jane, Gary McAvoy, and Gail Hudson. *Harvest for Hope: A Guide to Mindful Eating.* New York: Warner Wellness, 2005.

Grandin, Temple, and Catherine Johnson. *Animals Make Us Human: Creating the Best Life for Animals.* Boston: Houghton Mifflin Harcourt, 2009.

Gurian-Sherman, Doug. *CAFOs Uncovered: The Untold Costs of Confined Animal Feeding Operations.* Cambridge, MA: UCS Publications, 2008.

Imhoff, Daniel, *Farming with the Wild: Enhancing Biodiversity on Farms and Ranches.* San Francisco: Sierra Club Books, 2003.

Institute of Medicine of the National Academies, Food and Nutrition Board, Committee on Nutrition Standards for National School Lunch and Breakfast Programs. *School Meals: Building Blocks for Healthy Children,* ed. Virginia A. Stallings, Carol West Suitor, and Christine L. Taylor. Washington, DC: National Academies Press, 2009.

Intergovernmental Panel on Climate Change (IPCC). *Climate Change 2007: Fourth Assessment Report of the Intergovernmental Panel on Climate Change.* New York: Cambridge University Press, 2007.

Kaminsky, Pete. *Pig Perfect: Encounters with Remarkable Swine and Some Great Ways to Cook Them.* New York: Hyperion, 2005.

Kirschenmann, Fred. "Toward Sustainable Animal Agriculture." In *Putting Meat on the Table: Industrial Farm Animal Production in America*. A Report of the Pew Commission on Industrial Farm Animal Production. Washington, DC: Pew Charitable Trusts and Johns Hopkins Center for a Livable Future, Bloomberg School of Public Health, 2008.

Lappé, Anna. *Diet for a Hot Planet*. New York: Bloomsbury, 2010.

Lappé, Frances Moore. *Diet for a Small Planet*. 20th anniv. ed. New York: Ballantine Books, 1991.

Lefferts, Lisa Y., Margaret Kucharski, Shawn McKenzie, and Polly Walker. *Feed for Food-Producing Animals: A Resource on Ingredients, the Industry and Regulation*. Baltimore: Center for a Livable Future/Johns Hopkins School of Public Health, 2007.

MacDonald, James M., and William D. McBride. *The Transformation of U.S. Livestock Agriculture: Scale, Efficiency, and Risks*. Washington, DC: U.S. Department of Agriculture, 2009.

Manes, Christopher. *Other Creations: Rediscovering the Spirituality of Animals*. New York: Doubleday, 1997.

Manning, Richard. *Against the Grain: How Agriculture Has Hijacked Civilization*. New York: North Point Press, 2004.

Marcus, Erik. *Meat Market: Animals, Ethics, and Money*. Boston: Brio Press, 2005.

———. *Vegan: The New Ethics of Eating*. Ithaca, NY: McBooks Press, 2001.

McWilliams, James E. *Just Food: Where Locavores Get It Wrong and How We Can Truly Eat Responsibly*. New York: Little Brown, 2009.

Mellon, Margaret, Charles Benbrook, and Karen Lutz Benbrook. *Hogging It! Estimates of Antimicrobial Abuse in Livestock*. Cambridge, MA: UCS Publications, 2001.

Mendelson, Anne. *Milk: The Surprising Story of Milk Through the Ages*. New York: Random House, 2009.

Midkiff, Ken. *The Meat You Eat: How Corporate Farming Has Endangered America's Food Supply*. New York: St. Martin's Press, 2004.

Nabhan, Gary Paul. *Where Our Food Comes From: Retracing Nikolay Vavilov's Quest to End Famine*. Washington, DC: Island Press, 2009.

National Research Council of the National Academies. *Animal Biotechnology: Science Based Concerns*. Washington, DC: National Academies Press, 2002.

Niman, Bill, and Janet Fletcher. *The Niman Ranch Cookbook*. Berkeley: Ten Speed Press, 2005.

Niman, Nicolette Hahn. *Righteous Pork Chop: Finding a Life and Good Food Beyond Factory Farms*. New York: Collins Living, 2009.

Patel, Raj. *Stuffed and Starved: The Hidden Battle for the World Food System*. Brooklyn: Melville House Publishing, 2008.

Pew Commission on Industrial Farm Animal Production. *Putting Meat on the Table: Industrial Farm Animal Production in America.* A Report of the Pew Commission on Industrial Farm Animal Production. Washington, DC: Pew Charitable Trusts and Johns Hopkins Bloomberg School of Public Health, 2008.

Philpott, Tom. "From Concentrate: How Food Processing Got into the Hands of a Few Giant Companies." *Grist*, April 26, 2007.

Pollan, Michael. *In Defense of Food: An Eater's Manifesto.* New York: Penguin Books, 2008.

———. "Power Steer." *New York Times Magazine*, March 31, 2002.

Rollin, Bernard. *Animal Rights and Human Morality.* Amherst, MA: Prometheus Books, 2006.

———. "Farm Factories." *The Christian Century,* December 19, 2001.

Sapkota, Amy R., Lisa Y. Lefferts, Shawn McKenzie, and Polly Walker. *Feed for Food-Producing Animals: A Resource on Ingredients, the Industry, and Regulation.* Baltimore: Johns Hopkins Center for a Livable Future, Bloomberg School of Public Health, 2007.

———. "What Do We Feed to Food-Production Animals? A Review of Animal Feed Ingredients and Their Potential Impacts on Human Health." *Environmental Health Perspectives* 115, no. 5 (2007): 663–70.

Schell, Orville. *Modern Meat: Antibiotics, Hormones and the Pharmaceutical Farm.* New York: Random House, 1984.

Schlosser, Eric. "Bad Meat: Deregulation Makes Eating a High-Risk Behavior." *The Nation*, August 29, 2002.

———. *Fast Food Nation.* New York: Houghton Mifflin, 2001.

Scully, Matthew. "Fear Factories: The Case for Compassionate Conservatism—for Animals." *American Conservative*, May 23, 2005.

Singer, Peter. *Animal Liberation: A New Ethics for Our Treatment of Animals.* 3rd ed. New York: HarperCollins, 2002.

Starmer, Elanor, and Timothy A. Wise. *Feeding at the Trough: Industrial Livestock Firms Saved $35 Billion from Low Feed Prices.* Policy Brief No. 07-03. Medford, MA: Tufts University Global Development and Environment Institute, December 2007.

Steinfeld, Henning, Pierre Gerber, Tom Wassenaar, Vincent Castel, Mauricio Rosales, and Cees de Haan. *Livestock's Long Shadow: Environmental Issues and Options.* Rome: United Nations Food and Agriculture Organization, 2006.

Stier, Ken. "Fish Farming's Growing Dangers." *Time*, September 19, 2007.

Striffler, Steve. *Chicken: The Dangerous Transformation of America's Favorite Food.* New Haven: Yale University Press, 2005.

Stull, Donald D., and Michael J. Broadway. "Slaughterhouse Blues: The Meat and Poultry Industry in North America." In *Case Studies on Contemporary Social Issues*, ed. John A. Young. Belmont, CA: Wadsworth, 2004.

Thu, Kendall. "Industrial Agriculture, Democracy and the Future." In *Beyond Factory Farming: Corporate Hog Barns and the Threat to Public Health, the Environment and Rural Communities*, ed. Alexander M. Ervin, Cathy Holtslander, Darrin Qualman, and Rick Sawa. Ottawa: Canadian Centre for Policy Alternatives, 2003.

Tietz, Jeff. "Boss Hog." *Rolling Stone*, December 14, 2006.

ACKNOWLEDGMENTS

This book required standing on the shoulders of giants: activists and organizations, writers and publishers, scientists, funders, and public interest attorneys who for many decades have been battling against the wrongs of the CAFO system and the industrial meat, dairy, and egg complex. Many deserve special thanks, and please pardon us if we have unintentionally forgotten to list someone.

Thanks to all the authors who graciously donated their essays and many hours of editing, legal reviews, and revisions. Rebecca Spector and Andrew Kimbrell of the Center for Food Safety conducted much of the early research for this project, following their landmark book, *Fatal Harvest: The Tragedy of Industrial Agriculture*. Our project manager, Sharon Donovan, coordinated the final publication effort, along with a dedicated editorial team led by Mary Anne Stewart, who spent months polishing the manuscript. Christen Crumley and Emmett Hopkins of Watershed Media, Patty Lovera of Food and Water Watch, and Tom Butler and George Wuerthner of the Foundation for Deep Ecology provided essential research and editorial support. Janet Reed Blake proofread; Roger Myers kept us on a tight legal track; and BookMatters typeset the book.

Numerous scientists and industry experts helped us with technical reviews, including Larry Baldwin of the Neuse Riverkeeper Foundation; Dave Bard and Andrea Kavanagh of the Pew Environment Program; Joann Burkholder of North Carolina State University; Kendra Kimbirauskas; Bob Lawrence, Shawn McKenzie, and Leo Horrigan at the Johns Hopkins University Center for a Livable Future; Kathy Martin; Carole Morison; Doug Morton and Peter Griffith of NASA; Helen Reddout; Amy Sapkota of the University of Maryland; Doug Gurian-Sherman of the Union of Concerned Scientists; Sara Shields of the Humane Society of the United States; and Elanor Starmer of Food and Water Watch.

Thanks also to Jennie Curtis and the Garfield Foundation for their steadfast support of Watershed Media, as well as to the staff of the Foundation for Deep Ecology. And last, but certainly not least, to our principal collaborators on this intensely demanding project, Doug Tompkins, founder and president of the Foundation for Deep Ecology, and Roberto Carra, the graphic designer on this book's photo-format companion volume and my long-time collaborator who stayed true to the vision for the project and made sure we did our best to achieve it.

—*Daniel Imhoff, Editor*

CREDITS

Grateful acknowledgment is made to the following publications that previously published some of the material that appears in this book. Portions of "Farm Factories" were previously published in "Farm Factories," *The Christian Century*, December 19, 2001, and in *Animal Rights and Human Morality*, © 2006 Bernard E. Rollin, Prometheus Books. "Fear Factories" was adapted from "Fear Factories: The Case for Compassionate Conservatism—for Animals," originally published in *The American Conservative*, May 2005. "Cold Evil" was adapted from a lecture for the Twentieth Annual E. F. Schumacher Lectures, October 2000, Salisbury, Connecticut, © 2000, 2004, E. F. Schumacher Society and Andrew Kimbrell, edited by Hildegarde Hannum. "Renewing Husbandry" was excerpted from *The Way of Ignorance: And Other Essays*, © 2006 Wendell Berry, used by permission of Counterpoint. "Man, the Paragon of Animals?" was originally published in *Other Creations: Rediscovering the Spirituality of Animals*, © 1997 Christopher Manes, reprinted by permission of Doubleday, a division of Random House, Inc. "Power Steer" was adapted from "Power Steer," *The New York Times Magazine*, March 31, 2002. "Boss Hog" was adapted from "Boss Hog," *Rolling Stone*, December 14, 2006. "Watching the Chickens Pass By" was excerpted from *Chicken: The Dangerous Transformation of America's Favorite Food*, © 2005 Steve Striffler, Yale University Press. "The Milk of Human Unkindness" was adapted from *Milk: The Surprising Story of Milk Through the Ages, with 120 Adventurous Recipes That Explore the Riches of Our First Food*, © 2008 Anne Mendelson, used by permission of Alfred A. Knopf, a division of Random House, Inc. "Floating Hog Farms" was adapted from "Fish Farming's Growing Dangers" by Ken Stier, *Time*, September 19, 2007. "Old MacDonald Had Diversity" was adapted from *Taking Stock: The North American Livestock Census*, © 1994 D. E. Bixby, C. J. Christman, C. J. Ehrman, and D. P. Sponenberg, McDonald and Woodward Publishing Company. "Squeezed to the Last Drop" was adapted from "From Concentrate: How Food Processing Got into the Hands of a Few Giant Companies," *Grist*, May 2007. "From Farms to Factories" originally appeared in *Waterkeeper Newsletter*, Spring 2006. "Bad Meat" was originally published in *The Nation*, August 29, 2002. "CAFOs Are in Everyone's Backyard" was adapted from "Industrial Agriculture, Democracy and the Future," from *Beyond Factory Farming: Corporate Hog Barns and the Threat to Public Health, the Environment and Rural Communities*, Canadian Centre for Policy Alterna-

NOTES

INTRODUCTION

1. Erik Marcus, *Meat Market: Animals, Ethics, and Money* (Boston: Brio Press, 2005), 5.

2. Henning Steinfeld, Pierre Gerber, Tom Wassenaar, Vincent Castel, Maurice Rosales, and Cees de Haan, *Livestock's Long Shadow: Environmental Issues and Options* (Rome: United Nations Food and Agriculture Organization, 2006), xx.

3. James McWilliams, *Just Food: Where Locavores Get It Wrong and How We Can Truly Eat Responsibly* (New York: Little, Brown, 2009), 125.

4. Food and Water Watch, *Turning Farms into Factories: How the Concentration of Animal Agriculture Threatens Human Health, the Environment, and Rural Communities* (Washington, DC: Food and Water Watch, 2007).

5. Ibid.

6. Michael W. Fox, *Eating with a Conscience: The Bioethics of Food* (Troutdale, OR: NewSage Press, 1997), 13.

7. Ben Goad, "Obama Ends Slaughter of Sick Cows for Meat," *Press Enterprise (Riverside, CA)*, March 16, 2009. Estimate of downer cattle slaughtered is from *USDA's Mad Cow Disease Surveillance Program: A Comparison of State Cattle Testing Rates*, A Report by Public Citizen and the Government Accountability Project, July 19, 2001.

8. Victoria Kim and Mitchell Landsberg, "Huge Beef Recall Issued," *Los Angeles Times*, February 18, 2008.

9. Dave Murphy, "The Great Pig Debate: How CAFOs Stalk the Future President," *Animal Welfare Institute Quarterly* (Winter 2008).

10. Gurian-Sherman, *CAFOs Uncovered: The Untold Costs of Confined Animal Feeding Operations* (Cambridge, MA: Union of Concerned Scientists, April 2008), 1.

11. Elanor Starmer and Timothy A. Wise, *Feeding at the Trough: Industrial Livestock Firms Saved $35 Billion from Low Feed Prices*, Policy Brief No. 07-03 (Medford, MA: Tufts University Global Development and Environment Institute, December 2007).

12. Mary Hendrickson and William Heffernan, "Concentration of Agricultural Markets," Report, Department of Rural Sociology, University of Missouri—Columbia, April 2007.

13. Steinfeld et al., *Livestock's Long Shadow*, xxi.

14. Robert Goodland and Jeff Anhang, "Livestock and Climate Change: What If the Key Actors in Climate Change Are . . . Cows, Pigs, and Chickens?" *World Watch Magazine* (November/December 2009), 10–19.

15. Pew Commission on Industrial Farm Animal Production, *Putting Meat on the Table: Industrial Farm Animal Production in America*, A Report of the Pew

Commission on Industrial Farm Animal Production (Washington, DC: Pew Charitable Trusts and Johns Hopkins Bloomberg School of Public Health, 2008), viii.

PART ONE

INTRODUCTION

1. Bernard Rollin, "Farm Factories: The End of Animal Husbandry," *Christian Century* 118, no. 25 (December 19–26, 2001), 26–29.

PART TWO

INDUSTRIAL FOOD IS CHEAP

1. U.S. Geological Survey, "Chesapeake Bay: Measuring Pollution Reduction."

2. Karl Blankenship, "Analysis Puts Bay Cleanup Tab at $19 Billion," Alliance for the Chesapeake Bay, *Bay Journal*, December 2002.

3. Robert J. Diaz and Rutger Rosenberg, "Spreading Dead Zones and Consequences for Marine Ecosystems," *Science*, August 15, 2008.

4. Polly Walker, Pamela Rhubart-Berg, Shawn McKenzie, Kristin Kelling, and Robert S. Lawrence, "Public Health Implications of Meat Production and Consumption," *Public Health and Nutrition* 8, no. 4 (2005): 348–56.

5. Ibid., 349.

6. Doug Gurian-Sherman, *CAFOs Uncovered: The Untold Costs of Confined Animal Feeding Operations* (Cambridge, MA: Union of Concerned Scientists, April 2008), 64.

7. Pew Commission on Industrial Farm Animal Production, *Putting Meat on the Table: Industrial Farm Animal Production in America*, A Report of the Pew Commission on Industrial Farm Animal Production (Washington, DC: Pew Charitable Trusts and Johns Hopkins Bloomberg School of Public Health, 2008), 13.

8. "Robert F. Kennedy Jr. on Smithfield Foods Criminal Behaviour," CogitamusBlog.com, April 30, 2009.

9. Elanor Starmer and Timothy A. Wise, *Feeding at the Trough: Industrial Livestock Firms Saved $35 Billion from Low Feed Prices*, Policy Brief No. 07-03 (Medford, MA: Tufts University Global Development and Environment Institute, December 2007).

10. Jon Jeter, "Flat Broke in the Free Market: How Globalization Fleeced Working People" (New York: Norton, 2009), xii.

11. Larry Satter, "Amazing Graze," *Agricultural Research* 48, no. 4 (April 2000).

INDUSTRIAL FOOD IS EFFICIENT

1. Doug Gurian-Sherman, *CAFOs Uncovered: The Untold Costs of Confined Animal Feeding Operations* (Cambridge, MA: Union of Concerned Scientists, April 2008), 18.

2. Ibid.

3. Ibid.

4. Deborah Zabarenko, "One-Third of World Fish Catch Used for Animal Feed," Reuters UK, October 29, 2008.

5. Henning Steinfeld, Pierre Gerber, Tom Wassenaar, Vincent Castel, Maurice Rosales, and Cees de Haan, *Livestock's Long Shadow: Environmental Issues and Options* (Rome: United Nations Food and Agriculture Organization, 2006), 270.

6. "*E. coli* O157:H7 Season Is Nearly upon Us: Will It Be 2005 and 2006 or 2007 and 2008?" E. coli Blog, April 5, 2009.

7. "USDA Announces New *E. coli* Measures," *Food Nutrition & Science*, November 26, 2007.

8. Pew Commission on Industrial Farm Animal Production, *Putting Meat on the Table: Industrial Farm Animal Production in America* (Washington, DC: Pew Charitable Trusts and Johns Hopkins Bloomberg School of Public Health, 2008), 23.

9. Elanor Starmer and Timothy A. Wise, *Feeding at the Trough: Industrial Livestock Firms Saved $35 Billion from Low Feed Prices*, Policy Brief No. 07-03 (Medford, MA: Tufts University Global Development and Environment Institute, December 2007), 1.

10. Ibid.

INDUSTRIAL FOOD IS HEALTHY

1. P. Frenzen, A. Majchrowicz, B. Buzby, B. Imhoff, and the FoodNet Working Group, "Consumer Acceptance of Irradiated Meat and Poultry Products," *Agriculture Information Bulletin* 757 (2000): 1–8.

2. Pew Commission on Industrial Farm Animal Production, *Putting Meat on the Table: Industrial Farm Animal Production in America* (Washington, DC: Pew Charitable Trusts and Johns Hopkins Bloomberg School of Public Health, 2008), 13.

3. Polly Walker, Pamela Rhubart-Berg, Shawn McKenzie, Kristin Kelling, and Robert S. Lawrence, "Public Health Implications of Meat Production and Consumption," *Public Health and Nutrition* 8, no. 4 (2005): 348–56.

4. "Is Meat the Real Culprit in Heart Disease?" *Doctor's Guide*, November 19, 1997.

5. Walker et al., "Public Health Implications of Meat Production and Consumption."

6. Amy R. Sapkota, Lisa Y. Lefferts, Shawn McKenzie, and Polly Walker, "What Do We Feed to Food-Production Animals? A Review of Animal Feed Ingredients and Their Potential Impacts on Human Health," *Environmental Health Perspectives* 115, no. 5 (2007): 663–70.

7. Doug Gurian-Sherman, *CAFOs Uncovered: The Untold Costs of Confined Animal Feeding Operations* (Cambridge, MA: Union of Concerned Scientists, April 2008), 60.

8. David Brown, "Inhaling Pig Brains May Be Cause of New Illness," *Washington Post*, February 4, 2008; Centers for Disease Control and Prevention, "Investigation of Progressive Inflammatory Neuropathy Among Swine Slaughterhouse Workers: Minnesota, 2007–2008," *MMWR*, January 31, 2008, 1–3.

9. Pew Commission, *Putting Meat on the Table*, 29.

10. Food and Water Watch, *Turning Farms into Factories: How the Concentration of Animal Agriculture Threatens Human Health, the Environment, and Rural Communities* (Washington, DC: Food and Water Watch, 2007), 7.

11. Gurian-Sherman, *CAFOs Uncovered*, 60.

12. Pew Commission, *Putting Meat on the Table*, 17.

13. Susan S. Schiffman and C. M. Williams, "Science of Odor as a Potential Health Issue," *Journal of Environmental Quality* 34 (2005): 129–138.

14. Pew Commission, *Putting Meat on the Table*, 17.

CAFOS ARE FARMS, NOT FACTORIES

1. 1,000 "animal units" is the equivalent of 1,000 beef cattle, or 700 dairy cattle, or 2,500 hogs, or 10,000 sheep, or 55,000 turkeys, or 100,000 broilers or laying hens.

2. Susan S. Schiffman and C. M. Williams, "Science of Odor as a Potential Health Issue," *Journal of Environmental Quality* 34 (2005): 129–138.

3. Doug Gurian-Sherman, *CAFOs Uncovered: The Untold Costs of Confined Animal Feeding Operations* (Cambridge, MA: Union of Concerned Scientists, April 2008), 54; C. B. Roller, A. Kosterev, and F. K. Tittel, "Low Cost, High Performance Spectroscopic Ammonia Sensor for Livestock Emissions Monitoring," USDA Research, Education, and Economics Information System.

4. "Attorney General Lori Swanson and Minnesota Pollution Control Agency Jointly Sue Feedlot to Abate Public Nuisance and for Violations of Minnesota's Environmental Protection Laws," Office of Minnesota Attorney General Lori Swanson, press release, June 20, 2008.

CAFOS ARE GOOD FOR RURAL COMMUNITIES

1. John Ikerd, "Confronting CAFOs Through Local Control," Organic Consumers Association, October 29, 2007.

2. "The Cruelest Cuts: The Human Costs of Bringing Poultry to Your Table," *Charlotte (NC) Observer*, February 10–15, 2008.

3. Kerry Hall, Ames Alexander, and Franco Ordoñez, "The Cruelest Cuts: The Human Cost of Bringing Poultry to Your Table," *Charlotte (NC) Observer*, September 30, 2008.

4. Hamed Mubarak, Thomas G. Johnson, and Kathleen K. Miller, *The Impacts of Animal Feeding Operations on Rural Land Values*, Report R-99-02, College of Agriculture, University of Missouri—Columbia, May 1999, cited in Doug Gurian-Sherman, *CAFOs Uncovered*, 61.

5. Doug Gurian-Sherman, *CAFOs Uncovered*, 62,

INDUSTRIAL FOOD BENEFITS
THE ENVIRONMENT AND WILDLIFE

1. U.S. Dept. of Agriculture, NRCS-RID, *Acres of Cropland, 1997* (National Resource Inventory, 1997); ibid., *Acres of Non-Federal Grazing Land, 1997*

(National Resource Inventory, 1997); U.S. Dept. of Interior, Bureau of Indian Affairs, *15.034 Agriculture on Indian Lands* (Catalog of Domestic Assistance, 2002); U.S. Dept. of Interior, Bureau of Land Management, *Working Together for the Health of America's Public Lands, Annual Report*, 1997; U.S. Forest Service, *Forest Service Acres Grazed in All or Parts of Fifteen Western States (AZ, CA, CO, ID, KS, MT, ND, NE, NV, NM, OR, SD, UT, WA, WY)*, Rangeland Management: Profile of the Forest Service's Grazing Allotments and Permittees, U.S. GAO Public Lands Grazing Report RCED-93-141FS (Washington, DC: U.S. GAO, 1993).

2. Ted Williams, "Silent Scourge: Legally Used Pesticides Are Killing Tens of Millions of America's Birds," *Journal of Pesticide Reform* 17, no. 1 (Spring 1997).

3. James McWilliams, *Just Food: Where Locavores Get It Wrong and How We Can Truly Eat Responsibly* (New York: Little, Brown, 2009), 136.

4. Robert Goodland and Jeff Anhang, "Livestock and Climate Change: What If the Key Actors in Climate Change Are . . . Cows, Pigs, and Chickens?" *World Watch* (November/December 2009), 10–19.

5. U.S. Department of Agriculture Natural Resources Conservation Service and U.S. Environmental Protection Agency, "Unified National Strategy for Animal Feeding Operations," draft, September 11, 1998.

6. Food and Water Watch, *Turning Farms into Factories: How the Concentration of Animal Agriculture Threatens Human Health, the Environment, and Rural Communities* (Washington, DC: Food and Water Watch, 2007), 3.

7. Jeff Donn, Martha Mendoza, and Justin Pritchard, "AP Probe Finds Drugs in Drinking Water," *SFGate (San Francisco Chronicle)*, March 10, 2008.

8. Ibid.

9. John Robbins, FoodRevolution.org, "What About Grass-Fed Beef?" *The Food Revolution*.

10. Predator Conservation Alliance, *Wildlife "Services"? A Presentation and Analysis of the USDA Wildlife Services Program's Expenditures and Kill Figures for Fiscal Year 1999* (Predator Conservation Alliance, 2001).

INDUSTRIAL FOOD CAN FEED THE WORLD

1. Raj Patel, *Stuffed and Starved: The Hidden Battle for the World Food System* (Brooklyn, NY: Melville House, 2008), 1.

2. Jeremy Rifkin, introduction to *Feed the World*, Viva! (Vegetarians International Voice for Animals) Guide No. 12.

3. Ibid.

4. Ibid.

5. Vaclav Smil, "Eating Meat: Evolution, Patterns, and Consequences," *Population and Development Review* 28, no. 4 (December 2002): 599–639.

6. Ibid.

CAFO MANURE IS A BENIGN RESOURCE

1. Michael W. Fox, *Eating with Conscience: The Bioethics of Food* (Troutdale, OR:, NewSage Press, 1997), 37. This estimate was updated with information

from the Pew Commission on Industrial Farm Animal Production, *Putting Meat on the Table: Industrial Farm Animal Production in America* (Washington, DC: Pew Charitable Trusts and Johns Hopkins Bloomberg School of Public Health, 2008), 23.

2. "Behind the Odors from Factory Farms: What the Nose Doesn't Know," the diary of Stanley Cooper, image links compiled by Kathleen Jenks, MyThing Links.org.

3. Fox, *Eating with Conscience*, 39.

4. Pew Commission, *Putting Meat on the Table*, 16.

5. Robbin Marks, *Cesspools of Shame: How Factory Farm Lagoons and Sprayfields Threaten Environmental and Public Health* (Washington, DC: Natural Resources Defense Council and Clean Water Network, July 2001).

6. Wendell Berry, "The Pleasures of Eating," in *Bringing It to the Table: On Food and Farming* (Berkeley, CA: Counterpoint, 2009).

PART THREE

INTRODUCTION

1. Bill Niman and Janet Kessel Fletcher, *Niman Ranch Cookbook: From Farm to Table with America's Finest Meats* (Berkeley: Ten Speed Press, 2005), 46.

2. Humane Society of the United States, Farm Animal Statistics: "Meat Consumption, 1950–2007."

3. "Fish Farm Boom Strains Wild Stock, Study Finds: Up to Five Pounds of Wild Fish Needed to Raise One Pound of Farmed Salmon," MSNBC, September 9, 2009.

BOSS HOG

1. "Smithfield Foods Announces Third Quarter Results," Smithfield press releases, March 12, 2009.

2. "Smithfield Foods Production," *Smithfield Corporate Social Responsibility Report 2007/08*, 11.

3. U.S. Department of Agriculture, North Carolina Field Office, *September 2009 Hog Report*.

4. "Pork Producer Says It Plans to Give Pigs More Room," *New York Times*, January 26, 2007.

5. "Smithfield Foods to Convert Hog Waste into Diesel Fuel," *U.S. Water News Online*, March 2003.

6. "Smithfield Foods Reports Fourth Quarter Results," Smithfield press release, June 7, 2007.

7. "Coalition Clean Baltic," press release, March 3, 2004.

WATCHING THE CHICKENS PASS BY

1. Interview with poultry worker #26, August 10, 2001.

2. Measuring the relative danger of occupations is tricky, not only because

what is being measured can vary, but also because such statistics depend on companies to keep accurate records—a serious problem within the meat industries. Meatpacking is routinely among those industries with the highest rates of workplace injury (see U.S. Dept. of Labor, Bureau of Labor Statistics).

3. Human Rights Watch, *Blood, Sweat, and Fear: Worker's Rights in U.S. Meat and Poultry Plants* (Human Rights Watch, 2005), 24.

4. Interview with poultry worker #13, August 6, 2001.

5. Interview with poultry worker #3, September 20, 2000.

6. Interview with poultry worker #8, November 1, 2000.

FLOATING HOG FARMS

1. Alan Lowther, "Highlights from the FAO Database on Aquaculture Statistics," *FAO Aquaculture Newsletter*, no. 31 (July 2004).

2. Rosamond L. Naylor, Ronald W. Hardy, Dominique P. Bureau, Alice Chiu, Matthew Elliott, Anthony P. Farrell, Ian Forster, Delbert M. Gatlin, Rebecca J. Goldburg, Katheline Hua, and Peter D. Nichols, "Feeding Aquaculture in an Era of Finite Resources," *Proceedings of the National Academy of Sciences* 106, no. 36 (2009): 15103–10.

3. Juan Carlos Cárdenas and P. Igor, "Intensive Carnivorous Fin Fish Farming Industry: The Unrevealed Appetite for Destruction" (Centro Ecocéanos, Chile).

4. Brian Halweil, *Farming Fish for the Future*, Worldwatch Report No. 176 (Washington, DC: Worldwatch Institute, 2008).

5. Ibid. According to Brian Halweil of Worldwatch Institute, the aquaculture industry spends almost $1 billion each year on veterinary products.

6. Pilar Hernández Serrano, *Responsible Use of Antibiotics in Aquaculture*, FAO Fisheries Technical Paper No. 469 (Rome: Food and Agriculture Organization of the United Nations, 2005).

7. Ibid. The antibiotics are generally applied through food pellets, and research has found that 70–80 percent of the drugs enter the environment—rather than the fish they are intended to treat. Degradation time depends on the chemical makeup of the drugs and environmental conditions.

8. Ibid. A memorandum from the Centers for Disease Control and Prevention as early as 1999 identified that "use of antimicrobial agents in aquaculture has selected for antimicrobial resistance among bacteria in the exposed ecosystems. This resistance can disseminate through the environment and can be transmitted to a variety of bacterial species, including bacteria that can infect humans"; U.S Department of Health and Human Services, Centers for Disease Control, "Antibiotic Use in Aquaculture: Center for Disease Control Memo to the Record," October 18, 1999.

9. The U.S. Agency for Toxic Substances and Disease Registry reports that women who ate large amounts of fish contaminated with PCBs gave birth to babies that weighed slightly less than babies born to women who were not exposed. Babies born to women who ate PCB-contaminated fish were also more likely to have behavioral problems, "such as problems with motor skills and a decrease in short-term memory." High PCB concentrations can also cause skin and liver harm; U.S. Department of Health and Human Services, Agency for

Toxic Substances and Disease Registry, "ToxFAQs for Polychlorinated Biphenyls (PCBs), February 2001."

10. John Jane, "Results from Tests of Store-Bought Farmed Salmon Show Seven of Ten Fish Were So Contaminated with PCBs That They Raise Cancer Risk," *Environmental Working Group Research*, July 2003. A study published in the journal *Science* in 2004 also found that "concentrations of these contaminants are significantly higher in farmed salmon than in wild" (Ronald A. Hites, Jeffrey Foran, David Carpenter, M. Coreen Hamilton, Barbara Knuth, and Steven Schwager, "Global Assessment of Organic Contaminants in Farmed Salmon," *Science* 303, no. 5655 [January 2004]: 226–29). Some industry and academic critics have taken issue with these studies, while others have begun experimenting with vegetarian diets that could lower the PCB concentration in farmed salmon (Stephanie Cohen, "Raising Salmon on a Vegetarian Diet," *Berkshire [MA] Eagle*, February 16, 2004).

11. While John Volpe put the numbers of sardines killed at 75 percent, the Australian government estimates about 10 percent. The Australian government also reported that in 1998 another episode wiped out about two-thirds of the sardine population. Government of Western Australia, Department of Fisheries, "Commercial Fisheries of Western Australia: Pilchards."

12. John P. Volpe, "Dollars Without Sense: The Bait for Big-Money Tuna Ranching around the World," *BioScience* 55, no. 4 (2005): 301–2.

13. "Fishy Farms: The Problems with Open Ocean Aquaculture," Food and Water Watch, 2007. For more on whirling disease, see R. P. Hedrick, M. el-Matbouli, M. A. Adkison, and E. MacConnell, "Whirling Disease: Re-emergence Among Wild Trout," *Immunological Reviews* 166 (1998): 365–76.

14. Whirling Disease Initiative, "Frequently Asked Questions," Montana State University.

15. Cárdenas and Igor, "Intensive Carnivorous Fin Fish Farming Industry" (see n. 3).

16. Tom Seaman, "Half-Year Outlook: World Salmon Production Could Plunge 18%," *IntraFish Media AS*, June 5, 2009.

17. Ibid.

18. Eric Verspoor, Lee Stradmeyer, and Jennifer L. Nielsen, eds., *The Atlantic Salmon: Genetics, Conservation and Management* (Oxford, England: Blackwell, 2007), 361.

19. Ibid.

20. Randy Sell, "Tilapia," Department of Agricultural Economics, North Dakota State University, Alternative Agriculture Series, No. 2, January 1993. An analyses of a tilapia facility that would produce 80,000 pounds of fish per year determined that—in addition to the initial 50,000 gallons of water required to fill the holding tanks and other equipment—the system would require a constant supply of 3 to 5 gallons of water per minute. This results in a range of 1.63 million to 2.68 million gallons of water per year, or a range of 20 to 33 gallons of water per pound of tilapia.

21. Jack M. Whetstone, Gravil D. Treece, Craig L. Browdy, and Alvin D. Stokes, *Opportunities and Constraints in Marine Shrimp Farming*, Southern Regional Aquaculture Center Publication No. 2600, July 2002. This paper cites

a shrimp farm that had dramatically cut its water use from 4,500 gallons per pound of shrimp to 300 gallons per pound.

22. U.S. Geological Survey, "Estimated Use of Water in the United States in 2000."

23. Solon Barraclough and Andrea Finger-Stich, "Some Ecological and Social Implications of Commercial Shrimp Farming in Asia," United Nations Research Institute for Social Development Discussion Paper No. 74, March 1996.

24. Danielle Knight, "Groups Want Action on Destructive Shrimp Farms," *Third World Network*, April 25, 1999.

25. Cárdenas and Igor, "Intensive Carnivorous Fin Fish Farming Industry" (see n. 3).

26. Roz Naylor, interview by the author, September 2007.

27. Food and Agriculture Organization of the United Nations, Fisheries and Agriculture Department, *The State of World Fisheries and Aquaculture* (Rome: FAO, 2009), 17, 58.

28. Naylor et al., "Feeding Aquaculture" (see n. 2).

29. David Higgs, interview by the author, September 2007.

30. Richard Ellis, *Tuna: A Love Story* (New York: Vintage Books, 2008); Volpe, "Dollars Without Sense."

31. Brian Halweil, interview by the author, September 2007.

32. Reg Watson, Jackie Alder, and Daniel Pauly, "Fisheries for Forage Fish: 1950 to the Present," in *On the Multiple Uses of Forage Fish: From Ecosystem to Markets*, Fisheries Centre Research Reports, vol. 14, no. 3, ed. Jackie Alder and Daniel Pauly (Vancouver, BC: Fisheries Centre, University of British Columbia, 2006), 1–20.

33. FAO, *State of World Fisheries*, 17.

34. Naylor et al., "Feeding Aquaculture."

35. Anne Platt McGinn, "Blue Revolution: The Promises and Pitfalls of Fish Farming," *World Watch Magazine* 11, no. 2 (March/April 1998).

36. Ibid.

37. Ibid.

38. Food and Agriculture Organization of the United Nations, Fisheries and Aquaculture Department, "Fishery and Aquaculture Country Profiles: Peru"; International Fishmeal and Fish Oil Organisation, "Datasheet: The Production of Fishmeal and Fish Oil from Peruvian Anchovy," IFFO, May 2009.

39. Jennifer Jacquet, "Save Our Oceans, Eat Like a Pig: Let's Stop Wasting Tasty Fish on Animal Feed," *The Tyee*, April 17, 2007.

40. Antarctic Krill Conservation Project, "Increasing Demand for Krill."

41. Julliette Jowit, "Krill Fishing Threatens the Antarctic: Intensive Harvesting of the Tiny Crustaceans for Fish Food and Omega 3 Puts Ecosystem at Risk," *The Observer*, March 23, 2008.

42. Ibid.

43. Ibid.

44. Rashid Sumaila, interview by the author, September 2007.

45. Rick Parker, *Aquaculture Science*, 2nd ed. (Albany, NY: Delmar Thomson Learning, 2002).

46. McGinn, "Blue Revolution" (see n. 35).

47. "Learn About the U.S. Market for Seafood, with a Focus on Fresh," *Reuters*, January 20, 2009.

PART FOUR

INTRODUCTION

1. Temple Grandin and Katherine Johnson, *Animals Make Us Human: Creating the Best Life for Animals* (Boston: Houghton Mifflin Harcourt, 2009), 217.

2. Food and Agriculture Organization of the United Nations, Commission on Genetic Resources for Food and Agriculture, *The State of the World's Animal Genetic Resources for Food and Agriculture* (Rome: FAO, 2007).

3. Ibid.

4. Food and Water Watch, *Turning Farms into Factories: How the Concentration of Animal Agriculture Threatens Human Health, the Environment, and Rural Communities* (Washington, DC: Food and Water Watch, 2007), v.

5. Mary Hendrickson and William Heffernan, "Concentration of Agricultural Markets," Report, Department of Rural Sociology, University of Missouri—Columbia, April 2007.

OLD MACDONALD HAD DIVERSITY

1. C. M. A. Baker and C. Manwell, "Population Genetics, Molecular Markers and Gene Conservation of Bovine Breeds," in *Cattle Genetic Resources*, ed. C. G. Hickman (Amsterdam: Elsevier Science Publishers, 1991).

SQUEEZED TO THE LAST DROP

1. Ron Schmid, *The Untold Story of Milk: Green Pastures, Contented Cows, and Raw Dairy Foods* (Washington, DC: New Trends Publishing, 2007), 211.

2. Land O' Lakes 2008 Financial Results.

3. "The 35 Largest U.S. Companies: 29. Dairy Farmers of America," *Fortune*, 2008.

4. "Fortune 500 2008: 224. Dean Foods," CNNMoney.com.

5. "Gregg L. Engles," Forbes.com.

6. Mary Hendrickson and William Heffernan, "Concentration of Agricultural Markets," Report, Department of Rural Sociology, University of Missouri—Columbia, April 2007.

7. "Update 3—JBS Says U.S. Justice Cleared Pilgrim's Takeover," Reuters, October 14, 2009.

8. "JBS Eyes No. 1 Spot with Pilgrim's, Bertin Deals," Reuters, September 21, 2008.

9. *Smithfield Corporate Social Responsibility Report 2007/08.*

10. Mark Honeyman, "Iowa's Changing Swine Industry," in *Iowa State University Animal Industry Report 2006.*

11. "Hog Farming," *North Carolina and the Global Economy*, Spring 2004.

12. "EPA Offers Air-Pollution Immunity to Factory Farms," *Grist*, January 24, 2005.

13. Eric Schlosser, "Hog Hell," *The Nation*, September 12, 2006.

14. Human Rights Watch, *Blood, Sweat, and Fear: Worker's Rights in U.S. Meat and Poultry Plants* (New York: Human Rights Watch, 2004).

15. "Why 'the Market' Alone Can't Save Local Agriculture," *Grist*, August 2006.

ASSAULT ON NATURE

1. Barbara Gemmill and Ana Milena Varela, "Modern Agriculture and Biodiversity: Uneasy Neighbours," SciDev Net, February 1, 2004.

2. "Livestock a Major Threat to Environment," FAO Newsroom, November 29, 2006.

3. USDA National Agricultural Statistics Service (NASS), "USDA Report Assesses 2008 Corn and Soybean Acreage," USDA Newsroom, June 30, 2008.

4. USDA, "Vegetable Report," April 2009.

5. USDA National Agricultural Statistics Service, "USDA Report Assesses 2008 Corn and Soybean Acreage."

6. U.S. Environmental Protection Agency, "Major Crops Grown in the United States," September 10, 2009.

7. John J. VanSickle, "Vegetable Perspectives and 2008 Outlook," Electronic Data Information Service, University of Florida Institute of Food and Agricultural Sciences Extension.

8. U.S. EPA, "Major Crops Grown in the United States."

9. U.S. Fish and Wildlife Service, Mountain Prairie Region, Partners for Fish & Wildlife, "Tallgrass Legacy Alliance."

10. "Distribution and Causation of Species Endangerment in the United States," *Science* 22, no. 5329 (August 22, 1997): 1116–17.

11. See George Wuerthner, "Guzzling the West's Water: Squandering a Public Resource at Public Expense," in *Welfare Ranching: The Subsidized Destruction of the American West*, ed. George Wuerthner and Mollie Matteson (Washington, DC: Island Press, 2002).

CONSEQUENCES OF DIVERSITY LOSS

Narrowing of Poultry Breeds

1. "Poultry Industry May Need Genetic Restock," UPI *Science News*, November 5, 2008.

2. Temple Grandin and Catherine Johnson, *Animals Make Us Human: Creating the Best Life for Animals* (Boston: Houghton Mifflin Harcourt, 2009), 218.

Traditional Versus Industrial Beef and Dairy Cattle

1. Andrew Rice, "A Dying Breed," *New York Times*, January 27, 2008.

Demise of the Family Farmer

1. "Food and Water Watch," *Turning Farms into Factories: How the Concentration of Animal Agriculture Threatens Human Health, the Environment, and Rural Communities* (Washington, DC: Food and Water Watch, 2007), v.

Loss of Individual Farms

1. Doug Gurian-Sherman, *CAFOs Uncovered: The Untold Costs of Confined Animal Feeding Operations* (Cambridge, MA: Union of Concerned Scientists, April 2008), 17–20.

2. James MacDonald and William D. McBride, *The Transformation of U.S. Livestock Agriculture: Scale, Efficiency, and Risks*, Economic Information Bulletin No. EIB-43, A Report from the Economic Research Service (Washington, DC: USDA, January 2009), iii.

3. Gurian-Sherman, *CAFOs Uncovered*, 15.

PART FIVE

INTRODUCTION

1. Doug Gurian-Sherman, *CAFOs Uncovered: The Untold Costs of Confined Animal Feeding Operations* (Cambridge, MA: Union of Concerned Scientists, April 2008).

2. Eric Schlosser, *Fast Food Nation: The Dark Side of the All-American Meal* (Boston: Houghton Mifflin, 2001), 197.

3. Pew Commission on Industrial Farm Animal Production, *Putting Meat on the Table: Industrial Farm Animal Production in America*, A Report of the Pew Commission on Industrial Farm Animal Production (Washington, DC: Pew Charitable Trusts and Johns Hopkins Bloomberg School of Public Health, 2008), 13.

CAFOS ARE IN EVERYONE'S BACKYARD

1. Iowa State University and the University of Iowa Study Group, *Iowa Concentrated Animal Feeding Operations Air Quality Study: Final Report* (Iowa City: University of Iowa, 2002).

2. J. A. Merchant, J. Kline, K. Donham, D. Bundy, and C. Hodne, "Human Health Effects," in *Iowa Concentrated Animal Feeding Operations Air Quality Study*, 121–45.

3. Stephanie L. Dzur, *Nuisance Immunity Provided by Iowa's Right-to-Farm Statute: A Taking Without Just Compensation?* (Des Moines, IA: Drake University School of Law, 2004).

4. Rachel C. Avery, Steve Wing, Stephen W. Marshall, and Susan S. Schiffman, "Perceived odor from industrial hog operations and the suppression of mucosal immune function in nearby neighbors," *Archives of Environmental Health* 59 (2004): 101–8; Merchant et al., "Human Health Effects"; Kendall Thu, "Public Health Concerns for Neighbors of Large-Scale Swine Production Operations," *Journal of Agricultural Safety and Health* 8, no. 2 (2002): 175–84.

5. *South Dakota Code*, Disparagement, title 20, chapter 20-10A (n.d.).

6. Erik Marcus, *Meat Market: Animals, Ethics, and Money* (Boston: Brio Press, 2005), 121.

7. U.S. General Accounting Office, *Livestock Agriculture: Increased EPA Oversight Will Improve Environmental Program for Concentrated Animal Feeding Operations*, GAO-03-285 (Washington, DC: U.S. GAO, 2003).

8. D. Diamond, "Testing the Water of Illinois Politics: The Case of Industrialized Agriculture and Environmental Degradation" (master's thesis, Northern Illinois University, 2002).

9. W. Goldschmidt, testimony before the Senate Subcommittee on Big Business, Washington, DC, 1972.

10. R. Enslen, *Michigan Pork Producers et al. v. Campaign for Family Farms et al. v. Ann Venneman, Secretary of the U.S. Department of Agriculture*, 1:01-CV-34 (U.S. District Court Western District of Michigan Southern Division; October 25, 2002; Kalamazoo, MI).

PAYING THE POLLUTERS

1. Doug Gurian-Sherman, *CAFOs Uncovered: The Untold Costs of Confined Animal Feeding Operations* (Cambridge, MA: Union of Concerned Scientists, April 2008).

2. See, e.g., Kate Clancy, *Greener Pastures: How Grass-fed Beef and Milk Contribute to Healthy Eating* (Cambridge, MA: Union of Concerned Scientists, 2006).

3. Elanor Starmer and Timothy A. Wise, *Feeding at the Trough: Industrial Livestock Firms Saved $35 Billion from Low Feed Prices*, Policy Brief No. 07-03 (Medford, MA: Tufts University Global Development and Environment Institute, December 2007).

4. Elanor Starmer, *Industrial Livestock at the Taxpayer Trough: How Large Hog and Dairy Operations Are Subsidized by the Environmental Quality Incentives Program*, A Report to the Campaign for Family Farms and the Environment, December 2008.

5. See L. M. Risse, K. L. Rowles, J. D. Mullen, S. E. Collier, D. E. Kissel, M. L. Wilson, and F. Chen, *Protecting Water Quality with Incentives for Litter Transfer in Georgia*, Cooperative Services Working Paper #2008-01 (Georgia Soil and Water Conservation Commission and the University of Georgia, September 2008).

6. Alabama Cooperative Extension, *An Update for Alabama CAWVs [Certified Animal Waste Vendors] and Others Involved in Waste Management* (newsletter, Summer 2007).

7. Keeve E. Nachman, Jay P. Graham, Lance B. Price, and Ellen K. Silbergeld, "Arsenic: A Roadblock to Potential Animal Waste Management Solutions," *Environmental Health Perspectives* 113 (2005): 1123–24.

8. U.S. Department of Energy, "State Energy Program, Projects by State: Fair Oaks Dairy Farm Innovative Manure Digestion System," State Energy Program Special Project, Indiana, 2002.

9. See Environmental Working Group's Farm Subsidy Database. Information on Michael McCloskey and Timothy den Dulk provided at Bion Management Team profiles.

10. U.S. Citizen and Immigration Services Regional Center Programs, "The EB-5 Visa."

11. See "Iowa New Farm Family Project Overview," Iowa State Extension to Agriculture and Natural Resources.

12. Center for Rural Affairs, Corporate Farming Notes, "South Dakota Industrial Dairies Financed Through Bizarre Immigration Arrangement," Organic Consumers Association, February 21, 2008.

13. Peter Harriman, "Investors Trade Millions for Visas," *Argus Leader (Sioux Falls, SD)*, January 13, 2008.

14. *Waterkeeper Alliance v. EPA*, 399 F.3d 486 (2d Cir. 2005).

15. Revised National Pollutant Discharge Elimination System Permit Regulation and Effluent Limitations Guidelines for Concentrated Animal Feeding Operations in Response to the Waterkeeper Decision; Final Rule, *Federal Register* 73 (November 20, 2008): 70417–86.

16. A copy of the Michigan Department of Environmental Quality comments is posted on Scribd.com.

17. The EPA webpage for the Animal Feeding Operations Air Agreements is www.epa.gov/compliance/resources/agreements/caa/cafo-agr.html.

18. U.S. Government Accountability Office, *Concentrated Animal Feeding Operations: EPA Needs More Information and a Clearly Defined Strategy to Protect Air and Water Quality from Pollutants of Concern*, GAO-08-944, September 4, 2008.

19. "Attorney General Lori Swanson and Minnesota Pollution Control Agency Jointly Sue Feedlot to Abate Public Nuisance and for Violations of Minnesota's Environmental Protection Laws," Office of Minnesota Attorney General Lori Swanson, press release, June 20, 2008.

20. Archie Ingersoll, "MPCA Seeks Comments on Stricter Permit for TRF Dairy," *Grand Forks (North Dakota) Herald*, March 4, 2009.

21. See North Carolina Department of Environment and Natural Resources, Division of Soil and Water Conservation, Lagoon Conversion Program.

SLICED AND DICED

1. Author's note: This and all other quotations not footnoted are from interviews with the author, originally published in the following articles by the author: Christopher D. Cook, "Hog-Tied: Migrant Workers Find Themselves Trapped on the Pork Assembly Line," *The Progressive*, September 1999; Christopher D. Cook, "Revolt over Conditions and Poultry Plants," *Christian Science Monitor*, April 28, 1999; Christopher D. Cook, "Plucking Workers: Tyson Foods Looks to the Welfare Rolls for a Captive Labor Force," *The Progressive*, August 1998; Christopher D. Cook, "Fowl Trouble," *Harper's Magazine*, August 1999.

2. American Meat Institute, "Fact Sheet U.S. Meat and Poultry Production and Consumption: An Overview" (Washington, DC: American Meat Institute, April 2009).

3. Roger Horowitz, *Negro and White, Unite and Fight!: A Social History of Industrial Unionism in Meatpacking, 1930–90* (Urbana: University of Illinois Press, 1997).

4. Jimmy M. Skaggs, *Prime Cut: Livestock Raising and Meatpacking in the United States 1607–1983* (College Station: Texas A&M University Press, 1986), 190.

5. Louise Lamphere, Alex Stepick, and Guillermo Grenier, eds., *Newcomers in the Workplace: Immigrants and the Restructuring of the U.S. Economy* (Philadelphia: Temple University Press, 1994), 3.

6. This and other meat industry information, unless otherwise cited, is from Cook, "Hog-Tied." Sources for the data include the U.S. General Accounting

Office, the Department of Labor, the USDA, the Occupational Safety and Health Administration, and the National Institutes for Occupational Safety and Health.

7. These and other details about poultry factory conditions, when not otherwise noted, are from Cook, "Fowl Trouble."

8. Ibid.

9. "Hispanics in Iowa Meatpacking," *Rural Migration News* 1, no. 4 (October 1995).

10. "Union Charges at Poultry Plant Bring New Policy on Workplace Bathroom Rights," press release, United Food and Commercial Workers International Union, April 15, 1998.

11. "UFCW Vote Pays Off for Omaha ConAgra Workers," press release, United Food and Commercial Workers International Union, October 24, 2002.

DIET FOR A HOT PLANET

1. Frances Moore Lappé, *Diet for a Small Planet*, 20th anniv. ed. (New York: Ballantine Books, 1991).

2. Doug Gurian-Sherman, *CAFOs Uncovered: The Untold Costs of Confined Animal Feeding Operations* (Cambridge, MA: Union of Concerned Scientists, April 2008).

3. Review of Form 10-K filings from the largest agribusiness and meat processing companies, including Smithfield and Tyson.

4. Henning Steinfeld, Pierre Gerber, Tom Wassenaar, Vincent Castel, Maurice Rosales, and Cees de Haan, *Livestock's Long Shadow: Environmental Issues and Options* (Rome: United Nations Food and Agriculture Organization, 2006).

5. Nitrous oxide and methane carbon-dioxide equivalents based on a 100-year time scale, from Intergovernmental Panel on Climate Change, *Third Assessment Report: Climate Change 2001*.

6. Steinfeld et al., *Livestock's Long Shadow*, 79.

7. Figures on animal production from UNFAO, FAOSTAT.

8. Steinfeld et al., *Livestock's Long Shadow*.

9. Anthony J. McMichael, John W. Powles, Collin D. Butler, and Ricardo Uauy, "Food, Livestock Production, Energy, Climate Change, and Health," *Lancet* 370 (2007): 1259.

10. Most recent data can be found in the consumption data from the USDA/ERS. It is estimated that because of higher feed costs as well as gains in meat and poultry exports, per capita meat consumption in the U.S. may decline to 214 pounds in 2012–2014.

11. Steinfeld et al., *Livestock's Long Shadow*, 22.

12. Ibid., 99.

13. Cited in Gowri Koneswaran and Danielle Nierenberg, "Global Farm Animal Production and Global Warming," *Environmental Health Perspectives* 116, no. 5 (May 2008). Based on data from the U.S. Environmental Protection Agency, *Inventory of U.S. Greenhouse Gas Emissions and Sinks: 1990–2005*, 6-6 and 6-7.

14. Steinfeld et al., *Livestock's Long Shadow*, 274.

15. Koneswaran and Nierenberg, "Global Farm Animal Production and Global Warming."

16. Steinfeld et al., *Livestock's Long Shadow*, 87.

17. Ibid.

18. See, e.g., California Environmental Protection Agency, Air Resources Board, "Research on GHG Emissions from Fertilizer."

19. Koneswaran and Nierenberg, "Global Farm Animal Production and Global Warming," 4. Emissions per country are from the United Nations Carbon Dioxide Information Analysis Center, "Global Climate Change Links."

20. The U.S. Department of Agriculture, Economic Research Service, "U.S. Fertilizer Imports/Exports: Summary of the Data Findings," states: "U.S. nitrogen and potash supplies largely depend on imports. About 62 percent of nitrogen and 88 percent of potash consumed in the U.S. in 2006 was from imports. Because of limited domestic production capacity, increased fertilizer demand will have to be met largely by imports. In calendar year 2007, U.S. nitrogen net imports increased 27 percent, to 10.2 million tons, 2.2 million tons above 2006 net imports. From July to December of 2007, net imports of nitrogen increased 34 percent to 4.8 million tons."

21. Calculation based on fertilizer trade data from the USDA/ERS.

22. "Legume Versus Fertilizer Sources of Nitrogen: Ecological Tradeoffs and Human Need," *Agriculture, Ecosystems, and Environment* 102 (2004): 293. Quoted in Paul Roberts, *The End of Food* (Boston: Houghton Mifflin, 2008).

23. Most recent data available from USDA/ERS, "U.S. Cattle and Beef Industry, 2002–2007."

24. Pounds noted here are measured by commercial carcass weight; see USDA/ERS, "U.S. Red Meat and Poultry Forecasts." See also USDA/ERS, "U.S. Crops in World Agricultural Supply and Demand Estimates."

25. Andrea Johnson, "Successful Meat Exporting Countries Will Deliver What Consumers Want," *Farm and Ranch Guide*, June 25, 2005.

26. United States Department of Agriculture, Foreign Agricultural Service, Office of Global Analysis, *Livestock and Poultry: World Markets and Trade*, Circular Series DL&P 2-07, November 2007.

27. Bishal K. Sitaula, S. Hansen, J. I. B. Sitaula, and L. R. Bakken, "Effects of Soil Compaction on N_2O Emission in Agricultural Soil," *Chemosphere—Global Change Science* 2, nos. 3–4 (2000): 367–71.

28. Steinfeld et al., *Livestock's Long Shadow.*

29. IPCC, *Climate Change 2007: Fourth Assessment Report of the Intergovernmental Panel on Climate Change* (New York: Cambridge University Press, 2007).

30. Henning Steinfeld and Tom Wassenaar, "The Role of Livestock Production in Carbon Cycles," *Annual Review of Environment and Resources* 32 (November 2007): 274.

31. Steinfeld et al., *Livestock's Long Shadow*, xxvii. About 20 percent of the world's pastures and rangelands, with 73 percent of rangelands in dry areas, have been degraded to some extent, mostly through overgrazing, compaction, and erosion created by livestock action.

32. Ibid., xxvii.

33. Elisabeth Rosenthal, "As More Eat Meat, a Bid to Cut Emissions," *New York Times*, December 3, 2008.

34. Peter Allen, "Sheep Flatulence Inoculation Developed," *Telegraph*, June 4, 2008.

35. H. Alan DeRamus, Terry C. Clement, Dean D. Giampola, and Peter C.

Dickison, "Methane Emissions of Beef Cattle on Forages: Efficiency of Grazing Management Systems," *Journal of Environmental Quality* 32 (2003): 269–77.

36. Robert B. Jackson, Jay L. Banner, Esteban G. Jobbágy, William T. Pockman, and Diana H. Wall, "Ecosystem Carbon Loss with Woody Plant Invasion of Grasslands" *Nature* 418 (August 8, 2002): 623–26.

37. For a review of life-cycle analyses of various livestock production scenarios, visit the resources compiled by the Food Climate Research Network. See, for instance, the working paper from Tara Garnett, "Meat and Dairy Production: Exploring the Livestock Sector's Contribution to the UK's Greenhouse Gas Emissions and Assessing What Less Greenhouse Gas Intensive Systems of Production and Consumption Might Look Like." As of this writing, the other excellent discussion piece about comparative emissions from different modes of livestock production is from Danielle Nierenberg at the Humane Society of the United States. See, for instance, Gowri Koneswaran and Danielle Nierenberg, "Global Farm Animal Production and Global Warming," *Environmental Health Perspectives* 116, no. 5 (May 2008).

38. See Gidon Eshel and Pamela A. Martin, "Diet, Energy, and Global Warming," *Earth Interactions* 10, no. 9 (April 2006): 1–17.

39. Claude Aubert, "Impact of the Food Production and Consumption on Climate Change" (paper presented at the International Conference on Organic Agriculture and Global Warming, Clermont-Ferrand, France, April 17–18, 2008).

40. David Pimentel, *Impacts of Organic Farming on the Efficiency of Energy Use in Agriculture*, An Organic Center State of Science Review, Organic Center, August 2006, 9.

PART SIX

INTRODUCTION

1. Temple Grandin, *Animals Make Us Human: Creating the Best Life for Animals* (Boston: Houghton Mifflin Harcourt, 2009), 176.

ANTIBIOTIC DRUG ABUSE

1. "Penicillin," *Chemical and Engineering News*, June 20, 2005.

2. "Subtherapeutic": Below the dosage level used to treat disease.

3. U.S. Centers for Disease Control and Prevention, "Leading Causes of Death, 1900–1998."

4. Ibid., "Achievements in Public Health, 1900–1999: Control of Infectious Diseases," *Morbidity and Mortality Weekly Report* 48, no. 29 (July 30, 1999): 621–29.

5. Ibid.

6. World Health Organization, *Overcoming Antimicrobial Resistance: World Health Report on Infectious Diseases 2000*.

7. Ellen K. Silbergeld, Jay Graham, and Lance B. Price, "Industrial Food Animal Production, Antibiotic Resistance, and Human Health," *Annual Review of Public Health* 29 (2008): 151–69.

8. Xander W. Huijsdens, Beatrix J. van Dijke, Emile Spalburg, Marga G. van

Santen-Verheuvel, Max E.O.C. Heck, Gerlinde N Pluister, Andreas Voss, Wim J.B. Wannet, and Albert J. de Neeling, "Community-Acquired MRSA and Pig-Farming," *Annals of Clinical Microbiology and Antimicrobials* 5 (2006): 26.

9. Taruna Khanna, Robert Friendship, Cate Dewey, and Scott Weese, "Methi-cillin resistant *Staphylococcus aureus* colonization in pigs and pig farmers," *Veterinary Microbiology*, 128, nos. 3–4 (2008): 298–303.

10. Tara C. Smith, Michael J. Male, Abby L. Harper, Jennifer S. Kroeger, Gregory P. Tinkler, Erin D. Moritz, Ana W. Capuano, Loreen A. Herwaldt, and Daniel J. Diekema, "Methicillin-Resistant *Staphylococcus aureus* (MRSA) Strain ST398 Is Present in Midwestern Swine and Swine Workers," *PLoS ONE* 4, no. 1 (January 2009).

11. R. Monina Klevens, Melissa A. Morrison, Joelle Nadle, Susan Petit, Ken Gershman, Susan Ray, Lee H. Harrison, et al., "Invasive Methicillin-Resistant *Staphylococcus aureus* Infections in the United States," *Journal of the American Medical Association* 298 (2007): 1763–71.

12. Ibid.

13. Margaret Mellon, Charles Benbrook, and Karen Lutz Benbrook, *Hogging It: Estimates of Antibiotic Abuse in Livestock* (Cambridge, MA: Union of Con-cerned Scientists, 2001).

14. James Krieger and Donna L. Higgins, "Housing and Health: Time Again for Public Health Action," *American Journal of Public Health* 92, no. 5 (May 2002): 758–68.

15. M. Sunde and M. Norström, "The Prevalence of, Associations Between and Conjugal Transfer of Antibiotic Resistance Genes in *Escherichia coli* Isolated from Norwegian Meat and Meat Products," *Journal of Antimicrobial Chemo-therapy* 58, no. 4 (October 2006): 741–47.

16. Ramanan Laxminarayan and Anup Malani, *Extending the Cure: Policy Responses to the Growing Threat of Antibiotic Resistance* (Washington, DC: Resources for the Future, 2007).

17. Abigail Salyers and Nadja B. Shoemaker, "Reservoirs of Antibiotic Resis-tance Genes," *Animal Biotechnology* 17, no. 2 (November 2006): 137–46.

18. F. M. Aarestrup, A. M. Seyfarth, H. D. Emborg, K. Pedersen, R. S. Hen-driksen, and F. Bager, "Effect of Abolishment of the Use of Antibiotic Agents for Growth Promotion on Occurrence of Antibiotic Resistance in Fecal Enterococci from Food Animals in Denmark," *Antimicrobial Agents and Chemotherapy* 45 (2001): 2054–59.

19. H. M. Engster, D. Marvil, and B. Stewart-Brown, "The Effect of With-drawing Growth Promoting Antibiotics from Broiler Chickens: A Long-Term Commercial Industry Study," *Journal of Applied Poultry Research* 11 (2002): 431–36; Gay Y. Miller, Kenneth A. Algozin, Paul E. McNamara, and Eric J. Bush, "Productivity and Economic Effects of Antibiotics Use for Growth Promotion in U.S. Pork Production," *Journal of Agricultural and Applied Economics* 35, no. 3 (December 2003): 469–82.

20. Ian Phillips, Mark Casewell, Tony Cox, Brad De Groot, Christian Friis, Ronald Jones, Charles Nightingale, Rodney Preston, and John Waddell, "Does the Use of Antibiotics in Food Animals Pose a Risk to Human Health? A Critical Review of Published Data," *Journal of Antibiotic Therapy* 53 (2004): 28–52.

21. Silbergeld et al., "Industrial Food Animal Production" (see n. 7).

22. Kenji Sato, Paul C. Bartlett, and Mahdi A. Saeed, "Antibiotic Susceptibility of *Escherichia coli* Isolates from Dairy Farms Using Organic Versus Conventional Production Methods," *Journal of the American Veterinary Medical Association* 226, no. 4 (2005): 589–94.

23. Lance B. Price, Elizabeth Johnson, Rocio Vailes, and Ellen Silbergeld, "Fluoroquinolone-Resistant *Campylobacter* Isolates from Conventional and Antibiotic-Free Chicken Products," *Environmental Health Perspectives* 113 (2005): 557–60; Taradon Luangtongkum, Teresa Y. Morishita, Lori Martin, Irene Choi, Orhan Sahin, and Qijing Zhang, "Effect of Conventional and Organic Production Practices on the Prevalence and Antibiotic Resistance of *Campylobacter* spp. in Poultry," *Applied and Environmental Microbiology* 72, no. 5 (May 2006): 3600–3607.

24. U.S. Department of Agriculture, Agricultural Research Service, "FY-2005 Annual Report Manure and Byproduct Utilization: National Program 206, May 31, 2006."

25. Silbergeld et al., "Industrial Food Animal Production."

26. Ibid., 160.

27. Ajit K. Sarmah, Michael T. Meyer, and Alistair B. A. Boxall, "A Global Perspective on the Use, Sales, Exposure Pathways, Occurrence, Fate and Effects of Veterinary Antibiotics (VAs) in the Environment," *Chemosphere* 65 (2006): 725–59.

28. Shawn G. Gibbs, Christopher F. Green, Patrick M. Tarwater, Linda C. Mota, Kristina D. Mena, and Pasquale V. Scarpino, "Isolation of Antibiotic-Resistant Bacteria from the Air Plume Downwind of a Swine Confined or Concentrated Animal Feeding Operation," *Environmental Health Perspectives* 114, no. 7 (July 2006): 1032–37.

29. Silbergeld et al., "Industrial Food Animal Production," 159.

30. Ramana Laxminarayan and Gardner M. Brown, "Economics of Antibiotic Resistance: A Theory of Optimal Use," *Journal of Environmental Economics and Management* 42, no. 2 (2001): 183–206.

31. American Public Health Association, "Precautionary Moratorium on New Concentrated Animal Feed Operations," APHA policy statement, November 18, 2003.

32. World Health Organization, Department of Communicable Disease Surveillance and Response, *WHO Global Strategy for Containment of Antibiotic Resistance* (World Health Organization, 2001).

33. Pew Commission on Industrial Farm Animal Production, *Putting Meat on the Table: Industrial Farm Animal Production in America*, A Report of the Pew Commission on Industrial Farm Animal Production (Washington, DC: Pew Charitable Trusts and Johns Hopkins Bloomberg School of Public Health, 2008).

34. Ibid., 61.

FRANKEN FOOD

1. Pallavi Gogoi, "Why Cloning Is Worth It," *Business Week*, March 7, 2007.

2. U.S. Food and Drug Administration, Center for Veterinary Medicine, and U.S. Department of Health and Human Services, *Animal Cloning: A Risk Assessment*, January 8, 2008.

3. S. Rhind, W. Cui, T. King, W. Ritchie, D. Wylie, and I. Wilmut, "Dolly: A Final Report," *Journal of Reproduction, Fertility, and Development* 16, no. 2 (January 2, 2004): 156.

4. U.S. FDA, "Food Consumption Risks," in *Animal Cloning: A Risk Assessment.*

5. Ibid., "Executive Summary."

6. Eric M. Hallerman, "Will Food Products from Cloned Animals Be Commercialized Soon?" *ISB News Report*, November 2002, 1.

7. Jorge Piedrahita, as quoted in "Cloned Pigs Differ from Originals in Looks and Behavior," *ScienceDaily (North Carolina State University)*, April 16, 2003.

8. James C. Cross, "Factors Affecting the Development Potential of Cloned Mammalian Embryos," *Proceedings of the National Academy of Sciences* 98 (2001): 5949–51.

9. Rick Weiss, "Human Cloning Bid Stirs Experts' Anger: Problems in Animal Cases Noted," *Washington Post*, March 7, 2001.

10. Sharon Begley, "Little Lamb, Who Made Thee?" *Newsweek*, March 10, 1997.

11. Gregory M. Lamb, "How Cloning Stacks Up," *Christian Science Monitor*, July 13, 2006.

12. Lorraine E. Young, Kenneth Fernandes, Tom G. McEvoy, Simon C. Butterwith, Carlos G. Gutierrez, Catherine Carolan, Peter J. Broadbent, John J. Robinson, Ian Wilmut, and Kevin D. Sinclair, "Epigenetic Change in IGF2R Is Associated with Fetal Overgrowth After Sheep Embryo Culture," *Nature Genetics* 27, no. 2 (February 2001): 153–54; John Travis, "Dolly Was Lucky," *Science News* 160, no. 16 (October 20, 2001): 250–51.

13. Jacky Turner, *The Gene and the Stable Door: Biotechnology and Farm Animals*, A Report for the Compassion in World Farming Trust (Hampshire, England: CIWF, 2002), 6.

14. U.S. FDA, "Animal Health Risks," in *Animal Cloning: A Risk Assessment*, 121 (see n. 2).

15. Ibid., 114.

16. Ibid., 116.

17. Travis, "Dolly Was Lucky" (see n. 13).

18. Audrey Cooper, "Cloned Calves Die at California University," *Apologetics Press*, April 3, 2001.

19. Simon Collins, "Cloned Animals Dying at AgResearch," *New Zealand Herald*, November 14, 2002.

20. Jose B. Cibelli, Keith H. Campbell, George E. Seidel, Michael D. West, and Robert P. Lanza, "The Health Profile of Cloned Animals," *Nature Biotechnology* 20 (2002): 13–14.

21. Narumi Ogonuki, Kimiko Inoue, Yoshie Yamamoto, Yoko Noguchi, Kentaro Tanemura, Osamu Suzuki, Hiroyuki Nakayama, et al., "Early Death of Mice Cloned from Somatic Cells," *Nature Genetics* 30 (March 1, 2002): 253–54.

22. Gina Kolata, "Researchers Find Big Risk of Defect in Cloning Animals," *New York Times*, March 25, 2001.

23. Helen Pearson, "Adult Clones in Sudden Death Shock: Pig Fatalities Highlight Cloning Dangers," *Nature*, August 27, 2003.

24. Steve Johnson, "Cloning Prospects Multiplying," *San Jose (CA) Mercury News*, August 23, 2005.

25. Janet Raloff, "Dying Breeds: Livestock Are Developing a Largely Unrecognized Biodiversity Crisis," *Science News* 152 (1997).

26. "Duplicate Dinner," *New Scientist*, May 19, 2001.

27. National Research Council of the National Academies, *Safety of Genetically Engineered Foods: Approaches to Assessing Unintended Health Effects* (Washington, DC: National Academies Press, 2004).

28. Ibid., 64.

29. "The Cloned Cow Coming to a Farm Near You," *Guardian Newspapers*, November 15, 2002.

30. Center for Food Safety, "Not Ready for Prime Time: FDA's Flawed Approach to Assessing the Safety of Food from Cloned Animals," Center for Food Safety, March 26, 2007.

31. Rick Weiss, "Cloned Cows' Milk, Beef Up to Standard," *Washington Post*, April 12, 2005.

32. National Research Council of the National Academies, *Animal Biotechnology: Science Based Concerns* (Washington, DC: National Academies Press, 2002), 66.

33. Jean-Paul Renard, Sylvie Chastant, Patrick Chesné, Christophe Richard, Jacques Marchal, Nathalie Cordonnier, Pascale Chavatte, and Xavier Vignon, "Lymphoid Hypoplasia and Somatic Cloning," *The Lancet* 353, no. 9163 (May 1, 1999): 1489–91.

34. Karl B. Tolenhoff, ed., *Animal Agriculture Research Progress* (New York: Nova Science Publishers, 2007), 122.

35. Randolph E. Schmid, "Cloned Meat, Milk Identical to Normal Ones, Study Says," Associated Press, April 12, 2005.

36. National Research Council, *Animal Biotechnology: Science Based Concerns*, 65 (see n. 33).

37. European Parliament, "MEPs Call for Ban on Animal Cloning for Food," press release, March 9, 2008.

GENETICALLY ENGINEERED FARM ANIMALS

1. Scott Gottlieb and Matthew B. Wheeler, *Genetically Engineered Animals and Public Health: Compelling Benefits for Health Care, Nutrition, the Environment, and Animal Welfare* (Washington, DC: Biotechnology Industry Organization, 2008), 9.

2. S. Clapp, "Pew Report Stimulates Debate over Future of Biotech Regulation," *Food Chemical News* 46, no. 8 (April 2004): 9–11.

3. U.S. Food and Drug Administration, Center for Veterinary Medicine, "Regulation of Genetically Engineered Animals Containing Heritable Recombinant DNA Constructs," *Guidance for Industry* 187 (January 15, 2009).

4. Jeremy Rifkin, *The Biotech Century* (New York: Tarcher Putnam, 1998).

5. Presentation by Paul B. Thompson, W. K. Kellogg Professor of Agricultural, Food and Community Ethics, Michigan State University: "Ethical Issues in Animal Biotechnology," November 29, 2007, to USDA AC21 Committee. While this proposal was made partly in jest, it illustrates the kind of thinking that might promote such alterations as "ethical" changes in animals.

6. Reuters, "And This Little Piggy Was Environmentally Friendly," June 24, 1999.

7. Personal Communication between Jaydee Hanson and John Phillips, emeritus professor, University of Guelph and Enviropig developer, November 10, 2008.

8. Vernon G. Pursel, Carl A. Pinkert, Kurt F. Miller, Douglas J. Bolt, Roger G. Campbell, Richard D. Palmiter, Ralph L. Brinster, and Robert E. Hammer, "Genetic Engineering of Livestock," *Science* 254, no. 4910 (1989): 1281–88.

9. Stephen Nottingham, *Eat Your Genes: How Genetically Modified Food Is Entering Our Diet* (New York: Zed Books, 2003); Tara Weaver, "New Transgenic Pigs with Lean Pork Potential," USDA Agricultural Research Service News & Events, February 18, 1998.

10. Associated Press, "FDA Investigates Biotech Pigs," New York Times, February 6, 2003.

11. Sylvia Pagán Westphal, "Pigs Out," *NewScientist*, no. 2301, July 28, 2001; U.S. Food and Drug Administration, "Reminder to Scientists Involved in Research with Genetically Engineered Animals," *FDA Veterinarian Newsletter* 18, no. 4 (July/August 2003).

12. Personal communication at Pew Biotechnology Meeting in Washington DC, October 18, 2006.

13. See "FDA Approves Orphan Drug ATryn to Treat Rare Clotting Disorder," press release, February 6, 2009. The goat itself was cloned by Genzyme, which spun off its transgenic animal business as Genzyme Therapeutics and later renamed it GTC Biotherapeutics.

14. The FDA Blood Products Committee reviewed the safety of the drug excreted in the goat's milk, but not the safety of the goat itself or the appropriateness of the environmental confinement of the 200-plus goats. That committee received only a two-page summary of the environmental risk assessment of the goats.

15. "Birth of 'BioSteel' Goats Marks Major Manufacturing Milestone," Nexia Biotechnologies, press release, January 12, 2000, reprinted by Hidden Mysteries .org.

16. The company is a subsidiary of the Dutch firm Gene Pharming. It appears that William Velander at Virginia Polytechnic and State University and William Drohan of the American Red Cross in Rockville, MD, coordinate the project, according to "Building to Order: Genetic Engineering," *The Economist*, March 1, 1997, 81.

17. P. Smith, "A Community Struggles with a Transgenic Animal Facility," *Gene Watch* 13, no. 1 (February 2000): 12–13.

18. Tim Thornton, "Pharming Won't Process at Tech Corporate Center: Biotech Milk Plan May Be Souring," *Roanoke (VA) Times*, December 16, 2000. Pharming instead has created Vienna Farms outside Madison, Wisconsin, where it initially had a herd of at least 35 GE cattle for pharmaceutical production. On February 28, 2008, Pharming Group NV ("Pharming") announced that it has concluded a license agreement with Advanced Cell Technology Inc. to obtain exclusive rights on patents in the field of transgenic technology, to which it already had nonexclusive rights. These patents, previously owned by Infigen Inc., cover a wide range of technologies, including for Pharming relevant elements of somatic

nuclear transfer (cloning), an essential step in generating transgenic cattle. The agreement provides Pharming strict control over the generation of its transgenic cattle, while at the same time increasing the barriers of entry for others.

19. Liangxue Lai, Jing X. Kang, Rongfeng Li, Jingdong Wang, William T. Witt, Hwan Yul Yong, Yanhong Hao, et al., "Generation of Cloned Transgenic Pigs Rich in Omega-3 Fatty Acids," *Nature Biotechnology* 24 (April 1, 2006): 435–36.

20. ViaGen, "ViaGen Acquires Livestock Pioneer ProLinia: Deal Gives Genetics Company Patent Rights, Contract with World's Largest Hog Producer and New Scientific Talent," press release, June 30, 2003.

21. Andrew Pollack, "Cancer Risk Exceeds Outlook in Gene Therapy, Studies Find," *New York Times*, June 13, 2003.

22. Ibid.

23. National Research Council of the National Academies, *Animal Biotechnology: Science Based Concerns* (Washington, DC: National Academies Press, 2002), 12.

24. The FDA approved ATryn, the genetically engineered form of a human anticoagulant, despite the fact that it did not contain the same sugars as the human form and despite the fact that a large portion of the few patients treated with the drug suffered serious side effects. Moreover, even to approve the drug with such a small trial, the FDA had to change its "Choice of Margin," a statistical standard used for drug trials.

25. Pew Initiative on Food and Biotechnology, *Biotech in the Barnyard: Implications of Genetically Engineered Animals* (proceedings of a workshop sponsored by the Pew Initiative on Food and Biotechnology, September 24–25, 2002, Dallas, TX).

26. Ibid.

27. William M. Muir and Richard D. Howard, "Possible Ecological Risks of Transgenic Organism Release When Transgenes Affect Mating Success: Sexual Selection and the Trojan Gene Hypothesis," *PNAS* 96, no. 24 (November 23, 1999): 13853–56.

28. U.S. Food and Drug Administration, "Guidance for Industry on Regulation of Genetically Engineered Animals Containing Heritable recombinant DNA Constructs," Docket No. FDA-2008-D-0394, *Federal Register* 74, no. 11 (January 16, 2009): 3057–58.

29. "AgResearch Aims to Spread GE Animals Around NZ," press release, August 8, 2008, *Scoop Independent News*. The New Zealand Agricultural Research Center, AgResearch, saw its research funding for cloning research cut in 2008 by the New Zealand government but has requested instead blanket approval for its work genetically engineering animals for commercial interests. This would sidestep government controls and allow for the development of unlimited numbers of animals. The institute has already announced that it wants to genetically engineer llamas, alpacas, sheep, cows, pigs, goats, buffalo, deer, and horses. If the application for across-the-board approval is given, it may make it more likely that New Zealand could export genetically engineering animals in the future.

30. Pew Initiative on Food and Biotechnology, "Regulating Genetically Engi-

neered Animals," in *Issues in the Regulation of Genetically Engineered Plants and Animals* (Washington, DC: Pew Initiative on Food and Biotechnology, April 2004).

31. Ibid.

32. At the USDA Agriculture for the 21st Century meeting on December 17, 2008, Dr. Larissa Rudenko, the veterinary scientist in charge of the FDA reviews, announced that the FDA already had requests from foreign producers for import tolerances.

33. See Center for Food Safety, "Not Ready for Prime Time: FDA's Flawed Approach to Assessing the Safety of Food from Cloned Animals," Center for Food Safety, March 26, 2007.

34. See discussion of problems of environmental problems likely to be caused by transgenic animals in National Research Council of the National Academies, *Animal Biotechnology: Science Based Concerns* (Washington, DC: National Academies Press, 2002), 73.

NUCLEAR MEAT

1. U.S. Department of Agriculture, Food and Nutrition Services, "USDA Releases Specifications for the Purchase of Irradiated Ground Beef in the National School Lunch Program," press release, May 29, 2003.

2. Herbert L. DuPont, "The Growing Threat of Foodborne Bacterial Enteropathogens of Animal Origin," *Clinical Infectious Diseases* 45, no 10 (November 15, 2007): 1353–61.

3. Felicia Nestor and Wenonah Hauter, *The Jungle 2000: Is America's Meat Fit to Eat?* (Washington DC: Public Citizen, 2000).

4. "Ionizing Radiation for the Treatment of Food," *Code of Federal Regulations*, title 21: Food and Drugs, CFR §179.26 (December 2005).

5. Nestor and Hauter, *The Jungle 2000: Is America's Meat Fit to Eat?*

6. Peter Jenkins and Mark Worth, *Food Irradiation: A Gross Failure* (Washington, DC: Center for Food Safety and Food and Water Watch, January 2006).

7. D. Anderson, M. J. Clapp, M. C. Hodge, and T. M. Weight, "Irradiated Laboratory Animal Diets: Dominant Lethal Studies in the Mouse," *Mutation Research* 80, no. 2 (February 1981): 333–45.

8. L. Bugyaki, A. R. Deschreider, J. Moutschen, M. Moutschen-Dahmen, A. Thijs, and A. Lafontaine, "Do Irradiated Foodstuffs Have a Radiomimetic Effect? II. Trials with Mice Fed Wheat Meal Irradiated at 5 Mrad," *Atompraxis* 14 (1968): 112–18.

9. M. Moutschen-Dahmen, J. Moutschen, and L. Ehrenberg, "Pre-Implantation Death of Mouse Eggs Caused by Irradiated Food," *Journal of Radiation Biology* 18, no. 3 (1970): 201–16.

10. C. Bhaskaram and G. Sadasivan, "Effects of Feeding Irradiated Wheat to Malnourished Children," *American Journal of Clinical Nutrition* 28 (1975): 130–35.

11. P. R. Le Tellier and W. W. Nawar, "2-Alkylcyclobutanones from the Radiolysis of Triglycerids," *Lipids* 7 (1972): 75–76.

12. A. V. J. Crone, J. T. G. Hamilton, and M. H. Stevenson, "Detection of

2-Dodecylcyclobutanone in Radiation-Sterilized Chicken Meat Stored for Several Years," *International Journal of Food Science and Technology* 27 (1992): 691–96.

13. Henry Delincée and B. L. Pool-Zobel, "Genotoxic Properties of 2-Dodecyl-cyclobutanone, a Compound Formed on Irradiation of Food Containing Fat," *Radiation Physics and Chemistry* 52 (1998): 39–42; Henry Delincée, B. L. Pool-Zobel, and G. Rechkemmer, "Genotoxicity of 2-Dodecylcyclobutanone," in *Report by the Bundesforschungsanstalt für Ernährung*, BFE-R-99-01, Food Irradiation, Fifth German Conference, November 11 and 13, 1998, ed. K. M. Ehlermann and Henry Delincée (Karlsruhe, Germany: Federal Nutrition Research Institute; translated from the German by Public Citizen, Washington, DC, February 2001); Henry Delincée, Christiane Soika, Péter Horvatovichm, Gerhard Rechkemmer, and Eric Marchioni, "Genotoxicity of 2-Alkylcyclobutanones: Markers for an Irradiation Treatment in Fat-Containing Food," 12th International Meeting on Radiation Processing, Conference Abstracts, March 25–30, 2001, Avignon, France, 148–49.

14. Mark Worth and Peter Jenkins, *Hidden Harm: How the FDA Is Ignoring the Potential Dangers of Unique Chemicals in Irradiated Food* (Washington, DC: Public Citizen and the Center for Food Safety, 2001).

15. Ibid.

16. *AEC Authorizing Legislation, Fiscal Year 1970: Hearings Before the Joint Committee on Atomic Energy, Congress of the United States*, April 29–30, 1969 (Washington DC: Government Printing Office, 1970), 1692.

17. Shelley Emling, "DOE Finishes $47 Million Cleanup of Plant Contaminated by Cesium," *Atlanta Journal Constitution*, April 22, 1990.

18. "Food Irradiation Pioneer Sentenced for Lying to NRC," United Press International, October 12, 1988.

19. Wenonah Hauter and Mark Worth, *Zapped: Irradiation and the Death of Food* (Washington, DC: Food and Water Watch Press, 2008).

20. Food and Water Watch, "Fact Sheet: Irradiation and Vegetables Don't Mix."

PART SEVEN

INTRODUCTION

1. Pew Commission on Industrial Farm Animal Production, *Putting Meat on the Table: Industrial Farm Animal Production in America*, A Report of the Pew Commission on Industrial Farm Animal Production (Washington, DC: Pew Charitable Trusts and Johns Hopkins Bloomberg School of Public Health, 2008), 35.

2. Chad Smith, "Antibiotic Usage: Our European Observations" (paper presented at the Forty-Seventh Annual North Carolina Pork Conference, Greenville, NC, February 19–20, 2003).

3. Ibid.

TOWARD SUSTAINABILITY

1. Jared M. Diamond, *Guns, Germs and Steel* (New York: Norton, 2005); ibid., *Collapse: How Societies Choose to Fail or Succeed* (New York: Viking, 2005).

2. Aldo Leopold, "The Outlook for Farm Wildlife," in *Aldo Leopold: For the Health of the Land*, ed. J. Baird Callicott and Eric T. Freyfogle (Washington, DC: Island Press, 1999), 218.

3. Richard Heinberg, *Powerdown: Options and Actions for a Post-Carbon World* (Gabriola Island, BC, Canada: New Society Publishers, 2004); Paul Roberts, *The End of Oil: On the Edge of a Perilous New World* (Boston: Houghton Mifflin, 2005); Steve Sorrell, Jamie Speirs, Roger Bentley, Adam Brandt, and Richard Miller, *Global Oil Depletion: An Assessment of the Evidence for a Near-Term Peak in Global Oil Production* (London: UK Energy Research Centre, August 2009).

4. National Academy of Sciences, *Understanding Climate Change: A Program for Action*, Report of the Panel on Climate Variations (Washington, DC: National Academy of Sciences, 1975).

5. Cynthia Rosenzweig and Daniel Hillel, "Potential Impacts of Climate Change on Agriculture and Food Supply," *Consequences* 1, no. 2 (Summer 1995).

6. Lester R. Brown, *Plan B 2.0: Rescuing a Planet Under Stress and a Civilization in Trouble* (New York: Norton, 2006), 42–44.

7. "A Book Excerpt from *Slow Money: Investing as if Food, Farms, and Fertility Mattered*, by Woody Tasch," *Ode Magazine*, November 2008; Judith D. Soule and Jon K. Piper, *Farming in Nature's Image: An Ecological Approach to Agriculture* (Washington, DC: Island Press, 1992).

8. Perry Beeman, "Speakers Say Biofuel Boom Puts Pressure on Water," *Des Moines Register*, October 20, 2007.

9. "Neb. Republican River Plan on Fast Track," *Denver Post*, September 28, 2009.

10. W. J. Lewis, J. C. van Lenteren, Sharad C. Phatak, and J. H. Tuminson III, "A Total System Approach to Sustainable Pest Management," *Proceedings, National Academy of Sciences* 94 (November 1997), 12243–44.

11. Ibid., 12245.

12. John P. Reganold, Llloyd F. Elliott, and Yvonne L. Unger, "Long-term Effects of Organic and Conventional Farming on Soil Erosion," *Nature* 330 (November 26, 1987) 370–72; John P. Reganold, Jerry D. Glover, Preston K. Andrews, and Herbert R. Hinman, "Sustainability of Three Apple Production Systems," *Nature* 410 (April 19, 2001): 926–30.

13. Frederick Kirschenmann, "Potential for a New Generation of Biodiversity in Agro-Ecosystems of the Future," *Agronomy Journal* 99, no. 2 (March–April, 2007): 375.

14. Michael P. Russelle, Martin H. Entz, and Alan J. Franzluebbers, "Reconsidering Integrated Crop-Livestock Systems in North America," *Agronomy Journal* 99 (2007): 325–34.

15. Donald C. Lay Jr., Mark F. Haussmann, and Mike J. Daniels, "Hoop Housing for Feeder Pigs Offers a Welfare-Friendly Environment Compared to a Nonbedded Confinement System," *Journal of Applied Animal Welfare Science* 3, no. 1 (2000): 33–48.

16. For extensive peer-reviewed research on hoop barn performance, go to www.leopold.iastate.edu, click on "Ecology," and type "hoop barns" into the Search box.

CHANGING THE LAW

1. State of California: Elections, Initial Ballot Argument Against Proposition 2, July 11, 2008.

2. Ibid.

3. California Secretary of State, "Californians for Safe Food," Cal-Access Campaign Finance.

4. Ibid., "2008 Election: State Ballot Measures."

5. Clean Water Act, 33 U.S.C. § 1251 et seq.

6. Robert F. Kennedy Jr., "Statement of Robert F. Kennedy, Jr., Chairman of Waterkeeper Alliance Before the U.S. House of Representatives," Select Committee on Energy and Climate Change, December 11, 2008.

7. Under the Clean Water Act, only discharges of a pollutant from a "point source," a discernable, discrete source such as a pipe, ditch, or channel, require a permit (40 C.F.R. § 122.2 [2008]). "Nonpoint source" pollution, or pollution from runoff or other nondiscrete source, does not require a permit and is generally not regulated by the Clean Water Act (40 C.F.R. § 122.2 [2008]). There is an exception for nonpoint source pollution entering a state-designated polluted waterway. In these circumstances, the state may set total maximum daily loads (TMDLs) for certain pollutants (40 C.F.R. § 130.7 [2009]). For CWA-based oversight, then, it is crucial that a pollution-generating facility, such as a CAFO, be regulated as a point source and therefore be required to obtain a permit under the CWA.

8. *Waterkeeper Alliance v. EPA*, 399 F.3d 486, 506 (2d Cir. 2005).

9. 40 C.F.R. § 122.23(e) (2008).

10. 40 C.F.R. § 122.23(d)(2) (2008). As defined by the regulation, a "discharge" is the addition of any pollutant from a point source into the waters of the United States (40 C.F.R. § 122.2).

11. Tony Bennett et al., "Livestock Report 2006" (Rome: Food and Agriculture Organization of the United Nations, 2006); Robert Goodland and Jeff Anhang, "Livestock and Climate Change: What If the Key Actors in Climate Change Are . . . Cows, Pigs, and Chickens?" *World Watch Magazine* (November/December 2009), 11.

12. The EPA has determined that when manure is stored or treated in systems that promote anaerobic conditions, such as the liquid storage systems commonly found in CAFOs, decomposition produces great amounts of methane. This increases greenhouse gas emissions and concentrates them in the vicinity of the CAFO manure lagoon. However, when manure is handled as a solid and appropriately deposited on pasture, range, or paddock lands, it produces minimal amounts of methane. See, e.g., U.S. Environmental Protection Agency, "U.S. Greenhouse Gas Inventory Report: U.S. Greenhouse Gas Emissions and Sinks: 1990–2007: Agriculture" (2009); and Ad Hoc Committee on Air Emissions from Animal Feeding Operations, *Air Emissions from Animal Feeding Operations:*

Current Knowledge, Future Need (Washington, DC: National Academies Press, 2003), 54.

13. D. Marvin, "Factory Farms Cause Pollution Increases," *Johns Hopkins University Newsletter* (2004); Ad Hoc Committee, "Air Emissions," 52; D. Osterberg and D. Wallinga, "Addressing Externalities from Swine Production to Reduce Public Health and Environmental Impacts," *American Journal of Public Health* 94 (2004): 1703–08.

14. Clean Air Act, 42 U.S.C. § 7401 et seq.

15. 42 U.S.C. § 7401(b)(1).

16. *Vigil v. Leavitt*, 366 F.3d 1025, 1029 (9th Cir. 2004).

17. *Association of Irritated Residents v. Fred Schakel Dairy*, No. 1:05-CV-00707 (E.D.Cal, 2008); *Association of Irritated Residents v. C & R Vanderham Dairy, et al.*, No. 05-01593 (E.D.Cal, 2008).

18. Center for Agricultural Air Quality Engineering and Science, "Agricultural Air Pollution Fact Sheet," Texas Agricultural Experiment Station, http://caaqes.tamu.edu/Publications/Publications/AgAir.pdf (accessed February 13, 2009).

19. R. G. Hendrickson, A. Chang, and R. J. Hamilton, "Co-Worker Fatalities from Hydrogen Sulfide," *American Journal of Industrial Medicine* 45 (2004): 346–50.

20. B. Predicala et al., "Control of H_2S Emission from Swine Manure Using Na-Nitrate and Na-Molybdate," *Journal of Hazardous Materials Online* (October 2007); National Institute for Occupational Safety and Health (NIOSH), "Recommendations to the U.S. Department of Labor for Changes to Hazardous Order," Centers for Disease Control and NIOSH (May 2002): 86–88.

21. Comprehensive Environmental Response, Compensation and Liability Act, 42 U.S.C. § 9601 et seq.

22. Emergency Planning and Community Right-to-Know Act, 42 U.S.C. § 11001 et seq.

23. 40 CFR § 302 (2008); 40 CFR § 355 (2008).

24. 72 Fed. Reg. 73701 (December 28, 2007).

25. Numerous reports have addressed the impact of CAFOs on public health. See, e.g., Pew Commission on Industrial Farm Animal Production, *Putting Meat on the Table: Industrial Farm Animal Production in America*, A Report of the Pew Commission on Industrial Farm Animal Production (Washington, DC: Pew Charitable Trusts and Johns Hopkins Bloomberg School of Public Health, 2008); Osterberg and Wallinga, "Addressing Externalities from Swine Production" (see n. 13); S. Sneeringer, "Does Animal Feeding Operation Pollution Hurt Public Health? A National Longitudinal Study of Health Externalities Identified by Geographic Shifts in Livestock Production," *American Journal of Agricultural Economics* 91 (2009): 124–137.

26. *Waterkeepers Alliance, Sierra Club, Humane Society, Environmental Integrity Project, Center for Food Safety, and Citizens for Pennsylvania's Future v. EPA*, Petition for Review, United States Court of Appeals for the D.C. Circuit, Docket # 09-1017 (January 15, 2009).

27. Animal Welfare Act, 7 USC § 2131-2159.

28. Humane Methods of Livestock Slaughter Act, 7 USC § 1901-1906.

29. Factory Farming Campaign, "Farm Animal Statistics: Slaughter Totals," Humane Society of the United States.

30. J. Miller, "The Regulation of Animal Welfare in Food Production" (written work requirement, Harvard Law School), 51; David J. Wolfson and Mariann Sullivan, "Foxes in the Henhouse: Animals, Agribusiness, and the Law: A Modern American Fable," in Cass R. Sunstein and Martha C. Nussbaum, *Animal Rights: Current Debates and New Directions* (Oxford, England: Oxford University Press, 2004), 208.

31. See, e.g., *New Jersey Soc. for the Prevention of Cruelty to Animals v. NJ Dept. of Ag.*, 196 N.J. 366 (N.J., 2008).

32. Erik Marcus, *Meat Market: Animals, Ethics, and Money* (Boston: Brio Press, 2005), 57.

33. Nev. Rev. Stat. Ann § 574.200.6 (2007).

34. Marcus, *Meat Market*, 58. Quoting a personal communication with attorney David J. Wolfson.

35. *N.J. Society*, 196 N.J. at 366.

36. *Id.* at 399–402.

37. This is in contrast to many environmental statutes, which have private attorney general provisions, known as "citizen suit" provisions, which permit third-party enforcement of statutory violations when the government fails to act.

38. Pew Commission, *Putting Meat on the Table* (see n. 25).

39. United States Department of Agriculture, "USDA Farm Bill Forum Comment Summary and Background: Agricultural Concentration."

40. Packers and Stockyards Act, 7 U.S.C. § 192 (2007).

41. 7 U.S.C. § 192(b).

42. *London v. Fieldale Farms Corp.*, 410 F.3d 1295, 1304 (11th Cir. 2005) (holding that to prove violation of the PSA, the farmer must prove that the alleged violation adversely affects competition or is likely to adversely affect competition); *Adkins v. Cagle Foods*, 411 F.3d 1320, 1324-25 (11th Cir. 2005) (holding that Appellee failed to demonstrate discriminatory purpose).

43. *Wheeler v. Pilgrim's Pride Corp.*, 536 F.3d 455, 456 (5th Cir. 2008).

44. Oprah's Report on Mad Cow Disease, Oprah Winfrey Show, CBS, April 15, 1996; Sam Howe Verhovek, "Talk of the Town: Burgers v. Oprah," *New York Times*, January 21, 1998.

45. Oprah's Report on Mad Cow Disease; see *Texas Beef Group v. Winfrey*, 201 F.3d 680, 683–84 (5th Cir. 2000).

46. Oprah's Report on Mad Cow Disease.

47. Verhovek, "Talk of the Town: Burgers v. Oprah."

48. La. Rev. Stat. Ann. 3:4501.

49. A. J. Nomai, "Food Disparagement Laws: A Threat to Us All" (Free Heretic Publications, 1999).

50. About EU Law, "Process and Players," *Europa—EUR-lex*. In the EU, treaties (also called conventions) are the primary legislation, comparable to constitutional law in the United States. Treaties form the basis for secondary legislation: regulations, directives, and decisions. A regulation is a general measure, binding in all its parts, applicable to everyone in the EU. Regulations do not need to be implemented by each member state. A directive is specifically addressed to member states. A directive's main purpose is to align national legislation with the contents of the directive. A decision is a ruling on a particular matter. Decisions are binding only on those involved, such as specific individuals or member states.

51. Application of Community Law, "What Are EU Directives?" European Commission. EU directives outline end results to be achieved by member states. Member states must adapt their laws to meet these goals but are free to decide how to do so. Directives may concern one or more member states, or all of them. Directives specify a future date by which national laws must be adopted, allowing member states time to adjust current practices to those adopted in the directives and incorporate the new practices into their own laws. Member states are free to enact stricter laws. Note that in addition to directives, the EU uses regulations, which apply directly and need not be adopted or amended by member states. The general chemical law, REACH, is a regulation, for example, not a directive.

52. European Convention for the Protection of Animals Kept for Farming Purposes, March 10, 2006.

53. European Commission, "A New Animal Health Strategy (2007–2013) for the European Union Where Prevention Is Better than Cure," September 19, 2007.

54. Commission Directive 2001/88/EC of October 21, 2001, amending directive 91/630/EEC laying down the minimum standards for the protection of pigs.

55. Commission Directive 2001/93/EC of November 9, 2001, amending directive 91/630/EEC laying down minimum standards for the protection of pigs.

56. Council Directive 2007/43/EC of June 28, 2007, laying down minimum rules for the protection of chickens kept for meat production at Article (3)(2).

57. Council Directive 1999/74/EC of July 19, 1999, laying down the minimum standards for the protection of laying hens at Chapter II, Article 5 (2).

58. Norwegian Animal Welfare Act, No. 73 of December 20, 1974.

59. The Welfare of Farmed Animals: (England) Regulations 2007.

60. Council Directive 2008/119/EC of December 18, 2008, laying down minimum standards for the protection of calves.

61. Commission of the European Communities, Proposal for a Council Regulation on the Protection of Animals at the Time of Killing, 2008.

62. Food Marketing Institute, "Low-Level Use of Antibiotics in Livestock and Poultry."

63. Michael Kharfen, "Denmark's Phase-Out of Antibiotics in Livestock and Poultry Has Protected Health and Not Hurt Farmers, World Health Organization Concludes," Keep Antibiotics Working Campaign, 2003.

64. Food Marketing Institute, "Low-Level Use of Antibiotics in Livestock and Poultry."

65. "Danish Ban on Antibiotics Proves Successful," Food Production Daily, May 5, 2003; Testimony of Dr. Frank Møller Aarestrup and Dr. Henrik Wegener, National Food Institute Technical University of Denmark, Søborg, Denmark, for the U.S. House of Representatives Committee on Rules. Hearing on H.R. 1549, the Preservation of Antibiotics for Medical Treatment Act of 2009, submitted for the record, July 13, 2009, Washington, DC.

66. Directive 81/602/EEC; Directive 88/146/EEC; Directive 88/299/EEC.

67. Renee Johnson and Charles E. Hanrahan, "The U.S.-EU Beef Hormone Dispute," Cong. Res. Service (2009). This information is found in the summary of the document.

68. Council Directive 91/676/EEC of December 12, 1991, concerning the protection of waters against pollution caused by nitrates from agricultural sources.

69. Agriculture and Rural Development, "Agriculture and Climate Change," European Commission.

70. Pew Commission, *Putting Meat on the Table*, 77 (see n. 25).

71. Bailey Norwood, "Research in Farm Animal Welfare Development," Oklahoma State University Department of Agricultural Economics.

72. Pew Commission, *Putting Meat on the Table*, 38 (see n. 25). The Pew Commission on Industrial Farm Animal Production concluded: "Food animals that are treated well and provided with at least minimum accommodation of their natural behaviors and physical needs are healthier and safer for human consumption." This is likely because they are not as likely to contract diseases since the report further notes: "The intensive confinement practices that are common in industrial farm animal production so severely restrict movement and natural behaviors that the animal may not be able to turn around or walk at all. . . . The stress that results from these situations can result in animals that are more susceptible to disease and more likely to spread disease" (Pew Commission, *Putting Meat on the Table*, 13).

73. Margaret Mellon, Charles Benbrook, and Karen Lutz Benbrook, *Hogging It: Estimates of Antibiotic Abuse in Livestock* (Cambridge, MA: Union of Concerned Scientists, 2001), xiii.

74. Pew Commission, *Putting Meat on the Table*, 15.

75. Guidance #152, Evaluating the Safety of Antimicrobial New Animal Drugs with Regard to Their Microbiological Effects on Bacteria or Human Health Concern.

76. Kharfen, "Denmark's Phase-Out of Antibiotics in Livestock and Poultry" (see n. 63).

77. Guidance #152.

78. Elanor Starmer and Timothy A. Wise, *Feeding at the Trough: Industrial Livestock Firms Saved $35 Billion from Low Feed Prices*, Policy Brief No. 07-03 (Medford, MA: Tufts University Global Development and Environment Institute, December 2007).

79. Doug Gurian-Sherman, *CAFOs Uncovered: The Untold Costs of Confined Animal Feeding Operations* (Cambridge, MA: Union of Concerned Scientists, April 2008), 31.

80. Timothy Searchinger, Ralph Heimlich, R. A. Houghton, Fengxia Dong, Amani Elobeid, Jacinto Fabiosa, Simia Tokgoz, Dermot Hayes, and Tun-Hsiang Yu, "Use of U.S. Croplands for Biofuels Increases Greenhouse Gases Through Emissions from Land-Use Change," *Science* 319 (2008): 1238–40.

81. Agricultural Marketing Resource Center at Iowa State University.

82. Food Security Act of 1985, 16 U.S.C. § 3839.

83. United States Department of Agriculture, Economic Research Service, *2008 Farm Bill Side-by-Side:* "Title II: Conservation" and "Miscellaneous."

DISMANTLEMENT

1. David W. Moore, "Public Lukewarm on Animal Rights," Gallup News Service, May 21, 2003.

2. Glynn T. Tonsor, Christopher Wolf, and Nicole Olynk, "Consumer Vot-

ing and Demand Behavior Regarding Swine Gestation Crates," *Food Policy* 34 (2009) 492–98.

3. Moore, "Public Lukewarm on Animal Rights."

4. People for the Ethical Treatment of Animals (PETA), "Legislation Prohibiting or Restricting Animal Acts," September 21, 2005.

5. Humane Society of the United States, "Ballot Measures on Animal Protection Since 1990."

6. GoVeg.com, "Seaboard Farms Investigation."

7. "Three Men Plead Guilty to Animal Abuse in Beating Calf," Associated Press, July 26, 2002.

8. Organic Trade Association, "Industry Statistics and Projected Growth."

9. "How Many Vegetarians Are There?" *Vegetarian Journal*, May 15, 2009.

10. "The Most Expensive Free Lunch," NoJunkFood.org, October 14, 2008.

11. Institute of Medicine of the National Academies, Food and Nutrition Board, Committee on Nutrition Standards for National School Lunch and Breakfast Programs, *School Meals: Building Blocks for Healthy Children*, ed. Virginia A. Stallings, Carol West Suitor, and Christine L. Taylor (Washington, DC: National Academies Press, 2009).

12. Jennifer Talhelm, "Report: Public Lands Grazing Costs $123 Million a Year," Trib.com, November 1, 2005.

THE FARMER'S BIND

1. Elizabeth Gudrais, "Flocking to Finance," *Harvard Magazine*, May–June, 2008, 18–19.

INDEX